DATE DUE

Demco, Inc. 38-293

Hans Keller and Internment

Hans Keller aged 18, at the family summer house at Kritzendorf on the Danube. This photograph was taken in 1937, during their last holiday there before the Anschluss.

Hans Keller and Internment

The Development of an Emigré Musician,
1938-48

A. M. Garnham

with

'Hans Keller in the Early Days'
Donald Mitchell

edited by
Christopher Wintle

with translations from the German by
Irene Auerbach *and* Dorly Bailey

Plumbago Books
2011

Plumbago Books and Arts
26 Iveley Road,
London sw4 0EW

plumbago@btinternet.com
www. plumbago.co.uk

Distribution and Sales:
Boydell & Brewer Ltd.
PO Box 9
Woodbridge
Suffolk IP12 3DF

trading@boydell.co.uk
tel. 01394 610 600
www.boydellandbrewer.com

Boydell and Brewer Inc.
668 Mount Hope Avenue
Rochester
NY 14620, USA

A. M. Garnham,
Hans Keller and Internment. The Development of an Emigré Musician, 1938-48.
with: Donald Mitchell, 'Hans Keller in the Early Days'
Edited by Christopher Wintle
The Hans Keller Archive
General Editor: Christopher Wintle

First published 2011

ISBN: 978-0-9556087-7-3 (hardback), 978-0-9556087-8-0 (softback)

Typeset in Adobe Minion Pro and Adobe Cronos Pro

Printed by MPG Books, Bodmin

Contents

Note: Titles in inverted commas are Keller's, with the exception of the Epilogue, which is Donald Mitchell's. Keller's letters and essays are printed in a separate font throughout and as far as possible preserve the style of the times.

Preface

This book deals with what is still a relatively little-known episode in British wartime history. Despite the current dominance of the Holocaust and the Second World War in popular culture, the mass internment of those who fled to this country is rarely mentioned. In the spring and summer of 1940, however, as Britain braced itself for what seemed like an inevitable invasion by Nazi forces, the question of what to do with the foreigners in our midst was on everyone's lips.

In May and June of that year, the vast majority of the German, Austrian and Italian men in Britain, and some of their wives and children, were hurriedly rounded up and imprisoned in makeshift camps. Such was the haste with which this was done that there was initially little thought given to the conditions in which they were held, or any discrimination between refugees and fascists, between young and old, or between those who had recently arrived in the country and those who had been settled here for years. An outcry in Parliament began to effect improvements towards the end of July, but not before thousands had been deported overseas to the colonies, and several hundred drowned en route when their ship was torpedoed.

As the months passed, conditions in the camps improved, and the cumbersome machinery of government slowly began to process applications for release. Meanwhile, the émigrés in the camps organised themselves into an unprecedented flowering of middle-European culture, which was to have a profound effect on Britain in the post-war years.

Hans Keller, who arrived in London from Vienna at the end of 1938, was one of the most influential of the many German and Austrian émigrés who enriched British musical life after the war. He became the most brilliant and original music critic of his day, helping to shape a whole generation of musicians through his writing, his teaching and his work for the BBC, where he was a senior member of Music Division for twenty years. His first arrival on the British musical scene – as co-editor with Donald Mitchell of the short-lived but disproportionately notorious journal *Music Survey* – was a shock of fresh air to a musical establishment whose cautious conservatism and insularity had been increased by its war-time isolation from the rest of Europe.

When Keller first became well known, at the end of the 1940s, it was naturally assumed by many of his English colleagues that most of his insights – so different from their own received opinion – had been brought wholesale from Vienna. But in fact his enforced change of language and culture after he fled from the Nazis had altered him profoundly, and his first decade in England had been one of deep self-examination and reinvention. Though his writing was founded to a very great extent on two giants of the modern Viennese landscape – Freud and Schoenberg – his personal discovery of their work took place only in England and with the help of English collaborators. Indeed, the fact that he wrote about music at all was initially the product of his encounter with two English musicians: Benjamin Britten and Peter Pears. To them he owed the start of what was to become his life's work – as he told them in 1946, 'I don't think you'll find a great many people who are more lastingly grateful to you for your work than I am.'[1]

This process of discovery began during the nine months that Keller spent in British internment camps from June 1940 to March 1941. After the initial frightening confusion of the mass arrests and deportations was over, he became enormously stimulated by the richness of the talent by which he found himself surrounded. For a young man who had been prevented by the German annexation of Austria from going to university, the burgeoning intellectual life created by the internees in this strange vacuum was enormously important, heightening his awareness of the culture he had left.

This book is the story both of Keller's personal development as a musician and of the British internment of refugees in general. To approach a historical subject through the mind of a remarkable individual who lived it can be unexpectedly illuminating. Hans Keller was himself the most passionate individualist and, moreover, a believer in the paradoxical importance of seeking objective truth through subjective experience.

The story is told chronologically, but through a collage of different forms: sections of history and biography alternate with Keller's own letters and writings. The book falls into three main sections, the first of which deals with Keller's Viennese childhood, the Anschluss, his arrest by the Gestapo and his eventual escape to London. The middle section then tells the story of his internment in Britain, based on his own letters written from the camps, alternating between the details of his everyday life and the wider story of what was going on outside, where an intense political debate was taking place during Britain's 'finest hour' about the rights of the individual in times of national emergency, and who our friends and enemies actually were. The final section of the book then traces Keller's development as a musician and writer from his release until his *Music Survey* days, showing the effect of what had happened to him on his intellectual maturation, and ending with a moving recollection by Donald Mitchell of their exciting early partnership and its place amid Britain's post-war musical resurgence.

It is now 25 years since Hans Keller died, and 70 years have passed since he was interned in 1940. Some of his fellow-internees still survive, however, and they continue to contribute to the growing debate over the rights and wrongs of that wartime policy – and to other more contemporary discussions in which its echoes can still be heard. Meanwhile, the importance of the part that Keller and so many other interned émigrés have since played in the life of their host country is beyond all doubt. It is now time to consider the creative effect of the internment camps on this cultural gift to Britain.

Alison Garnham

Acknowledgements

This volume is the product of many hands. My first thanks go to the many members of Hans Keller's family who have supported it at different stages and in various ways. It was his cousin Inge Trott, née Kompfner, who discovered the existence of Hans's letters from internment and donated them to the archive at Cambridge University Library. She and Hans grew up together, and she has been able to provide many memories of their early life in Vienna. I am extremely grateful for all her help, and that of her daughter Nina. Hans's niece, Ena Blyth, née Franey, has also been of great help; as the elder daughter of Hans's sister Gertrude ('Mowgli') and Roy Franey – to whom Hans and all the family owed their escape from Vienna – she was only a child at the time of Hans's internment, but she has nevertheless been able to give a considerable amount of background information, and access to many family photographs. She and her husband have also very kindly read much of this volume in manuscript, and I am very grateful for all their comments. To Hans Keller's widow, Milein Cosman, I also owe the warmest thanks, for permission to publish these letters, for allowing us to include some of her wonderful drawings, and for her generous support and friendship over many years.

I am also very grateful to Donald Mitchell, one of Keller's oldest and closest English friends, for sharing with me his memories of their early partnership during their *Music Survey* days, and for permission to include in this volume a transcript of his 2001 conversation on the subject with Christopher Wintle – a conversation that brought home to me the crucial importance of their meeting to Keller's understanding of Schoenberg's music.

Given the limitations of my own knowledge of German, this book would have been impossible without the help of Irene Auerbach and Dorly Bailey. When the letters were first discovered, it was Dorly Bailey, the widow of my grandmother's cousin, who helped me produce a preliminary translation, initially with a view simply to selecting a few of these letters for inclusion in *The Letters of Hans Keller* (forthcoming from Ashgate). Sharing the story of the young Hans's experiences with Dorly was a very happy time, and it was her enthusiasm for the letters that first led me to think of them as a possible book. When the opportunity arose to publish them as a complete series, Irene Auerbach undertook a professional revision of the translations. Having already worked with Christopher Wintle on his edition of Keller's *Music and Psychology,* she was familiar with Keller's early style of writing in both German and English, and her experience was invaluable. I am very thankful for the pains she took to produce a meticulously accurate translation; she also consulted others, and I should like to thank those whose knowledge and advice have helped us with the fine details, in particular Gwendolyn Tietze and Laurence Dreyfus for advice on Viennese and Yiddish linguistic peculiarities respectively. I am also grateful to both my translators for many insights into the life of a refugee in wartime England. Since Dorly was herself a Jewish refugee from Hitler, leaving Berlin only days before the war broke out, and Irene the child of political refugees who had to leave Germany in 1933, their help with this book naturally extended far beyond translation.

I should also like to express my gratitude to Jennifer Taylor of the Research Centre for German and Austrian Exile Studies in the University of London. When she and I first met, the Research Centre's excellent yearbook on internment[1] – with Jennifer's article on camp journals – was in press, and I am very grateful for the guidance that she and her colleagues have given me. I should also like to thank Martin Anderson of Toccata Press for his interest and support, and for permission to reprint Keller's final version of 'Vienna, 1938'. I am very grateful to Ashgate Publishing for permitting the publication of this volume ahead of the larger collection of Keller's letters on which I was already engaged for them, and for their patience with the inevitable delay that resulted.

To the editor and publisher of this volume, Christopher Wintle of Plumbago Books, I owe the most profound thanks for help and support beyond measure over many years. Although I had come across Hans Keller's writings when I was an undergraduate, it was Christopher who effected the 'formal introduction' as it were, and drew me to join the many people who have been involved with the Hans Keller Archive and its publications over the last twenty years. In the words of the composer Hugh Wood, Keller 'taught a whole generation' of musicians,[2] and it is thanks to Christopher that his writings are being collected and preserved to contribute to the education of generations to come. In one way or another, Christopher has been responsible for almost all the research into Keller's legacy that has gone on since his death; his founding of Plumbago was an imaginative and courageous step – allowing the publication of books which other publishers could not take on but whose success has shown him justified.

I should like to offer my final thanks to Hans Keller himself. We never met, but I have been reading his words for twenty years now. For all he has taught me, and for all I have been given by his friends and the incomparable Milein Cosman, I am more grateful than I can say.

The book is dedicated to Chris and Will, with my love.

Alison Garnham

Editor's Preface

A text that combines letters (some in translation), reprints of essays, illustrations, commentary and copious scholarly notes, where each category has a house-style to itself and the whole is arranged with the author's words in one typeface and the subject's in another, demands sustained attention to detail. So I am grateful to all those who have contributed to the production process in addition to those mentioned by Alison Garnham: the readers, Hugh Wood (formerly the Fellow in Music at Churchill College, Cambridge) and Daniel Snowman (of the Institute of Historical Research, London), both of whom helped fix the overall shape, and, above all, our creative and tireless typesetter, Julian Littlewood. The Cosman and Keller Art and Music Trust have generously met the printing costs; and our distributors, Boydell & Brewer, have been exceptionally patient in awaiting a long-promised volume. I formally acknowledge the copyright-owners of the photographs and paintings for permission to reprint, and less formally, but no less gratefully, people within the organizations who have been so helpful: Tom Sloan of Getty Images, Nathan Pendelbury of the Walker Gallery (National Museums, Liverpool) and Peran Dachinger, son of the painter Hugo. In fact, Hugo Dachinger became a friend of Hans Keller's in the Huyton and Mooragh internment camps, and his cover picture is entitled, appropriately, 'A Mad, Mad World'.

Christopher Wintle

A sketch of Keller playing the violin in Huyton Camp, August 1940, drawn by an unidentified fellow internee. 'I keep having my portrait painted … People here [haven't] managed to reach agreement yet as to whether my bearded face looks like a rabbi, a Spanish aristocrat, or an Indian prince.'

*Hans Keller
and Internment*

Josef Grotte = Sofie Stern

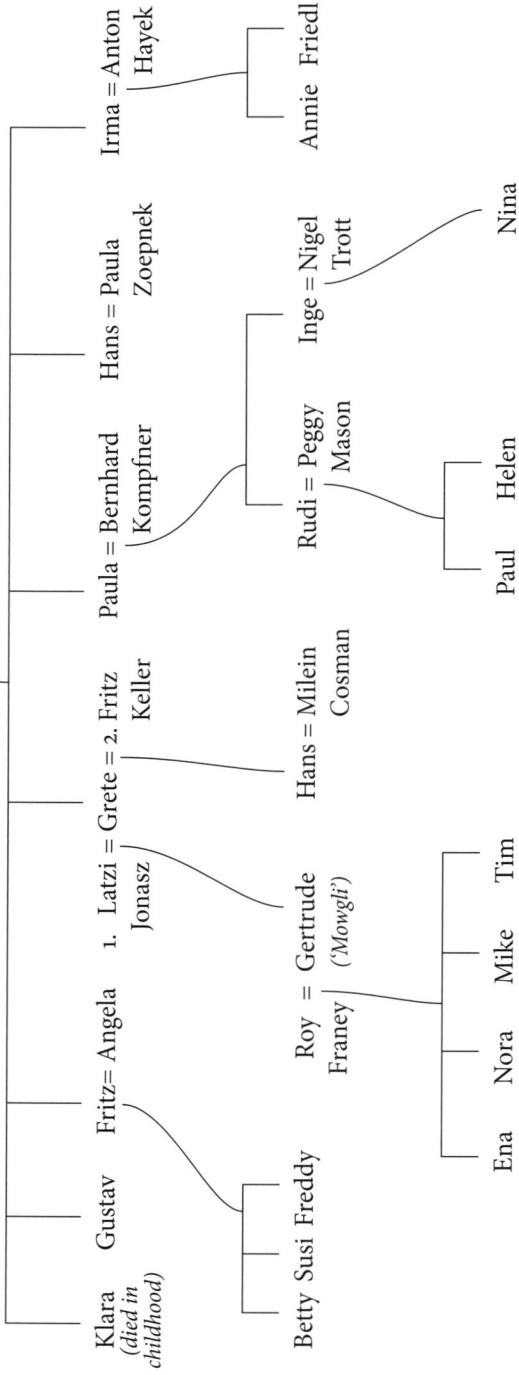

- Klara *(died in childhood)*
- Gustav
- Fritz = Angela
  - Betty
  - Susi
  - Freddy
- 1. Latzi = Grete = 2. Fritz Keller
  - Jonasz
- Roy = Gertrude Franey *('Mowgli')*
  - Ena
  - Nora
  - Mike
  - Tim
- Hans = Milein Cosman
- Paula = Bernhard Kompfner
  - Rudi = Peggy Mason
    - Paul
    - Helen
  - Inge = Nigel Trott
    - Nina
- Hans = Paula Zoepnek
- Irma = Anton Hayek
  - Annie
  - Friedl

1   *Looking Back*

I'm not sure what Hans Keller would have made of this book. He was famously suspicious of history as an academic discipline – he once described it as 'frighteningly haphazard, an inevitable victim of the personal equation'.[1] Biography is naturally even more vulnerable to the compromises that individual personalities inflict on the truth, and dubious motives may well lie behind the act of delving into the life of somebody else. Keller himself was merciless in pointing out the less honest part of its appeal:

> There is only one thing that's more interesting than my family background, and that is your interest in it – its motivation, which is your own family background: I am to be the material for your phoney psychology, your projected self-analysis and self-therapy. Be my guest, but not without a brutal clarification of the psychological situation.[2]

As a writer, Keller has a personality that leaps off the page. But despite the direct way in which he placed himself before the reader, he cannot really be called an autobiographical writer. It was ideas, rather than the details of his life, that he wanted to communicate. But there were occasions when he did write autobiographical pieces, none more striking than the talk he gave in 1974 in the Radio 4 series *The Time of my Life*. Keller chose as his subject 'Vienna, 1938', describing what happened to him between his 19th birthday in March that year, which coincided with Hitler's annexation of Austria, and his escape from Vienna nine months later.

It was a memorable broadcast, all the more effective for its dispassionate tone – Keller himself called it 'a mere report'[3] – and the remarkable insights with which it concluded. The response it drew was considerable, and though Keller patiently wrote individual answers to the hundreds of letters he received, he was doubtful about the ultimate value of the work. 'I have come deeply to suspect my successful pieces,' he wrote shortly afterwards:

> Altogether ['Vienna, 1938'] elicited well over 300 letters, and although I answered most of them, I don't think I liked many of them. What I

disliked was not any of the writers, but that which they all seemed to have in common – one or the other type of moral satisfaction at being able to be horrified at the past, which was safely past enough to make the illusory exercise worthwhile: it can't happen nowadays, it can't happen in this country, it couldn't have happened in this country, we must make sure that it never happens in this country etc. – all reactions which got their bearers out of the present, out of the need to do something here and now. If there is any lesson to be drawn from any crime against humanity, it is that its sources, inevitably, are actively around us all the time, and within us too, otherwise it could not possibly have happened. But the last thing we want to do when confronted with despicable human behaviour is to find it as near to us as we possibly can. We passionately turn every experience, the most distasteful included, into a source of pleasure, and there is little pleasure to be derived from realising that what, say, the Nazi story teaches me is that I am behaving wrongly to my subordinates, or not wrongly enough to my superiors.[4]

Keller's imprisonment by the Gestapo was mercifully brief, but it was one of the defining experiences of his life. Of his nine months' subsequent imprisonment by the British, however, he did not write publicly. Indeed it is remarkable how relatively little anyone in Britain referred to the internment of refugees in print during the first thirty years after the war ended. More recently, the release of the relevant government files in the 1970s and 1980s has provoked a number of historical studies of the issue, beginning with Peter and Leni Gillman's *Collar the Lot!* and Ronald Stent's *A Bespattered Page?* in 1980,[5] and including a major academic conference in 1990, marking the fiftieth anniversary of the 1940 round-up.[6] Still, as the editors of the publication that followed the conference pointed out, the wartime internment of civilians had yet to penetrate far into British public consciousness. Official Second World War commemorations around the same time made this abundantly clear: when looking back to 1940, it is the bravery and communal spirit represented by the Blitz, Dunkirk, and the Battle of Britain that the British wish to remember, not the injustice of the *Arandora Star* tragedy. Britain's role in the Second World War has been heavily mythologised (not least by Churchill himself, the myth's embodiment), and the defining notes of 1940 are British moral pre-eminence and national unity – neither of which sits easily with the internment story.

Understandably, the internees themselves were reluctant to criticise their adopted country once the war was over, both out of a sense of gratitude for their asylum, and also a disinclination to mark themselves out as anything other than British, since many of them were now applying for naturalisation. It is also true that the suffering caused by this episode had become dwarfed by that of the war as a whole, especially once the enormity of the Holocaust became known. The journal of the Association of Jewish Refugees, for example, published almost nothing on internment for twenty years, and even when it did decide to mark that anniversary, it stipulated that contributions should be personal rather than political: 'Whilst it is not visualised to deal with this emergency measure after the fall of France from the political angle, some readers may have personal interest.' The sort of material requested was along the lines of 'short episodes, camp bulletins, references to "Camp Universities" etc.'.[7]

The post-war silence on the British internment and deportation policy of 1940 is all the more notable given the considerable amount of criticism that was published about it at the time. One of the best books on the subject remains one written during the summer of 1940 and published as a Penguin Special in the autumn of that year: François Lafitte's *The Internment of Aliens*. Given the wartime conditions under which he was working, and the difficulty of obtaining accurate information (especially from government departments), this is a remarkable work, and indeed, when it was reissued nearly half a century later, Lafitte found, to his own surprise, that 'with the knowledge and hindsight of 1988 I find astonishingly little that I would wish to rewrite.'[8]

François Lafitte was actually a near neighbour of Keller's family in Herne Hill, South London, where his home became something of a centre for Austrian refugees during the war. Lafitte's own parentage and upbringing were distinctly cosmopolitan: his father, whom he never knew, was American and his mother a Frenchwoman who became the second wife of the famous sexual psychologist Havelock Ellis, whose works Keller read so assiduously during the 1940s,[9] and whom Lafitte clearly remembered with deep respect: 'I was reared under his wise, intellectually wide-ranging, unpartisanly radical, cosmopolitan influence in a home replete with the world's finest literature.' Several years of study in France, Switzerland, Weimar Germany and Vienna had given Lafitte a thoroughly European outlook, which helped him see, perhaps more clearly than his more English contemporaries, the difference between the Second World War and previous conflicts:

> [This] war is not a war of conflicting nations (though this is its outward form), but an international civil war. Hitler's allies and Hitler's enemies are to be found in every country.[10]

Lafitte attributed the pressure for mass internment to the failure on the part of many in the Army and security services to grasp this difference: 'Too many of our Generals simply believe that this is a war of England against Germany (and Austria), so that all "Huns" are enemies.' Many other campaigners against mass internment made the same point – this, for example, was how the Bishop of Chichester put it in the House of Lords in August 1940:

> The present war is not a war on a primarily national basis, but is, as British statesmen have often stated, a war between ideologies and principles. Therefore the question who is Britain's friend or enemy cannot any more be answered under the aspect of 'passport nationality' but must be answered in terms which take into account the new character of the present war, in terms of ideological citizenship.[11]

Although historians have detected a profound shift in British attitudes towards foreigners in the second half of the nineteenth century, culminating in the Aliens Act of 1905,[12] it was the First World War that caused the greatest acceleration in the development of immigration control in Britain. That war also brought Britain's first experience of mass internment on home ground when the Aliens Restriction Act of 1914 led to the arrest or deportation of thousands of expatriate Germans and Austrians. After the sinking of the liner *Lusitania* on 7 May 1915 caused a popular outcry, what had previously been a selective (and in some cases temporary) policy became universal, destroying the German communities which had been a feature of Victorian Britain. As well as the internment and repatriation of Germans, the government had

> closed down German restaurants, newspapers and clubs, … and forced the closure of German businesses. Large sections of the public and press, meanwhile, had developed its hostility towards enemy aliens to such an extent as to view them as pariahs. Such attitudes had led to widespread dismissal of German employees from their jobs and the destruction of their property by rioters. This combination of factors meant the disappearance of German London, German Bradford, German Liverpool and German Manchester.[13]

E. M. Forster, in the little epilogue he appended to his novel *A Room with a View*, shows the intensity of anti-German feeling during the First World War when his heroine gets into trouble for playing Beethoven: 'Hun music! She was overheard and reported, and the police called.' There is another amusing vignette at the end of the novel:

> A quiet little party was held on the outskirts of [Alexandria], and someone wanted a little Beethoven. The hostess demurred. Hun music might compromise us. But a young officer spoke up. 'No, it's all right,' he said, 'a chap who knows about those things from the inside told me Beethoven's definitely Belgian.'

Soon after the end of the First World War, the government began to plan how it might deal with the 'aliens' problem in future wars. At that stage, however, the primary concern was not Germany, but communist Russia, and the Committee of Imperial Defence looked with anxiety on Britain's 90,000 Russian residents, many of whom were Jewish refugees from earlier pogroms. In 1920, it seems to have been agreed that, in the event of war, the 'Russians' in the East End would have to be interned en masse.[14]

No doubt alarmed at such a possibility, Jewish leaders were keen to involve themselves in the Home Office's work with immigrants during the inter-war period. The influx of refugees after Hitler came to power in 1933 was managed at first by constant dialogue between the Home Office and voluntary organisations like the Jewish Refugees Committee and the Jews' Temporary Shelter. In return for the opportunity to contribute to the shaping of the government's policy on Jewish immigration, these voluntary organisations took it upon themselves to offer an extraordinary guarantee that 'all expense, whether temporary or permanent accommodation or maintenance, will be borne by the Jewish community without ultimate charge to the state.'[15]

This guarantee held good until the Anschluss in March 1938. At that point, the Jewish community in Britain realised that it could no longer afford to offer unlimited assistance to the flood of refugees that was now anticipated. The British government was not prepared to admit thousands of possibly destitute Austrians, and therefore responded by reintroducing a visa requirement, for the first time since 1927. For many Austrian Jews, already stripped of much of their property by the Nazis, this was an insuperable barrier.

Hans Keller had the good fortune to have been born into a wealthy family – but even better was the fact that he had family connections in England. Despite his father's money, it is doubtful whether that alone would have sufficed to get him a visa, because nearly all the family's property was confiscated by the Nazis (though his cousin did manage to arrange for some furniture and personal effects to be shipped to England – including their Bösendorfer and Bechstein grand pianos).

What saved Keller's life was his half-sister's marriage to an Englishman, Roy Franey – 'without him, the gas chamber would have been an absolute certainty'.[16] Before Keller's parents met (through their playing of piano duets, apparently),[17] his mother Grete had been married to Latzi Jonasz, with whom she had her first child, Gertrude Gerda, known to the family as 'Mowgli' – a reference to Kipling's Jungle Book, because of the darkness of her skin at birth (the midwife apparently exclaimed 'Ooh, we have another Mowgli here').[18] Keller was born in 1919, ten years after his half-sister, so there was a considerable age-gap. 'I can strongly recommend this set-up: it makes for a smashing childhood,' he wrote later. 'Whenever anything goes wrong between you and your parents, you have a mediator at hand, an acting mother as it were.'[19] Keller was also lucky enough to have a playmate nearer his own age, in the shape of his cousin, Inge Kompfner, the daughter of Grete's younger sister Paula Kompfner. The Kompfners lived round the corner from the Kellers' house in Nusswaldgasse in Döbling (the artistic quarter of Vienna), and Hans and Inge therefore grew up together: 'We lived quite near each other, about five minutes' walk – we grew up like brother and sister,' remembers Inge, who was one year younger than her cousin, and rather looked up to him: 'I remember, when I was a child, I couldn't imagine marrying anybody I didn't know as well as Hans; he certainly was a strong influence.'[20]

The young Hans's very first piece of published writing was a story written for Inge. It was printed in a children's newspaper ('all papers had a children's section', Inge recalls), when he was seven and she was six. Fifty years later, Keller remembered the moment of its publication as marking the start of his ambition to be a writer:

> I was in bed with measles, not allowed to get up or do anything; I just had to wait for the temperature to abate. I slank to the bathroom, got myself plenty of lavatory paper and, on it, wrote a story called *Inge's Journey through the Clouds* (Inge is a cousin of mine, one year younger than I am), whose precise structure was not even recovered in self-analysis, so it must have been even lousier than I am prepared to admit. When it was completed, I got my sister to post it to the *Prager Kinderzeitung*, the 'Prague Children's Newspaper', which was the only market I knew.
>
> I was still in bed when, one morning a week or two later, my father came in grinningly, the open paper in his hands. There, in fantastically black type, it said '*Inge's Journey through the Clouds* – by Hans Keller (7½)'. I have never seriously accepted the reality of 'happiness' or indeed the interest of the concept which, I think, is an invention of the depressive mind, but if there is anything remotely resembling such a state, this was it. Thenceforth, I was a writer, and have never stopped writing until the present day, though the change of languages at the age of 19 (retrospectively a blessing) was, of course, a major crisis.[21]

The actual story is long lost – not surprising, if it was written on toilet paper – and Inge does not remember its contents either. But she does remember her cousin's passion for writing:

> Yes, he loved writing, always. … I remember him being conscious of writing and having his writings remembered. And he wrote to me and he said 'Keep my letters'. But my mother read all my letters … and when Hans knew that he said he wasn't going to write any more to me.[22]

Inge had an older brother, Rudi, who was born the same year as Mowgli; they too had been brought up together. Inge suspects that her own birth, a year after Keller's (and so long after her brother's), may have been the result of her mother following her older sister's example: 'Mutti had Hans and soon afterwards my mother had me, and Mutti always said she imitated her.'[23]

Keller's mother Grete was known as 'Mutti' by the whole family, not only by her own children. Although physically quite small and slight, she had by all accounts a powerful and magnetic personality, and was quite a daunting figure to the children: 'I was terrified of her, and so was my brother,' Inge remembers. 'She would look at you and you would shrivel up. It wasn't until I came to this country and after my mother died that I eventually made friends with her.'[24] Towards her son, however, Mutti was enormously proud and fond – and, as his cousin says, 'she must have been a powerful influence on him'.[25] Grete Keller kept open house in Vienna to many gifted artists, writers and musicians, among whom she apparently had several admirers: 'Peter Altenberg and the composer Franz Schreker had been in love with my mother,' remembered Keller later; 'Mahler's wife was her girl friend, and writers like Alfred Polgar, Egon Fridell and Franz Theodor Csokor were regular visitors to our house.'[26] After the death of Keller's father, Grete's first husband appeared in London and proposed re-marriage to her, according to her niece: 'He wanted to marry Mutti again, but she wasn't having it.'[27]

Fritz Keller, Hans's father, was an architect ('he built the biggest house in Vienna, the Hochhaus,' says Inge) and he was also 'a self-taught pianist who could reproduce, on the piano, anything he had heard up to and including Bruckner'.[28] He was a gentler character than his wife, 'a lovely man,' remembers Inge, 'Mutti never really appreciated him. He was very musical. He played the piano, and I'll never forget that he introduced me and my mother to opera.'[29] 'Owing to my father,' wrote Keller later, 'thought … became a magical concept in my childhood. On Sunday mornings, he'd walk around the garden for hours, his hands behind his back, and wouldn't want to be disturbed. … Sunday morning after Sunday morning, I would silently walk behind my father, for hours, hands on my back, trying to think.'[30]

Grete's daughter Mowgli met her future husband, an English surveyor called Roy Franey, in 1929, at the Alpine motor rally, to which she went with her father, Latzi Jonasz, who was a motoring correspondent. Roy was driving one of the cars, and because Mowgli (having had an English governess) could speak English, she was seated at dinner next to him and his co-driver.[31] They were married four years later and settled in Herne Hill in South London, in a house designed for them by her stepfather Fritz Keller and her cousin Rudi Kompfner, Inge's older brother. Rudi Kompfner also moved to London around this time and took a job in Roy Franey's company, 'Almond Franey and Son Ltd, Estate Managers and Builders, London', in which he was serving

as Managing Director at the time of his internment.[32] He supervised the
building of the new house for his cousin and her husband, the architecture
of which has been described as 'admirable'.[33] When it was finished it featured
in a small book celebrating modern domestic architecture published by the
Architectural Press in 1937.[34]

One of the bedrooms at No. 32 Herne Hill was kept for Mutti, who came to
visit Mowgli and Roy regularly. She was there at the time of the Anschluss in
1938, and thus immediately divided from the rest of the family. Although she
was persuaded to remain in London with the Franeys, she was desperately
anxious about her family in Vienna, particularly her son Hans, now nineteen.
Since the British government had immediately reinstituted the visa barrier
for Austrians, the rest of the family was prevented from joining Grete in
London. Roy Franey made strenuous efforts to secure visas, and luckily he
was able to provide the financial guarantees required. Even so, it was not
an easy process. Family papers which survive in the Hans Keller Archive
in Cambridge University Library show that Roy actually went himself to
Vienna to pursue the matter of Keller's visa with the British Embassy there,[35]
but that six weeks later the Home Office was still not prepared to grant him
the document. Even after Roy had satisfied the British Passport Controller
of his ability to maintain his brother-in-law financially, the visa was still
withheld: 'I am directed by the Secretary of State to say that before reaching
a decision in this case, he desires to learn what plans Mr. Franey has in
view for his brother-in-law after he has completed the proposed course of
education in this country.'[36] When permission to enter Britain was finally
granted in July, it was only temporary. Roy Franey was told, 'The visa has
been authorized on the understanding that arrangements will eventually be
made for your brother-in-law's emigration.'[37] At that stage, the Home Office
was still attempting to control the flood of visa applications from Austria and
somehow ensure that those who applied to come to Britain on a temporary
visa would indeed stay only temporarily:

> Desperate for any document enabling them to escape, people applied
> for visitors' visas, signing the requisite form of undertaking that they
> would not seek to extend their stay. The immigration authorities soon
> realised that many of these people, once they had achieved the object of
> gaining admission, would plead that they could not go back to Germany
> or Austria. In a bid to intercept these cases, preferably before they were
> given leave to land, PCOs [Passport Control Officers] were told in June
> 1938 to mark the passports of persons who signed these undertakings
> with a secret signal, which would be picked up by officials in the United
> Kingdom. However, the futility of demanding such undertakings
> in the absence of the will to enforce them subsequently was finally

acknowledged in August, when the Home Office decided to abandon their use in refugee cases.[38]

As the political situation of Austrian Jews deteriorated, the pressure on the British diplomatic mission in Vienna increased. Downgraded to a Consulate after the Anschluss, and 'reduced to a fortnightly diplomatic bag via Berlin, of which it was now an outpost',[39] it was having to cope with thousands of requests for refuge:

> Visas granted in the first half of 1938 alone to Austrian subjects totalled 2,740, refusals approximately 420, and 545 cases, including some already disposed of, had been referred for decision to London. The number of staff dealing with visas in Vienna had been increased from four to fifteen. Locally engaged staff were employed as reception clerks to manage the crowd. By September, staff were dealing with 200 enquiries a day about emigration to various parts of the British Empire and accepting over 100 visa applications daily. From May to September 1938 the Consulate had also given out 16,000 forms in connection with possible emigration to Australia.[40]

Even more difficult than persuading the British to accept Keller, however, was the task of persuading the Germans to let him go. As he wrote in October to a schoolfriend in Switzerland, it was not the British visa which ultimately held him back: 'You are wrong if you think I haven't got a visa. I've had one for over two months; the thing which I haven't got, or haven't got *yet*, is a passport. But I hope to get this in the near future, that is if you take the idea of "near" as a rather elastic concept.'[41] This unfortunately meant that he and all the rest of the family were still in Vienna at the time of the notorious Kristallnacht pogrom a month later.

What happened to Keller on that day, and the dreadful days that followed, is best told in his own words – in his 'Vienna, 1938' broadcast, the text of which forms the next chapter of this book. To add to that account, however, his cousin Inge has given a vivid description of what was happening to the rest of the family while Keller was imprisoned. She herself was then living in Keller's family home in Nusswaldgasse, after her own home had been requisitioned by a Nazi officer. Grete Keller being in England, the household at Nusswaldgasse at that time consisted only of Keller and his father, who was by then an invalid (he had prostate cancer), and his father's nurse.

> [My parents and I] were living in a flat nearby, and the flat was allocated to a German officer. He appeared one day and said "This flat has been allocated to me" – a flat where I'd grown up and lived all my life – so we

had to move out. But they had allocated some flats for the Jewish people. [Ours] was much too small, and it was still wet: it wasn't really fit to be lived in, and it was too small for me as well, so I stayed with [Hans and his father]. ... [Hans] was taken by the Gestapo, and we didn't know where he was. It was a terrible time...

We had to queue for all sorts of things ... before we could get the visa. And in one of these queues they came and took all the men, I think, and he never came back home. ... We didn't know what had happened. And he had a girlfriend at that time, Erika, and she was absolutely beside herself not knowing what had happened to him. I had a contact with my religious instruction teacher who was working at the Kultusgemeinde [Jewish Community Centre], which helped people to emigrate, and we both went to see him and said, "Do you know what happened to the people who were rounded up outside your office?" and he said, "They're fine, they're being treated very gently." He wasn't supposed to say anything, he was told by the Nazis. And I remember Erika being quite reassured, but of course it was all lies. ...

[While I was living at Nusswaldgasse] I used to go and have breakfast with my parents. And I had just gone there to have breakfast [that morning], when I heard these men, these SS men rushing up the stairs. My knees went. And they said, "Where's Mr Kompfner?" And my mother said, "In the office." "Where's the office?" So she told him exactly where the office was. And Mrs Seidl, our help, was there at the time – she wasn't Jewish – and she immediately got a taxi and went to the office and brought my father home. And from there we went to Nusswaldgasse. So we were all in Nusswaldgasse when they came there. ... And they said, "Where's Keller?" And the nurse said, "He's in bed, dying." And she refused to let them go upstairs. So they went [away]. But they took my father.... [He was released later that day] because he was over sixty. But he had to stand for hours and hours, and he didn't know what was going to happen. And the younger men, they were put in concentration camps, Dachau at that time.[42]

One of the things that Inge remembers Keller describing to her when he finally returned from imprisonment was the impression made on him by the orthodox Jews with whom he had been held. This he described later as 'one of the deepest experiences of my life', and it is the subject of his first adult publication. Orthodox Judaism had held a certain fascination for Keller throughout his adolescence. His maternal grandmother had been orthodox, though his parents were very liberal: 'While there were plenty of Jews around,' wrote Keller of his childhood home, 'the atmosphere was typical of "emancipated" Jewry which had left the ghetto behind. ... At the same time, in view of Austria's steadily mounting antisemitism, my parents had decided very early on to impress on me, as naturally as possible in the circumstances, that there was nothing wrong with being a Jew.'[43]

After his first taste of 'antisemitism in the flesh' (being beaten up on the way to school by Catholic boys for being a 'murderer of Christ'), Keller became much more consciously Jewish as a teenager: 'Far from wishing to hide my Jewishness, I was intent upon showing it wherever I could.'[44] His cousin remembers that Keller was 'very much more consciously Jewish than I was. But he looked more Jewish, and he got picked on.'[45] Keller attended synagogue and made frequent visits to Leopoldstadt, the Jewish quarter, 'walking behind gesticulating orthodox Jews ... and trying to listen to what they were saying'. Part reaction to antisemitism, part genuine fascination and 'strong metaphysical leanings', this teenage religious phase was also, Keller thought later, part rebellion against his liberal parents:

> It was now quite clear to me that my father wasn't Jewish enough, that my mother could only just pass, and that in this respect, my uncle was really the only wholly dependable member of the family; why, in private – not in court – he even sported a strong Jewish accent, which was held up to me as an anti-model by my parents, especially my father, who preferred 'beautiful German'. I decided, first unconsciously, then jolly consciously, to move nearer to him. My mother was the emotional bridge: he was her favourite sibling (out of five), and she was his, except that she was 'too intelligent for a woman'. But, once again, I wasn't going to have any model; in fact, I was going to outdo my uncle's Jewishness by turning into a believer.[46]

His father's reaction surprised him:

> He started worrying about the Jewish problem, quite genuinely so. On the level of Association Football, it was merely amusing: he would come with me and my uncle to those boring *Hakoah* matches – relegation fights year in, year out – and amuse himself by pulling our legs in view of our involvement. However, there he was, almost every Sunday, even if the temperature was 10 centigrades below zero, freezing pitiably. But there were other levels: what he found so objectionable about Theodor Herzl's *Jewish State* was its location – Palestine. He had been there, and did not consider the climate suitable for the flowering of thought. He promptly started to read every available book on Zionism, and to write a counter-book, called 'The European Jewish State', which he never finished. I'm afraid I forget where that European Jewish State was supposed to be

situated ... Suffice it to say that were he alive, I would give him half a point: it may not have happened in Europe, but Israel is pretty much a European Jewish State all the same.[47]

The very Jewish uncle whose Jewishness the young Keller was determined to outdo was Hans Grotte, Grete's youngest brother, who, as 'Uncle Hans', is one of the most vivid characters in Keller's letters from internment. He was a lawyer and a veteran of the First World War who had fought on the Eastern Front and been taken prisoner by the Russians. At the end of the war the Austrian government had been too impoverished to bring home all its prisoners-of-war, and Uncle Hans was lost for some time. Eventually his whereabouts was discovered by a ship's captain who knew the family (his wife having been treated by Grete's eldest brother, who was a gynaecologist). He made enquiries at Vladivostok, and Uncle Hans was brought home as if from the dead.[48] According to Keller's niece, Ena, Uncle Hans in later years said that this experience had taught him that survival in such circumstances depended on keeping one's head down and never volunteering for anything – advice which he apparently passed on to his nephew while they were interned together.[49]

Another major influence on the young Keller who was also later interned with him was Oscar Adler, a medical doctor and violinist, and a close friend in his youth of the young Arnold Schoenberg. Despite being of a similar age, Schoenberg later described Adler as his first musical teacher:

> Only after I had met three young men of about my own age and had won their friendship did my musical and literary education start. The first was Oscar Adler, whose talent as a musician was as great as his capabilities in science. Through him I learned of the existence of a theory of music, and he directed my first steps therein... All my acquaintance with classical music derived from playing quartets with him, for even then he was an excellent first violinist.[50]

For Keller, too, Adler was his first and most profound musical influence:

> From my early childhood I lived in his chamber-musical world, first passively, later actively. He did not care two hoots about analysis, but his uniquely organic and motif-conscious way of playing taught me more about the essentials of chamber-musical forms and textures than any analytical teacher could possibly have done.[51]

When Keller was a child, Adler was in his fifties and a very striking musical personality. He was often at Keller's parents' house in Nusswaldgasse, as his cousin Inge remembers: 'Mutti discovered him ... She kept open door for all artists and musicians and they played chamber music.'[52] Inge describes his playing as 'beautiful ... a bit like a gypsy; I remember him playing freely, improvising – there are bits in Haydn and Mozart where the first violin goes off.'[53] Adler was all the more important to the young Hans because at that time, according to Inge, 'Hans learned with a [violin] teacher who was not very good.' She and Hans also used to go to Adler's house, where Inge took piano lessons with his wife, Paula, and they both would listen to Adler's quartet rehearsals:

> And of course the Adler Quartet played in the Adlers' house, and after I had my piano lessons I was invited to stay and listen, and that made an indelible influence on me. ... The Adler quartet had Franz Schmidt as the 'cellist, who was the principal 'cellist of the Vienna Philharmonic. ... He also played the piano brilliantly, Schmidt, and he played at Hans's house, on one of the big pianos. That was the first time I heard him and I was so impressed. The *Trout*, he played ... They had two pianos – a Bösendorfer and a Bechstein – in a big music room and [Hans and I] played on two pianos. We played Beethoven's piano concertos. I think I played the higher part ... But there was one mistake I kept making – I can still hear it. I knew it was wrong, but I kept hitting the wrong key, and Hans didn't like that at all!

It was Roy Franey who was responsible for the escape from Vienna of both Adler and his wife. After they got to London, they were regular visitors to No. 32 Herne Hill (and later No. 30, when Grete Keller moved into the house next door). There the quartet-playing continued. One English visitor who took part in it was Esther ('Tess') Simpson, assistant secretary (and prime mover) of the Society for the Protection of Science and Learning, founded by a group of British academics in 1933 'to help University teachers and investigators of whatever country who, on grounds of religion, political opinion or race, are unable to carry on their work in their own country':

> In London I met Mrs. Keller, a Viennese 'cellist, to whom I was introduced by a very close Viennese friend, Dr. Lydia Sicher, a psychiatrist, whose husband, Professor Harry Sicher, had a regular string quartet in Vienna – he himself was a violinist – with a medical, Dr. Oscar Adler, well-known in Vienna as a quartet leader and mentor. Dr. Adler was now living in London and playing regularly with Mrs. Keller and her teenage son, Hans, and I was invited to join them. Yes, it was *the* Hans Keller, who later became so well known for his work with the B.B.C. Sometimes Harry Sicher played with us, with the Kellers in string

quartets and string quintets. I sometimes played the violin, sometimes the viola, joined sometimes by Gertrud Kaldeck from Vienna.[54]

Another musician who joined them after the war was Michael Graubart, who had got to know the family through his father's connection with Uncle Hans:

> My father had been an officer in the Austrian army in the First World War and, wounded on the Eastern Front, had been a prisoner-of-war in Siberia together with a Viennese lawyer called Dr Grotte – Hans's uncle. It was through these unlikely circumstances (all of us having ended up in London as refugees) that I was invited to a quartet evening in West Hampstead.
>
> The quartet had a slightly flexible membership. There was a German or Austrian couple called, I think, Dr and Mrs Weiss, who played second violin or viola; Hans himself played viola or second violin; Hans's mother was the 'cellist; and there was the leader, an impressive old gentleman with a splendid head of white hair, to whom everyone deferred: 'We do this with an upbow!' – 'Oh yes, Dr Adler, we do this with an upbow!' How was I – who had probably not even heard of Schoenberg! – to know what suddenly dawned on me years later: that this was Dr Oskar Adler, Schoenberg's boyhood friend and first teacher?[55]

Many years later, Inge's daughter Nina (now a violinist herself) would also listen, as her mother had done in Vienna, to Adler's quartet-playing:

> I remember quartets at number 32, because that's why I wanted to play the violin. [My mother] used to go round there and turn pages for people, and I used to sit there and draw and listen. And there'd be Hans, Adler, Mutti … I was only five then. But everybody was always talking about Dr Adler: 'Dr Adler this, Dr Adler that'… He was a huge influence on Hans. He was a huge influence on Schoenberg.[56]

He was evidently a huge influence on everyone who was lucky enough to hear him play. Another listener to the quartet-playing at Herne Hill in the years after the war was Keller's future wife, the artist Milein Cosman. She vividly remembers the extraordinary Oscar Adler: 'He was like Socrates re-born'.[57]

~

Writing many years after he left Vienna, Keller attributed his 'joyful temperament' to his 'sunny early years' as a child in Vienna.[58] The manner of his leaving the city of his birth seems, paradoxically, to have reinforced this aspect of his character; at the end of his 1974 broadcast 'Vienna, 1938' he relates a significant decision (as will be seen in the next chapter), the effect of which, he says, he continued to feel for the rest of his life.

It is essential to read Keller's letters from his British internment in the context of his earlier arrest in Vienna, because his first imprisonment, under the Nazis, had a deep effect on the way he experienced his second. Naturally there are no letters from the time of Keller's detention in Austria, and even those few which survive from immediately afterwards, while he was trying to get out of Vienna, contain no reference to what had happened to him, for fear of reprisals – writing to a friend in Switzerland three days after his release, for example, he explained his silence by saying that he had been in hospital.[59]

Once he had arrived in England, however, the silence could be broken. Another letter, written in February 1939 to the same friend, Fritz Schonbach (by then also in London), shows that Keller had now explained what lay behind his previous dissembling:

> I thank you for the only possible reaction: don't be sorry for me. ... At the moment, I'm fine, as ever – more so because after the beatings during my imprisonment, and having given up hope of survival (as I did at that time), I am now happy *to be alive*. – Nevertheless I am not complaining about what is now past: should you ever get to see 'Das Neue Tagebuch', Paris, of 7 January, then you will find set out – in an article penned by yours truly (entitled '... for they know not what they do') – the reason why I was able to see a metaphysical benefit in the time of my captivity and thus be moved to the statement made above.

The 'article' mentioned in that letter was Keller's very first publication (apart from his childhood story). It is here reprinted for the first time, and follows the text of the 'Vienna, 1938' radio broadcast. Written and published 35 years apart, these two pieces are very different in purpose, style and content; reading them together is illuminating. Keller's brief, anonymous '... for they know not what they do' is an immediate emotional reaction to his imprisonment, and it must have been written as soon as humanly possible, for it was in print a fortnight after his arrival in London. By contrast, 'Vienna 1938' (which here appears first, for reasons which will become obvious), was a product of his maturity, originally broadcast on Radio 4 on 3 February 1974. Such was the attention it received that an abridged version was reprinted in *The Listener* on 28 March, and the broadcast was repeated on 24 August. Keller returned to it three years later, when he published the full text as Chapter One of his book *1975 (1984 minus 9)*.[60]

There is no better way in which to tell the story of such traumatic events than in Keller's own words. Such is the quality of the writing, moreover, that to start with this remarkable broadcast will serve to explain to any reader who may be unfamiliar with Keller's later achievements why the story of this particular internee should be of such interest.

2   'Vienna, 1938'

In 1938, I was due to take my matriculation exam – my A Levels, if I may translate meaningfully. For years I had been scared of this event – as indeed had all other schoolboys, good or bad: in German-speaking countries, the matriculation was one of life's major traumas, and people had matriculation dreams right up to their death, while books were written about suicides which took place out of matriculation-fear. Franz Werfel's *Der Abituriententag* ('The Matriculation Day') was one outstanding novel about such a suicide.

But in March of that year, a month or two before the date of the examination, the Nazis invaded Austria. The Austrian Chancellor, Kurt von Schuschnigg (whose brother was to become Austrian radio's head of music after the war), abdicated on my birthday, March 11, ("to avoid the shedding of fraternal blood" – *Bruderblut*, as he called it), and the Nazis proceeded to invade Austria. On March 12, Hitler made his entry into Vienna. While it was, of course, carefully stage-managed, the difficult question remains how far the Austrians welcomed the Anschluss. In any event, their enthusiasm tends to be underplayed nowadays. There had been a strong illegal Nazi party; there had been thousands if not millions of more passive sympathisers. It's not for me to guess proportions. Anyhow, the Vienna correspondent of the *Völkische Beobachter* went through the usual motions:

> The streets of Vienna are ablaze with a veritable fire-storm of frenzied enthusiasm which beggars description. The crowds are beside themselves with delight. As news came of the German troops' approach, people openly embraced and hugged each other in the streets. They still can't quite believe that they have won. The German city of Vienna, and with it the whole of Austria, has arisen. Swastika flags flutter from every window and balcony. Austria is a National Socialist State! Outside the official German tourist office, whose windows display a photograph of the Führer, the crowds gather. The sparkling, happy eyes of the people are the most moving thing I have ever seen.

With the Nazi invasion, the imminent trauma of my matriculation suddenly ceased to exist: from the moment go, one was, intermittently, running for one's life, and the school and study aspect of it assumed, to put it mildly, a dream-like quality: if one passed one's matriculation, one would not, as a Jew, be allowed to enter university anyway, while abroad – if one was lucky enough to get out – an Austrian or German matriculation certificate would not be recognised. Nevertheless, one did one's empty duty. After all, one had been preparing for this event for eight years; besides, going to school and doing as if one cared about the matric created the illusion, however thin, that life was going on as usual, that one might eventually survive. For many, though, life was not going on, not at all as usual anyway. According to an official enquiry carried out after the war into the events of those days,

> the best available estimates are that the very first wave of arrests in the days of March 1938 caught more than 7,000 people. Thereafter, a regular trickle of arrests and disappearances continued.

The father of a girl friend of mine was arrested on March 13: he had, as a barrister, conducted and won an action against the *Völkische Beobachter*. He was taken to Dachau concentration camp, and slowly tortured to death. Friends who met him there in later months were unable to recognise him.

Now, in view of the large Jewish contingent in my own school, the physical separation of the form into Aryans and Jews, the former yelling "Heil Hitler!" when the uniformed form-master entered (who had replaced our Jewish form-master), was not too frightening: it was easier, at that adolescent stage, to stand by silently and think "You fools!" if there were many of you. But when we heard that our former Jewish form-master, whom we all venerated, had been savagely beaten up and his flat plundered, the thought of 'You fools!' wasn't quite good enough. He is now a university professor in America – doing better, no doubt, than he could ever have done without the holocaust. This is the paradox, but it only affected that tiny proportion of German and Austrian Jews who were not, eventually, gassed.

The matriculation came, and I passed without noticing, as it were. But one thing I did notice, and that was the official reaction to my German essay. For the Aryans, there were five titles for choice, four of them on such subjects as 'Adolf Hitler's *Mein Kampf* and the Concept of National Socialism'. The fifth subject, the only one for the Jews, was 'An Analysis of Poetic Realism in German Literature'. Well, when it came to the prize-giving stage, the German teacher, a physical cripple in SA uniform, made a speech in which he pointed to the deplorable fact that mine had been by far the best German essay: "It's high time for Austrian culture to be rescued. We must have reached a low point in degeneration if it is possible for a Jew to write the only outstanding German essay."

The ensuing months were spent on unsuccessful attempts to get out of the country, and on being beaten up in between. My father, who was wealthy, was dying – and it was his money which made it difficult for me to obtain a passport.

Soon after the Anschluss, this order appeared in the Austrian Legal Gazette:

The Commissioner for the Four Year Plan and the Minister for Internal Affairs of the German Reich decree as follows:

Para. 1   Every Jew is ordered to declare his entire property, both at home and abroad, valued as of the date of this decree.

Para. 2   Property within the meaning of this decree means the total and entire possessions of those affected, irrespective of whether they are liable to tax or not.

Para. 3   Whoever fails, negligently or with malice aforethought, to comply with the above instructions, will be liable to a fine and/or 10 years' penal servitude. In addition to the punishment, the Court may order confiscation of the property.

My father had made a full and frank declaration, and the official view was that where so much had been declared, there must be much more, undeclared, where that had come from. So long as the Nazis did not feel sure that they were getting hold of every penny available, I would not get my passport. I remember my father calling me into his bedroom and saying that anyway, he was glad that we had lost all our money: he had always been worried by my growing up as the son of wealthy parents, and by the danger of my attributing an importance to money which it did not, in reality, possess: "Only when one realises that money's of no importance whatever, does one begin to live." He himself had been both poor and (as a successful architect) wealthy in his own life, and from the point of view of life's real values, he hadn't noticed the difference. He said he didn't care two hoots about losing all his money; he didn't, incidentally, know that he was dying.

In order to try and get a passport, one had to queue up at various places to obtain the necessary documents, and what usually happened was that one queued up all night without achieving any result, except that the SA or SS came to visit these queues occasionally, for the purpose of beating them up. As an official contemporary report to Police Headquarters had it:

Sympathy for Jews, or compassion with their fate, was manifested only rarely, and where such feelings were nevertheless expressed, however hesitantly, the majority of onlookers turned on those concerned with great energy. Any who showed excessive sympathy with the Jews were pointed out to the Police. Some of these were themselves arrested.

One such occasion sticks vividly in my memory, because at that stage I felt as if Western civilisation had abandoned us: this time, I queued up in order to obtain my British visa, or rather the document confirming it (since I had no passport to put it in) – something which very few people were able to obtain, and which I was fortunate enough to have been granted because my sister was married to an Englishman who had undertaken, if necessary, to support me for the rest of my life, so that I wouldn't be a burden to the state. Now, I had to queue up outside the British Consulate in order to get this document. We were a small and eminently beatable queue, and we talked, with some excitement, about the chances of our being beaten up while we stood there. In due course, an English Consulate official came out and asked us in a stern voice to behave in an orderly fashion, and not to make so much noise. I took the opportunity to step forward and ask him why it was necessary to stand out there in the road, when it was extremely likely that we would be beaten up sooner or later: couldn't we wait inside, since there were so few of us? "This is quite out of the question," he said, and vanished through the door, which was duly and audibly locked. Within an hour, we were beaten up.

There were other pleasantries, such as being arrested for short periods in order to clean some Nazi barracks; if one said that one wanted to ring home, where one had a dying father, in order to tell him that one would be late, one was told "Let him die".

At least, I was released. Such arrests could have more serious consequences, as witness a circular by the Gestapo of 24th May, 1938:

TO: All district commissariats in Vienna.
SUBJECT: Arrest of Jews.
ENCLOSURES: Interrogation sheets and index cards.

It has been decreed that undesirable Jews, especially those with a criminal record, are to be arrested and transferred to Dachau concentration camp. The arrests are to be organised by District Police Commissariats. Only German – that is, Austrian – and stateless Jews are affected. Jews of more than 50 years of age are to be arrested only in special circumstances.

Some 2,000 Jews were arrested following this order and transferred to Dachau.

On November 1938, a junior official at the German Embassy in Paris, Ernst vom Rath, was shot by a 17-year-old Polish Jew, Herschel Grynspan, whose parents had been expelled from Germany and sent back to Poland. Rath did not immediately die – and I thought to myself that if he died, a violent pogrom was an extreme likelihood. I therefore decided to follow the news closely, in order to stay at home or go into hiding when the news of his death came. The day after his death, however, I overslept: I had wanted to be at the Jewish Community Centre, where I would get one of the necessary documents for my passport, at 6 a.m., in order not to be at the end of one of those enormous queues; but woke up at 7. I hastily dressed, put the unread *Völkische Beobachter* into my coat pocket, ran out into the street, and caught a taxi. The unread paper contained the news that Rath had died. At the corner of the little street where the Community Centre was, I paid off the taxi – to find, to my surprise, that the street looked peaceful and abandoned: I didn't see any queues. But there was a Jew standing at the street corner, and I walked up to him and asked him whether the Centre was open, and whether one could queue up for the document in question. "Yes," he said, with a sad face, "just walk over there, right up to the main door." A pity that I did not, at this stage at least, have a look at my paper. I walked along to the main door, outside which stood another Jew. I walked up to him and said: "It looks terribly quiet around here. Is the Centre really open? I want to queue up for my document." "Yes," he said with an equally sad face, "just step in here." I opened the door but, instead of Jewish officials, I faced an SA man who threw me against a wall with considerable zest. When I picked myself up, I found myself in the company of a number of Jews who had just had the same experience. "Vom Rath is dead?" I asked one of them. "Of course," he said. The Jewish guides outside the building had been posted by the Nazis; whoever refused to play the game would be shot.

   This was the notorious November pogrom, the Kristallnacht, from which, eventually, only a small proportion of Jews escaped with their lives; the vast majority rotted away or were tortured to death in concentration camps, or were ultimately exterminated, gassed. Here is a confidential report by one Lieut. Fast of the SS, who was in charge of a small detachment taking part. It is dated November 12, 1938, and is addressed to one of his superiors at the SS headquarters for Lower Austria:

> After my detachment had been detailed for special duty at midnight on November 9, I was ordered to report to the office of the District Commissioner at 1 a.m. Also present were leaders of other SS detachments, representatives of the SA and of the police, as well as the Special Commissioner for the Aryanisation of Jewish property. The District Commissioner gave us a strict briefing. In response to the cowardly Jewish assassination of Third Secretary vom Rath in Paris, fierce popular indignation had already turned its wrath upon the Jews of Germany. Among other things, several synagogues had been set on fire. It was essential, the District Commissioner continued, that in Austria, too, popular indignation should rouse itself against the Jews this very night. If, as a result, any building and property belonging to the Jews should catch fire, this would be a matter for the local fire services, and detachments of the National Socialist movement were not obliged to take a hand. Within the framework of the operation, the police would have the following duties: (1) Looting was to be prevented, and so was the destruction or damage of Aryan property. (2) Towards the end of the operation, the Jews were to be taken into custody for their own safety – especially those of working age. Popular indignation was to be given full reign until 6 o'clock in the morning; until that hour the police were to avoid all confrontation with the demonstrators. Care should be taken that all those involved in the operation should wear civilian clothing.

At the time, I knew none of this, of course. After a few hours in the Jewish Community Centre, we were taken, in lorries, to various primary schools which had been allocated for the purpose and set up as temporary prisons. Upon arrival, we had the first of several Gestapo interviews. The Gestapo officer had a printed form before him, from which he read his questions. Among the questions I remember were the following: "Since when have you been a homosexual?" "I am not a homosexual," I replied. "Did I ask you whether you were, or did I ask you since when you have been one?" When I did not reply, he wrote in 'five years'. "How many Aryan girls have you seduced?" "I haven't seduced any Aryan girls," I replied. "Did I ask you whether you had, or did I ask you how many you had seduced?" Again, when I didn't reply, he wrote in 'five'. After this comprehensive survey of my biography, he turned the sheet round and said "Sign". I started reading it – whereupon he said, "Did I say read, or did I say sign?" I duly signed, and the document was carefully filed away.

Between 150 and 200 of us were then driven into a classroom which would normally have space for 20 or 30, and which was to be our abode for the next six days. For three days, we didn't get any food, but the fact that we didn't get any water for more than a day was worse. There were various types of beatings, and what was, perhaps, most interesting psychologically was that in the middle of every night appeared a special SS detachment, called *Verfügungstruppe*,* which consisted of unpaid volunteers (unpaid, that is, for this special task) who went through a violent beating exercise purely for the fun of it. At the other end of psychological interest was the composure and behaviour of the orthodox Jews, of whom I was not one. Quite often, we were chased through corridors, with SS men with rifles on either side, who beat us with those rifles while we ran through. What *I* did when such a corridor was in sight was to stop and wait until I had a long free space before me; then I bent down, covered my head with my hands, and ran through the corridor as fast as I could, so that I got most of the knocks on my behind. The orthodox Jews were above any such evasive action. They slowly walked through those corridors, in an upright position, with the result that you couldn't identify them when they came out at the other end – but, at the same time, without showing the slightest sign in their behaviour of having been touched, telling each other the same Jewish jokes at the other end as they had before the operation started. I was stunned: this was one of the deepest experiences of my life, about which I later published an article, a few weeks after my escape from Austria. There they were, people who seemed quaint, curious figures in ordinary life, now behaving in a detached manner which was far beyond the rest of us. In particular, I remember a newspaper boy whom I had known because I always bought my papers from him. He must have been about sixteen or seventeen. When he came out at the other end of such a corridor, I literally didn't recognise him; it took me minutes to discover who he

---

*   [HK:] 'Disposal Squad' – which may not mean much, but then *Verfügungstruppe* didn't mean much either.

was. But his behaviour was of the orthodox kind, and when I asked him how it was possible for him to behave like that, he laughed and answered, "Well, we have had a few thousand years' training, haven't we? What difference does one more such incident make? These people haven't reached the stage where they know what they're doing so you can't even blame them." Then he told me a Jewish joke which was appropriate to the occasion.

After three days, we got our first food, paid for by the Jewish Community. Most people were sick after it; I myself wasn't hungry any more by that stage and ate very cautiously and little. On, I think, the fourth day, one chap suddenly went beserk, if beserk you can call it, and started shouting "Criminals, murderers, sadists ..." He was shot dead, whereupon another chap, likewise, decided that he had had enough, and jumped out of the fourth-floor window. Now this wouldn't do at all, having a Jewish corpse in the street, so we were told to stand with our faces against a wall, by way of punishment, without the slightest movement; whoever moved would be shot: the SS stood with their rifles behind us. This exercise lasted about four hours – in which circumstances it was amazing to note how much you could move without moving, by gradually shifting your weight from one leg to the other.

As for events in the outside world, here's the Nazis' own statistical survey:

> In Vienna, 17 synagogues and 61 prayer houses (described by the newspaper *Der Stürmer* as 'not real houses of God, but dens of iniquity') were set on fire. 7,800 Jews were arrested, including 1,226 who already had permission to emigrate or who were listed as wishing to emigrate at the centre for Jewish emigration. 4,083 Jewish shops were plundered and closed down, 1,950 dwellings ransacked. In Germany as a whole, damage amounted to 25 million marks, and 7½ thousand shops and stores were destroyed.

These figures were revealed at a meeting of representatives of the Ministries of Finance and Economic Affairs. Hermann Göring, who presided in his capacity as Commissioner for the Four Year Plan, exclaimed: "Good heavens! Why couldn't you have killed off a couple of hundred Jews instead of destroying so much valuable property?" In fact, 91 Jews were killed during the pogrom according to the official German statistics. The number of those who committed suicide has never been established. Göring later made a speech in which he promised that within a year, Vienna would be *'judenrein'* – free of Jews and clean. *That* kind of promise the Nazis tended to keep.

Now, to give a full description of the events of those days of imprisonment would be repetitive and boring; suffice it to say that more often than not, when something frightening was in store for us, we were told of it beforehand, so that we could fully savour our anxiety for hours before the event. As a result, when, on the sixth day, we were told: "Tomorrow, at 6 a.m., you will be castrated, and at 8 o'clock you will be executed", we believed it. By that time, mind you, most of us were beyond the will to survive – almost too tired to be capable of fear. Nevertheless, at one moment during that night, the thought flicked through my mind: "If, by any remote chance, I should succeed in getting out of here, and in dying in a bed, I swear to myself that I'll never again be in a bad mood, whatever the circumstances of my life or death." I'll come back to this one later.

We were not castrated at six o'clock nor executed at eight. Instead, we were transported to a proper police prison, where we met proper, ordinary criminals – veritable saints compared to our guards and officers. In the course of the morning, after a series of the usual violent incidents, there was another interview. This time, the atmosphere *seemed* slightly more courteous. "Sit down," the officer said as I approached his desk. I could not believe my ears, and was right not to: as I sat down, the chair was of course, pulled from under me. Nevertheless, the questions seemed less Kafkaesque than at previous interviews, and I decided to be on my guard, just in case there was some point in giving a skilful answer.

"Why are you bleeding all over?" "Oh, well, I fell down a whole flight of stairs as I came up here." "Fell? You fell down a flight of stairs?" "Yes, I stumbled and fell." "Did anybody beat you?" "No." "Did you see anybody beat anybody?" "No." "Nothing at all?" "No." He adopted a more solemn voice: "Have you any complaint about the treatment you received?!" "None whatever." While I answered, I heard an excerpt from an interview at the next desk: "Do you know why you are in here?" "I believe because I am one of the murderers of vom Rath." "That is correct." My own interrogator now proceeded to a series of questions which could not but raise hopes in my mind: "If we released you, how soon would you be able to leave the country?" "Immediately, and I would leave tomorrow." That, of course, was a lie: for more than eight months I had tried, in vain, to obtain a passport. "Have you any proof that you can leave immediately?" "It so happens I have," I said. "I have a British visa and I have the relevant document on me." I pulled the British Consulate's confirmation out of my pocket. He read it carefully, then shouted: "Form 'B'." In due course, four identical forms were placed in front of me which, this time, I was required to read. They said that in no circumstances, for the rest of my life, wherever I was, would I say a word about what I'd seen and experienced while being imprisoned, and that I was aware that if, at any stage, I were to disclose what I had seen and experienced, I would meet with just punishment, wherever I was. I signed, perjuring myself joyfully: unless this was another funny game there really was hope. The officer then shouted "D!", which made my heart sink again, because I thought it might mean Dachau. I was pushed into group 'D', then, and the excitement about a possible release had totally overcome my exhaustion. Where, a day or two before, I had wholly given up, accepting the end without much difficulty, the desire to survive had come back explosively.

Group 'D' was pushed into one of the corridors we knew so well, again with SS lined up on either side, complete with rifles. But though we were chased through the corridors, nobody touched us this time which, of course, reinforced hope. This operation continued for a considerable time: we were chased through a vast variety of corridors, up and down staircases, almost always with SS lined up on either side, and always being left unharmed. We were, however, reaching exhaustion point, and wondered how long we would be able to continue. I happened to be the first in my particular group, the front runner, as it were, and running along a corridor, I came to face a glass door without being able to stop before it. I crashed into it, and as I picked myself up and got through the door, I was standing in the street. This, I realised, was my discharge from prison.

There is an excerpt, not readily comprehensible to me, from the minutes of the Regional Economic Committee for Vienna, drafted by an SS Captain by the name of Seeliger – and interesting as a psychological document, rather than as a factual report on what he calls 'the population at large'.

> As for the popular reaction to the events of 10th November and the following days, the unanimous view was that it had been one of revulsion and horror, and that in the execution of the operation, scandalous scenes had been enacted which did great damage to the prestige of the Party and the Government. Two of those present declared that if another party existed in Germany, it would be the duty of every right-thinking man and woman to support it. All those present declared unanimously that pogroms and vandalisms were not suitable means for solving the Jewish question, and that the destruction, looting and devastation which had taken place had filled not only the population at large, but even large sections of the Party, with disgust and shame.

Well, neither I nor any of my fellow Jews were in touch with any of this 'revulsion and horror', 'disgust and shame'. Anyway, the first thing I wanted to do as I was out in the street was to ring my father to tell him that I was alright. As I tried to do this, I noticed the effect of what one might call a traumatic neurosis: diagonally across the road I saw a telephone box, but in order to reach it I would have had to pass an SS man who was posted outside the prison. I tried to get myself to pass him, explaining to myself that at this stage he would not possibly harm me, since I was obviously a released person, and as care had always been taken not to show the outside world what was happening to prisoners. In spite of several mental attempts, however, I could not bring myself to pass him; instead, I walked right round the block, in order to reach the telephone box from the other side, without the necessity of having to pass an SS man.

Now, the Gestapo were not as well organised as they were reputed to be, and I should not, in fact, have been released: from another Gestapo headquarters, a warrant for my arrest had been issued before I was freed. I came to know about this fact through bribing an SS officer to look up my files: he had been an acquaintance of a half-Jewish cousin of mine, through whom I advanced the payment to him. The information was that I was to be arrested because my father had money in Hungary and England, which he had not declared – neither fact true, incidentally, but that did not, of course, make any difference, and there was no point in trying to establish the truth. One consequence which seemed to flow from this state of affairs had been that I had been told, before my arrest, that a large sum of English money (I forget the actual amount, I think it was about £1,000) was needed, in addition to the official 'escape tax' which comprised all my father's available money, in order for me to obtain one of the documents needed to get my passport. My brother-in-law had duly paid the money, but I never got the document. As a matter of fact, the Jews themselves were made to pay compensation to the German Government for the damage and devastation caused to their own property. At the meeting of representatives of the Ministries of Finance and Economic Affairs, presided over by Göring (which I've already mentioned), the following was decreed:

> (1) German Jews must make restitution for all damage caused by the pogrom and reimburse insurance companies for any payments they have been obliged to make. (2) As an atonement for the death of Councillor vom Rath, a fine is to be levied on all Jews totalling one thousand million marks. (3) All Jewish enterprises, shops and factories are to be taken over compulsorily by non-Jews – the sale price to be paid into blocked accounts.

Fortunately, my father still had enough money left to pay this 'restitution and atonement tax' too. Well, in full possession of the information in my file after my release, I was, of course, determined to be extremely cautious in order not to be arrested again. I rarely slept at home and, generally, made myself as unfindable as possible. At the same time, I had to continue to try to get the necessary documents for obtaining my passport, and indeed the passport itself. Each attempt was, of course, fraught with danger since, in theory, I should have been arrested each time I appeared at one of the relevant police or emigration departments. Fortunately, inefficiency prevailed. I remember one particular instance, when the official in question looked at my name, repeating "Keller, Keller … I know your name: I ought to know your face." I remained silent; he had, no doubt, been given or shown a copy of the warrant, but had forgotten his instructions. "Ah," he suddenly said, "I seem to remember. You probably were one of the Jews downstairs whom we employed to sift documents, and that's where I know your name and face from." I joyfully agreed, although, of course, I'd never been in the place.

In the end, I did actually obtain all the necessary documents, and my passport. But by this stage I and my uncle-adviser, a barrister, were very doubtful about how to manage my departure, for the border police, as well as the officials at Vienna airport, would be in possession of the warrant for my arrest: that much we knew from the information about my file. However, another event occurred which caused the absolute need for my immediate escape – or my immediate attempt to escape, anyway: my father died, and I became his sole heir. It was obvious that as soon as the fact of his death was known, there would be redoubled attempts to arrest me and not to let me go.

My uncle and I finally decided for me to try a flight from Vienna rather than a train journey. For one thing, emigration by aeroplane was rare at that time, and one might possibly hope that I would be expected at a border rather than at the airport; for another, my uncle, if he accompanied me to the airport, would know if the escape succeeded, and would be able to notify my mother and sister in London. I bought myself an air ticket for the next plane and, next morning, proceeded to Vienna airport with my uncle. As we waited in the airport lounge, we sat back to back, because we thought that two Jews being seen together at the same time might arouse suspicion. We were talking over our shoulders, when I suddenly heard a stern voice ask my uncle: "What are you doing here?" "I'm waiting for a friend who is arriving on the plane from Prague." "What's his name?" My uncle invented a name. There was a short silence, and then the voice said "Come with us."

As I was passing through the passport control (or trying to, anyway), the officer, looking at my name and picture said, "Keller, Keller … I know that name and I know that picture; there is something wrong with you." I shrugged my shoulders in bafflement, hoping to God that he had forgotten his instructions, as his predecessor had at that emigration office, and that he would be equally disinclined to tell his superiors that he had forgotten. "Ah," he said, after a short pause, "I think I remember: you didn't surrender your driving licence when all Jews were ordered to." I had never driven a car, and I had had no driving licence, but I immediately confessed: "Yes, this is quite true, but I have apologized and did finally surrender it. I simply had forgotten, and I think my apology was accepted." He shook his head musingly, and finally said, "Come with me." I was taken into an empty room, where I was told to undress, and every inch of my clothing was carefully examined – as, of course, was my luggage. The whole operation took a very long time, and the departure time of my plane had passed, but through a window, I still saw the plane standing on the runway. Eventually, the investigation having yielded a negative result, the officer who had taken me into the room said, "Alright, then. Dress and get into the plane." As the plane took off, there was the overwhelming consciousness of survival, but, at the same time, extreme anxiety about my uncle's fate. He was going to ring my mother and sister upon my departure, so I thought that if they were at the airport in Croydon, that meant that he had been released; and if they weren't, that he hadn't been. Unfortunately, when I arrived in Croydon, there was no trace of them. I was now certain that my uncle was on his way to a concentration camp. Eventually, however, I found my family: they had gone to the wrong door. My uncle had been released after an hour's interrogation, and had telephoned them.

I was fortunate; thousands of other Jews – eventually millions, six million Jews – weren't. They did not die in the war, as part of the cruelty of war, in battle; they were exterminated – the vastest extermination of human beings in the history of the world. Against this background, let's hear what Dr Josef Goebbels, Germany's Minister of Propaganda and a man with literary, 'cultural' aspirations, had to say in an official statement in that selfsame month of November, 1938:

> The cowardly assassination by the Jew Grynspan has provoked, in the entire German people, a most understandable indignation which, in view of the unexampled turpitude of the deed and the unbelievable impudence with which it was carried out, manifested itself in anti-Jewish demonstrations. If, despite the highly justified fury of all Germans, not a hair on the head of a single Jew was so much as touched, the world should give due recognition to the German people's sense of discipline and decency.

Two conclusions emerge – one of them what I learned to regard as sour grapes. For a long time, I thought that if one happened to survive it all, it was important to have had this experience, because, otherwise, one would not really be aware of what human beings were capable of. That's to say, if my best friend had told me about the things I had witnessed – about this indiscriminate, enthusiastic, collective sadism – I should not have believed him. The trouble is that, psychologically, this realisation of what human beings are capable of at the most primitive level simply does not work in the long run. Today, although I know, purely intellectually, what I experienced, the emotional awareness of it has been repressed – or, to put it differently, I am just as incapable of appreciating this level of reality emotionally as I would have been if I had never experienced it. This type of repression is probably the most dangerous obstacle along the road towards an ethical improvement of society. It's all very well to be intellectually aware of what people are capable of, but if you don't feel it in your bones, you are likely not to do enough about preventing recurrences of such sadistic climaxes.

But the other conclusion, equally psychological, has remained reality. I've mentioned the thought which flashed through my mind at the very stage when, rationally, I had given up all hope – that if, against all realistic expectations, I was going to survive, I would never again be in a bad mood. This one, surprisingly, still works. Whenever there is motivation for a bad mood, it is enough for me to remind myself of this thought, and the attendant emotion comes back with it, the result being a grateful elation about being alive.

3   Testimony, 1939

After his release, Keller was determined to break his promise to the Gestapo as soon as possible, by writing publicly about his experience. The full account printed above was not written until many years later, but he did write at the time a short piece which appeared in an émigré journal just after his arrival in England – his first adult publication. As he said in a letter to a Roman Catholic nun 35 years later:

> Immediately upon my arrival in England, I cleared my conscience by confirming my perjury ('I shall never tell anybody …') in an article in a Paris weekly, in which I described what I had experienced, and pointed out that the joyful martyrs amongst the orthodox Jews, though no doubt passionately anti-Christian, were, in ethical essence, the truest Christians I had ever come across.
>
> I was much concerned in my teens with the thought that religions, their causes and effects, were most similar in the very respects in which they thought they differed most; perhaps I still am.[1]

The 'article' is in fact in the form of a letter to the editor, which Keller signed simply 'HK, London'. It appeared anonymously in *Das Neue Tage-Buch* on 7 January 1939. The published version is a heavily edited and condensed version of the original, which was nearly twice the length. *Das Neue Tage-Buch* ('*The New Diary*') was a reincarnation in exile of the Berlin independent weekly *Das Tagebuch*. Originally founded in 1920 by the Viennese theatre critic Stefan Grossmann, it was a publication that Keller would have known in Vienna as one of the more influential radical magazines of the Weimar Republic. In 1933, when the Nazis came to power, the journal was being edited by the Frankfurt-born Leopold Schwarzschild, Grossmann having withdrawn from the editorship in 1927 due to ill health. Schwarzschild fled to Paris, where he immediately re-established the journal under the name *Das Neue Tage-Buch*. Grossmann escaped arrest in 1933 because of his state of health, but was expelled from Germany. He returned to Vienna, where he died in 1935. Schwarzschild continued publishing *Das Neue Tage-Buch* in Paris until the fall of France in 1940, providing a invaluable means of expression for German opposition opinion during the Nazi era: it was later described as 'far and away the best of all German émigré publications' and its shrewd analysis and anti-appeasement warnings (Winston Churchill was a regular contributor from 1933) were 'read by the chancelleries and general staffs of Europe … and debated in the Parliaments of Britain, France and Holland'.[2]

Keller's letter was published under the title, given it by the journal, '… denn sie wissen nicht, was sie tun' ('… for they know not what they do'), the words of Christ on the cross.[3] It survives in two versions: a carbon copy retained by Keller of his original letter as sent to *Das Neue Tage-Buch*, and the published version as edited by the journal. The latter is reproduced here, together with the editorial comments with which it was prefaced and followed.

'… for they know not what they do'

A letter received by the NTB from a former inmate of a German prisoners' camp has made a deep impression on us. It is a letter which contains nothing concrete. But there are things which so obviously come straight from the heart, that they reach others' hearts immediately. This is the text:

> Dear Editorial Board,
>
> As a Jewish former 'protection prisoner' in a German holding camp I should like to take the liberty of sending you a few lines, the publication of which is close to my heart.
>
> During the time of my imprisonment I had the opportunity of getting to know the mass of Jewry, the majority, namely the much-maligned *'Polish'* orthodox Jews. The stance which these Jews took in the face of the sufferings laid upon them moved me to tears. Indeed, I can now say that I am grateful to fate for allowing me to live through this time. Just as I should never have thought it possible that there could be so many abysmally evil people as I was forced to encounter during my imprisonment, I should never have thought it possible that there could be so many people of the highest moral and spiritual calibre as I had the opportunity of meeting during my imprisonment.
>
> I am speaking on the one hand of the persecutors, and on the other of those who are being persecuted.
>
> The *hate- and revenge-free* attitude of the tormented Jews finds only *one* equivalent in history: Jesus Christ. It may appear paradoxical, but it is understandable to anybody who gives the matter thought: National Socialism,

that embodiment of the Antichrist, is opposed by Jewry – and in particular orthodox Jewry – as the embodiment of Christ.

Never ever before did I have the opportunity (and I am unlikely ever to have it again either) to see the phrase 'Lord, forgive them, for they know not what they do' *come true*[4] in such a noble form as during this time of my imprisonment. I do not think that it is necessary to go into detail, or list examples. Such impressions have to be lived through: if described their effect will be fragmentary.

In any case, the deeply moving fact that the most maltreated part of Judaism persecuted today not only harbours no feelings of hate against its persecutors, but even prays to God for *them*, is, I think, an observation worth sharing.

We felt obliged to allow this voice that wished to bear witness, to speak. It shows up a new, so far unknown trait in the drama, a trait that must move everybody: but which must give particular satisfaction to those circles within the Christian Church who have recently been dedicating themselves to charitable work on behalf of this suffering of strangers.

*Keller's cousin Rudi Kompfner, with his niece Ena Franey,
supervising the building of the house at Herne Hill for Roy and Mowgli, c.1936.*

4   *London, 1939*

Keller arrived in London on 20 December 1938, and joined his mother at his sister's house in Herne Hill, the house which his cousin Rudi Kompfner had designed with Keller's father. Rudi Kompfner was living nearby, working for Roy Franey's building company, engaged to Peggy Mason, an English girl, and anxiously awaiting the arrival of his parents and sister, Inge. The Kompfners emigrated by train, arriving in London on Christmas Day after a frightening journey, during which they were all taken off the train and searched, their valuables confiscated, and they themselves detained until they had thought the train would have left without them. The family feared particularly for Bernhard Kompfner, Rudi and Inge's father, whom the Gestapo had already arrested once and apparently wanted to interview again – but, as in Keller's case, inefficiency fortunately prevailed, and he was allowed to leave. Mr. Kompfner's fragile state of health had prevented his travelling ahead by air as Keller did, but in the end the stress of the train journey also proved too much. He died in January 1939, just two weeks after his emigration.[1]

Keller's brother-in-law, Roy Franey, worked tirelessly to help as many as possible of his wife's family and friends leave Vienna, and he succeeded in getting about fifteen people to London, including Grete Keller's youngest brother Hans (the barrister uncle who saw Keller off at the airport in Vienna) and Oscar Adler and his wife. The financial cost of this was considerable, because as well as the charges for visas and German emigration taxes, he had to act as guarantor for everyone he brought into Britain.

Roy Franey's fifteen émigrés were among over 60,000 people from Germany and Austria who had sought refuge in Britain by the time war broke out. For the British government, the question of what to do with them was an increasingly pressing concern. Some 30,000 German nationals had been interned in Britain during the First World War, and many thousands were deported, a policy that had not been much questioned at the time. Twenty years later, however, British attitudes to Germans living in their midst were less negative. Growing awareness of what was happening in Germany, and in particular the dreadful events of Kristallnacht, had generated considerable public sympathy for the Jewish refugees. In any case, the government had already concluded that little had been achieved for the war effort by the indiscriminate internment and deportation policy of the First World War, and Sir John Anderson, the Home Secretary, was keen to avoid a repetition. The policy which he decided upon for 1939 was therefore much more benign. All German and Austrian nationals were required to appear before a local tribunal, which would judge whether they were likely to pose a threat to British interests. The tribunals divided the cases before them into three categories: category A were to be interned immediately; category B were doubtful cases who were left at liberty but under certain conditions (such as being prevented from travelling more than a few miles from home, or having to obey an evening curfew); category C – the vast majority – were termed 'friendly enemy aliens' of no threat to Britain, and allowed to go on with their lives without restriction.

When war broke out in September 1939, Keller was on holiday at the house which his sister's family had rented at Angmering-on-Sea in Sussex.[2] Immediately, the planned restrictions on German nationals came into force, with the Home Secretary's announcement in Parliament of the Aliens Order on 4 September 1939: 'The new Order requires all enemy aliens (that is, Germans and Austrians) ... to report to the police, and provides that they must obtain police permits for change of residence, for travelling, and for possession of certain articles, including cameras and motor cars.'[3] On 7 September Keller received a letter from the local police requiring him not to move from his current address without permission, which he duly requested on 16 September before returning to London.[4] He was summoned to appear before his tribunal on 11 November 1939, and placed in category C, as were the rest of the family.[5] Life then continued much as normal during the 'phoney war' period: Keller lived at his sister's house in Herne Hill, playing the violin (taking lessons from Max Rostal), reading, preparing for his LRAM diploma, and trying to make a decision about his future. From the evidence of a letter which he received on 19 December from the Careers Section of the *Jewish Chronicle*, it seems that he was contemplating university study in either philosophy or medicine – although, as the *Chronicle* pointed out to him, 'if you wanted to study medicine ... the difficulty, of course, would be the permission to practise when you had qualified ... As an alien it would be next to impossible for you to get that permission in present circumstances.' As for philosophy, 'unless you were exceptionally brilliant, it would, I think, be most difficult to earn a living as a philosopher.'[6] Subsequent correspondence shows Keller attending Science, Radio Technology and Television classes at the Norwood Technical Institute, as well as embarking on lessons in Yiddish and Stenotyping.[7]

In addition to his educational pursuits, Keller was involved after September 1939 in volunteer war work and charity concerts. His later letters from internment refer to 'Brixton casualty ARP work' and 'Red Cross concerts'. He also seems to have signed up to join the ranks of the many hundreds of refugees who were being drafted into agricultural work to help with wartime food production.

> Since the number of workers on the land had declined at the rate of 12,000 men a year between 1921 and 1937, with two million less arable acreage at the outbreak of this war than in 1914, it was soon realised that there would be an almost unlimited demand for agricultural labour. It was optimistically supposed that all refugees not otherwise employable would become skilled farm workers and that they might play a fairly useful part in the government's ploughing-up schemes.'[8]

One of the most successful efforts to involve refugees in the British war effort – and thus protect them by establishing them as useful members of the community – was initiated by Yvonne Kapp (neé Mayer), who was then working as Assistant to the Director of the Czech Refugee Trust Fund, established with British government money after the invasion of Czechoslovakia. This was the only refugee organisation to be funded by the British government – its existence perhaps a British guilt-offering after Munich:

> Britain had obtained the peace it craved – refugees had paid the price. A significant section of the British public considered their nation to be under a moral obligation to mitigate the Czech refugee crisis. For these reasons the British government – which steadfastly refused to finance the exodus from Germany and Austria – decided to fund relief and resettlement for refugees from Czechoslovakia.[9]

Kapp, who was born in South London to a Jewish family, had been working as a journalist up until the 1930s, when events on the continent awakened her political conscience: in an interview in the 1980s she said that it had been because of 'fascism in Germany and the burning of the books that as a liberal, and a Jewish liberal at that, I began to feel really involved'.[10] She threw herself into refugee relief work and political campaigning, joining the Communist Party as a result of a visit to the Soviet Union in 1935. Initially, she began helping individual refugees in a voluntary capacity, offering assistance and accommodation in her own home, but in 1938 began to work full time for the cause, first for the Jewish Refugees Committee, and then for the Czech Refugee Trust Fund.

Sensing the political importance of refugees being seen to make a contribution to the war effort, Kapp 'set about devising a programme for those of active age to be drafted into industry or agriculture, including retraining for such occupations.' She was so successful that 'by the early spring of 1940, hundreds of the Germans, Austrians and Czechs had been drafted into factories, foundries, mines, forestry and farming.'[11] From the reference to 'the farm' in Keller's letter of 17 July 1940, it appears that he had been about to become one of these refugee agricultural workers when his plans were interrupted by the sudden change in government policy towards 'enemy aliens'.

~

Throughout his early months in England Keller was also busy writing. His reading as a young man was evidently voracious, and he engaged passionately with every idea he encountered. As he wrote to his schoolfriend Fritz Schonbach, 'I am reading Schopenhauer at the moment, but I do not just stick to this passive activity; I am writing polemics against his work. It is not easy to say whether these polemics are more stupid than long, or longer than stupid.'[12] It was not only his reading that provoked him to put pen to paper: almost any experience could be a subject – the lavatory in a Lyons Corner House, for example ('They stand there in quiet reverence neatly lined up: notice their bodies. By entering a pissoir you learn what the Temple of the Body is like ...'), or an amusement arcade ('It would hardly be possible to describe these places or their details to anyone living in Paris'). A visit to a Zionist youth group in April 1940 provoked so much thought during the tube journey home afterwards that Keller next day produced a lengthy report on it, together with recommendations for the group's reorganisation.[13]

Unsurprisingly, Keller's writing at this time was often concerned with contemporary political events and issues of nationality and identity – including of course Judaism and the 'most burning and topical question' of whether or not National Socialism could be said in any way to be 'typically German'.[14] Keller's treatment of such issues was never narrowly political, however: he was always most interested in their psychological and ethical implications, drawing all the time on his philosophical reading. At this time, Keller seems to have thought of himself primarily as a philosopher; but although this might have been true of his reading, it was not true of his writing, which already contained plenty of evidence of his inclination for psychology. At this date, however, it seems that he had not yet read much of the psychological literature, despite his connections in Vienna (Oscar Adler's wife Paula was the niece of Sigmund Freud). Even some years later, when he was in the midst of rectifying this omission, he still seems to have considered philosophy to be the ground of his thought – much to the surprise of his then collaborator, Margaret Phillips:

> I have been puzzled ever since in one of your early letters you spoke of yourself as coming from philosophy, for while it is obvious that you are a psychologist through and through, you have never yet said anything which suggested to me that you had arrived at any of your values with the help of philosophy.[15]

Another indication that Keller had not yet realised his own character as a writer lies in the disparity between what he was actually writing and what he professed himself intending to write. His preference for short forms – essays, short stories and aphorisms – is clear from his surviving manuscripts, but his correspondence from around this time shows his desire to be the author of something more substantial. There are frequent mentions of the current 'book', 'dissertation' or 'treatise' on which he was engaged, though the variety of titles and the absence or fragmentary nature of such manuscripts suggest that he found this sort of extended writing difficult. In February 1939, for example, he told his schoolfriend Fritz Schonbach that 'I am at the moment writing a book. Title: 'On the Renaissance of Naivety within present-day intellectual Judaism.' Whether it will succeed, I shall have to wait and see. At the moment, I am gathering material and ideas, by far the most pleasant part of such work.'[16] Other subjects mentioned for book-length treatment were 'The Psychology and Logic of Wit'[17] and 'A Treatise on Vanity',[18] of which Keller confessed 'I've only got as far as the introduction'. None of these manuscripts survive, but there are others which appear to have been intended to be longer works, including '*Ursache und Schuld*: Roman von Hans Keller'.[19]

Although none of these projected 'books' advanced beyond a few pages, Keller's output of shorter pieces was considerable. As well as all his varied essays and stories, he produced many hundreds of aphorisms, for which he had a pronounced gift:

> Aphorisms are not valuable on account of their substance, but on account of their function. They transmit little truth, but they provoke the desire for it.

> An artist needn't know what he has to say as long as he says it.

> The fool is simple without being profound, the mediocre is profound without being simple.

> There are three spheres of life where pity is much more immoral than indifference: Love, Art, Science.

> Both the dreamer and the poet see things as they aren't. But only the poet sees them as they could be.[20]

These particular examples are among the earliest instances of Keller's writing in English, and date from around 1941, the same year in which his next publication appeared – a set of (German) aphorisms which were printed in the London-based Austrian émigré magazine *Zeitspiegl*, under the rather untranslatable title 'Schonend, weil in Kürze'.[21] Keller continued to write aphorisms all his life, and his later writings are full of such striking sentences – one 1949 essay, for example, opens with the thought-provoking statement that 'Art arises where the arbitary and the predictable are superseded by unpredictable inevitability'.[22] In his first years in England, however, he wrote a particularly large number of aphorisms, many of which he polished and collected into sets. Writing English aphorisms was evidently one of the ways in which he came to terms with the language and formed his style. Perceptive insights, paradox and verbal play came more\naturally to Keller than the formal development of an extended argument; using English allowed him to play more consciously with language, and also helped him write more concisely.

In later life, Keller professed himself grateful for his enforced change of language, reflecting that English suited his personal style better than German would have done.[23] At the time, however, it was 'a major crisis'.[24] As he wrote to a friend, 'I find it extraordinarily difficult to leave the German language behind and take on the English language.'[25] He was already so committed a writer by the time he left Vienna that such a change could hardly be accomplished with ease. Aphorisms apart, he continued to write mostly in German for nearly five years after his arrival in England. In the same way he remained musically within refugee circles for even longer.

Nevertheless, he was immediately curious about the new culture he was entering, as the following essay shows. Written in German, most likely early in 1939, it survives in two versions, the more complete of which is printed below.[26]

'An Emigrant Searches for England'

Far from wanting to come up with popular and mindless generalizations, I nevertheless believe in the existence of an 'English character', a belief that makes me want to draw attention to a number of emotional features typical of a large part of the population.

There is a well-known anecdote of the pupil who asked the rabbi whether humans live from the outside inwards or from the inside outwards, to which the rabbi responded with a thoughtful 'you could say: yes'. Ever since I've lived in England the ideas behind that question have gained new significance: for the Englishman, as opposed, for example, to the uninfected German, lives from the outside inwards. In Spengler's terms he is similar in this context to the man of civilization: his energy goes outwards, not inwards (as would be the case with a man of culture). He develops concrete thought to an extraordinary degree; isn't it remarkable that philosophy, this most abstract of all sciences, experienced the highest development of its *concrete* branch, inductive logic, with John Stuart Mill, an Englishman? In this country people think concretely with extraordinary consistency. Even religion here becomes a matter of *things*, it is placed on a real, plastic level, and apart from Hume no Englishman ever seems to have been bothered by doubts that threaten his understanding. This tendency of thought *seems* to extend the scientific horizon to the same degree as it apparently limits that horizon from the perspective of the theory of cognition. This tendency to out-turned energy can be observed right down to the smallest detail: nowhere else will you see such thorough study of daily newspapers as is cultivated in this country.

This matter-of-fact, vivid way of thinking is matched by a tendency to categorize without major complications, to layer, to simplify the tangled problems of life. Here is religion, there is life; here are the ideals, there is reality. Whereas Goethe (in *Tasso*) resignedly withdrew from the world of appearances into one of dream-images, Shelley finds nothing objectionable in a double life, conducted on the one hand in the real environment and on the other in the ideal, fictional dreamland of poetry. Nor does he shed a single tear over the lack of relevance of his imaginary world to the world about him. In this he understands classical aesthetics much more deeply than did any German classicist who, with mounting despair, confronted the diffusion of the opposing areas of thought and feeling. This naive attitude towards the deepest problems of life must remain unintelligible to the 'sentimental', intellectual German. Shelley was an atheist. As a German (if you permit me this fantastic assumption) he would have been a decadent metaphysician. Yet as an Englishman he was capable of very neatly separating the irrational world in which he spoke and felt as a poet from the surrounding society, *into which* he thought in a materialistic way, and for this reason he deemed it permissible to call himself 'atheistic'.

This leaning towards a schematism rooted in concrete thought (which in the area of philosophy – with Wolf, for example – appears exceedingly strange) is the criterion of an original naivety that surprises the foreigner mightily. At first you think you are faced with a nation of fools; soon you realize your mistake, only to fall victim to the opposite error: to make a habit of finding naivety only in the idiot and the sage, but never in the intellectual or moral make-up of the man-in-the-street; then you seek the genius in every Englishman, only to come to the final conclusion that almost every member of this race bears naive traits independent of his or her intellectual or moral capacities. Schiller used to read detective novels in his uncreative moments; Shelley liked going to the pond to sail tiny boats in just the way that we do to amuse our children.

The dislike of every complication in the problems of life (or of knowing about the complications) leads on the one hand to the neglect, or at least the simplification, of philosophical questions, but on the other hand to an intensification of detailed studies of the human being as well. The highest development of this process we find in Shakespeare, whose character studies outstrip many a psychoanalytical dissertation.

Those of us who have lived in Germany have always thought that Germans have a special access to certain complexes of thought, which, if they haven't invented, they've nevertheless discovered. However, it turns out that certain ethical problems, whose treatment through Kant on the philosophical side and Schiller on both the philosophical and poetic sides we have all felt to be specifically and uniquely German, have been addressed just as deeply by Wordsworth and Coleridge from an artistic point of view. In this we are repeatedly surprised by a healthily naive manner of thinking. The intellectual German, no matter how unproductive he may be, is complicated; the Englishman, no matter how creative he is, remains naive and simple, without being primitive. How typical it is in this context that Dostoyevsky, the complicated fanatic of naivety, loved the English so dearly (but hated the French); maybe he found among the English the figures he had dreamt up, Prince Myshkin or Aljoshca Karamazov, at least to some extent.

The fading of any wellspring of judgment leads the Englishman to an unconditional and reactionary clinging to these romantic explosions and revolutions. Individual revolution you find only as a reaction against the dark sides of limited development: against conservatism that is suffering from hardened arteries, against fossilised tradition, against convention, and against conventional piety. Surely the over-developed consciousness of class and status, together with their fossilised conventions, are unwelcome developments. However, the innate worth of a Lord is as crucial and significant as is the acquired worth of a Gauleiter: today, with regard to these stratified relations we are prepared to make concessions. Even if the 'thank you' and the 'sorry' that you hear constantly from the mouth of an Englishman can be considered at least in part a convention, I find it much more attractive if one agrees to say 'thank you' as often as possible rather than to kick each other. If modern Germany continues along its present path, then it might well be that it is the kick that becomes the convention. We will judge this kick as severely as we appreciate the 'thank you' of the Englishman. A fossilised 'sorry' remains greatly more attractive than a living kick.

As a reaction against the social ossification mentioned above, certain individuals among English intellectuals stand out: the matter-of-fact (how could he be otherwise?) philosopher [William] Godwin, Wilde, and above all Byron who so completely falls out of my English framework and whose romantic cynicism, similar to that of Disraeli's, reminds us far more of Heine's than that of any other English poet. Shelley, who also revolted against English society, and like Byron fled it, did so on the basis of naive (though also intellectually distinguished) opinions, which would have had to lead back to the conserving and fossilised society in some vicious circle, were it possible to put these judgments to the test; they appear to be categorical and static, incapable of development or withstanding changes brought about by time and circumstance.

That inconsistency which on the side of genius has brought the Germans so much good and on the side of the devil has brought them so much bad, is, as I have said, totally alien to the English. This manifests itself again in a manner that is at once pleasant and unpleasant especially in the English educational system. Here [the English] hold fast to good and bad practices with steadfast stubbornness; one-sided work, training the memory in great detail, which in an earlier age of a limited educational system might have had its point, is cultivated to this day and paid for dearly by the neglect of general topics offering an overview of life. Here the Englishman works inductively: from paying attention to detail he may go on to comprehend the whole, whereas the German is used to starting from the general insight and working deductively towards the detail. This latter way of teaching, however, rarely lacks a dangerous encouragement to superficiality.

A naive race creates no music. Music, the most romantic, metaphysical, 'sentimental' of all the arts reaches its highest watermark in Germany. There one yearns and bursts through barriers (upwards, as in [Goethe's] *Faust*, downwards as in [Rosenberg's] *Myth of the 20th Century*); it is such a constitution that breathes life into music. Here in England they merely achieve a limit. There is hardly an important composer here; I personally think Purcell is still the relatively outstanding one. But alongside the lack of musical fertility there is a fundamental and harmonious love of music, of which Handel, Haydn, Mozart, Beethoven, and Mendelssohn happily took note. This harmonious love, which today is strangely focused on Bach in particular, has nothing in common with the searing Bach fanaticism of the musical German. If the German nevertheless seems to understand Bach more deeply, then the reason for this must lie in the fact that the unhappy lover who yearns passionately for the beloved, but can never reach her, feels for her perhaps more deeply than does her happy husband. Thus the musical Englishman is happily married to Bach – so happily that Bach almost becomes a habit for him. German listening to music always bears a creative, active character, whereas English listening to music is entirely passive.

Thus the Englishman unconsciously represents a classical ideal, one for which Germans have always yearned in vain, without realizing how unclassical even the yearning is. In England physical training of the body is accorded outstanding importance, in this country sport enjoys an edified culture that has nothing to do with the enforced physical training of the hordes found in the Germany of today. Apollonian feelings and activities dominate this island, which is free from the deformation of dionysiac orgies: [the subjective idealist and nationalist] Fichte would have been impossible here; his grandchildren, the National Socialists, even more so; an enthusiastic, tolerant patriotism takes the place of an ecstatic, keenly destructive nationalism.

Everywhere we look in English intellectual life we find clear, intelligent, original minds and observant eyes. Lawrence's polemic against Freud left me dumbfounded. It is a polemic fought with weapons of the mind that have nothing in common with Freud's and which until then had been totally alien to me. Reading Lawrence's work left me rather confused. These two men would never be able to understand each other; to try to decide which of the two was right would be an infantile exercise: nothing would ever come of it.

In Germany the lower criminal murders, the higher and nastier one demonstrates intellectually the use of the non-use of morals and calls himself Nietzsche. Here, in England, such formally perfect disfiguration of human abilities is unknown, here you are simply either decent or not decent, but usually decent. The tendency towards schematics and layering of which I spoke at the opening is not a drive towards ranking, but to a classification of things put beside each other. The different areas of life are juxtaposed equally but harmoniously: a skilful footballer is as 'clever' as a wise philosopher.

The Englishman hates the turbulence of a Faust just as he hates the seduction of a Gretchen (though occasionally he pays lip service to moral codes and the awareness of moral codes). The straightforward, open, intelligent attitude of this people might yet show it can have positive effect, even in the near future.

5   Internment, June 1940

Everything changed in the spring of 1940. As the German Blitzkrieg swept across the rest of Europe, it seemed only a matter of time before Britain too would be invaded. Rumours of the role played in the fall of Norway and the Low Countries by German spies planted there ahead of the troops' arrival made Britons begin to look on their own 'enemy aliens' with more suspicion. As in May 1915 after the sinking of the *Lusitania*, in May 1940 an unreasoning panic over foreign nationals gripped the nation, orchestrated by a determined campaign in some parts of the popular right-wing press, where the 'refu-spy' was portrayed as a real danger.[1] The attempts of the Home Office to preserve a liberal policy crumbled as responsibility for internment passed into the control of the secretive Swinton Committee,[2] and those elements within the security services and the War Office which had long been pressing for mass internment now held sway.

The patient work of the nationwide network of tribunals was swept aside as the panic mounted, and views previously confined to a minority flowed into mainstream opinion: 'Don't trust a German,' the readers of the *Daily Herald* were advised,[3] and the *Daily Mail* agreed: 'Every German is an agent.'[4] 'I have German friends,' wrote one columnist in the *Sunday Chronicle*, 'but I would very willingly see them all, yes all, behind bars, and I have told them so to their faces.'[5] 'Act! Act! Act! – Do it now,' demanded the *Daily Mail*: 'All refugees from Austria, Germany and Czechoslovakia, men and women alike, should be drafted without delay to a remote part of the country and kept under strict supervision.'[6] The BBC had done much to fuel this frenzy of suspicion when it allowed Sir Neville Bland, former British Minister in the Hague, to broadcast to the nation (and reprint in *The Listener*) a talk about fifth columnists in Holland helping the advancing Germans: 'I hate to have to say this to you,' he told his listeners, 'but I find it my duty to say it, and say it I will: Be careful at this moment how you put complete trust in any person of German or Austrian connections. If you know people of this kind who are still at large, keep your eye on them; they may be perfectly all right – but they may not, and to-day we can't afford to take risks.'[7] Within government circles, Bland's language was even more alarmist: in a memorandum on the 'Fifth Column Menace' circulated in Whitehall on 14 May, he assured ministers that 'I have not the least doubt that, when the signal is given, as it will scarcely fail to be when Hitler so decides, there will be satellites of the monster all over the country who will at once embark on widespread sabotage and attacks on civilians and the military indiscriminately. We cannot afford to take this risk. All Germans and Austrians, at least, ought to be interned at once.'[8]

In this atmosphere, it was not only the émigrés themselves who were viewed with suspicion, but also those who were helping them. Roy Franey came to the attention of the Metropolitan Police for bringing into the country such a large number of 'enemy aliens', and he was interviewed at Brixton Police Station under section 18B of the Defence (General) Regulations 1939, (the same regulation under which Sir Oswald Mosley and other British fascists were interned). This threw the family into panic – Roy's daughter remembers Mrs Adler crying in the kitchen at Herne Hill, asking "what will become of us all if Roy is imprisoned?".[9] They were, of course, all completely dependent on him: he had secured their visas, vouched for them, and was now supporting everyone financially, at a time when employment opportunities for aliens were extremely limited.

The tribunals had put everyone Roy Franey had helped into category C, which was supposedly a declaration that they were officially accepted as genuine refugees, but it was not long before this was overturned. Internment of those not in the 'A' category began immediately after Churchill became Prime Minister on 10 May – and the importance of Churchill's personal support for the new policy should not be underestimated. The round-up started with those from categories B and C who were living anywhere near the south or east coast of the British Isles. With the German army now occupying the continental Channel ports and posing an additional threat from Scandinavia, the government was anxious to ensure that there could not be any help for invaders from resident fifth columnists. The coastal strip declared 'protected' was wide enough to include Cambridge, several of whose academics now found themselves arrested, together with some of their students and their colleagues from the London School of Economics, since that institution had been evacuated to Cambridge. The strip reached as far as Dorset in the west and Inverness in the north, and so encompassed more than 2,000 men, some of whom had only been on holiday at the time. (Indeed, had Keller and his family been in Angmering in May, they could all have been interned at that point.) Within days the first 2,000 were joined by another 2,000, when the order was given to intern all men in category B, no matter where they lived. Shortly afterwards, this was extended to include B category women.

The rapid acceleration of internment caused enormous practical problems, as accommodation had to be found for many more than had been originally envisaged. At the same time, the war was going badly, and it is not surprising that the evacuation of British troops from France and preparations for possible invasion took priority over the provision of facilities for imprisoned foreigners – whose terms of imprisonment were not, after all, covered by the Geneva Convention on the treatment of prisoners-of-war. Conditions in the camps quickly deteriorated. Italy entered the war on 10 June, and Churchill ordered the internment of Italians with his infamous phrase 'Collar the lot!'. This was easier said than done: unlike the German-speaking community who had all been through the tribunal system, there were no comparable data on Italians living in Britain, and their internment was even more haphazard and disorganised. Finding somewhere to put the thousands of supposedly dangerous 'aliens' was a tremendous task. Given that they were considered a security risk, a remote location was desirable, but the Isle of Man, which had served this purpose during the First World War, was not prepared to take such numbers. Interning many thousands of foreigners on the mainland was thought to be too dangerous, and Churchill declared at Cabinet on 24 May that 'he was strongly in favour of removing all internees out of the United Kingdom'.[10] Although there was no Cabinet discussion of any scheme to effect this, somebody must have moved quickly, since just over a fortnight later a surprised Cabinet was told that negotiations had been completed and arrangements were now being made to ship 7,000 internees to Canada.[11]

A similar agreement with Australia, concluded a few days later, increased substantially the number who could be sent overseas – just in time for the final fall of France, which prompted the government to take the decision to imprison the rest of the German and Austrian men in Britain. This order, which was conveyed to Chief Constables around 21 June (the same day on which the first deportation ship, the *Duchess of York*, sailed for Canada), poured another 13,000 men into the overflowing camps – including Hans Keller.

Keller was arrested on or around 21 June,[12] and was taken to the temporary aliens collecting station which had been set up at Kempton Park racecourse. Here internees were handed over to the military and after a few days' wait (in most cases, though some were there for weeks) they were moved to more permanent accommodation. Keller was lucky enough to be held together with his uncle Hans Grotte, cousin Rudi Kompfner, and Oscar Adler who, at 65, was one of the oldest internees. Here is a contemporary description of the conditions which they would have experienced there:

> At Kempton Park, the 'collecting station' for the London region, men were billeted in the Tote buildings (large office rooms with pigeon-holes

for betting transactions), in the stables (some underground) and, at one time, in tents. Conditions here appear to have been typical of a great many other camps. Men slept (often on stone floors) on thin mattresses with two thin blankets, sometimes packed a hundred to a room, with no chairs, no cupboards, nowhere to hang clothes. There was no common room – one could only lie on one's mattress, or sit in the grandstand and watch the sentries, or stroll about the enclosures.[13]

The circumstances of individuals' arrest could vary widely: in some cases it was a relatively civilised affair, with police giving notice and allowing the internee time to pack and say his farewells. Others were taken away much more suddenly and unhappily:

> As for the people to be interned, they were fetched away in the middle of the night or in the early hours of the morning. Sometimes the police took them at once; sometimes they graciously allowed one or even two hours for packing. ... At one Aliens' Collecting Station the officer in charge told them: 'After all, you have had eight months to get out of the country.' One refugee tried to explain that they had hoped to be allowed to help Britain in the war against Fascism. But the officer found this difficult to grasp.[14]

From Kempton Park, Keller was transferred to Huyton Camp in Liverpool, where he arrived at a time of huge confusion and overcrowding. Thousands of newly-arrested internees were being brought in, and many more were being deported overseas, some to the Isle of Man, but more to Canada and Australia. Keller was still with his uncle and Oscar Adler, but had been separated from Rudi Kompfner, who was shipped to the Isle of Man without, it seems, any opportunity of telling his family members interned with him where he was going. He probably did not know himself.

Huyton Camp was formed from an unfinished housing estate which was commandeered and fenced off. Most internees were accommodated in the houses, which were at least dry, though there was practically no furniture. During the period of maximum overcrowding this accommodation was supplemented with tents, in which up to a third of the inmates were lodged, and which were apparently frequently waterlogged. Keller and his uncle were originally put in tents, but Oscar Adler was lucky enough to be given a place in a house, probably because of his age. Even in a house, he would have slept on a sack stuffed with straw and shared a room with several other men. As well as no furniture, there were almost no cleaning implements available, and the houses quickly became dirty. It was just as difficult to keep oneself clean: as one contemporary reported, one could 'bath only in cold water and in a dirty tub. Sanitary arrangements equally deficient. No paper of any kind, either toilet or newspaper.'[15]

Communication with the outside world was almost impossible at this time – which caused enormous anxiety. Newspapers and radios were forbidden in the camps, and letters were censored. Since the postal system for internees was anyway in complete disarray, and the task of trying to keep track of the enormous shifting population of the camp was overwhelming the authorities, the chances of a letter reaching the internee to whom it was addressed were not good. Internees were permitted to write two letters a week – in theory – but at this time supplies of the official notepaper were intermittent and the delays in the censor's office meant that a letter could take weeks to reach its destination. For those who were interned earlier, therefore, their only information about what was happening in the outside world came from those who were interned after them – and the tidings were all bad. Keller's 'generation' of internees brought to the camps news of the evacuation of the British Expeditionary Force from Dunkirk and the fall of France, the entry of Italy into the war on Germany's side, and the internment of category B women. The internees could see for themselves the Luftwaffe's bombing raids on Liverpool (all the more frightening as no air-raid shelters were provided in the camp). The deportation ships departing to unknown destinations together with the disorganisation of the camp itself only added to the sense of chaos. Indeed, some thought that the lack of food and basic facilities in the camp was a sign that the Germans had already landed.

The effect of all this on the internees may be imagined. Many of them, having fled for their lives from Germany – from concentration camps in some cases – were in despair. According to the very few of Keller's letters which survive from this early period of his internment, he managed to keep up his spirits remarkably well – though it must be remembered that these are censored letters, which were written to reassure his mother. The following extracts from the diary of another Austrian internee who arrived at Huyton just before Keller give a rather more negative picture:

> [27 June] Since yesterday there are new people arriving all the time. Most of them are 'C' class from London. [Keller is likely to have been one of these.] Our hopes for release are down to zero. The newly arrived say that even the women will be interned soon. ...

> [28 June] All the time now masses of men arrive from London. ...

> [1 July] 780 new arrivals. Among them very old men, invalids. One gentleman is 68 years old, suffers of serious heart failure and only with the greatest effort could I find him a place in one of the houses. All the

others have to sleep in tents. During dinner-time, that is six o'clock, suddenly intensive anti-aircraft fire was to be heard and the men grew nervous. I shouted that it is only the wind clattering the roof of the tents, because I was afraid of a panic which would have had unthinkable effects, because we had 490 men pressed into one tent, so that there was almost no space to move. ...

[2 July]   The catastrophe has come. A certain Mr. Schiff has committed suicide in the cloak-room. It has gripped us all. For a minute we stood still in memory of him before sitting down for lunch. ... The man who committed suicide is almost 60 years old and has been in a Concentration Camp for two years. Our position is desperate: Will we fall into the hands of Hitler again? What is happening to our wives, children and parents? ...

[3 July]   690 men have been sent away with unknown destination this morning. All of them are single, between 20-40 years old. Many say that they will be sent to Canada, others that they might go to the Isle of Man or to the Shetland Islands. ...

[6 July]   So much has happened until to-day that it would fill the pages of a tragic novel. Another suicide, a man became mad and many who turned melancholic. We are afraid now that they might attempt suicide. Another transport with unknown destination is being arranged for. They say that all men between the ages of 20 and 50 will be deported. This caused great unrest. A meeting was called and the married men protested against being deported and leaving their wives and children behind in uncertainty. We decided rather to be shot than deported. ...[16]

For those with no dependants to worry about, however, deportation to the colonies may have seemed the lesser of two evils: at least it would remove them further away from Hitler. One of the biggest fears of the internees at this time was that the Nazis would invade Britain – to find the German Jewish refugees all neatly penned up ready for them:

For they knew how thousands of German and Austrian refugees, who had been interned all through the war in the *Stade Buffalo* near Paris, had simply been handed over for certain death to the Gestapo by the Paris police. They knew the terrible significance of Article 19, Clause 2, of the Compiègne Armistice terms: 'The French Government to hand over all German subjects indicated by the German Government who are in France or French overseas territory.'

At this point, when all was uncertain, they were locked up and cut off from all reliable news from the outside world. Would Britain follow France and sell out to the Nazis? Would they – the internees – be handed over, as in France? Little wonder that wild rumours circulated in all the camps.[17]

This ban on any news reaching the internees was a particularly painful deprivation, and it was initially carried to extraordinary lengths, according to one contemporary report:

When 600 [internees] were transferred to Prees Heath, near Whitchurch, an officer was sent in advance through Paignton to tear down all hoardings, posters, newspaper headings, etc., which might give information as to news.[18]

In the House of Commons on 10 July, Eleanor Rathbone MP protested vociferously at the absurdity of such treatment of civilian refugees, instead of enlisting their services on Britain's behalf. The vast majority of internees, she pointed out, were desperately opposed to the German regime, so could have been of considerable help to the British war effort:

They ... knew their own countrymen and had watched the growth of Nazi and Fascist tyranny, [so] they perhaps had something that they could teach us about how to master those evils, and how to keep up the morale of our own countrymen. Instead of that, not merely are their services rejected, but they find themselves treated as dangerous people ... so dangerous that they may not even receive newspapers or listen to the wireless and they live in conditions very similar to those of a convict prison. Is all that really necessary? Is there no better way?[19]

Outside Parliament, H. G. Wells made the same point:

Even while we are actually at war with the Axis Powers and their subjugated 'allies', people in positions of authority and advantage in this country are allowing the collection, internment and ill-treatment of all those disaffected subjects of our enemies who would be most willing and able to organise internal resistance in their own countries on our behalf.[20]

There were many others who agreed with Wells that, as well as the humanitarian argument against internment, there was also a strategic one. As the author of one contemporary polemic put it:

> I am not concerned in this book with the humanitarian aspect of the
> Government's refugee policy, but with its influence on war strategy. ...
> We must find means of co-operating with the oppressed peoples [of
> Europe]. We shall not win without their help.[21]

This book was one of a series of 'Victory Books' published by Victor Gollancz
during the summer of 1940. It was one of the darkest moments of the war,
and Gollancz's authors – many of whom wrote under Latin pseudonyms like
'Cato', 'Scipio', 'Miles' and 'Judex' – argued passionately for urgent changes to
government policy, without which, they said, defeat was inevitable.

The humanitarian case against internment was presented by 'Judex' in a
book called *Anderson's Prisoners* – whose title rather unjustly implied that it
was Sir John Anderson who was primarily to blame for the mass internment
policy. The strategic argument was put forward in a book called *100,000,000
Allies – If We Choose* (originally entitled simply *How to Win*, by 'Miles').
In it, the author – now calling himself 'Scipio' – argued convincingly for a
redefinition of what Britain was fighting for. Rather than the simple self-
interest of one nation defending itself against another, he wrote, the British
should instead see the war as an international conflict of values, and thus
enlist in their defence everyone in Europe who wished to oppose Hitler:

> We cannot win this war on our own insular British terms; we can only
> win it provided men and women of other nations are willing to risk their
> lives inside the Third Reich. And they will not do that for the sake of
> a typical English compromise which treats their revolutionary activity
> merely as a convenient method of saving the British Empire. European
> revolution entails a revolution in our own outlook. We ourselves
> must recognise the character of this Civil War and our own place as
> Europeans, on a level with the other peoples of Europe.[22]

Seen from this point of view, locking up thousands of Hitler's most bitter
enemies was almost insanely counter-productive:

> Of all groups in this country that of the German and Austrian refugees
> is one in which the fanaticism of the active Fascists and the defeatism
> of the passive capitulator are least likely to be found. Men, women and
> children, who have lost everything through Nazi persecution and who
> can only expect the concentration camp if Hitler defeats this country,
> are *prima facie* unlikely to be either ardent Nazis or inclined in a crisis
> to give active leadership to a movement for capitulation. And yet, it is
> precisely this group which the Home Office, on the command of the
> War Office, has selected for wholesale internment. ...

Hitler's racial mania dealt a deadly blow at the strength of the Third Reich. By condemning the German Jews to starvation and exile, he dismissed from the service of his country, men and women of the greatest distinction ... Here was an opportunity for the democratic countries. They could take advantage of the talent Hitler was wasting on principle; more, they could create, outside the Third Reich, a free Germany in startling contrast to the slave Germany inside its frontiers.[23]

In a nation stunned by the speed of the German advance and the rapid capitulation of its continental allies – and which, during the First World War, had been taught only a generation earlier to fear Germans as scarcely human – this was perhaps too much to hope for. As the British waited for Hitler to cross the channel, the fate of the refugees who had fled from him was not at the forefront of their minds.

～

Hans Keller was interned during the last of the mass round-ups, so this early, most alarming and chaotic period of internment lasted a relatively short time for him. Newspapers began to filter into the camps from around 17 July, by which time Grete Keller had been able to send a suitcase of clothes and the first of her lavish weekly food parcels. A week later, Keller also had his violin and a few books, and life began to improve. The supply of official letter-paper also became better, and Keller was able to send out regular letters, though they could still take a very long time to reach their destination.

Internees' letters had to be written on officially-issued notepaper, which was designed to be folded and posted without an envelope, unsealed and with the flap simply tucked in. They were sent via the military censor's office in Liverpool from which they emerged sealed by the censor's sticker. At the beginning of Keller's time in the camps, the exponential rise in the number of internees (and British prisoners-of-war held in Germany after Dunkirk), meant that the system was in disarray, and many letters were lost or delayed for weeks. When Osbert Peake, Undersecretary of State at the Home Office, inquired into the state of the military postal system on 5 August 1940, he apparently found a backlog of nearly 100,000 letters from internees in the Liverpool censor's office. As Peake explained to the House of Commons on 22 August 1940:

Until May, the prisoners of war department of the postal censorship had a very small amount of correspondence to handle, but after Dunkirk there was a considerable number of British prisoners in German hands. All their correspondence, obviously, has to be censored for security reasons with extreme care, because letters passing from this country to Germany and from Germany to this country are a very probable source of communication with agents of the enemy. In addition, these large numbers of civilians were thrust into internment in the month of June, so the postal censorship was confronted with an enormous task at very short notice. We found these 100,000 letters from the camps awaiting censorship...[24]

In order to ease the censor's task, internees were permitted to send only two letters a week, each of which could be a maximum of 24 lines long. Internees were also instructed to write clearly, 'in the Roman characters if possible ... in plain language, of which the meaning was clear.'[25] At the beginning of his internment, Keller therefore printed his letters in a style quite unlike his normal hand. He also wrote his first few letters in English, though this was not a formal requirement: as he told his mother in the one uncensored letter in the collection, 'It's quite all right to write in German – for you, too; I only write in English when I've got a lot to get in, as English is shorter.'[26] As his internment lengthened, Keller's writing gradually became less clear, and the censor didn't seem to mind. The restriction on the length of letters did not ease, but Keller became adept at squashing more and more words into the 24-line limit, in increasingly tiny handwriting. His first letter contained 240 (English) words. By his fiftieth letter he was getting over 500 words into the same number of lines – and those were German words (which tend to be longer: our English translation of that letter contains over 600 words).

With a very few exceptions, all the letters Keller wrote from the camps were addressed to his mother, who would then pass on the news to and from other friends and family members. Grete Keller kept every one of her son's letters from internment (or at least all those that managed to reach her), including the few he wrote to others in the family. She preserved them carefully in a bundle labelled 'Hansel Briefe', and numbered them in date order. This numbering is reproduced here, with the addition of editorial numbers in square brackets to those few items which, for one reason or another, Mrs Keller did not include in her numerical sequence. Unfortunately, apart from one or two drafts of her own telegrams which she kept with the letters, none of her side of the correspondence survives. She kept the bundle of Hansel Briefe until 1954, when she had a clear-out of her son's papers, Hans having by that time moved to Hampstead with Milein Cosman. Most of his papers ended up in their loft in Hampstead (where he evidently never looked at them again, since they were still sealed inside their 1954 newspaper wrappings), but some were passed to his cousin Inge, and it was among these, half a century later, that Hans Keller's letters from internment were found.[27]

~

1.   **26 June 1940, postcard from Kempton Park.**
        In English.

> We are at Kempton Park Internment Camp and all well.
> We shall let you know our permanent address as soon as possible.
> Uncle Hans, Oscar, Rudi, Hans

2.   **5 July 1940, Huyton.**
        In English.

> Dearest mother, – Roy and Mowgli, as British subjects, are permitted to visit me and uncle Hans provided that they obtain the permission from the Home Office. They, or one of them, should do so at once. They should bring, or you should send me immediately the following things in face of the fact that I don't know how long I stay in this camp: warm underwear, a warm cap (ski-cap), warm gloves, a violin with reserve strings, fruits, cheese, chocolate and other eatables (I probably have not to carry my luggage for long distances), some soap, perhaps ski-shoes with warm stockings, about 10 £ and my training suit [tracksuit]. I have made an application for release to the War Office, but as this will take months till it is there, I ask you urgently to make an application, too. I am told that my face-neuralgia, my hayfever, my nervous and physically infirm constitution as well as my testifiable pro-British attitude, and the fact that I am a jew, that I have volunteered for casualty service etc. will be considered as valid reasons. Oscar is with us, though in a house; he and we are quite all right. Send my things in a case. Mention in the application my having been in a Nazi Concentration Camp. Write soon. Try to speak to Uncle Rudi's friend, Mr. Vansittart about the application. For the rest don't worry about me. Yours affectionately, Hans.

[2a].   Telegram *(date illegible)*, Huyton.
In English.

188 2 188 2.20 LIVERPOOL LHX
KELLER 32 HERNE HILL LONDON SE 24 =
AM AT SAME ADDRESS LOVE =HANS AIC HUYTON

Undated draft on reverse of [2a] of a telegram from Grete Keller. *In English.*

wire whether you received registered letter with 10 £ which I sent
fortnight ago otherwise I have to inquire
how is Oscar?

[2b].   Undated draft of telegram from Grete Keller.
In English.

H. H. K.
A. I. C. 9, 2 NR 75107

No news since your telegram wire how you are whether received
registered letter with 10 £, books, music, violin, food. love mother

3.   13 July 1940, Huyton.
In German.

Dearest Mutti, I was really happy with the parcel and suitcase which
I received today. Please send me a food-parcel like that every week.
I haven't yet received the violin. Please send cornrings and plasters.
The important facts for the application for release are my relations
in the British Army: Peggy's brothers and father, in future Roy. Shall
I volunteer to go overseas? Would you perhaps come as well?
Please send me the address of the Australian lady who was with
Hamilton in Kritzendorf. The relations in the army are also important
for Uncle Hans. Please send slippers with space for my corns, and
a cushion. Please pursue our applications [for release] vigorously.
The Home Office is in charge of this. Oscar is well. Please send lots
of oranges and apples etc for Uncle Hans. Concerning Australia or

any journey abroad, make enquiries at the Home Office. I managed to have a temporary filling done on the tooth. Uncle Hans wants glycerine suppositories. You can telegraph important matters. In myself I am feeling well; I read and wait for the violin. It is likely that accompanying relations in Australia or overseas generally will also be interned initially. Roy or Mowgli should bring the Bach solo sonatas and Rode studies, along with the Beethoven concerto. Many many kisses, Hans.

[3a].   Undated draft of telegram from Grete Keller.
In English.

HANS HEINRICH KELLER
A. I. C. 009,2 NO. 75107 TENT 220
CAMP 2 HUYTON nr. Liverpool

Please wire whether any change of address and whether received money and 2 parcels
Love Mutti

Undated draft on reverse of [3a] of another telegram from Grete Keller. *In English.*

Do not want you to go to Australia as I am not at all well letter follows
Mother

~

It is clear from these first few letters and telegrams just how difficult it was to communicate. Two short, censored letters, one postcard and one telegram were all Grete Keller received in nearly four weeks. Whenever Keller and his mother were apart later in the war, he wrote to her almost every day (Keller remained a most assiduous letter-writer all his life). So it can be imagined how difficult both would have found such a sparse correspondence as they were forced to have now.

The first of the two letters gives Keller's address as 'Tent 220', which gives some idea of the size of the camp at that time. These tents apparently had 'no groundsheets and only thin straw mattresses on the bare ground,' so damp was a constant problem: 'At Huyton, two-fifths of the refugees living in tents found it practically impossible to keep their belongings dry. Early in July they were flooded out.'[28] Hence Keller's request that his mother should send warm clothes.

The address given on the second letter indicates that Keller had now been moved out of his tent into a house, 138 Parbrook Road, which became available as other internees were deported. By the date of that letter, the deportation policy was already being reconsidered, though Keller's question 'Shall I volunteer to go overseas?' indicates that he was not yet aware of any change. This question should not be taken as an indication that deportation was only voluntary. Some refugees were indeed keen to leave the country (especially during the period when a German invasion seemed imminent), and it was of course easier for the authorities to take volunteers. Nevertheless, considerable pressure was put on internees to volunteer, including all sorts of promises about things like automatic release on arrival, or relatives being allowed to follow. In the event, the number of volunteers was insufficient, and so many of those deported had to be sent by force, as this report from a British refugee official visiting one of the camps shows:

> The Commandant told me that he has to produce 1,000 men at a time to fill a ship; the men do not know to which country they are to go. If only 700 put their names down for going, he has to make the list up at random and their relations know nothing.[29]

The first ships to depart had contained the highest number of those sent by force, the concern of the War Office being simply to dispatch the requisite number as quickly as possible. After protests from the Home Office, more effort was put into obtaining volunteers, but promises about things like relatives being allowed to go too (which Keller had clearly heard), turned out to be false. That some internees feared this would be the case is shown by an anguished telegram received by Antony Eden, Secretary of State for War. It came from a group of men interned on the Isle of Man who were down to be deported to Australia, but who clearly distrusted the promises they had been given about their families. The telegram also makes clear how dangerous were such long voyages in wartime:

IN THIS VERY LAST HOUR WHERE WE ARE TO LEAVE THIS COUNTRY WHICH RECEIVED US ONCE AS FRIENDS WE MARRIED INTERNEES OF ONCHAN INTERNMENT CAMP ISLE

OF MAN IMPLORE YOU TO ASSURE US THAT UNDER ALL CIRCUMSTANCES SHALL WE BE TRANSPORTED WITH OUR WIVES AND CHILDREN TO THE SAME DESTINATION STOP IF AN EMERGENCY SHOULD ARISE WE WANT TO SHARE THIS EMERGENCY TOGETHER WITH OUR DEAR ONES STOP PLEASE REALIZE THAT WE HAVE LOST EVERYTHING FREEDOM FATHERLAND PROPERTY STOP DO NOT TAKE FROM US THE VERY LAST WHICH PRESERVES OUR WILL TO LIVE STOP LEAVE US OUR WIVES AND CHILDREN TO LIVE OR DIE WITH TOGETHER.

THE MARRIED INTERNEES OF ONCHAN CAMP[30]

It is likely that these men had not seen their families since their arrest, as it was extremely difficult to obtain permission to visit an internee. As to Keller's mention of a possible visit to the camp by Roy and Mowgli (the British citizens of the family), it is not known whether they ever managed to get the necessary permit, although there is evidence that an application from Roy was being processed by the authorities in August.[31] As will be seen, however, Keller managed to smuggle out an uncensored letter in mid-July, which is probably an indication that he did have a visitor. Such an early visitor is more likely to have been his solicitor, however – and indeed later letters do refer to visits from 'Greig' (Mr William Fairchild Greig, of Fairchild Greig & Co., 177 Fleet Street, EC4).[32] One contemporary polemic on internment reported that 'It is almost impossible for even the nearest relative to enter a camp. One method is through a lawyer. An internee has the right to see his solicitor, who may be accompanied by the refugee's wife or next of kin. Solicitors' charges are, however, necessarily heavy; clearly it is not a method open to many. The only other way is to obtain a permit from P.W.2, the Department of the War Office concerned. This is by no means easy and it is reported that personal influence is usually necessary to obtain one.'[33]

The possibility of release was naturally at the forefront of all internees' minds. Amid all the uncertainty, and lack of reliable information, people were desperate for any means of convincing the authorities to let them go. Keller's attempts to use ill-health, previous service, possible emigration, relatives serving in the British army and his detention by the Nazis as reasons for release were typical, as was his evident conviction that friends on the outside were in a much better position to do something positive than he was. Contacts in high places were potentially valuable – 'Mr Vansittart' may refer to the diplomat and vociferous anti-appeasement campaigner Robert Vansittart, formerly permanent under-secretary at the Foreign Office, and now chief diplomatic advisor to the government. But any friends on the outside, whatever their status, could be a comfort – hence the request for 'the address of the Australian lady who was with Hamilton in Kritzendorf'. (Hamilton was a friend of Roy Franey's, and Kritzendorf the place where Keller's family had had a summer house on the Danube.) If Keller was going to end up deported to the other side of the world, he wanted to feel that he had at least one friend he could contact who was near at hand.

Back at No. 32 Herne Hill, Roy Franey was the only male member of the family left at home, but they all knew that it could not be long before he was called up into the forces, in which the father and brothers of Rudi Kompfner's new wife, Peggy, were already serving. According to the National Service (Armed Forces) Act passed at the outbreak of war, all men between the ages of 18 and 41 were liable for conscription, but so far only men in their early twenties had received their papers. Roy and Mowgli now had two young daughters, Ena and Nora. Still living with them in the Herne Hill house was their grandmother Grete Keller, while Inge Kompfner and her mother Paula were living just round the corner at 40 Oakbank.

One other member of the family who now managed to get to London, by a most perilous route, was Dr Rudolf Keller. He was the brother of Keller's father and a prominent member of the German-speaking intelligensia in Prague. 'An important scholar and world-renowned biochemist',[34] he was also the former editor of the *Prager Tagblatt* and *Neue Leipziger Zeitung* ('the most radical anti-Hitler papers of Central Europe', as he himself described them)[35]. He had escaped with difficulty after the German invasion of Czechoslovakia, spending many months making his way across Europe. He had been in considerable danger, for the *Prager Tagblatt*, being a German-language paper of international reputation that was not yet directly threatened by the Nazis, had become something of a refuge after 1933 for émigré German writers, until it was closed down in 1939 when the Nazis took Prague. Rudolf Keller was apparently on a Gestapo wanted list, which he thought may have contributed to his nephew's difficulty in leaving Vienna: 'I am afraid he was persecuted by the well informed Gestapo, because he is my only relative of this name.'[36] Hans Keller's remark in his letter of 15th August that he was 'very pleased about Uncle Rudi', from whom he had just received a letter, might refer to the news that Rudolf Keller had finally arrived in London, though such a late arrival would have been fraught with difficulty. Czech nationals were not routinely interned, and Uncle Rudi seems to have escaped the camps.

As well as family members, there are references in Keller's letters to several of his Viennese friends, most frequently 'Georg', 'Muni and Kollmann', and Gertrud Marle. Georg Stroh was a former schoolfriend of Keller's, who had been in the middle of his medical studies when he had to flee Vienna with the help of Roy Franey. (He later became a well-known child psychiatrist, with whom Keller remained close friends.) 'Muni' was another friend, now in America, and 'Kollmann' was Eric Kollman (as he later spelled his name), Keller's former schoolteacher, the 'Jewish form-master whom we all venerated'. He also managed to get to America and in 1944 he became Professor of History at Cornell College, 'doing better, no doubt, than he could ever have done without the holocaust', as Keller points out in 'Vienna, 1938' above.

Keller's cousin Inge remembers Eric Kollman well: he began to teach Keller when Keller changed schools at 16:

> [Hans] went to the Gymnasium, the boys' school. He got thrown out of it … when he was 16, and he went to the Landerziehungsheim in Döbling where we lived, where naughty boys were sent. I don't know why – that's funny. He certainly did his last exam at the other school – and there he had a teacher who was very influential on him. … Kollmann, the teacher was called at the school where he went when he was 16, who was very influential, and became a friend.[37]

Kollman taught German literature, but he was also very musical, as Inge recalls:

> He used to come to the Adler quartets. And I remember going home with him on the tram, and I didn't know very much music apart from quartets, and he said, 'There's so much more!'

In 1944, Keller described his relationship with Kollman to his psychological colleague Margaret Phillips. They were studying the workings of social groups, and in a letter discussing the nature of group leadership Keller gave the example of 'the nature of the authority & leadership exercised in my school class':

> In this group the Jews were in the majority and the main teacher was a Jew … the latter was a man of unusual educational and intellectual capabilities. Leadership was twofold: (1) The main teacher, who tried to lead the life of at least a number of the boys outside his official educational domain, exerted an influence which to the more mature boys was on many occasions primary. (2) The (elected) class leader who, through his intimate friendship with the teacher, was in a position to serve as a perfect connecting link between the teacher and the boys, undertook to influence the boys wherever infantile opposition against the teacher made it impossible for the latter to exert sufficient immediate influence. ((Private addition: the class leader was, as you probably know, myself.))[38]

Gertrud Marle was the sister of Erika, Keller's girlfriend in Vienna. The two sisters had left Vienna for England the day after Keller was released by the Gestapo; it is possible that they were also helped to emigrate by Roy Franey. They kept in touch with Keller after he reached Britain, but his relationship with Erika did not continue. The sisters lived a long way from London, having found accommodation and work in Cornwall – probably as domestic servants. Domestic service was one of the few employment opportunities open to aliens at this time, so the war saw many highly qualified people working as maids and chauffeurs.

~

The next letter that Grete Keller received was different. It is clearly uncensored (as evinced by its content, the plain paper on which it is written, and the fact that Keller uses his normal hand, not the clear printing he adopts elsewhere for the censor's benefit). It is the only uncensored letter in the collection; how Keller managed to send it is not known, but one frequent method of getting uncensored messages out of the camps was for a visitor to smuggle them out.

[3b].   17 July 1940, Huyton.
In German.

Dearest Mutti,
I assume that you will be interested in a more detailed letter, for which reason I'm making use of a rare chance to write to you in the normal way.* Most importantly: in spite of the adverse conditions I feel by no means unwell, which, however, does not mean that you should not do absolutely everything to secure our release. Your real original nobodies do get released here – one of them apparently because his English bride cried at the Home Office for so long that they ordered his release (this was a perfectly ordinary Jew without a key position), the other because a prominent person produced a letter of recommendation for him etc. I only want to say by this that it really must be *possible*, with close relatives who are English, relatives in the Army, the hardship of the separation and infirmity,** to achieve something, if one just puts enough effort into it and makes use of every possible connection, like Greig's friend at the Home Office, *Vansittart*, and

all English friends. After all, I know your energy and I am therefore not worried in that respect, only I fear that that you might be discouraged by a negative (meaningless) decision by a junior civil servant, or by Greig's opinion etc.

I slipped out of the last transport to Canada; I did that 1) because of the torpedoing of the Star-Andora [sic], 2) because of release in Canada being unlikely, and the possibility of release in England, 3) because one has no idea what it would be like in Canada. On the other hand, of course, there are lots of arguments in favour of deportation, but as I still have time for that, and since it is uncertain whether I should ever see you again if I went overseas, I've kept my head down for the time being. The next transport, which will go to Australia, leaves at the end of July; I am still undecided. Nobody will be forced to go (as was the case with the last transport), i.e. one can put to the commander the reasons why one doesn't want to go, and he will then decide. We've been told that from now on the ships will be going in convoy till they are through the danger zone (that's the way it was with the last ship), close relations will probably be allowed to go, too, but not necessarily on the same ship – something I put to you because this might be the only possibility for you to get abroad. I am writing this to you anyway, though I know that you won't contemplate parting from Mowgli nor a six-week journey by boat. Whether I should go, I can't decide with the best will in the world. – Where Rudi is you probably know better than we do: he was separated from us in Kempton Park. There's a letter here for him from Peggy, which was wrongly forwarded here from Kempton Park; as the post here, like all other institutions, is run by refugees, they have no idea where Rudi is, so I do not know what will happen to the letter. Don't worry if you don't receive any news for a while, because although officially we are allowed to write 24 lines twice a week, we only get writing paper very irregularly. It goes without saying that you mustn't mention this letter in your letters to me. Please send me toilet paper, and more good things to eat; I'm really happy with your first food parcel. You've decided on the various types of food and their quantities in a most admirable way. I'm looking forward longingly to receiving the violin – have you sent it yet? [Illegible name] is just sketching a rough picture of the conditions here, about which, however, you need not worry on my account, as you know that I don't mind the lack of certain comforts; it wouldn't have been any better on the farm. The only thing that is unpleasant is that one is constantly without one's freedom, not knowing how long this will go on, and contemplating an uncertain future. So be it. They give us bromide in our grub here (against sexuality), so we sleep a lot. Oscar is well; he has already started giving lectures; his only worry is his wife. – I myself am in a really good mood, I had only one (short) crisis, when I felt pretty rotten, but now nothing can upset my equilibrium any more. – We were not allowed newspapers until today; today we got a few. Please send saccharin, because the tea, though it is sugared, is made salty by the bromide. The long woolly hat was a wonderful idea; I am also using it as a night-cap. The tracksuit I wear day and night. The ski-cap is unfortunately too small already, but I can still wear it with the ear-flaps down. Have Kollmann and Muni written? If so, give them the news briefly, please. Oscar has received both the cards from his wife. Please send me, direct through the bookshop, 1 book by Chesterton, 1 book by John Stuart Mill, the Dvorak Violin Concerto. I have just received Muni's letter; she and Kollmann (whose address she knows) should write to me. Please write to her immediately, she is worried. What's going on at home? I (we) shall be very grateful for every letter. In my room sleeps the gentleman (with a duodenal ulcer) who sold you that radio in Vienna, he remembers you and the Steyr [the Kellers' car] really well, a nice Pole. Let's see how life goes on, Mutschi, don't worry. Lots of kisses to Mowgli, the children, Roy, Paula. It's quite all right to write in German – for you, too; I only write in English when I've got a lot to get in, as English is shorter. The mailing with the things I asked for will tell me that you've received this letter. So once more many kisses, Mutschili; – Your Hans.

* and using an abnormal route
** the fact that I was in a concentration camp, am a Jew etc.

4.   **18 July 1940, Huyton.**
In German.

Dearest Mutti, I received your telegram just now. We are only allowed to telegraph in urgent cases. I have received two parcels so far, not the money yet. Have you received my 2 letters? Confirmation of one I had through the parcels, but the other one, in which I asked about cushion etc, may have got lost? Mrs Rathbone spoke in the House of Commons about her sympathy for those who were forced to abandon their studies, so we should also mention in the application that I was about to take my L.R.A.M. exam at the Royal Academy. Further, don't forget: my relations in the British Army, Peggy's brothers, father, and in future Roy, my state of health after the Nazi concentration camp, the hardship of the separation from you, my provable pro-British attitude, the fact that I am a Jew and was in a Nazi concentration camp and beaten up. Please find out immediately about the possibility of going to Shanghai: if I could go abroad I should certainly be released. Oscar is well. I have received Muni's letter – why still none from you? Write to her, and she should then write to Kollmann. Have you received the house key? Please send lots to eat. Have you heard from Georg? Some of his colleagues are here, but they do not know where he is. I am feeling well. Many kisses, Hans.

5.   **20 July 1940, Huyton.**
In English and German.

Dearest Mutti, The following statement was announced here today: 'Every alien who has not appeared before the Advisory Committee of the Home Office for his case to be reconsidered may appeal to the Committee for a hearing and may write out a memorandum setting out the grounds upon which he claims to be released. Any alien who prepares such a memorandum should hand it to his Company Officer and his Commandant will see that it is forwarded at once to the Committee.' I am writing this memorandum today, but this should not make your efforts any the less. In order to send the urgent telegram which you will have received I applied for permission, which was granted. Send me the exact Christian names and addresses of Peggy's father and brothers who are in the army. We have no hot water, and that's why an electric cooker, 230 volts, would be beyond all treasure. Unfortunately I have still not received the violin: have you sent it yet? I've just now received your second food parcel and am immensely happy with it! Please go on sending food as regularly! As you are still using tent 220 as the address, it looks as if you still have only received one letter from me. I haven't received a single one from you. Oscar is fine; Uncle Hans has a cold; I had one; here in the camp that sort of thing gets passed from one nose to another. Otherwise I continue to feel fine in myself; I'm reading Descartes. Many, many kisses, Hans.

6.   **24 July 1940, Huyton.**
       In German.

Dear Mutschili, I've just received your letter (of 10 July). Haven't got the money yet, but it will probably come soon. I have also received: your 2nd telegram (on 22 July), thank you very much; the Daily Telegraph (always a day late) is no longer necessary, because we have got it here now – touch wood, the parcel with toilet paper on 22 July, many thanks, and the violin yesterday, thank you many, many times. Please send me: a further set of strings in the next parcel, or direct though the music shop, namely A and E-strings of pure steel, D and G-strings metal-covered, as high quality as possible, because of the climate; the G-string arrived broken, and both the A-strings are unplayable as they produce 2 notes at the same time. I am already practising. If you pay 4/6 per day, you can get a bed on which to lay your straw sack, a table, a chair, normal food and other comforts. We have so far refused this: what do you think? Please send me a tin-opener, a screw one like the one in our kitchen. Yesterday we were escorted on a short walk outside the camp – 'taken walkies' as it were. For the application: my volunteering before and during the war for National Service (Casualty Service etc.). Could you possibly have the Cowling System Finger-Training Course sent me direct from the Institute? More food parcels, please. I was enormously pleased with your letter and all the other mailings. Many kisses, Hans.

[6a]. **25[?] July 1940, *[date stamp is unclear]* telegram, Huyton.**
       In English.

197 2.30 LIVERPOOL 21 =
KELLER 32 HERNE HILL LONDON SE 24 =
AM QUITE ALL RIGHT RECEIVED MONEY BOOKS MUSIC VIOLIN
FOOD DON'T WORRY MUCH LOVE = HANS +

7.   **27 July 1940, Huyton.**
       In English.

Dearest mother, please don't hesitate to inquire about a visa (immigration) to Shanghai for me and uncle Hans. I learn from a most reliable source, i.e. Hr. Hüttenbach ('cellist) who wanted to go to Shanghai some time ago himself, that the only profession in which there is a serious shortage in Shanghai is the musical profession, and any musician is badly wanted and needed there. So please reconnoitre, which I'll do at the Overseas Department in this Camp, too. Just after I had sent my letter on July 24th, I received the two books. On 25th inst. I received the parcel with the tin-opener (for which I had asked in my letter of the day before) and the other delicious things: thank you very very much. From Gertrud Marle (16 Gerard Rd., S.W.13) I received some sweets and cigarettes, by which I was moved very much; please let her know that. To-day we make, once again, an application for release to the Under Secretary of State, Home Office. Please send me adjuster ('Feinstimmer' in German) for the steel a-string, which I am waiting for. I shall soon play String-Quartet with Oscar and Hüttenbach. Is there any news about our release? Recently Miss Rathbone, M.P., delivered a consolatory speech here. Much love, Hans.

~

'Miss Rathbone MP', whom Keller describes giving a 'consolatory speech' to the internees at Huyton, was one of the most important of the Parliamentarians who spoke up for the interned refugees. Born in 1872, Eleanor Rathbone had already been a prominent crusader for social justice for nearly half a century. Her major focus hitherto had been on women's rights (both in Britain and abroad) and on poverty, with her longstanding fight for family allowances bearing eventual fruit in the 1945 Family Allowances Act. She had been involved in the women's suffrage movement from her days as a student at Somerville College, Oxford, in the early 1890s, and she succeeded Millicent Garrett Fawcett in 1919 as President of the National Union of Women's Suffrage Societies. She entered Parliament in 1929 as MP for the Combined English Universities – hence her special concern, mentioned by Keller in his letter of 18th July, for refugee students in particular. During the 1930s she had become increasingly worried by political developments in Europe and campaigned vigorously against fascism in Spain, Germany and Italy. An early critic of appeasement, she predicted in 1936 that 'only a "real National Government" led by Churchill and backed by Labour would effectively stand up to the fascist powers'.[39]

The internment of refugees from Nazism was naturally repugnant to Rathbone's sense of justice, and she was a tireless campaigner against the policy. According to her biographer, she became 'locked in combat with Herbert Morrison [Anderson's successor as Home Secretary] and his under-secretaries both about policy and about individual cases.

Her persistence and expertise made her at the same time respected and (in some cases) disliked by the officials and ministers whom she badgered almost daily. So strained did her relations become with Morrison in particular that Rathbone, fearing that his hostility would jeopardize particular cases, began working through other MPs.[40]

Later in the war, when news of the Nazis' extermination policy began to reach Britain, Rathbone threw herself into pressing the British government to try to find ways to save the threatened Jews, founding the National Committee for Rescue from Nazi Terror in 1942.

As will be seen in the next chapter, public opposition to the mass internment and deportation policy was mounting rapidly, and at the beginning of July it received further fuel from the tragedy of the *Arandora Star*. This was the second of the ships deporting internees to Canada: on 2 July it was torpedoed in the Atlantic by a German U-boat and sank with the loss of 700 lives. Despite the newspaper ban, some news of this evidently filtered back to the camps, as is shown by the reference to 'Star-Andora' in Keller's uncensored letter. According to Lafitte, the news provoked two more suicides in Huyton camp.[41] The Cabinet was told the day after the event, at a meeting at which Neville Chamberlain (now Lord President of the Council and a member of Churchill's War Cabinet) had – ironically – been already due to report on his efforts to carry out his successor's instruction to send as many internees abroad as humanly possible. He now had this disaster to add to the list of problems he was encountering, which included opposition from the American government and fears of potential German reprisals against British prisoners-of-war. The Cabinet discussed whether to halt the deportations forthwith, but concluded that it was too late. Even as they were meeting, internees were already boarding the *SS Ettrick* at Liverpool, and the *Sobieski* sailed from Glasgow the following day.

The one ship that probably could have been stopped was the *Dunera*, the only ship to carry internees to Australia, which set sail from Liverpool a week later. Keller was lucky not to have been among the 2,542 (mainly German and Austrian) internees on that voyage. Crammed together for two months on a ship intended for a maximum of 1600 (including crew), in appallingly insanitary conditions, the internees were also scandalously abused by some of their guards, who may have been under the impression that they were guarding Nazi prisoners-of-war (though the fact that the average age of the *Dunera* prisoners was nearly 50 makes this questionable).

Unknown to Keller, one of his schoolfriends was unfortunate enough to be on the *Dunera*. Fritz Schonbach, with whom Keller had been corresponding while he was trying to escape from Vienna, was studying in Switzerland at the time of the Anschluss. He also made his way to England, where he was interned and then deported to Australia. There he was put in the hot and dusty internment camp at Hay, New South Wales, along with many other 'Dunera boys', as they became known.[42] Despite the scandal of their mistreatment on the voyage, the internees at Hay remained for some time suspended in a bureaucratic tangle as Britain and Australia wrangled over what to do with them, and tried to trace their lost or stolen papers and belongings. The imprisoned men were left to organise themselves, and apparently created a 'cultural and intellectual life [that] was richer even than Onchan or Hutchinson on the Isle of Man'.[43] Their ironic comment on the pointless absurdity of their position was displayed clearly on the banknotes they designed to use as internal currency: each note was 'bordered by barbed wire into which had been woven the refrain: "We're here because we're here because we're here."'[44] When they were eventually freed, only about half elected to return to Britain. Many of the others, Schonbach among them, volunteered for service in the Australian military, after Pearl Harbor awoke the Australians to their potential value to the war effort.

Back in Britain, even after the deportations had stopped, emigration was still one of the only routes out of internment. Pressure was put on refugees to re-emigrate if they possibly could, including the withdrawal of financial support from those who had the opportunity to leave and were not doing so. According to the historian Louise London, 'The departures of at least 10,000 refugees in 1940 were "voluntary" in name, but the circumstances were often close to expulsion.'[45] Most, like Keller, had been given only temporary visas, and it was repeatedly emphasised that there would be no guarantee that they would be allowed to remain in Britain when the war was over. As 'Scipio' put it in his *100,000,000 Allies* book for Victor Gollancz,

> The vast majority were given entrance permits on the condition that they had reasonable prospects of re-emigrating to other countries overseas. The only exceptions were women and married couples willing to work as domestic servants, capitalists with sufficient money to keep themselves for life, and those with special knowledge which enabled them to establish industries. Our attitude throughout this period to the victims of Nazi persecution and to the democratic fighters against Hitler could be expressed in one sentence: 'They can stay here if they make us rich: otherwise they must get out as soon as possible.'[46]

In the circumstances, it is not surprising that Keller should have seriously considered going as far as China. Shanghai at that time was 'the only city in the world where refugees could enter without visas; in 1939 every third European in Shanghai was a German-Jewish refugee.'[47] Only those with definite travel plans could hope to be released from the camps, however, so

Keller would have needed to show that arrangements had already been made for him to make an immediate departure.

~

In the meantime, life in Huyton began to become slightly more settled in the second half of July. The most chaotic period of panic, rumour, and innumerable arrivals and departures was gradually drawing to a close, although conditions were still far from satisfactory. With the deportations halted, and little immediate prospect of release, it now seemed to the occupants of Huyton that they were likely to remain in the camp for some time. Many therefore started making the best of things:

> The camps were so full of men of learning and artistic merit that most of the camps by the end of July were developing into centres of free German culture. In many of the camps the scientists and university teachers, usually without the necessary books or paper, began to organise 'People's Universities'.[48]

Another Huyton internee, Ernst Schaefer, who was a lawyer in civilian life, remembered his time there as enormously stimulating:

> Internees came from all walks of life. They included a remarkable number of intellectuals, scholars, scientists, artists, lawyers and the like. Very soon individual lectures and planned courses in various subjects were organised, so that the weighty name of 'camp university' was not quite unjustified. In particular, many courses were devoted to the study of English, including beginners' and conversation classes as well as systematic lectures on phonetics, English literature, etc. Other languages, such as Spanish, were taught as well. Of legal subjects I remember a most interesting course at Huyton camp on Private International Law, given by a young Cambridge lecturer.[49]

Much of the intellectual life of Huyton in the early days was apparently co-ordinated by David Josef Bach, a friend of both Arnold Schoenberg and Oscar Adler. Bach, Schoenberg later recalled, was 'a linguist, philosopher, a connoisseur of literature, and a mathematician', as well as being 'a good musician', and he had considerable influence on his friends. Schoenberg credits him (along with Adler and Alexander von Zemlinsky) with starting 'my musical and literary education'. Bach also 'greatly influenced the development of my character by furnishing it with the ethical and moral power needed to withstand vulgarity and commonplace popularity'.[50]

Writing to Schoenberg after the war, Adler recalled Bach's time in Huyton:

> I can tell you something about Bach, with whom I was interned. He has lost nothing of his liveliness. In the internment camp immediately a kind of cultural club was formed under his direction. There were lectures to which I was able to contribute.[51]

As well as giving lectures, Adler naturally led a quartet, which just as naturally included Keller as second violin. They were lucky enough to have at Huyton the excellent 'cellist Otto Hüttenbach, with whom Keller continued to play chamber music in London after their release. Their quartet seems to have included various viola players, including the conductor Karl Haas, who went on to found the London Baroque Ensemble. Books and scores were a problem, though. Keller's request for books to be sent 'direct through the bookshop' reflects the fact that internees were not allowed to have their own books. As the anonymous author of the Gollancz anti-internment polemic *Anderson's Prisoners* explained, 'Their own private books might not be sent (for fear of code markings). They could only receive new books, prohibitively expensive in the case of university textbooks, or secondhand books through the Y.M.C.A.'[52]

Communication with the outside world was now getting easier. Letters to and from family and friends could still be subject to lengthy delays, but there were now enough stocks of the official writing paper to send out one's two letters a week, and access to the news was now permitted. This included the welcome tidings of a possible change of heart on the part of the government, with the appearance of the Home Secretary's first White Paper on the release of civilian internees. Hopes rose further when August brought the first few actual releases.

∿

8.   3 August 1940, Huyton.
      In English.

> Dearest mother, you will have read in the White Paper that your illness is a ground upon which I can be released. You must apply and enclose a Medical attest. I received: on August 1st parcel with

spoons, Black Magic etc., on 27th music, money, on 31st pillow and corn plaster (and parcel for Uncle Hans) on 2nd letter from Georg (Private, 13801007, 87th Coy. AMPC, Chard, Somerset), he is expecting a letter from me, but I can't write him as I send you my two letters weekly. This week was an exception, because I wrote Tuesday's letter to Mr. Winston Churchill, expounding the Jewish refugee's attitude and present state generally, and uncle Hans' and mine specifically. Just now I received Cowling's Course, thank you for all things, very much! I'm playing quartets with Adler and Hüttenbach daily, but have up to now refused to give a concert. Today Dr. Necker, who came from another camp, became our neighbour. Just received your letter of 20th, chips are unfortunately rancid, all other things nice; had a kind card from Tess.[53] Shanghai: 1) Bank of England must permit transfer of 400 Dollar (preferably money which has been brought into this country) to Shanghai-Hong-Kong-Bank, Shanghai. 2) Then landing-permit would be granted. Particulars at 52 Bloomsbury Way, W.C.1., Palestine and Orient Lloyd, Dr. JAKOBOWITZ, recommended by Dr. NEUMANN. What do you think of it? For the rest I'm quite O.K. and cheerful, yesterday I played Handel with Landauer (B.B.C., formerly Radio Vienna).[54] Just received a letter from Gertrud. Thanks for writing to Muni. Much love Hans.

9.   7 August 1940, Huyton.
In German.

Dear Mutschili, On the 5th I received your parcel with the cooker, and on the 6th strings, the music (Bach, Rode), Mowgli's letter, Inge's letter. Many thanks to all. What did Mowgli want from Miss Tooth? Inge should continue practising straight away on my second violin. Since it will get colder here in time, please send me a warm blanket. The cooker is already marvellously useful to us: yesterday we prepared ourselves a first-class tea which consisted of cocoa, toast and jam. All the things which you send us are most useful to us, you know better what we need than we do. We played Beethoven Opus 132 yesterday; next week I shall give a concert with a young violinist: 2 Handel double sonatas, Bach double concerto. Oscar is well: we're playing quartets almost every day. Please send a music stand (next to finding the space to play, this is our greatest difficulty). I shall need more toilet paper before long. Please pass on my thanks to Inge for her efforts. Uncle Hans, in his desperation at having nothing to do, has started to read again. Besides that, he is already a member of the local football club, Arsenal. I myself live nearly the same sort of life as I do in London (basically): violin, reading etc. However, real practice is unfortunately not possible: imagine 17 people in a house that is half the size of ours. It was difficult even at home to find somewhere for me to play where I didn't disturb anyone else. Servus,[†] Mutschi, many, many kisses. Hans

[†] *Translators' note: 'Servus' is an Austrian/Bavarian expression meaning 'goodbye', 'so long', 'cheerio'. This has been left untranslated where it occurs.*

10.   10 August 1940, Huyton.
In German.

Dearest Mutschili, I've never eaten so well in my life – this cake (which I received today with the parcel of tins) is an absolute dream; did it come from Aunt Paula? All the things in this parcel, like in the earlier ones, are wonderfully useful. I received the adjuster yesterday, thank you very much. Could you send me: a little medicine kit with essential basic remedies, such as iodine etc., and furthermore a duster (what do you say to that: I'm asking for a duster!). Otherwise, everything for me is quite acceptable objectively, and subjectively completely marvellous. We're playing quartets daily; both technically and in the way in which it understands Oscar's intentions, the quartet is much better than it ever was in London. The first movement of Beethoven's Op. 132 is really going very well already. Uncle Hans has already been appointed President of the local football association, he plays frequently too, and is the Prima Donna. I've heard that you are unhappy, which I don't quite understand: your poor little son will not have his head bitten off by a little straw-mattress-sleeping; clearly one would rather be free than locked up, but it will not last for ever. One has another benefit here: I am getting to know some very distinguished and charming people. Otherwise don't keep thinking that we are at death's door whenever we write asking you to work hard on pursuing the application vigorously: we want to be free to help the country in whatever way we can, in order not to be looked upon as worthy only of internment.
Lots of kisses, Hans

[10a].   15 August [1940], draft of telegram to Hans Grotte from Grete Keller.

In English.

Wire your and Hans Bl. house Registration No. and whether I shall send canvas campbed or proper springbed.
How are you.
Love Margret

11.   15 August 1940, Huyton.

In German.

Dear Mutschili, Have received: on the 12th your letters of 3rd and 6th; on the 14th your card about the bed (a canvas camp bed, please), Uncle Rudi's letter and your letter to Uncle Hans of the 10th. Send your letters postage paid 'Internee's Mail, Free of Charge'. Your questions: washing is being done by the refugee laundry; we're now quite well supplied with food, so you do not need to send something every week; things like cake and Liptauer cheese are of course always very welcome, also fruit. Yesterday received parcel with sardines. Bread I can buy. I agree with your not agreeing about Shanghai. Crate makes a wonderful table (at which I'm now writing). We are at present 16 in the house, 5 to a room. I am in no way neglected: Hans even checks that my little top collar button is always fastened. I don't need any clothing or underwear. Cushions have come. I have seen Greig's friend and have found out that he has written to you about my beard – but so far I have only a little beard. Very pleased about Uncle Rudi. I will have patience as long as you want. The 4/6 'bed and breakfast' doesn't look as though it's going to materialise, but it is not at all necessary. I'm really happy with all the letters. The Liptauer cheese was a dream. We can buy eggs here occasionally. After your and Uncle Rudi's letter I feel optimistic. Tomorrow we shall play the Brahms sextet. Yesterday I ate so much of all the good things you sent me for my dinner that I felt quite sick. Practise the 'cello; I'll be able to play quartets with you when I come to London. Apart from Hüttenbach, all the professional 'cellists here are not as good as you are.
Many, many kisses, Hans

12.   **17 August 1940, Huyton.**
         In German.

Dear Mutschili, I received your letter of the 10th on the 15th. Three different people play the viola in turn; the conductor, Haas (formerly of Radio Stuttgart), Dr Grünbaum, Dr Zanker. Necker is not in our room, but in the house next door. I don't want the bed because [the floor] is too hard, but because I'm suffocating in the dirt (I'm in a ground floor room with direct exit to the lane outside and nowhere to wipe your feet); moreover my (thin as air) straw mattress only stretches 2/3 of my length and just about my width. Nevertheless up until now I haven't slept badly; with bed-linen it will be paradise. Necker has a bed (for many weeks he had to sleep in a tent with 8 people). New slippers will soon become necessary, since the old ones are nearly worn through. Inge should write and tell me what she's practising and what doesn't work, then I'll send her short instructions. Uncle Hans has settled in now, thank God, for which reason 'married life' with him, which isn't simple anyway, has become easier for me. I think that living with someone who has interests so diametrically opposed to mine in every respect is very educational for me, and I reckon it a point in my favour that so far I haven't had a single quarrel with him, though he is not the easiest to get on with. (This is the first letter I've written which he hasn't read as well.) Today about 40 people were released: it was a wonderful sight, many of them cried like children with happiness and didn't know what to do with themselves. These releases give me new hope that perhaps it will be my turn some time. I keep having my portrait painted. The violin rash on my neck has healed since I grew the beard. Oscar is sitting next to me and making himself a coffee on the cooker. Many, many kisses, Hans.

[12b].   **17 August 1940, telegram, Huyton.**
         In English.

5.10 OF 16 TH LIVERPOOL 29
KELLER 32 HERNE HILL LONDON SE 24 =
UNCLE HANS NUMBER A 5877 MY NUMBER SEE MY
REGISTRATION BOOK IN MY DOCUMENTS PORTFOLIO
CANVAS BED SUFFICIENT ARE QUITE ALL RIGHT LOVE = HANS +

13.   21 August 1940, Huyton.
        In German.

Dearest Mutschili, Yesterday received your letter of the 15th and parcel with cucumber etc. What do you mean, 'My God, what do you look like?'? Haven't you ever seen an old Jew before? I don't need a suit. We have moved; our old room is needed as the A.R.P. room. Oscar must feel wonderful? Next week we have a quartet recital: Jekel, Keller, Haas, Hüttenbach. I can't start my own quartet just yet, as I can't dance at two weddings, nor do I want to compete with Jekel. We all miss Oscar very much (me most of all), at the same time we're all happy that he's been released. I saw him step out into the open through the barbed wire gates. What is left of the musicians is sad (to listen to). The sandwich spread is excellent, so are the little filled chocolate balls, Black Magic and everything else. I don't know what upsets you so much about the beard. What makes you so hopeful about Miss Rathbone's letter (apart from the fact that new categories may be created)? The pears are really excellent. I've had an answer from the First Lord of the Treasury via the Prime Minister's office to my letter, saying that it has been forwarded to the Home Secretary. From today we are eating kosher: much better, and a much more pleasant atmosphere. Yesterday we attended a speech by Rabbi Dr Ochs (Oscar knows him): really excellent. Every day many are being released: just now our former room-mate the radio salesman came to say goodbye. I am happy for everyone. Uncle Hans thinks it really important that Uncle Rudi speaks again to Mr Vansittart, and that the application doesn't become dormant. Is Inge practising? What are the children doing? How is Susi? Are you practising? Are you feeling happier yet? Play quartets with Oscar and Tooth. Servus Mutschili, many, many, many kisses, Hans.

~

Although he was obviously trying to reassure his mother (and one must also remember the censor), it does seem from these latest letters that Keller was beginning to enjoy himself – to the extent of describing his interned life as 'subjectively completely marvellous'. Of course he was keen to get out of the camp, but being interned was not altogether a negative experience. The amount of music he was now playing, and its quality, recalled the glories of Vienna – at least while Oscar Adler was still there: 'both technically and in the way in which it understands Oscar's intentions, the quartet is much better than it ever was in London'. The repertoire which emerges from Keller's internment letters, both the works he mentions playing and the music he asks his mother to send, gives some idea of the musical landscape in which he grew up. In Huyton, the musical environment was clearly a familiar one, with Haydn, Mozart, Beethoven and Brahms at the centre of his experience, supplemented by some Bach and Handel on the one hand and occasional references to Dvořak, Weber and Tchaikovsky on the other.

Socially and intellectually, the company in the camps was also most agreeable: 'I am getting to know some very distinguished and charming people'. As historian Daniel Snowman has described in *The Hitler Emigrés*, the internment camps were full of the most gifted people:

> Many of the leading figures in post-war British musical life spent time in internment: composers and musicologists like Hans Gál, Egon Wellesz, Franz Reizenstein and Hans Keller, while performers included the popular pianists Rawicz and Landauer and three-quarters of what was to become the Amadeus Quartet. Kurt Jooss was interned, as were his choreographer Sigurd Leeder and designer Hein Heckroth. Internees included a future editor of the *Financial Times* (Fredy Fisher), a future Controller of Radio Three (Stephen Hearst), the journalist Sebastian Haffner, the Dada artist Kurt Schwitters, economists, sociologists, publishers, psychologists, photographers, physicians, classicists, cartographers and a critical mass of top scientists.[55]

A large number of these people passed through Huyton camp at some stage, and Keller met several of them. For a young man who had been prevented from going to university, and until the Anschluss had never lived away from his parents, Keller's period in internment may have served some of the purposes of university for him, in terms of widening his horizons and strengthening his intellectual independence.

He was not the only one who could see a positive side to life in Huyton. Here is Leo Kahn's account of his time in internment, published twenty years later:

> Once we had conquered our first dismay at finding ourselves behind barbed wire, it was not even an altogether unpleasant experience. In fact, if you listen to some ex-internees exchanging their reminiscences, you might get the impression that they had the time of their lives. They will boast of clandestine and joyous parties after 'lights out', of their skill on the football field, of the wonderful meals they managed to make from

meagre rations. They will talk of concerts, produced on an ancient piano in an overcrowded room, with an uncritical enthusiasm that they would never show at the Royal Festival Hall. Lectures, prepared from memory without the benefit of a library, are remembered as stimulating events of the first order – as indeed, under the circumstances, some of them were. ... Only, of course, we did not know that all would be well in the end ...[56]

The pianist Paul Hamburger, whom Keller met later on the Isle of Man, certainly seems to have had the time of *his* life in the camps, 'which eye-witnesses remembered his enjoying to the point of refusing to leave'.[57] In general, however, it has to be said that this positive side to internment was only really perceptible to the young. It was undoubtedly easier for the youthful internees to adapt to their uncomfortable situation than for men who were older and more established in life, with wives and children and ruined careers to worry about. For Keller, like other young internees, the stimulating effect of meeting so many 'distinguished and charming people' was paradoxically enhanced by the difficult circumstances in which they were thrown together. 'In an internment camp,' Leo Kahn observed, 'as in army life, you get to know a person better in a few days than you normally do in years.'

6   Protest, July 1940

Although the invasion-fever which had fuelled the mass internment policy was widespread, there was nevertheless considerable opposition to the idea of interning refugees, from within government circles as well as outside. The national security arguments behind the policy naturally held back some of this censure for a while, but as reports of conditions in the camps began to circulate, together with distressing individual case histories, the government's critics found their voice.

If there was one single event which might be said to have mobilised the opposition, it was the sinking on 2 July of the *Arandora Star*, and the consequent death of hundreds of innocent civilians. The shock of this event was profound, and did much to bring home to the public the appalling consequences of the indiscriminate 'enemy aliens' policy. To make matters worse, however, some of the survivors from the *Arandora Star* were then immediately re-deported to Australia on the *Dunera*, on which they endured a nightmarish voyage, including a near miss with another torpedo. When the *Dunera* finally arrived two months later, evidence of the internees' maltreatment during the voyage shocked the Australians, and led to the court-martialling of the ship's captain.

It was, as the Home Secretary, Sir John Anderson, was forced to concede, 'a matter which touches the good name of this country'.[1] As one MP pointed out, the mass internment policy was even allowing German propagandists to claim that Britain was 'now starting to pursue the Nazi policy of interning every Jew in the country'.[2] The first major Parliamentary debate on internment took place on 10 July, initiated by the Conservative MP for Chippenham, Major Victor Cazelet. Eleanor Rathbone was one of the principal speakers: 'Many of us have wanted for a long time to raise this question in debate,' she told the House of Commons, 'but we have been restrained by two considerations, first our sense of the terrific pressure and strain on all Government Departments and reluctance to add to it, and, secondly, by a reluctance to give publicity to a matter which reflects unfavourably on our country's reputation for humanity, liberality and efficiency. We are compelled to do it now by the mass of evidence pouring in upon all of us of the widespread misery and fear suffered by refugees, many of them anxious to serve our country's cause. ...'[3]

From that point onwards, the internment policy was in retreat – though initially not very quickly. The administration of the camps was transferred from the War Office to the Home Office on 18 July, signalling the beginning of a parallel shift in influence over policy towards the internees – though the liberal instincts of the Home Office took some time to re-emerge. The first White Paper published on the subject appeared on 31 July, and although it was subtitled 'Categories of Persons Eligible for Release from Internment and Procedure to be followed in Applying for Release' and gave a list of eighteen such categories, most of these were little more than descriptions of those who should never have been interned in the first place.[4] Category 1, for example, was given as 'Persons under 16 and over 70 years of age', and category 3 was 'The invalid or infirm'. Announcing his new policy in the House of Commons on 23 July, the Home Secretary did admit that errors had been made during the mass round-up in June: 'There have been cases of mistake in interpreting instructions which necessarily had to be carried out under a great sense of urgency. In particular persons have been interned who should have been exempted on grounds of ill-health or infirmity. These mistakes must be rectified with the least possible delay.'[5] In August, therefore, there began a small trickle of releases, Oscar Adler among them. But there was as yet little to encourage internees who were young and fit to think that there would be any prospect of a quick release for them. As has been seen, there were two categories that caught Keller's eye: number 17: 'Persons about to embark for emigration overseas', and, (in view of his mother's recent telegram saying that she was ill) number 18: 'Special cases of extreme hardship, e.g., where a parent, wife or child is dangerously ill.' But his chances of success with either of these applications were slim. His mother's illness was not sufficiently serious, nor were his plans for re-emigration anywhere near concrete enough. Internees released for emigration were taken under guard to the actual port of departure, so everything had to be organised beforehand. As François Lafitte described it:

> 'Persons about to embark for emigration overseas' are 'released' in the following way. The re-emigrant is interned at Lingfield Race-course Camp and only allowed out to attend interviews at the U.S. Consulate. [America was the most frequent destination of re-emigrants.] On the day his ship sails 'the alien is taken to the port of departure' where, presumably, he meets his wife and children and becomes a free man when he sets foot on the American 'soil' of the ship.[6]

To some of the government's critics, Sir John Anderson's speech to the Commons on 23 July and his subsequent White Paper marked the end of the matter – or at least the beginning of the end. There had been a public acknowledgement of the suffering caused, and something official was being done. Procedures for releasing some internees were being drawn up, advisory committees established, and before long an inquiry was launched into the selection of internees for deportation on the ill-fated *Arandora Star*.[7] The Archbishop of York, for example, who had just written to Winston Churchill of the 'feeling of shame … that saps devotion to the national cause' which the 'wholesale Internment of Refugees' had created, hastily withdrew his criticism: 'Now I have heard of Sir John Anderson's statement … I wish I had not posted my letter; please ignore it.'[8]

Other critics of the government were not so easily appeased. Many thought, like François Lafitte, that 'Sir John's "new" policy was not new at all: he merely proposed to correct the mistakes the police had made in carrying out his original policy, but showed no signs of modifying that policy.'[9] And indeed, the Home Secretary continued to assert that the internment of civilians was necessary:

> There can be no question at the present time of reverting to a position in which the internment of men of enemy nationality shall be the exception rather than the rule.[10]

Anderson's White Paper, as Colonel Wedgwood, the MP for Newcastle-under-Lyme remarked, 'misses the whole point'. Far from wanting 'categories to be left out of unjust imprisonment', the opposition was seeking to question whether mass internment could be justified at all.

Significantly, a large number of the critics of internment were to be found at the very heart of Whitehall, and in the most highly educated and influential circles:

> John Maynard Keynes, who took up the cases of several interned fellow economists, claimed he had 'not met a single soul, inside or outside government departments, who is not furious at what is going on'. Indeed, civil servants supported François Lafitte in compiling his denunciatory study, *The Internment of Aliens*.[11]

François Lafitte wrote his book under the auspices of PEP (Political and Economic Planning), whose staff he had joined in 1938 at the age of 24. PEP was a rather remarkable institution at that time; it has been variously described as a 'think-tank' or research institute (and it is a direct forerunner of the Policy Studies Institute),[12] but these are scarcely adequate descriptions of the dynamic force which was PEP in the 1930s:

PEP was born in the crisis year of 1931, brought into life by leading personalities – industrialists, financiers, businessmen, academics, scientists, civil servants, journalists and just a few unusual politicians – with a common concern at the intellectual barrenness of governments confronted with economic slump and growing international tension. Located at the heart of Whitehall, it was a high-prestige institution *sui generis* – at once a West End club, a standing discussion group (or group of groups) and a research institute, yet not any one of these things as then conventionally understood. Its wide-ranging publications commanded high respect; and they were all anonymous, being the products of many minds. ... Among much else, PEP can fairly claim to have been one of the major intellectual influences preparing the way for the National Health Service and the Beveridge social security system instituted in the aftermath of the war.[13]

The immediate catalyst for the formation of PEP had been a report written by the young assistant editor of the *Weekend Review*, Max Nicholson, and published in that paper in February 1931. In common with many others, Nicholson was in despair at what he saw as 'a world apparently falling apart'.[14] Britain's tentative economic recovery after the end of the First World War had been dashed by the General Strike, after which the worldwide collapsing markets and political turmoil in Europe seemed to herald nothing but disaster. In the face of this emergency, the government's apparent lack of sufficiently co-ordinated policies led Nicholson and others to advocate centralised economic planning as essential to the survival of the nation. In the words of the TUC report of the same year, 'Only by comprehensive planning of our economic development and regulated trading can the needs of the present day be met.'[15] Nicholson's contribution to the debate was *A National Plan for Great Britain*. Its publication was a landmark event, and immediately attracted heavyweight support, including Israel Sieff, of Marks and Spencer, who became PEP's first chairman, and the Dartington philanthopist Leonard Elmhirst, who was PEP's chairman when Lafitte joined its staff.

According to Lafitte, Elmhirst was 'enraged at the internment of Kurt Jooss, Sigurd Leeder, and many other talented dancers and musicians at the Dartington Arts Centre, for no better reason than that Dartington came within one of the "protected" coastal zones that had just been proclaimed.' His rage was shared by Professor Alexander Carr-Saunders, Director of the London School of Economics, who had likewise 'just witnessed a wholesale round-up of scholars, however eminent, and of many students who happened to be of "enemy" origin.' Supported by Carr-Saunders and 'all the senior PEP personalities', Elmhirst asked Lafitte to investigate urgently what was being done to refugees from Nazi persecution:

My book was produced in that setting. But because it dealt with a very urgent problem demanding wide publicity and immediate action, PEP waived its normal procedures of thorough discussion by an expert study group (impossible to assemble during a military emergency) and of anonymous authorship. Instead, though I did in fact draw heavily on the knowledge and collective wisdom of PEP members, the book was to be my own and was to be issued as a 'Penguin Special'. ('Specials' were specially commissioned titles on current affairs, produced and published at speed, and with a higher print-run than most other Penguins.)[16]

With the help of PEP members, MPs from the Parliamentary Committee on Refugees and his many friends among the Austrian refugees, Lafitte quickly established an impressive network of information sources. Important among these were Bloomsbury House in London, the headquarters of all the main refugee welfare organisations, and also the Austrian Centre and the *Freier Deutscher Kulturbund* (Free German League of Culture), which had been set up in London in 1938 by prominent refugees (under the chairmanship first of the Berlin theatre critic Alfred Kerr, and then the painter Oskar Kokoschka). There were also many civil servants and academics among Lafitte's informants: 'As news of my assignment spread, I was spurred on and offered help by many others.' He even had a journalist from the *Daily Mail* supply him with a dossier of the iniquities of the Rothermere newspapers' anti-aliens campaign.

Particularly vital for Lafitte, however, was first-hand intelligence gathered from the internment camps themselves. This was naturally not accessible through official channels, but one of Lafitte's Austrian friends, an enterprising Viennese medical student called Eva Kolmer, managed to build up an extraordinary amateur intelligence service 'which, through local informants, smuggled out of every camp almost every day the latest news of what was happening; and through part of June and all July and August copies of these reports, typewritten on flimsy paper, were passed to me through Eva.'[17]

Lafitte digested all this information at top speed, and by September the book was ready for publication. Penguin books, acting with similar alacrity, managed to get it out only nine weeks later. It thus played its part in the maintenance of pressure on the government to resolve the internees' plight. The book sold nearly 50,000 copies, was widely reviewed and discussed, and the many positive letters Lafitte received from MPs and other influential figures encouraged him to think that his efforts had not been in vain. But what pleased Lafitte most was to hear that his book had been smuggled into the internment camps, 'where internees organised reading sessions – from the Isle of Man to Australia.' One internee later presented Lafitte with a souvenir of those reading sessions:

What I cherish most of all is a three-inch strip of the barbed wire which surrounded the Onchan internment camp in the Isle of Man. On his release the writer and journalist, the late Heinrich Fraenkel (whom I had not previously known), presented this memento to me in a little cigar box on behalf of his fellow internees. That symbol of their 'chains' has remained on display in my study bookcase ever since.[18]

~

The *Arandora Star* disaster had done something to soften the public mood towards the 'enemy aliens', but still the threat of a German invasion remained. Government progress on the release of internees was hindered both by the need to prioritize the nation's defences against invasion, and by the public's lingering fear that there might still be dangerous spies among the refugees. This fear seems to have remained longer in the public mind than in the government's, and Churchill himself is recorded as saying in Cabinet as early as 1 August 1940 that it was now possible 'to take a somewhat less rigid attitude in regard to the internment of aliens'.[19] Although he went on to say in the House of Commons that he had 'always' felt the danger of spies to be 'somewhat exaggerated',[20] the juggernaut set in motion by his order only two months earlier to 'collar the lot' was not so easily put into reverse. For some time to come, the burden of proof still lay with the internees to prove their loyalty beyond doubt in order to have any hope of release.

Hitler's intention was to invade Britain early in September 1940 and throughout the summer the tension mounted. As beaches were cordoned off to prevent advance landings, signposts were removed to confuse an invading army, the Home Guard drilled in parish halls, and government leaflets with titles like *If the INVADER comes : what to do and how to do it* dropped through letterboxes, a frightened public watched and listened for any sign of the enemy. Rumours swept the country, and the police received continual reports of suspicious activity. In this febrile atmosphere, anything odd could be interpreted as evidence of possible espionage – as Midge Gillies has described in her book *Waiting for Hitler*:

In times of extreme nervousness the human eye seeks out bizarre interpretations of everyday phenomena: the face of Christ in a fried egg, or a terrorist's profile in a plume of smoke. The summer of 1940 was one of those times. The authorities felt obliged to investigate every suspicious incident – or, at least, to listen to the person who hurried into their local police station with a tale: a trail of blue string might lead to a radio transmitter, or a municipal flowerbed had been planted in such a way that the blooms would form a white arrow to guide enemy bombers to a munitions factory.[21]

It was not a time to be or do anything that was different – including, of course, to be a foreigner. And no doubt there were occasions when the reports about spies provided an opportunity to settle old scores – or indulge old prejudices. The Jewish community, ever fearful of antisemitism, issued instructions to refugees on how to blend in, urging new arrivals not to be heard too much speaking German.[22] Such caution was lasting: it is noticeable from Keller's surviving correspondence that, even several years later, he always wrote to his mother in English when sending open postcards.

Throughout July and August, the Luftwaffe concentrated its bombing attack on the RAF's airfields, trying to ensure that when 'Operation Sealion' (as the invasion plan was called) launched itself across the channel, it would not be vulnerable to attack from the air. Industrial targets in major cities like Birmingham and Liverpool were also attacked, threatening those living nearby (including the internees at Huyton). When, in late August, stray bombs landed on north-east London, and the RAF retaliated with a raid on Berlin, Hitler's anger at the ensuing civilian casualties led to a change of policy, and the Luftwaffe switched to bombing British cities in an attempt to demoralise the population. Ironically, the consequent relief of pressure on the RAF airfields was a major contributory factor in the Luftwaffe's failure to gain air superiority, leading to the indefinite postponement of Operation Sealion on 17 September.

Although the London Blitz did not begin in earnest until 7 September (after which the capital was bombarded daily over the next two months and frequently until the following May), the Luftwaffe's attacks in August were already frightening the civilian population, and separated families worried constantly about each other's safety. Keller's relatives in London and the internees in Liverpool needed regular news to allay their anxiety for each other.

[13a].   21 August 1940, telegram, Huyton.
In English.

97 11.27 LIVERPOOL 10
KELLER LONDON BRIXTON 3383 =
WIRE WHETHER ALL RIGHT LOVE = HANS +

[13b]. 24 August [1940]. Draft of telegram from Paula Kompfner to Hans Grotte. *In English.*

HANS GROTTE
75106 'B'-Coy 099,2, Camp I
33 Sheptonroad
Huyton

No news since 5. August your sister and I very worried wire whether allright and whether Hans received the campbed
Kisses Paula

14.   23 August 1940, Huyton.
In German.

Dearest Mutschili, The bed is here! It came yesterday, while I was having a quartet rehearsal; Uncle Hans and another room-mate, a certain banker called Oppenheimer, wanted to surprise me, and they put the bed up all ready and waited for the big moment when I came back home. Unfortunately, I'm not a very observant sort of person, and although the room is extremely small and I used a number of things that were on the bed, I didn't notice it until they drew my attention to it. As to the new categories, the one called 1) 'People who were engaged in specially useful work' etc. should be mentioned (Red Cross Music), of course it depends on how the Berend matter is getting on; 2) my anti-Nazi activities: a) the article in *Das Neue Tage-Buch* which can be found in one of my folders, b) my membership of the Harand movement, and of the *Vaterländische Front*, both anti-Nazi movements, c) my uncle Rudolf Keller, my being actively friendly towards the Allied cause: volunteering for National Service (I have here confirmation of the Brixton A.R.P. casualty service), Red Cross Music etc. Bearing in mind my age, one can hardly expect me to have been involved in more official activities. The most important point remains the original one of your illness, as far as I can judge from here. Sleeping on this bed is like heaven. I haven't put the straw mattress on this bed, but *ad acta*. Jekel and Hüttenbach told me today that they had never met such a mature musician of my age. Lord Lytton is wrong if he thinks that a table and a chair had been provided for each room. Please tell Oscar that he doesn't know how wonderful such a bed is, because he once said that such things didn't matter to him on principle. The kosher cooking is in a class of its own. Greetings to everyone. Many, many, many kisses, Hans.

The 'new categories' to which Keller refers in this letter were announced by the Home Secretary during the second major parliamentary debate on internment, which took place on 22 August, the day before this letter was written. In contrast to his statement the month before, Sir John Anderson now addressed the central question of whether or not the mass internment policy was justifiable.

I have seen it stated that this is a policy which cannot be defended. There is an influentially signed letter in the 'Times' this morning which contains that statement. I am here to say that the policy can and must be defended, and I shall try to make clear … why in my view the policy was necessary and why it must, for the time being, at any rate, in all essentials be maintained.[23]

He reminded MPs of the liberal nature of his initial policy, announced at the outbreak of war, which had left the majority of German nationals at liberty by using tribunals to distinguish 'refugees from Nazi oppression from other categories of enemy aliens':

My statement on 4th September was a statement of policy which gave me personally the greatest satisfaction. I thought it was in accordance with the best traditions of the country. It was with the very greatest reluctance and regret that I departed from the policy which I enunciated, a policy which at the time commanded the approval of Members in all parts of the House and the support of public opinion outside.

His change of heart, he insisted, was purely 'a matter of military necessity':

The military authorities came to me, late one evening, and represented that, in view of the imminent risk of invasion, it was in their view of the utmost importance that every male enemy alien between 16 and 70 should be removed forthwith …

Describing how internment had expanded from the initial coastal strip into a nationwide policy, mirroring 'the enemy's rapid march' and hastened by the feeling in the country that 'no unnecessary risk must be taken', Sir John protested that he had had no choice. 'My postbag was full of letters urging me to go further,' he told MPs, adding that, after the arrest of the first internees in May, 'There was not a responsible newspaper on 13th May who did not applaud what had been done.'

Despite such applause in May, Anderson's speech on 22 August shows how much he now felt the pressure of the anti-internment campaign. Sensing that the 'military necessity' argument was not enough, he fell back on the issue of passport nationality. Alongside the familiar claim that 'enemy agents' might be hidden among the genuine refugees, he also seemed to imply that, however anti-Hitler they might profess themselves to be, a German was still a German, and thus not really to be trusted when the chips were down:

> Is it not the case that a fair proportion of those friendly aliens still have friends and relations in Germany, still have material interests in Germany, and as a result might be subject to pressure which would lead them, perhaps at the hour of our greatest peril, to take action, on an impulse it may be, which afterwards they might greatly regret? Further, is it not the case that these enemy aliens include quite a large number who, perhaps because of the experience they have gone through, are fundamentally defeatist, who, if it appeared that the enemy was making progress in an attempt to land on our shores or by parachute, would lose heart, would be a source of weakness, and would tend to lower the morale of the people around them, and might be tempted in the last resort to try to make terms?

Nevertheless, the new White Paper, when it was published on 26 August, did include a new category for the release of anyone who could 'show that by his writings or speeches or political or official activities he has consistently, over a period of years, taken a public and prominent part in opposition to the Nazi system and is actively friendly towards the Allied cause'.[24] Thus did Britain acknowledge that it had indeed locked up some of Hitler's most bitter enemies. Keller's attempt to gain release on the basis of his own 'anti-Nazi activities', however, was very unlikely to succeed. Despite his plea that, 'bearing in mind my age, one can hardly expect me to have been involved in more official activities,' his involvement seems to have been peripheral, rather than 'prominent', and neither of the organisations he mentions here were really what the authors of the White Paper had in mind. The 'Harand-movement' refers to the followers of Irene Harand (1900-75), a prominent Austrian Catholic campaigner against antisemitism in the 1930s. The *Vaterländische Front* was an Austrian nationalist party, founded by Chancellor Engelbert Dollfuss in 1933 when he merged the parties of his coalition government and suspended the Austrian parliament. It was anti-Nazi in that it opposed Austrian membership of a greater German Reich, and was banned after the Anschluss, but otherwise had much in common with Italian fascism.

Keller's uncle Rudolf, who certainly was a 'prominent' opponent of the Nazis, did not seem to have thought of his young nephew as a particularly active politician: 'He has done absolutely nothing politically, was strongly pro-British, but lived only for his musical studies'.[25]

Keller's mention of a category of 'Persons engaged in especially useful work' may be a confusion of category 6 ('Persons … engaged in work of national importance', which would have meant practical work for the war-effort and did not include music), and category 13 ('Persons engaged in refugee organisations which are still functioning'). The Austrian Centre and the *Freier Deutsche Kulturbund* were both still functioning, and the German composer and conductor Fritz Berend was involved in their concerts. It seems that Keller had previously played in charity concerts with Berend's orchestra ('Red Cross Music'), and the category mentioning refugee organisations encouraged him to hope that release might possibly be obtained that way.

Conditions at Huyton Camp had been the subject of repeated questions in Parliament as well as a Departmental Inquiry launched by the Secretary of State for War, so despite Keller's remark that 'Lord Lytton is wrong', the noble lord might have been forgiven for thinking that something had been done to improve things by now. It was, after all, six weeks since Eleanor Rathbone had first asked, 'Is it right … that at such a camp as the Huyton camp, which has been going for weeks, they should still be almost entirely devoid of chairs, tables and beds, so that elderly people have to sleep on the floor on mattresses, or, as I have been told, on heaps of straw? … Is nobody authorised to cut the red tape and drive to Liverpool, which is about four miles away, and order immediately a few things of that sort?'[26]

Lord Lytton was now chairing one of the two advisory bodies on enemy aliens which Sir John Anderson had announced in his statement to the House on 23 July. His Advisory Council was the larger of the two bodies, with perhaps the wider remit. It was part of the Refugee Department of the Foreign Office, and included among its members Sir Herbert Emerson (High Commissioner for Refugees) and Sir Neill Malcolm (former Commissioner for Refugees from Germany), together with several MPs (including Eleanor Rathbone) who also served on the Parliamentary Committee on Refugees. It was charged with advising the Home Secretary on the welfare of refugees in the camps, and its terms of reference included the requirement 'to suggest measures for maintaining the morale of aliens in this country so as to bind them more closely to our common cause'.

Sir Herbert Emerson and Sir Neill Malcolm also sat on the other new body announced by Anderson in July: the smaller Advisory Committee chaired by Sir Cyril Asquith. Its role was also advisory rather than executive, and, as François Lafitte complained, this advice was limited to matters referred to them by the Home Secretary:

Neither body is competent to discuss and advise on questions of general internment policy unless the Home Secretary chooses to refer such questions to it. General questions about the whole nature of internment are excluded from their scope, unless the Lytton Council cares to recommend that the most obvious method of 'maintaining the morale of aliens in this country so as to bind them more closely to our common cause' is to release all who are not suspect and make some attempt to redress the harm done to them.[27]

~

In public, the government clearly wished to maintain its official position that mass internment was justified and would continue. Although forced to acknowledge their critics, ministers tried to confine discussion to the periphery of the issue, ceding only minor points about the practical implementation of their policy, not the central question of the policy itself. The limitation of the *Arandora Star* inquiry to 'the method of selection of aliens to be sent overseas' is a case in point.

In private, however, there are several indications that the will behind the policy had gone, even before the second Parliamentary debate on 22 August. Winston Churchill himself no longer seemed to believe in the alien threat; after his announcement to the War Cabinet on 1 August that Britain's position was 'consistently more secure than in May', allowing a 'less rigid' treatment of aliens,[28] he wrote the following day to Lord Lytton in similar terms. His words made clear that things had changed, and that the quiet release of 'considerable numbers' was now the order of the day:

> We were in great danger two months ago, and it was absolutely necessary for their own sake to round up a great number of aliens. I think my view and yours will not diverge on the way they should be treated and on the liberation by more refined processes of considerable numbers, now that we are feeling a good deal firmer on our feet.[29]

The Intelligence historians F. H. Hinsley and C. A. G. Simkins are sceptical that the government's relaxation of its position on internment really sprang from any great improvement in the military situation – after all, at this date, 'the Battle of Britain had not yet reached its climax, the threat of invasion (Operation Sealion) was at its peak and public apprehensions were far from being allayed.' They look elsewhere for the real reasons:

On the one hand ministers were anxious about Parliamentary opinion and on the other was the fact that the interrogations and other intensive investigations carried out had produced no evidence for espionage or sabotage by Fifth Column elements, let alone the existence of an organised Fifth Column movement.'[30]

Shocked by the fall of Norway and the extraordinary speed of the Blitzkrieg, the British had simply been unable to bring themselves to believe that their enemies could have achieved so much without help, or that their allies could have crumbled so quickly without betrayal on a massive scale. Such fears had made Churchill's new government easy prey to the press scares about a network of spies infiltrating the country. But when the round-up was completed, and the authorities could look clearly at what they held, there was no Fifth Column in their hands, only frightened civilians – and in the country at large a thoroughly frightened public, which now made it politically very difficult to do what justice demanded.

~

15.   27 August 1940, Huyton.
In German.

Dearest Mutschili, I only received today your letter of the 11th that you sent through the Home Office. I've already answered all questions in my last letters. Today I got a letter from Georg and a little parcel (Black Magic) from Gertrud. I should like to thank her very much, but she shouldn't incur great expenses on my account. How is the tired eater – and his wife? Together with his room-mate the banker, I often think sorrowfully of the time when we could tease him because of his habit of jumping out of bed at night. At the moment, we have more reason to be worried about you than you about us. Do you stay in bed during the raids or do you always go to the shelter? Today we are having a Goethe Celebration, which we shall frame with the slow movement of the *Froschquartett* and Mozart's Adagio and Fugue. On Saturday we have a quartet recital: *Froschquartett*, Adagio and Fugue, Brahms C major [*sic*]. The cornplasters are excellent, but already used up, please send me some more. I hope you're practising the cello and are making efforts to get into a quartet? 28 August: just now, in the middle of a rehearsal and to my great joy, I received your parcel with the music stand and duster – and used the former immediately. I am subjectively and objectively very well, and apart from sadness about separation and lack of freedom, nothing disturbs my peace. Is Inge practising? Have you heard anything from Liane? Has the Berend offer any chance of being accepted and put into practice? I should love to hear something from Muni and Kollmann. Today – miracle of miracles – we have sunshine and no storm, which hardly ever happens here. How are the children? Might not Uncle Rudi have some chance of a post in the Czech government? Then he could grant me, the old Czech, Czech nationality. Kisses, Hans

Keller's father and his father's two brothers Rudolf and Hugo had all been born in Bohemia, hence Keller's reference to Czech nationality. Czechs were not routinely interned in Britain – indeed their designation as friendly aliens while Austrians were enemy aliens was an indication of the British government's acceptance of Hitler's claim to Austria. After Hitler annexed Czechoslovakia in 1939 many Czechs fled to London, where a Czech government in exile set up its headquarters. Keller was not joking about the possibility of Uncle Rudi being given a post in it: after the First World War he had been offered the Ministry of Education by President Masaryk, who was keen to involve prominent German-speaking Czechs in the new government. Rudolf Keller, to whom the offer apparently came as a great surprise, 'declined the invitation because he thought, reasonably enough, that the man who was to be responsible not only for the German but above all for the Czech schools must know more Czech than he did'.[31]

Rudolf Keller's newspaper, the *Prager Tagblatt* has been described as 'a fluorescent institution with the best news service in Prague'.[32] The excellence of its journalists and its editorial team was complemented by the many well-known literary figures who chose to contribute to its pages, who included Berthold Viertel, Max Brod, Rudolph Fuchs and Franz Kafka, who apparently read the paper daily and knew many of its staff. It was a liberal paper, with a wider readership that its older competitor, *Bohemia*, for which Kafka had written his first articles and which was rather more exclusively Germanic than the *Tagblatt* and 'less friendly to the Czechs'. 'The readers of the *Prager Tagblatt* were predominantly German-Jewish, though the paper – the largest in Bohemia – also reached a considerable number of Czechs who could read German.'[33]

In 1939 Kafka was long dead, but still living in Prague when the Nazis arrived was his former mistress, the writer and journalist Milena Jesenská. She immediately became involved with the Czech Resistance, working to smuggle out of the country those who were particularly in danger. The Nazis pursued an open policy of eliminating the Jewish presence in Prague, initially by heavy pressure on Jews to emigrate:

> The majority of Jews could have departed openly. Their difficulty was not so much in leaving the country as in finding a refuge abroad. On the other hand, the Germans attempted to prevent the departure of political opponents … who were therefore generally able to emigrate only by illegal channels.[34]

Jesenská's group was one of the illegal channels used by those who were wanted by the Gestapo. She was eventually arrested herself and ended up in Ravensbrück concentration camp – but not before she had helped save many lives, including that of Rudolf Keller.

In Ravensbrück Milena Jesenská met Margarete Buber-Neumann, on whom she made a profound impression. They remained imprisoned there together in dreadful conditions from 1940 until 1944, during which time Jesenská told Buber-Neumann the story of her eventful life. Jesenská died in the camp in 1944, but Buber-Neumann survived, and on her release wrote a memoir of her friend, which she called *Mistress to Kafka: The Life and Death of Milena*.[35] Here is the section in which Jesenská recalls the invasion of Prague:

> On the night of March 14th, 1939, Milena, like thousands of other Czechs, had no sleep. With despair in her heart she stood at her window, gazing down at the familiar scene. The street lamps formed the usual pattern, and the star-shaped square into which seven streets converged was as usual deserted. The only difference was that from three o'clock onwards more and more lights were turned on – in the flat next door, on the opposite side of the street, upstairs, downstairs, and all the way down the street. So they knew too. At four o'clock the Czech wireless began broadcasting at regular five-minute intervals the same brief announcement; the German army was advancing from the frontier on Prague, and calling on the population to remain calm, go to work, send their children to school as usual. That is how great events come to pass, quietly and unexpectedly, with dawn creeping gloomily over the house-tops, a vivid moon peeping from behind the clouds, people's faces haggard with sleeplessness, coffee simmering in the pot, and regular announcements coming over the wireless. At last it had come. We had expected it too long for it to be a surprise.'[36]

Jesenská started ringing round her Jewish friends immediately. 'It was as though Milena were born to face violent catastrophes,' wrote Willy Haas, one of those whom she telephoned that night. 'The more alarming the situation, the calmer and more composed and greater she became.'[37] She joined forces with a young Prussian, Count Joachim von Zedtwitz, who had just completed his medical studies in Prague, and together they formed a group of people dedicated to getting well-known Jews and anti-fascists out of the country. Zedtwitz had a car, and their plan was that he would drive the fugitives to the Polish border, while Jesenská would arrange to hide them in Prague until their turn came to make the journey.

Every trip to the Polish frontier was a risky enterprise. One day Zedtwitz's passengers were Rudolf Keller, the editor of the *Prager Tagblatt*, and Holosch, of the *Prager Mittag*. The first incident took place a few miles east of Prague. Zedtwitz knew that the Germans had set up a series of check-points round the city, but, driving at speed round a corner, he was brought up sharply by one of them; it was too late to turn and try another way. He told his companions to leave all the talking to him, got out and as though it was the most natural thing in the world, raised the bonnet to show the engine number, the usual procedure for an ordinary check by the traffic police. "But, when I looked at the German soldier, I started, because he had a real crook's face," he said. "However, our luck held; the man's reactions were slow, and my behaviour put him off his stride. Eventually he pulled himself together and asked me whether I had a Browning with me. I snapped back in my best Prussian manner that I was sorry, but had no use for such a thing. We were let through without any more questioning."

To avoid more check-points, they travelled by side-roads. All went well until they reached Moravia, but then it began to snow, and one snowdrift followed another until finally they were stuck. After this second mishap, Holosch lost heart, made his way to the nearest station, and went back to Prague by train. Rudolf Keller and Zedtwitz went on till they reached the place where they hoped to find another guide to take Keller over the frontier; by now they had missed their appointment with the original guide. Zedtwitz left the car by the roadside and went and knocked at the appropriate house. An old woman opened the door and told him in an agitated whisper that the man he wanted had been arrested for smuggling people over the frontier. Zedtwitz hurried back to the car, and to his horror found Rudolf Keller standing with a frontier guard in the light of the headlamps. Zedtwitz walked up to them and wished them a friendly good evening. The frontier guard, who was suspicious, demanded his papers, and Zedtwitz produced those he had. "But this gentleman has no papers," the frontier guard said. "Don't worry, he'll find some," Zedtwitz said reassuringly. Keller, who was sixty-eight, spent a long time fumbling in his pockets, and finally produced an old Austrian identity card dating from 1886. While the policeman examined it Zedtwitz, expecting the worst, tried to save the situation. "But Uncle Rudi," he exclaimed, "how can you think of going about without papers in times like these?" Then, turning confidentially to the policeman, he went on: "You know, we'll never be able to cure him. He still believes the Emperor Franz Josef is on the throne." Keller picked up the cue, and played the part of a senile old gentleman to perfection. The frontier guard began to laugh, asked where on earth they were going at this time of night, and Zedtwitz told him a long story about having had to visit some dairies and having lost their way. After a few more jests about old people who did not know what times they were living in, the man finally let them go.

There was nothing for it but to go back to Ostrava. They drove on for a while in silence, and then Keller asked Zedtwitz to stop and let him out. Why should Zedtwitz risk his young life for an old man like him? He proposed to lie down in the ditch by the wayside and take poison. Zedtwitz replied that there was plenty of time for that, and suggested that they should have a good dinner first and then think it over. A little while later they reached a hotel, where they dined. After that Keller felt better. Next day they found a guide to take him over the frontier.[38]

According to Zedwitz's testimony given to Yad Vashem on 8 April 1994, Rudolf Keller crossed the border at Moravská Ostrava to the English transit station at Katovice. But once in Poland the danger was not at an end. Poland could not offer a permanent refuge and its government did not wish to admit fugitives who could not move on immediately to other countries. The British Committee for Refugees from Czechoslovakia began to facilitate onward movement to Britain and the Empire by setting reception centres in Poland at the end of March 1939. But progress was slow, hindered both by the reluctance of the British government to issue enough visas, and the difficulty of arranging safe transport – particularly for those, like Rudolf Keller, who were wanted by the Nazis and therefore had to keep clear of German soil, coastal waters or air-space.

Most of the ships from Poland to western ports went through the Kaiser Wilhelm Canal. The political refugees could not risk travelling by that route. Special arrangements had to be made, again at great expense, to divert the ships round the Skagerak. Special ships were chartered to take refugees first to Sweden, whence they came to England. The delays grew worse – and were fatal. When the German army invaded Poland in September 1939 a small band of those who had escaped Hitler in

Germany, Austria, the Sudeten areas, who had survived the invasion of Czechoslovakia, who had reached Poland after hazardous journeys, exhausted, starved and wounded, were finally trapped. There were some 1,600 refugees from Czechoslovakia in Poland; about 500 of these had already – either in Prague before the *Einmarsch* or in Poland – been accepted for immigration into the United Kingdom, but had been defeated by the delays.[39]

~

In the context of such horrors, Keller's next letter to his mother is understandable:

16.   31 August 1940, Huyton.
In German.

Dearest Mutschili, I've just been talking to Greig, who told me that you are still very worked up ('You know how she is'; 'I know' was my response). Gradually, in spite of the pain of being apart from you, I'm getting really annoyed with you: why do I write you letter after letter that we are well? And now you've also talked to Oscar, who has surely told you that we're not at death's door, you know that basically I lead the same life as in London, you know that Uncle Hans has settled in, so what more do you want? That we're longing for release is not the result of bad living conditions, but the natural result of being locked up, even though it's quite a comfortable prison. But to get really worked up about this in times like these is a real luxury. If we don't get upset, then you certainly have no reason to do so. Your being unable to get a medical certificate is something I can't quite understand, surely one would issue such a thing to a poor old Jewish woman without a gall-bladder and with other pains?[40] But surely you are much better informed about that. We must hope for a new tribunal, and if that doesn't happen, we'll know how to console ourselves. On the 28th, I received a parcel with apples, Liptauer etc. Thank you very much. Greig tells me that you're all well, which comforts me a great deal. He was actually very excited and a little confused and slow in his head, so that it was difficult to get a complete sentence out of him – or inject one into him. Please send me in a case my dark bow (there's a light and dark one, which is the worse one, in my violin case). In the long run, this violin is not very pleasant, and if this internment goes on for much longer I shall ask you to send me the other one (the one that Inge had for a bit). How is Rudi Kompfner? Are you still practising and playing, pray? I shall really tell you off if you aren't. After all, why did we let Oscar leave here? Servus, Mutschili, love, many kisses, Hans.

17.   **4 September 1940, Huyton.**
In German.

Dearest Mutschili,
I hear from Zoepnek[41] that you are already reassured and no longer so worried, which, unless it's just silly talk on her part, reconciles me with you. Please don't send the loose cheese any more, it goes mouldy immediately. Greig was kind enough to leave us a food parcel here: we should like to thank him appropriately. Haas is released. Tell Adler that he should speak to Baron Fuchs about whether something couldn't be done using my position in the Centre. Fuchs is, as far as I know, also friendly with Baron Frankenstein.[42] Is there the slightest chance with the Berend Orchestra? Could one possibly, through Berend or the Kulturbund, do anything using my position in the latter? I'm writing to you all the ideas which come into my head, however laughable they might be. Our commander, who gave another speech the other day (about the White Paper) is one of the most charming people I know. I'm trying to write something in English: 'A Treatise on Vanity', though I've only got as far as the introduction. The fact that for long periods of time one doesn't even clap eyes on a woman has a peculiar effect on the younger ones and on the sensitive: I can now just about imagine what a monastic atmosphere is like, where people can't even get it out of their system by telling coarse jokes and drawing naked women. Do you spend most of the day in the cellar? Or only if it's banging and crashing? The post is getting rather bad again. You can see the camp is getting emptier: nearly 700 have already been released, and I have worked out that if this continues at the same rate, at worst my turn should come in a few weeks. But it won't continue at this rate, and one day these mass releases will stop. Uncle Hans is baking in the sun. I had a sharp discussion with Prof. Liebert about Goethe and Kant. Many kisses, Hans.

18.   **10 September 1940, Huyton.**

In German.

Dearest Mutschili, Received the parcel with the lovely slippers and even more lovely cake. You don't need to send tins any more, as one can get them here for 8 or 9d. Nor should you save any more sugar, as we have enough for the time being. On the 7th I sent you a birthday telegram. Received your 9th letter of the 5th. Tomatoes can't be got here, fruit rarely, everything else sporadically and very expensive. I've only received a single Cowling mailing. Music stand and duster as written already. Please subscribe to the Jewish Chronicle for me. Oppenheim the snorer is released, so we are now 3 in the room. I've asked Oppenheim to ring you: did he do that? If you write to Muni, tell her that in our room our room-mate has hung up a board which says, 'The sun is always shining behind the darkest clowd' [*sic*]; the writing and decoration are like on the Alt-Ausseer chamber-pots 'Make sure you do it in the middle, because that's the way we do it here'. She will be able to imagine what heart-warming comfort is provided by the continuous sight of this board in these difficult times; nothing is as inappropriate as an appropriate witty saying. Recently the 'Internee Art Exhibition, Art behind Barbed Wire' opened here; among other things there is a painting of the Adler quartet, composed of Adler, Keller, Grünbaum, Hüttenbach. We are now playing quartets only as a threesome (Jekel, me, Hüttenbach), because Zanker, when he's not under Adler's thumb, becomes coarse, so it's much more harmonious as a trio. I believe that the Berend application has no chance; I hope I'm wrong. How are you feeling during the bombing? Do you not get much sleep? How does it affect the children? And the Adlers? Has Muni written yet, or Kollmann? The post is going to get faster again, as the commander has gone to the Home Office about it. Kisses, Hans.

19.   **13 September 1940, Huyton.**

In German.

Dear Mutscherle, Can you send us the folding seats and the folding table you wrote to us about? It would be really nice if one of the folding chairs could be the sort with arm-rests. We have received your parcel to Uncle Hans with soap-dish etc. We should like to have an electric stove (the type that radiates out), not too small, and a triple adapter. If because of air raids etc. it isn't easy for you to leave the house, or you don't have much time for packing and sending, we will of course be patient as long as you like. Mowgli will remember the film 'Bombs on Monte Carlo' and the hit song 'Pilot: greet the sun for me'; I'm playing this and other popular songs with the composer, who made every single UFA film before the Nazis, in a musical show. Received Inge's letter of the 3rd and thank her very much for it. She should treat the 2nd and 4th position with the same intensity; many an excellent violinist is a bit scared of these two positions, because when he first started playing he neglected them in favour of first and third, or learnt to master these long *before* the other two. I have seen all the acquaintances about whom you and Inge have on occasion asked me; the camp is not big and the number of people not that high any more either. Please send a small comb for my beard. (I sleep with the beard under the blanket.) Of course it worries us every time we read that South-East London has been bombed, which is why we ask for more frequent if short signs of life. Sandwich spread and bread are excellent. Please could you send a new cooker because the other one keeps breaking down. Servus, Mutschi, many, many kisses, Hans

20.   17 September 1940, Huyton.
In German.

Dearest Mutschili, Table and easy chairs arrived one day after I had written my request for them. Life was immediately transformed by them. Naturally, it doesn't make sense now to send another chair with arm-rests. Parcel with toothpaste and -brush received. Today again somebody from our house was released: his wife had made a hardship application. I now play regularly in the variety shows here; though a little training in palm court orchestra-playing can't do me any harm, neither I nor my fellow musicians intend to act the Shames[43] for ever and ever, when everyone else, from the person who designs the scenery to the orchestra porter gets paid, which is why Jekel, Hüttenbach and I are going today to the C.E.C. (Camp Entertainment Committee) to make clear that either we get paid or we won't play any more. We had a gala première yesterday, all the officers were invited and came, we asked for an entrance fee of 6d per person (I would not have gone myself even if I had been given a ticket for free). It was a great success, for reasons that are a mystery to me. I indulged myself in particularly elaborate ornamentations around the choruses of whichever popular song we were playing. Our quartet of three about which I've already written to you is now playing the Rasumovsky Quartets; next week we have an orchestral performance of the Kleine Nachtmusik. -Naturally I now wish doubly hard that I was at home. Are the Adlers very nervous? I can well believe that Roy is calm (also Mowgli, if the crashes aren't as loud as in Carmen), and that you have a smoothly running system of shelter and alarm routines set up, complete with rules. Are you getting short of sleep? Are the children very disturbed? How are Paula and Inge taking the raids? I won't be able to send you portraits of me, because as far as I'm aware we're only allowed to send letters from here. Nor have people here managed to reach agreement yet as to whether my bearded face looks like a rabbi, a Spanish aristocrat, or an Indian prince. Many kisses, Hans

20(a). 20 September 1940, Huyton. To Roy Franey.
In English.

Dear Roy, I was very glad to receive your letter (and Mutti's) of 13ᵗʰ. The close raid-experience must have been rather exciting. As to our air-raids, we have, of course, much less to suffer than you. Though there are, daily and nightly, many alarms and much A.A. [anti-aircraft] fire (during the day we are able to watch the precise work of our gunners), generally nothing but A.A. shells drop in this camp. We had only three unpleasant nights, when incendiary bombs were dropped within camp lines, and high explosive bombs close by. – Could you tell Mutti that I received plaid and cornplaster, but no mattress up to now. We would very much like to have the brown bread sent as before. The parcels (which are always censored before my eyes) contain the index always. That Oscar and his wife are cheerful I cannot quite understand: they used to tremble every time an alarm sounded? That the Londoners are marvellous I can imagine very well, thus possibly this war will sooner be won than we think. Where (in which room) do Paula and Inge sleep? I suppose Mutti is in high spirits; as far as I know her she is only in a nervous state when danger is possible, not when it is imminent. Has the shelter been enlarged? How is it possible that 7 persons (or five and two halfs) sleep in it? In the 'music hall' which we perform almost every day, the following joke was made yesterday: 'The Home Secretary has announced that two further categories for persons eligible for release have been added: those boys under 18, whose grandchildren are serving with the army, and those over 65, the grandfathers of whom are waiting for them in front of the camp to take charge of them'. Much love from Uncle Hans. Yours affectionately, Hans

⁓

Unlike houses and apartment blocks in continental Europe, British houses built after the turn of the century did not tend to have cellars or basements. The protection of the population of London during the Blitz was therefore a major concern. In the absence of anywhere better, many Londoners made for Tube stations during raids. The government had misgivings about this, as it was thought that the lack of toilet facilities in the underground stations would encourage the spread of disease. Some kind of domestic shelter was obviously desirable and the Home Office had commissioned and distributed two designs, which it named after Home Secretaries Sir John Anderson and Herbert Morrison.

The Anderson Shelter, distributed in the months leading up to the outbreak of war, was constructed of galvanised corrugated steel panels, buried at least four feet deep in the garden. A deep layer of soil covered its roof (which efficient householders digging for victory would often plant with vegetables). The Morrison Shelter, distributed later during the war, was for indoor use. It had a solid steel plate top (to withstand falling debris), wire mesh sides and a mattress floor. Both shelters were distributed free to those on low incomes, with better-off householders paying a charge of a few pounds. Midge Gillies has described the 'hobbit-like' Anderson Shelters as 'a DIY nightmare to assemble', which 'precipitated an endless battle against damp. A sheet of sacking, saturated with water and hung across the doorway in the belief that it would mitigate the effects of poison gas, contributed to the mustiness, and the eighteen inches of soil piled on top, which soon sprouted flowers and vegetables, gave the impression of an animal's burrow'. The Morrison Shelter was not much better: 'a steel cage ... which held its own claustrophobic horrors'.[44]

Keller's family did not need either of these shelters. Built as it was by Austrian architects, the house at 32 Herne Hill did have a cellar, and despite Keller's doubts that 'five and two halfs' could sleep down there, there was actually quite a bit of room. The published plans of the house in the Architectural Press's *Small Houses*[45] show that the cellar contained three rooms (workshop, boiler room and meter room), plus a cupboard under the stairs leading up to the front door. Keller's niece Ena remembers being put to sleep with her sister Nora in that cupboard: since the front-door steps above were made of concrete, it was considered the safest place.[46] Inge and Paula Kompfner were resident at No. 40 Oakbank, nearby, but they were now sleeping at Herne Hill so as to be able to shelter during the raids.

~

The 'Art Behind Barbed Wire' exhibition at Huyton, which Keller mentions, was probably organised by the young artist Hugo Dachinger, who became a close friend of Keller and drew several portraits of him. Dachinger was moved with Keller to the Isle of Man, where he held another 'Art Behind Barbed Wire' exhibition in Mooragh Camp in Ramsey. When he was finally released, he refused to go without his pictures, which he later used to mount another 'Art Behind Barbed Wire' exhibition in London. Naturally there was not much in the way of artists' materials in the camp, and inmates had to make do with whatever resources they could find. Many of Dachinger's most remarkable paintings were done on newspaper, and he sometimes allowed the newsprint to show through in effective ways – as in his painting of rows of internees eating in a dining shed, through which the headline 'Vitamins Enlisted to Win The War' can be clearly read.

After Oscar Adler's departure, the violinist Max Jekel took over the leadership of Keller's quartet. Hüttenbach the 'cellist was still there, but Karl Haas and the best of their other viola players had now been released, leaving Keller and his colleagues reduced to playing as a trio. Keller doubtless missed Adler very much, but there were still many gifted musicians in the camp, including some well known popular performers. Walter Landauer, the 'BBC and Radio Vienna' pianist with whom Keller mentions playing Handel, was one half of the piano duo Rawicz and Landauer, who later built up an immense following playing popular classics in Britain after the war. He and his partner, the Polish pianist Maryan Rawitz, had already met with some success touring Europe in the early 1930s before they moved to England in 1935. There their career took off, helped by the fact that they were particular favourites of Edward VIII. The UFA composer with whom Keller mentions playing film songs was probably Werner Richard Heymann, a prolific writer of film and cabaret music who was closely associated with UFA (Universal Film AG) during the years of the Weimar Republic, when it was the principal film studio in Germany. It closed down in 1945, having been completely taken over by the Nazi party during the war, ruining its previously high international reputation.

All this, together with the regular 'music hall' shows kept Keller pleasurably busy, despite his complaints about the lack of payment and the type of music he had to play.

21.   **27 September 1940, Huyton.**
         In German.

Dear Mutschili, My last letter went to Eden, the Musical Entertainment organiser. Received: 3 Sept. parcel, mattress, letters of the 10th and 15th, telegram ('All right, unchanged'), letter from Ella. I have Liane's letter. The old Hamburger is here, quite cheerful, no question of him being despondent. Please send me a warm pair of pyjamas. As to your letter replying to mine telling you off, I deign to acknowledge its receipt but must put right that *I* have never despaired (except for 2 hours when I feared being deported). Received the First Aid kit some time ago and acknowledged it. We have all sorts of newspapers. The best paper that I have ever read is the Manchester Guardian, which I would warmly recommend to you. Our last room-mate will be released today, so that now at last, touch wood, we'll have one room for the two of us. He is a B-case and was probably released because of his beautiful eyes – I can't imagine any other reason. In view of the mass releases I have come to the conclusion that Greig is the greatest bumbler under the sun. Our show is happily at an end; they did Viennese songs with updated texts, e.g. 'My little mother is a Viennese girl and therefore I am interned', or 'Today I'll black out my window, put out that bloody light, put out that bloody light'(That's what the soldiers always shout) etc. or 'There will be a Huyton, and we'll be outside, there'll still be lists, & we won't be alive any more...'[47] Life just as a twosome will be really pleasant. Do write frequently, so that we need not worry. Have you heard anything from Berend? Many, many kisses Hans

22.   **1 October 1940, Huyton.**
         In German.

Dear, dear Mutschili, Received your card of the 24th and parcel of 4th September. Uncle Hans received your letter with the news of Karli's death today. Terrible. We're now only seven in the house (another one was released today) and we are beginning to prepare for winter.

As said winter is likely to be somewhat nippy (exceptionally as every year), I'd like to ask you for a warm pair of trousers and two pairs of warm leggings. I'd like you to ask Adler if I'm right in my belief that women perform and hear music mainly horizontally, while in men we more often find a preference for the vertical. This shows up even in extreme examples: coloratura (exclusively melodic) is only used by women, though it might be just as useful for men; the analogy, the concerto cadenza, which also has a harmonic dimension, is something typically male. Please be sure to ask and write the answer. I'm writing my next letter to Muni, if in the meantime there's nothing noteworthy to report. It's already rather cool, but thanks to the blankets we sponged off those who have been released, we are not cold at all. What do you do all day? Sleep? If it's not too much trouble and doesn't cost too much money, and you have no other worries, I should be very glad to have the famous D major Concerto by Mozart

etc.

sent direct from a music shop. But it isn't absolutely necessary. Don't start worrying again, I'm not smoking a lot, nor am I thin or otherwise close to death. Many, many greetings and kisses to everybody (do you get out of the house much?). Hans

23.   4 October 1940, Huyton.
In German.

Dearest Mutschili, Received: collapsible chair with armrests, cooker, all Cowling System courses, pyjamas, 2 Jewish Chronicles (it says an enormous amount about us that you don't find anywhere else), your 13th letter of the 23rd: I don't know Oppenheim's address, but it's not important. Margarine and butter we've always received. I've got the cream (and beard comb); till your letter arrived I didn't know whether I should spread it on my head, on the beard or between my toes. I don't need either towels or handkerchiefs. Nobody has mended my socks so far (they're not very torn: I wear the ski shoes all the time), and anyway Uncle Hans is a first class and enthusiastic sock-darner. It is said here officially that next week, on Wednesday at the earliest, most of the camp (including Uncle Hans and me) will be transported to the Isle of Man. We shall of course do our best to join Rudi and, God willing, we'll be successful. In spite of the definite official statements, my private opinion and experience is that this may be altered another 50 times and finally cancelled, so I would advise you not to take it as certain. I couldn't care less about the whole question – it doesn't matter where I sit, here or there. Rosch Haschonah with the orthodox community here was a unique, indescribably moving experience. Never unpacked the cooker, but am taking it in its packing to the Isle. Morrison, as the Home Secretary, is giving us grounds for hope. When I come out, I'm going to learn the clarinet. Servus, dearest Mutschili, greetings to everyone. Your Hans

24.   8 October 1940, Huyton.
In German.

Mutschili, my dear, dear one, I'm writing before our transfer to the Isle of Man tomorrow (if the whole thing isn't postponed or cancelled at the last minute). We haven't succeeded in being allocated to where Rudi is living, we're going to Ramsey, but possibly we shall be able to apply from there for a transfer to Douglas. With great pleasure I received Mowgli's letter of the 24th with your headnote of the 28th. The doctor's certificate is at least a step forward. Our luggage (9 pieces, the packing of which we have worked on for the last 2 days) has already been taken away. Uncle Hans will travel with a little hand case, me just with violin case and music stand: the violin is wrapped in the towel and pyjama trousers, soap is in the resin compartment, cigarettes in the same place. Mr Holiday I can easily picture.[48] Don't forget to mention in your hardship application your only brother Hans, also Papa's death, your brothers' deaths. Now the time has come for saying goodbye yet again, after I have made many a deep personal friendship here (something Uncle Hans probably doesn't even know about). But probably it will be much nicer over there than here. Hopes of release have risen again since Morrison. When I eventually get home, you will be able to sleep the whole night. I shall be happy to stay awake at night and sleep during the day, as you know. I have received your telegram ('All well'). Servus, Mutschi, many kisses, Hans

Grete Keller had three brothers, of whom only the youngest, Hans, survived the war. Gustav, the eldest, had died of a brain tumour before the Anschluss. He was a gynaecologist, one of whose patients was the wife of the ship's captain who had helped to trace Uncle Hans after the First World War. Fritz, the second son, was a dentist in the Czech Sudentenland. As can be seen from the family photograph on page 146, he was fair and rather Aryan-looking, and he apparently managed to conceal for some time the fact that he was Jewish. His eventual fate is no longer known, though a postcard sent by him to Grete Keller on 22 September 1938 still survives, which shows him still living in Košice.[49] He had two young daughters, whom Roy Franey managed to get to England early in 1939. They shared their father's Aryan looks – indeed, according to their cousin Inge, who was there when they arrived at Herne Hill, they did not actually know that they were Jewish. They came to London thinking that they were only on holiday, and it was Grete Keller who broke the news that they were now refugees. Their father's concealment of his family background had been so successful that the two girls had unthinkingly absorbed some of the antisemitism common among Sudeten Germans at that time. Their discovery that they were Jewish themselves was therefore quite a shock, compounded by the horrible realisation that they would be unable to return home.[50]

To secure the girls' position in England, the family found them work as domestic servants in the house of Lady Susi Jeans, the Viennese-born musician and wife of the mathematician and astronomer Sir James Jeans. The girls had never done any domestic work before, and Roy Franey's daughter Ena remembers much family hilarity over the mistakes they made.[51] Their situation was not uncommon, however. By the beginning of 1939 over 7,000 Jewish women had escaped to Britain as servants, and most of them were unqualified for their new role. To quote one example given by the historian Tony Kushner, 'out of 500 women rescued by the Cambridge Refugee Committee on domestic permits, only two were found to have suitable experience'.[52] Since their mistress had been born in Vienna, it is to be hoped that these particular girls met with some sympathy for their plight; all too often, however, the employers of refugee servants had little understanding of their new maids' and cooks' backgrounds, and harsh treatment sometimes resulted from the servants' failure to give immediate satisfaction.

Grete Keller's final sibling, Irma, was also able to conceal her ethnicity from the Nazi authorities, shielded by her marriage to an Aryan husband. She remained in Vienna throughout the war and survived. When the Russians entered the city in 1945, the family house in Nusswaldgasse was burned down. Flats were later erected on the site, and Irma moved into one of them.[53]

～

Keller and his uncle finally left Huyton internment camp on 9 October 1940. The camp was being run down and as many as possible of its remaining inmates were being transferred to more permanent accommodation elsewhere. Keller knew by now that his cousin Rudi Kompfner was on the Isle of Man, so when he discovered that he would be going to the island himself, he naturally hoped that they might be able to be together. However, he and Uncle Hans were sent to Mooragh camp in Ramsey, whereas Rudi Kompfner was in the Central Promenade camp in Douglas – where he apparently shared quarters (and discussed physics) with the mathematician Wolfgang Fuchs.[54]

As Keller mentioned in his letters of 4 and 8 October, the beginning of that month had seen a change of Home Secretary. Sir John Anderson had been the target of recent parliamentary and press criticism, particularly over his handling of civilian defence during the Blitz. His opposition to the building of deep shelters for the general public (on the grounds that the country could not afford to divert the necessary resources from the invasion preparations) was proving very unpopular, and Churchill took the opportunity of Chamberlain's resignation as Lord President of the Council to move Anderson into that role, making way for the experienced Labour politician Herbert Morrison to take over as Home Secretary.

Morrison was well known to Londoners, having been leader of the London County Council for most of the 1930s, and his response to their needs during the bombing was altogether more effective than Anderson's:

> This department [the Home Office] was ideal for him. ... The skills, techniques, and flair evident at the LCC were transferred effectively to a more extensive brief. He responded to the blitz with administrative flair and with a sensitive grasp of popular feelings. His visits to devastated cities, his responsiveness to local needs, and his characteristically careful discussions with officials produced new policies for civil defence and a radical reorganisation of fire services.[55]

The internees hoped that Morrison would deal with their situation with a similar energy and effectiveness. He was known to have fairly liberal views and the fact that he was a Labour politician also encouraged them to think that he would be more sympathetic to their plight than the Conservative Anderson – the political opposition to internment having come overwhelmingly from the left rather than the right wing of British politics. What was not true, however, was the rather widespread impression that Sir John Anderson was to blame for the policy. The title of the anti-internment polemic, *Anderson's Prisoners* (whose author, 'Judex', was actually the leading Fabian and later Labour MP Hector Delauney Hughes) reflected a common view of Anderson's responsibility – but, as has been seen, Anderson's original ideas were much more liberal, yielding only when Churchill came to power and, with the creation of the Swinton Committee, effectively took matters out of Anderson's hands. A. V. Hill, in a memoir defending his friend Sir Alexander Maxwell (Permanent Under-Secretary of State at the Home Office at the time), was very clear that the policy was primarily Churchill's: 'Naturally people assumed that Maxwell and Anderson shared some of the responsibility of the decision on internment. They did not; it was a panic stroke (or at least a typical impulsive act) of Churchill himself.'[56]

Many felt, however, that Anderson could still have been more robust in standing up to his political colleagues. François Lafitte was another critic who took this view (though he didn't realise at the time that the new Prime Minister was so prominent among those whom Anderson had to resist). His book *The Internment of Aliens* went to press just as the change of Home Secretaries was announced, and Lafitte added a topical dedication:

To

MR. HERBERT MORRISON,

Home Secretary and Minister of Home Security, formerly Ruler of London, in the hope that he will succeed where his predecessor, SIR JOHN ANDERSON, formerly Ruler of Bengal, has failed.

7   The Isle of Man, October 1940

Keller's transfer to 'The Island of Barbed Wire'[1] – apart from the uncomfortable journey he had to endure to get there – was very much a change for the better. Unlike Huyton, which functioned primarily as a transit camp, the camps on the Isle of Man were intended to serve as the permanent destination of the internees assigned to them. Mooragh Camp in Ramsey was one of the first to be set up on the island and was composed mainly of seaside boarding houses, hurriedly requisitioned in May 1940 (the name comes from Mooragh Promenade, the street facing the sea which was cordoned off to make the camp). Despite the island's role in the First World War, when the camps at Knockaloe near Peel had held over 20,000 internees, the Isle of Man had not been among the locations originally picked out to house internees in 1939. The panic and thousands of arrests of May and June 1940 led the War Office to instruct the Lieutenant-Governor of the island to make rapid preparations, and the owners of the Ramsey boarding houses were apparently given less than a week to vacate their premises, leaving behind 'all furniture, bedding, linen, cutlery, crockery and utensils'.[2] Mooragh Camp was therefore a vast improvement on the bare houses and straw sacks of Huyton. Here a more settled and domestic existence was possible, with the men catering for themselves in their houses – though for many of them, Keller included, this was a new experience for which they were unprepared. As François Lafitte explained, the fact that the internees were staying in hotels and boarding houses did not mean that Mooragh, Hutchinson and Onchan were like holiday camps: 'the men were not cared for by seaside landladies', and there were still many difficulties:

> The houses were commandeered, a minimum of furniture was left in them, and the internees were left to run things themselves. ... Each house had a common room with a table, chairs, a light and blacked-out windows. The remaining rooms were used for sleeping and contained beds with mattresses, but no chairs, cupboards, tables or light. Half the men in each house would sleep on palliasses on the floor, or in some

cases on couches. In theory there were two blankets per man, but the camp suffered from a chronic under-supply of blankets, and sheets of course were not available. Most houses had bathrooms, but warm baths were only available if and when – as rarely happened – coal was issued. The camp stores issued food rations for each man, and the men in each house had to do their own cooking. The kitchens mostly contained gas-stoves, but inadequate supplies of utensils and crockery. Since most of the men are naturally inexpert at cooking this arrangement caused considerable hardship and wastage of food. The food supplied was a just adequate minimum to avert hunger, but was not dietetically well balanced and tended to be monotonous. It consisted mainly of cabbage, potatoes and other vegetables, rice, plenty of kippers and fresh herrings, meat occasionally, bread and a little milk. No sugar, fruit or eggs were supplied. Invalids were able to get some extra food and milk. The camp stores also issued soap and other necessities to internees. The canteen, run by a staff of internees, sold such things as tooth-paste, razor-blades, notebooks, tobacco. It also sold – at intervals – apples, chocolate, and bread. Jam and marmalade were not available. Canteen prices were high, and although destitute internees received one shilling a week from the canteen profits and could apply for the payment of telegrams, it was not at all clear what happened to the greater part of the profits, since proper accounts were not kept. It is believed that they go to the Manx Goverment. Recreation facilities were good. ... There was an ample supply of interned medical practitioners working under a competent English doctor, but there was the usual shortage of medical equipment (though not nearly as bad as Huyton in June). The most seriously ill were sent out to hospital, where accommodation was severely limited. The camp was run in the usual way by house-leaders, under group leaders and camp supervisors who worked with the military staff, most of whom were intelligent and helpful.[3]

The cultural life of the internment camps on the Isle of Man is now legendary. As the broadcaster Andrew Marr put it, 'For a short period of time, one of the great centres of European intellectual life was the Isle of Man!'[4] Even in the more trying circumstances of Huyton, the extraordinary range of concerts and lectures mounted by the internees had led to the camp being nicknamed 'Huyton University'. The more settled conditions on the Isle of Man were even more conducive to intellectual activity:

At one Isle of Man camp a typical week's worth of activities in October 1940 included, *inter alia*, history lectures on Metternich, the Rise of English Democracy, Church History, Medieval Culture and the

British Empire; science lectures on bacteriology, physical chemistry, mathematics and aspects of nutrition; a philosophy series on the Ancient Greeks; lectures on French and German literature, and various literary and musical recitals. What could one do, Fred Uhlman wrote later, 'if Professor William Cohn's talk on Chinese theatre coincided with Egon Wellesz's Introduction to Byzantine Music? Or Professor Jacobsthal's talk on Greek Literature with Professor Goldmann's on the Etruscan Language. Perhaps one felt more inclined to hear Zunz on the *Odyssey* or Friedenthal on the Shakespearean stage.'[5]

In many of the Isle of Man camps, the internees produced a camp journal, and these publications – such as the *Onchan Pioneer*, the *Central Promenade Paper* and *The Camp* (published in Hutchinson Camp) – give a vivid picture of what was going on. Unfortunately the *Mooragh Times* fell foul of a particularly authoritarian Camp Commander, and its first issue (published on 12 August 1940, two months before Keller arrived there) turned out sadly to be its last.[6]

~

25.   10 October 1940, Mooragh Camp, Ramsey, Isle of Man.
In German.

Dear, dear Mutschili, Here we are happily in yet another camp. The journey was somewhat uncomfortable as the sea was 'very rough'; ship of 1200 tonnes licensed for 220 people was filled with 1000, and in addition not all facilities were accessible. The rest I leave to your oh so seamanlike imagination; would only add that today we are feeling OK again. (Arrival last night, sea journey 5 hours instead of the normal 3.) Uncle Hans is quite OK. I have still got muscle pains from vomiting and trying not to vomit, and blue bruises. When the ship seemed to be standing on its head, I would slide over my fellow-passengers' vomit from one end to the other, where I stayed lying down until I slid back again. But that was still better (lying on the floor and sliding) than sitting up, as practised by Uncle Hans, who I admit was warmer and not vomited over by others as much, and undertook less sliding around in other people's vomit, but who would surely have felt better if he had done as I did. I did wear the life jacket as I was told to, but I also used it as a pillow, so that my head stayed clean. (Only once did a pianist friend of mine throw up right into my face.) Here it's quite nice; hotels by the sea and no air-raids. Please send me warm leggings; those you sent me a while ago are too small. I can only do up the lowest button. Wonderful periodicals (from 1860) with philosoph. articles are available to read here. Kisses Hans

26.   13 October 1940, Mooragh Camp, Ramsey, Isle of Man.
In German.

Dear Mutschili, Please send all the things which we ordered from Huyton here now. Besides that we'd like a good medicine against seasickness: if we're released (God willing), we'll really need to have that, as we can't choose our sea crossing and are only released right by the ship itself. Send the result of the hardship application *no matter what the outcome* as soon as you get it, even if it's turned down. You would be ever so pleased to see me regularly doing all manner of jobs here. I hear that Jaray has already been released because of illness. From him you will be able to find out all about what it's like here. I've even started to play football again in my old age. We get newspapers a day late. Unfortunately for the time being we have neither our luggage nor our money. From experience I expect that will take some time yet. We are very short of fruit and also coffee: please send a pound in a good tin. Food parcels please, as regularly as in the past. Also I should like to have: soup spoon, fork, two large coffee cups (preferably unbreakable). Furthermore, laxatives and a small rubber hot water bottle, just in case, God forbid, one should be unwell; that would be a great luxury. How are you, Mutschi? I should love to be back in London with you, in spite of the bombs. Huyton supplied some very elementary training in this, as occasionally even there the bombs whistled round one's ears. Anti-aircraft fire was de rigueur day and night, but one got completely used to it. Here it is 100% quiet. Uncle Hans, thank God, has his bridge partners again. From the beginning he has been unbelievably nice and kind to me, and that smoothes over any conflicts in our interests. I keep thinking that the longer the internment lasts, the more wonderful the day of release will be; in addition, the whole thing is bound to be a good education for me, as long as I make the most of it. Mowgli's letter was very funny: please thank her a lot for it. Many, many greetings to all the others, many, many kisses to you. Hans.

The 'hardship application' which Keller mentions in this letter was his application for release under Category 18 of the August White Paper: 'Special cases of extreme hardship'. The White Paper specified that 'Full particulars of the circumstances should be given in the application, and, in cases of illness of a near relative, the application should be accompanied by a medical certificate.'[7] Keller had made this application on the basis of his mother's illness, starting the process at the beginning of August (see his letter of 3 August). It had taken his mother two months to secure the required medical certificate, so the application had only recently been submitted. Meanwhile, others were being released; 'Jaray' was probably Rudolf Jaray, whose sister Mariedl Jaray was a close friend of Mowgli's from the days when they were medical students together in Vienna.

Uncle Hans, who had been having prostate trouble, was hoping to be released under Category 3, 'The invalid or infirm'. For release under this category, internees did not have to make their own application. 'In any case in which the state of health of an internee is such that he is not fit to remain in internment,' said the White Paper, 'the medical officer of the camp will furnish to the Home Office a certificate to that effect and release will be authorised without delay.' Unfortunately this was not in practice quite the simple process that it sounds. Despite the White Paper's assertion that 'Internees receive medical attention in the internment camps', this was mostly provided by the internees themselves, whose numbers included quite a few refugee doctors. During the chaos of the initial stages of mass internment, the inadequacy of the medical care provided by the army forced the internees to take matters into their own hands, and even when conditions became more settled they continued to be heavily relied upon. Lafitte's report on the medical services in Huyton in June describes the situation as 'appalling'. Quite apart from the lack of proper beds and medical equipment, there were simply not enough qualified personnel:

> Only one Army doctor was available for a population which seldom fell below 3,000 and was often much greater. The refugee doctors interned in the camp saved the situation by putting their services at the disposal of the medical officer and organising a camp hospital and out-patients department. On June 28, 1940, they drew up a memorandum for the camp authorities revealing, among other things, (1) that accommodation and nursing facilities for men suffering from acute diseases and for helpless invalids was totally inadequate. There were very few beds, no bed-linen at all, no nursing materials, no skilled nurses and no hot water. Men with infectious complaints like tonsilitis were sleeping on the floor. (2) The 300 beds (without mattresses) then available for 4,000 men [i.e. the total number of beds available in the camp] were completely

insufficient for the large numbers of elderly invalids suffering from heart diseases, hernia and other conditions. (3) There was a total absence of first-aid accessories, even of bandages, splints and thermometers. (4) The supply of drugs was completely insufficient. Insulin – a vital necessity for the numerous diabetics in the camp – was available only for those who could pay for it. ... (5) They reported an increasing number of men suffering from psychological disturbances due to internment conditions ... Two men had committed suicide. By July 12 another two had taken their lives and there had been two unsuccessful attempts.[8]

On the Isle of Man in October things were not as bad as this, but still the vast bulk of the medical work was done by the internees. Naturally, they would have no say in who should be released, so would have to refer any serious cases to the English medical officer in charge. Getting to see 'the English doctor' was therefore vital, but due to the sheer numbers of cases it could take a while to achieve.

At this point, Mowgli and Roy Franey, their daughters and Grete Keller abruptly left the house at 32 Herne Hill and moved round the corner to 40 Oakbank, London SE23, where Inge and Paula Kompfner had been living. They sent a telegram to the Isle of Man, announcing the change of address, but unfortunately did not give the reason. As will be seen from Keller's next letter, the internees naturally assumed, given the nightly bombing raids on London, that the house at Herne Hill had been hit. The truth, when it came, was therefore a relief – especially, one would imagine, to Rudi Kompfner, after all his work on the building of the house. The family had in fact moved out only temporarily, while an unexploded bomb, which had fallen nearby, was made safe.

Meanwhile, the opportunity to play football on the Isle of Man was doubtless a big plus for Keller, who retained a passion for the game throughout his life. As a child in Vienna he had been 'a fanatical supporter of the Jewish football club, Hakoah ('strength' in Hebrew)'[9] and in later life he wrote and broadcast frequently – and idiosyncratically – on the game.

27.   14 October 1940, Mooragh Camp, Ramsey, Isle of Man.
   In German.

Dear Mutschili, Please send saccharin, please write whether we should lug the cooker back home if we are released or whether we may leave it here. *Tuesday:* I've just received your telegram that you have moved to Oakbank and have to conclude that Herne Hill has been bombed. We hope that it was only an incendiary bomb with comparatively little damage. I hope to get a letter soon with all the news in respect of this. *Wednesday*: Just now we received letter and card from Zoepnek, from which we understand that Herne Hill wasn't bombed and that it was only a time-bomb. Immediately the world looks much better for us. Next time something happens, please send a telegram with the reason, so that we don't worry because we're kept in the dark. *Thursday*: I'm waiting really eagerly for a letter from you, Mutschi, I miss you terribly all the time – but there are worse things these days. We've already got our luggage (nearly undamaged, only the handle of my large suitcase is torn off), though not our money yet, but we can borrow some here. For the time being, Morrison doesn't seem to want to change the internment policy either. We're looking forward very much to the next parcel. Where have the Adlers gone? I'm extremely sorry for you: those constantly disturbed nights etc. Have you heard from Muni and Kollmann? I haven't yet received her letter you told me was on the way; I'll only write when I have it. Meanwhile I've heard that since the middle of June there has not been a storm in the Irish Sea like the one on the day we came here. Misfortune upon misfortune.[10] How is Uncle Rudi? What do you do all day? What sort of mood is Roy in? Mowgli! Has anyone heard from Georg? Just now I've received Ena's and Mowgli's letter of the 4th. Will answer Monday. *Many* kisses, Hans

28.   20 October 1940, Mooragh Camp, Ramsey, Isle of Man. To Ena Franey. *In English.*

DEAR LITTLE ENA, I WAS VERY PLEASED WITH YOUR LETTER INDEED, AND I THANK YOU VERY MUCH FOR IT. WOULD YOU PLEASE TELL MUTTI THAT I RECEIVED HER PARCEL OF OCTOBER 1ST, ZOEPNEK'S PARCEL, AND MUMMY'S LETTERS OF OCTOBER 4TH, AND OCTOBER 8TH. I WAS GLAD TO HAVE MUMMY'S LETTERS AND I SHALL WRITE HER IN A FEW DAYS, BUT THIS LETTER I WRITE TO YOU. IT IS VERY NICE HERE, ONKEL HANS AND I ARE LIVING JUST AT THE SEA, AND WE ARE FEELING AS IF WE WERE IN ANGMERING. BUT I IMAGINE THAT IT MUST BE VERY NICE IN LONDON, TOO, SLEEPING EVERY NIGHT SOMEWHERE ELSE, AND HAVING A LOT OF EXCITEMENTS, WHICH YOU ENJOY VERY MUCH, AS I KNOW.

TELL MUTTI, PLEASE, THAT I THINK IT VERY ADVISABLE TO
WRITE TO MR. SCHIFF REPEATEDLY (AS SHE DOES) AND TO
WRITE TO MISS RATHBONE, SHOULD ANYTHING NOT BE
SUCCESSFUL, AND I THANK HER VERY MUCH FOR ALL SHE
(AND MUMMY) IS DOING FOR MY REUNION WITH YOU
ALL, FOR, THOUGH IT IS BEAUTIFUL HERE, I WOULD VERY
MUCH DESIRE TO BE WITH YOUR AND MY MUMMY ONCE
AGAIN. HOW IS NORA? I THANK HER VERY MUCH FOR HER
SIGNATURE IN YOUR LETTER. DO YOU KNOW THAT I HAVE
A BEARD? I'M SURE YOU WILL NOT RECOGNIZE ME, ONCE I
COME BACK. YOU AND NORA WILL HAVE BECOME QUITE
GROWN UP. KISSES HANS

Note to the Censor: The addressee of this letter is a child, hence the
remark about the pleasure of being interned etc.

29.   24 October 1940, Mooragh Camp, Ramsey, Isle of Man.
In German.

Dear Mutschili, I have received Roy's letter, Gertrud Marle's letter,
and Mowgli's letters, which I confirmed in my last letter to Ena. I
thank Roy and Mowgli very much, but I can't answer them today,
because I'm most concerned about the Artist application, which I
ask you urgently to make. Testimonials and letters from: Prof. Ernest
Read, Royal Acad. of Music, York Gate, Marylebone Rd., N.W.1,
Free German League of Culture (Berend Orchestra) 36, Upper Park
Road, N.W., nr. Hampstead St[ation]., Generalmusikdir. Dr F. Berend,
Austrian Centre (& *Circle for Arts and Science*) (Knepler, Baron Fuchs,
possibly also get in touch with Adler, who should write a letter to
the Circle), Anthroposophic Soc., Rudolf Steiner House, Park Road
(possibly also through Adler), Ethical Society, Holborn, 2nd alleyway
on the right beyond Holborn St[ation], if you're coming from the
Thames; if possible a letter from the *Red Cross* concerning the opera
at Sadler's Wells (through Berend), letter from Adler (on behalf of
the Circle) about the second violinist in his quartet, letter from
Rostal (?), Dr Redlich (through Berend). All these should also be
enclosed right away, rather than just naming the referees. Refer to
my age, also to the fact that without a work permit I could only give
concerts within the frameworks of refugee centres or for charitable
purposes. After release: participation in the Berend-Red-Cross-Orch.

Programme of the première of the Roger quartet can be found in one of my folders; the following Saturday, the Telegraph printed a review, could this critic give a short statement? Pro-British, anti-Nazi attitude as already described. Before making the application read through the White Paper on artists. In my opinion it doesn't matter if this application and the hardship one are running at the same time. Thank you ever so much. In the near future I shall ask for a few pounds: I always like to have £10 in reserve. Buy a lot of food. Many, many kisses Hans

Despite Keller's disappointment that 'Morrison doesn't seem to want to change the internment policy either', his hopes were raised by the publication in October of a revision to the August White Paper.[11] As well as various minor amendments, this revised White Paper created three new categories for release. Two of them ('Students who, at the time of their internment, were pursuing a course of study at a university' and 'Any person … [who] has, since his early childhood, or for at least 20 years, lived continuously, or almost continuously, in the United Kingdom') did not apply to Keller (though he did try the 'student' route on account of his LRAM studies). The third, however, was of great interest to him and to all the intellectuals in the camps:

20. Persons of eminent distinction who have made outstanding contributions to Art, Science, Learning or Letters.

(At the request of the Home Secretary special committees to consider the cases of artists, architects and men of letters and submit recommendations to him have been set up by the Royal Academy, the Royal Institute of British Architects and the P.E.N. Club. Committees to consider and submit recommendations relating to the cases of musicians and lawyers have been appointed under the chairmanship of Dr. R. Vaughan Williams, O.M. and the right Honourable Lord Justice Scott, respectively. Applications for release under this category will be referred by the Home Office to the appropriate Committee.)

Ralph Vaughan Williams, who since Elgar's death had rather assumed the mantle of England's national composer, had been actively championing the cause of refugee musicians for some time. As chairman of his local refugee committee in Dorking, he had got to know and deeply respect several of the continental musicians who came to him for aid.

The arrest and internment as 'enemy aliens' of friends like Robert Müller-Hartmann shocked him deeply, particularly when he learned of the conditions in which they were being kept. He began immediately to campaign for their release. But as time went on, and the first White Paper in July failed to make much difference to their situation, Vaughan Williams grew frustrated, and sought to enlist the help of fellow musicians. On 21 August 1940, he wrote to his friend the composer (and former Professor of Music at Birmingham University) Granville Bantock, copying his letter to Sir Hugh Allen, Lord Berners, Sir Adrian Boult, H.C. Colles, Edric Cundell, Sir Walford Davies, Thomas Dunhill, George Dyson, Constant Lambert, Stanley Marchant, Ernest Newman, William Walton and W.G. Whittaker – a list of names that, as Hugh Cobbe has commented, 'constituted perhaps Vaughan Williams's view of the British music establishment in 1940'.[12]

> Dear Bantock,
>   I feel that it is time that British musicians got together and looked for the release of their fellow musicians which are interned.
>   Musicians do not appear to come under any category in the White Paper and this makes it difficult for us, but perhaps by a joint letter we could persuade the authorities to broaden their interpretation of 'work of national importance' (see 'White Paper' section 8) and to point out that to fructify the life of the country is of national importance and the fact that artistic and intelligent people who will spread the gospel of anti-Nazism are an asset to the country.
>   Perhaps you have read Professor Rosenberg's report on the appalling conditions in his internment camp. This does not of course affect the injustice or otherwise of internment, but it does make it imperative, unless conditions have enormously improved, to release those who ought to be released immediately. Could we have a meeting to discuss the question?[13]

Vaughan Williams's assertion that 'to fructify the life of the country is of national importance' would have met with assent in some quarters of government. Even in 1940, during 'our darkest hour', there were some who were still thinking of the arts. Duff Cooper, for example, had written to Churchill only a few weeks before to suggest the creation of a 'Ministry of Fine Arts':

> We have never had a Ministry of Fine Arts in this country and we have often been taunted with our neglect of them. I have had recently brought to my notice a case of the London Philharmonic Orchestra which I am told is the best in the country, and which must shortly go into liquidation if it receives no financial support.

Part of our case is that we are fighting for civilisation, to which the Germans reply that in every city in Germany there is a state-subsidised opera, whereas we are unable to support even a single orchestra. That is good propaganda in the United States amongst a people who have a superstitious reverence for culture. ...

There is a great deal to be done in this direction. Plays for instance which can be produced for a few hundred pounds which can have a tremendous influence on popular morale, exhibitions and pictures which can be arranged, etc., and many other subjects which we cannot say are of definite or immediate importance from the point of view of the conduct of the war, but which should form part of a long-term policy.

No better Chairman for such an institution could possibly be found than Lord Lytton, who has long been so closely concerned with the movement for a National Theatre and who has always been an enthusiastic patron of the Arts.[14]

Not everyone agreed, however. Duff Cooper's letter arrived on Churchill's desk accompanied by a terse memo:

P.M.

I believe the idea of state-aided and directed 'culture' is abhorrent to most Englishmen. It certainly is to me.

I cannot think that the present, when we are fighting for our lives, is a proper time to think of wasting public money on these projects.[15]

In the long run, though, the author of this memo turned out to be swimming against the tide. The London Philharmonic may have had to keep body and soul together during the war by joining forces with Malcolm Sargent (a conductor with whom its players had very acrimonious relations at that time)[16] on his Blitz Tour of bombed British cities, but state-aided culture was enthusiastically embraced by the British after the war. Lord Lytton's 'movement for a National Theatre' did not bear fruit until 1963, but the Arts Council was born in 1945, growing directly out of the wartime Committee for Education, Music and the Arts, and the enormous public enthusiasm for culture which that had helped to foster. The war had brought a new seriousness to all levels of society, and the wish to 'build a better future' was strongly felt everywhere. The same post-war idealism that was to produce the 1945 Labour landslide, the National Health Service and universal secondary education also produced the abundance of new orchestras, festivals and

sundry other artistic organisations that sprang up all over the country at that
time. The new BBC Third Programme, which began broadcasting in 1946
with a remit to 'enable the intelligent public to hear the best that has been
thought or said or composed in all the world'[17] was another manifestation of
this post-war flowering of public interest in the arts.

Lord Lytton, however, was destined for another role, and it was just after
this letter was written that he was appointed to chair the new Advisory
Council on Aliens announced by Sir John Anderson in the Commons the next
day. It will be remembered that this was one of two new bodies created at that
time to advise the Home Secretary; the other was the Advisory Committee
chaired by Sir Cyril Asquith, and it was to him that Vaughan Williams went in
search of help for his interned musicians. Writing again to Granville Bantock
a week after his original letter, Vaughan Williams was able to tell him that 'I
have had a promise from Sir Cyril Asquith that the case of musicians shall be
"sympathetically considered".'[18]

Vaughan Williams' meeting of musicians was duly held at the Royal
Academy of Music on 4 September, and together they drew up a list of the
interned musicians they knew about, and discussed what action could be
taken to secure their release. Several weeks of lobbying produced the new
category of 'Persons of eminent distinction' in the October revision of the
White Paper. Vaughan Williams was then asked to chair the 'Committee
for the Release of Interned Alien Musicians' which was to advise the Home
Office on which musicians were of sufficiently distinguished to merit release
from the camps.

Keller and many of the musicians with whom he was playing in Mooragh
made immediate applications under this category. To support his application,
Keller needed to gather evidence of his 'distinction', and the letter above lists
various people who he thought might support him. As well as Georg Knepler
and Fritz Berend of the Austrian Centre and the Freier Deutscher Kulturbund,
his former violin teacher Max Rostal and, of course, Oscar Adler, Keller also
sought recommendations from English contacts like the conductor and
educationalist Ernest Read, who taught conducting at the Royal Academy of
Music. Read was the founder of two of the first youth orchestras in Britain:
the London Junior Orchestra in 1926 and the London Senior Orchestra in
1931, in which it is possible Keller may have played before he was interned.

Two of the letters of recommendation written for Keller in support of his
'Artist Application' have survived:[19]

> Herewith I state with great pleasure that Mr. Hans KELLER born
> in Vienna 1919, in spite of his youth may be signified as one of the
> best chambermusicians [sic]. His high and pure gifts in connexion
> with his great enthusiasm may be mentioned in particular.

Mr. Hans Keller has been these three years a member of my own String-Quartett [*sic*] as Second-Violinist and he was able to contribute a good deal to our success in performances given (of course only) in private and refugeecercles [*sic*] as in the „Austrian Centre, the Ethical Society („Refugee – At homes") etc.

It would be regrettable to see the development of this talent so sadly cut off. To justify this certificate of mine I beg to enclose some criticisms (copies) on Vienna concerts.

Dr. Oskar Adler

Hans Keller has repeatedly performed for our Club members. He is an exceptionally gifted young musician. I don't hesitate to express my opinion that interruption of study and practice – as internment would doubtlessly mean for him – will severely impair his career.

AUSTRIAN CENTRE
Dr. Georg Knepler
19th Nov., 1940

Interned with Keller at Mooragh Camp at that time was the Austrian pianist and composer Ferdinand Rauter, who was well known throughout Europe, especially for his recitals with the Icelandic singer, Engel Lund. They were particularly noted for their performances of folk songs from many different countries, for which Rauter composed the accompaniments. Vaughan Williams was naturally sympathetic to a musical interest in folk song, and Ursula Vaughan Williams worked with Rauter to prepare the songs for publication. At the end of December, Vaughan Williams secured Rauter's release, after which Rauter devoted considerable efforts to helping his fellow internees. Vaughan Williams invited him to join the Committee for the Release of Interned Alien Musicians, where his knowledge of Austrian musicians was invaluable.

After his release from internment Rauter also formed the Austrian Musicians' Group, with the aim of helping all Austrian musicians in exile. He asked Vaughan Williams if he would consent to be its patron. Despite his respect for Rauter, and his huge efforts on behalf of many Austrian musicians, Vaughan Williams hesitated:

Dear Dr Rauter,
Your letter has opened up a great problem. I find it difficult to state, but I want as a preface that nothing contained in this letter affects my

personal affection for my many Austrian friends; nor my admiration for their art.

The great thing that frightens me in the late peaceful invasion of this country by Austria is that it will entirely devour the tender little flower of our English culture. The Austrians have a great musical tradition, and they are apt to think that it is the *only* musical tradition and that everything which is *different* must be *wrong* or *ignorant*; they think moreover that they have a mission to impose their culture wherever they go as being the only one worth having.

Now this seems to me to be all *wrong*. We cannot swallow the strong meat of your culture whole (even if we wished to) our stomachs are not strong enough – indigestion and finally artistic putrefaction would result.

To try and make England, musically, a dependancy of Austria could kill all the musical initiative in this country – destroy all that is vital and substitute a mechanical imitation of your great art – which will have no vitality, no roots in the soil and no power to grow to full stature.

What do I suggest therefore? – We want your art and we want your help. – Become Englishmen – try to assimilate our artistic ideals and then strengthen and fertilize them from your own incomparable art. – But do not force a 'Little Austria' on England – keeping itself apart from the 'untouchables' and having its own musical life without reference to the life going on around. ...[20]

'There is a tendency among the English,' Vaughan Williams went on, 'to assume that if you are called Schmidt you are musical but not if you are called Smith'. As will be seen later in this book, Vaughan Williams's description precisely matches the attitude among English musicians that struck Keller so forceably in the 1940s – and which he diagnosed after the war as 'musical group self-contempt (nemesistic displacement)'. Keller was still encountering this tendency in English musicians (and arguing against it) at the BBC twenty years later. One instance that provoked him then to action was a radio talk given by Peter Maxwell Davies shortly after Keller joined the Corporation in 1959, on 'The Position of the Composer in Britain Today'. Maxwell Davies was highly critical of 'the reluctance of English musicians to face up to the problem posed by the legacy of the last century' and their 'complete ignorance' of developments on the continent. English compositions, he said, 'usually show a serious lack of ideas, content and technique; when one compares them with a more serious work by Schoenberg – or even by Bartók – they become unlistenable'. Keller immediately commissioned other English composers to broadcast a series of 'counter-blows against Davies'.[21]

Ferdinand Rauter was understanding when he received Vaughan Williams's worries, saying that although he and other Austrian refugees had as yet had little opportunity acquaint themselves with English music, they were determined to do so and to appreciate its different virtues. He re-formulated his group as the Anglo-Austrian Music Society, promoted concerts which featured both English and Austrian musicians, and Vaughan Williams duly became its patron.

~

After the incident with the unexploded bomb, Roy and Mowgli decided that it was time to leave London, and the whole family, including Paula and Inge Kompfner, moved to the Lake District. Initially they went to Ambleside, where Oscar and Paula Adler were already living, and stayed at a guest house there while they looked for more permanent accommodation. Before long they had found Glebe House, a former café on the Promenade at Bowness-on-Windermere, and there they decided to settle.

30.   **27 October 1940, Mooragh Camp, Ramsey, Isle of Man.** *In German.*

Dear Mutschili, Received: 1 parcel through Inge, your and Mowgli's letter of the 19th, the telegram. My application for a return telegram was refused. I'm so happy that you are there. Stay there. I've been able to take all my things with me. There is no quartet. I was supposed to have given a sonata recital here with Rauter, whom I know from Vienna and London as a marvellous pianist (and who knows of me by hearsay), but I refused because of the poor violin, and I'll give a chamber music evening with him, Brahms piano quartet in C minor, Beethoven trio. I shall earn something from that. However, my hands aren't in the best condition because of lugging sacks of coke and other things. For a viola, we're using a violin with viola strings. – We do each have our own room, but it's so small that one person hardly fits in. Please send bow if it's not too troublesome. Received trousers, jacket in Inge's parcel. It should be possible for the testimonials for the artist application to be requested in writing from there, I suppose. Should you have the opportunity, please have a suitcase sent to me. I am so happy every time I get detailed letters from you all, please do thank Mowgli for me. I don't consider the letter from Bloomsbury House to be very hopeful, but it is probably a standard letter; however, perhaps we shall be lucky in the end. We live in a kosher house, all proletarians, only a few speak German, just Polish, Russian, English, Yiddish. Military discipline is much stricter here than at the end of my Huyton time; we're all weeping for our commander there. Today Lord Lytton is coming here; he came to Huyton in Oscar's time. The Isle of M. must be really lovely if one is not interned; one should come and live here. Apart from the sea journey… Mutschi I hope you'll recuperate well there, it would be stupid to live in London when it is not necessary. Many kisses, Hans

31.   30 October 1940, Mooragh Camp, Ramsey, Isle of Man. *In German.*

Mutschili, my dear, I forgot to send my thanks for the wonderfully warming, irreplaceable gloves (apparently knitted by Paula) in the last parcel from Inge. In the meantime the first parcel from Bowness also arrived here today; the censoring officer remarked that he had never set eyes on such a beautifully packed parcel. Ad applicationem, it occurred to me that Berend should not fail to try to get in touch with Vaughan Williams personally about my case (of course this is not *instead of*, but *alongside* my application); this could be a step of paramount importance. I've received Inge's letter of 24th and was particularly pleased with it; she really writes as she does *not* speak.[22] Incidentally, many thanks for the thoughtful (and loving) choice of parcel contents. Please send some cocoa. Just received (1. Nov) the Mozart concerto, and, to be quite honest, I nearly cried with joy. – After looking through the new White Paper, I don't have anything to add to my statements so far. I have resigned from the position of leader in the orchestra here, as I had to interrupt every bar five times, which was unbearable in the long run. Rehearsing the Brahms quartet, I am very strict, but it is still not going too well: I'll turn to playing sonatas after all. The Jewish Chronicle is a real joy, the only newspaper from which you can get news about us. Uncle Hans is quite delighted with his hypertrophic prostate; he should soon be presented to the English doctor. Could you write to the Jewish Chronicle that it should be sent here, not to Huyton. Servus Mutschili! Hans

32. **6 November 1940, Mooragh Camp, Ramsey, Isle of Man.**
In German.

Dear, dear Mutschili, I was over-overjoyed with your two detailed letters of the 29th which I received yesterday; thank you very much! I shall try to answer everything in one letter. Cowling is excellent, I understand it all. Received the Mozart Concerto (as I've already written) and have already practised and played it. At the moment we don't get any fruit at all, but this will improve, as Lord Lytton is supposed to have promised. I have *not* received any hot water bottle. Received and already acknowledged cutlery, 2 coffee cups etc. I'm sending my very best regards to the Adlers, I'm already looking forward very much to meeting up with them again. Actually, you are not very far from us, just opposite us, in a manner of speaking, though at an angle. My heart is a lot lighter since you've been there and are having a pleasant time. I, too, got to know Felix Braun in Huyton. By the way, Bruno Heilig was here, but released before my arrival. I'm fundamentally pessimistic about the application, but at the same time I fervently hope for the best. I'm appalled by Georg's illness. I have enquired of our charming kosher 'GP', Dr Kohn (a former doctor for the poor in Berlin), and he thinks it depends on which part of the spine the inflammation is in, also one can hope for a number of years of remission. I've brought bed and mattress with me (I've already written that). I have the opportunity to play some music, and shall very shortly earn some money by it. Today, one of the most appealing characters in our house was released, thank God, a 64-year-old Pole who looks like a miniature incarnation of a Moische Rebbenuh*. All day he did nothing but pray, look at the sea, was always of a friendly and sunny disposition, and he would help anybody whenever he could; he hardly ever spoke a word, except when leading prayers. Otherwise, a cloth merchant from Manchester. Kisses, Hans

---
 * Note to the Censor: This is a Hebrew term and means 'Mose our Rabbi'.

33. **9 November 1940, Mooragh Camp, Ramsey, Isle of Man.**
In German.

Dear Mutschili,
As we cook our own breakfast and afternoon tea, we need coffee, cocoa and jam again, which one cannot buy here. I am glad that

Roosevelt has been re-elected.[23] Since my last letter I haven't received one from you. Rauter, with whom I make music here, is (as he says) 'an intimate friend of Mariedl'. Mariedl, he reports, is in Spain. 10 Nov: could you send me some sort of cover for my head which goes over my ears: the ski cap is much too small, as is the woolly hat, and anyway, as I always wear it on the back of my head as my 'Sabbath lid' in this house, I seem to have lost it. Two or three pairs of ordinary socks wouldn't do me any harm either. Now for a few funny things which are happening here: you know the orthodox separation of milk and meat is based on the sentence 'thou shalt not seethe a kid in its mother's milk'.[24] Uncle Hans, who gets annoyed by the interminable fuss about this separation, is now trying to convince all the Talmud scholars here that he has invented a much more ethical sentence: 'Thou shalt not cook the chicken in the fat of its aunt (the goose)'. For the mother goat does not have to be killed for us to get her milk, but the fat you can only get from the slaughtered goose. One ultra-orthodox has already admitted that Uncle Hans's law follows logically from the other, and moreover is more moral. A rabbi from another house always greets me with a deep bow, because he believes (because of the beard) that I am at least the chief rabbi of New York. *Many* kisses, Hans

Keller was clearly enjoying life in a kosher house. He was happy in the company of the 'proletarian' East European orthodox Jews – they were, after all, the same sort of people who had made such an impression on him during his imprisonment in Vienna. Despite the problems of communication, and the relatively little they probably had in common, at that time their company was less stressful than that of Germans, as Keller explained to a psychologist colleague two years later:

There was [in the camp] a small section of Germans (Gentiles), consisting of political and ideological refugees. Often Jews would not have anything to do with them, on account of the strong associations which persisted in their minds between those who had almost beaten them to death and those who, though fanatically opposed to the present German regime, were nevertheless members of the dreaded people. I know from my personal experience that I had very great difficulty, often hard to overcome, to meet proper Germans with the same attitude with which I met fellow-Jews, although I reproached myself with the fact that these Germans were among the strongest enemies of Nazism. The wounds resulting from physical and psychic persecution have left far-reaching scars, not really cured, on me and others.[25]

Although Keller does not mention it, there were of course a few actual Nazis in the internment camps, and one of the major complaints of early campaigners like Eleanor Rathbone had been that Nazi prisoners were imprisoned alongside their victims: 'Can we be assured,' she asked Anderson in July, 'that Nazis and Fascists shall not be allowed to mix with the victims of Nazi and Fascist oppression?'[26] According to Lafitte, this had been a particular problem in the early stages of internment:

> A general complaint in the early days was the herding together of Jews and other non-Fascists with Nazis, semi-Nazis or Italian Fascists. Until deportation took away most of the Nazis and Fascists this factor led to much avoidable misery. … The authorities did nothing about it. From May onwards they were able to plead in Parliament that the new 'intakes' of internees made separation of Nazis and non-Nazis impossible for the time.[27]

Since Keller was interned in the last of the mass round-ups, any exposure he might have had to Nazi internees was likely to have been limited to the first few weeks. His correspondence does not mention them, but his letters were scarce at that time, and in any case comments about such a political matter might have failed to get past the censors.

Despite his respect for the orthodox Jews, Keller also enjoyed Uncle Hans's legalistic arguments with them. His teenage fondness for his barrister-uncle left a permanent mark on him as he grew up. Throughout his life, Keller always had a passion for the law, and relished the aggressive logic of courtroom argument. In later life, this could make him difficult to work with, as he would pursue issues relentlessly, in nit-picking detail, and would never compromise on matters of principle. 'You ought to run our legal department,' one of his publishers told him in 1954 after a long-running book contract negotiation.[28]

Uncle Hans's influence is also discernible in Keller's rhetorical literary style. And certainly a courtroom atmosphere is detectable in much of his famous defence of undervalued composers. In articles like 'Schoenberg and the Men of the Press' and 'Britten and Mozart', Keller cross-examined the opposition like a defending barrister, sometimes springing on his reader-jurors surprise witnesses, like the contemporary critics of Mozart whose complaints mirror – with uncanny similarity – what was said about Britten a century and a half later.

Keller's hopes for release now received a set-back with the refusal of the 'hardship application' he had made on the basis of his mother's illness. He took it well, but he had nevertheless still harboured some hope of release this way, as is shown by the fact that he waited until this point before trying another route out of the camp – one that had actually been available to him ever since the first White Paper in July. Category 11 (12 in the subsequent White Papers) provided for the release of 'internees who are accepted for enlistment in the Auxiliary Military Pioneer Corps'.

The AMPC (whose name was officially shortened simply to 'Pioneer Corps' at the end of November) was the section of the army which provided auxiliary services such as light engineering, stores handling, stretcher-bearing, and the clearing of bomb debris in blitzed cities. It was formed out of the Works Labour Companies set up at the outbreak of war. Its members were non-combatants, so it was the obvious section of the army where internees could be used – naturally the authorities were not keen on enemy aliens wielding guns.

Keller decided to enlist on 16 November, immediately after receiving the news of the failure of his hardship application. As it happens, Herbert Morrison was planning to make a statement in the House of Commons some ten days later, in which he was to make it clear that the AMPC was now to be the principal route for release for the remaining internees.[29] Announcing the results of an enquiry by the Asquith Committee into the question of how to release 'friendly enemy aliens', he acknowledged that 'the main problem concerns men who are friendly to the Allied cause but cannot bring themselves within any of the categories set out in the White Paper.'

> The Asquith Committee has studied with great care the question whether provision should be made for the release of all such persons as could demonstrate to a carefully constituted tribunal their steadfast adherence to the Allied cause. It is probable that, if such a scheme were to be adopted, the great majority of those who are interned would make application to such a tribunal, and the committee estimate that the investigation of these applications would require 10 tribunals working for nearly a year.

Having dismissed this solution as 'quite disproportionate', Morrison announced his decision to channel men through the existing mechanisms:

> There are, however, already in the White Paper three categories in which release is directly or indirectly dependent on a loyalty test. In addition to the provision for those who can show that they have taken a prominent part in opposition to the Nazi and Fascist régimes, and to the provision relating to those who have resided here for 20 years and can show that

they have thrown in their lot with this country, there is a provision, more important numerically than either of these, namely the provision for enlistment in the Auxiliary Military Pioneer Corps. The normal age limits for enlistment are 18 and 50, and for all men between these ages there is an opportunity clearly to demonstrate their friendliness to the Allied cause by offering their services to the Corps. ... I want to make it clear that the Government regard this opportunity as the appropriate method of providing for such men. They should not, therefore, defer offering their services to the Corps in the expectation that there may be enlargements, affecting them, of the existing categories set out in the White Paper.

Morrison's presentation of enlistment in the Pioneers as a 'loyalty test' is in rather marked contrast to what Sir John Anderson had said in the Commons on 22 August:

I do not want to be either hard or cynical, but a young man in internment who accepts an alternative offered to him of joining the Pioneer Corps is not in quite the same position as the ordinary volunteer.[30]

Morrison's statement can therefore be seen as another indication of the shift in government policy – lowering the 'loyalty' bar to get the majority of the internees out of the camps as conveniently as could be managed.

Although this statement made it clear that the Pioneers were realistically Keller's best chance of getting off the Isle of Man, it was not made until some 10 days after Keller had signed up – which suggests that it was not this but the failure of his hardship application that triggered his decision. Despite his statement in the next letter that 'I had expected the refusal of my application as something completely certain', the timing of his enlistment betrays his lingering hopes. Evidently he was not particularly keen on the idea of military life, not least because of the long periods without his violin it would necessarily entail. It is also possible that he feared family opposition – in which context it is interesting to note that in all the correspondence with his mother about the various means of release the Pioneer Corps is never mentioned, until Keller's announcement on 16 November that he had actually joined up. The fact that he did not discuss his decision beforehand with Uncle Hans either makes it more likely that he knew the family would not approve.

Grete Keller, as is abundantly clear from this correspondence, was enormously caring and protective towards her son. The list of creature comforts which she managed to send into the camps is really impressive: folding chairs (with and without arm-rests), folding tables, kitchen utensils, toiletries and clothes, two electric ovens, Keller's violin, music and numerous books, and even the folding bed. There cannot have been many internees who were better provided for, although it is notable how often the clothes Grete sent were too small – perhaps a sign that she was still thinking of her son as younger than he actually was. The sheer amount of food, and its variety, is striking when one remembers the rations on which wartime families were living. As a young boy, and indeed later in life, Keller was always very thin, and when he was a child he was apparently a rather picky eater. Ever concerned for his health, his mother indulged his whims, as his cousin Inge remembers:

> He was always a bad eater, because his mother, whenever he liked something, she would give him only that, until he was fed up with it. … She was worried he was too thin. [When she went to London, his father's] nurse carried on the mother's concern for his feeding, and he used to tip it out of the window for the dogs.[31]

It is not therefore surprising that food should be such a dominant theme in these letters – nor that Keller might be anxious about his mother's reaction to the news that he had signed up for military service, even in a non-combatant role.

34.   16 November 1940, Mooragh Camp, Ramsey, Isle of Man.
In German.

Dear Mutschili, I have received your letter of 7 Nov. I had expected the refusal of my application as something completely certain. Hope you did, too. A description of the day: 8.30 (until the day before yesterday 8 am) roll-call, followed by breakfast. Make beds, tidy room. Practice or rehearsal. 12.30 lunch. Twice a week carry coal. 2 o'clock fetch rations for our house. Practice or rehearsal. 4 pm afternoon tea. Practice or rehearsal. 5 pm Roll-call. 7 pm evening meal and washing up afterwards. Then performance or socialising. – Today I joined the AMPC, which I would have done weeks ago if I hadn't been put off by the circumstances and recruiting methods. It isn't easy to sacrifice the violin, but I have done it and I am pleased with myself. Medical examination probably next week. The timing of the call-up is difficult to predict. I hope that, as a first class Balmerchome*, I shall get my first leave in about half a year. I hope I shall be sent to London to clear up bomb debris. I took this decision totally by myself and even only told Uncle Hans when I had already signed up. The work which the Pioneers are doing now (repairing bomb damage) suits me. Servus Mutschi, Kisses, Hans

---

* Note to the Censor: Jewish Expression for 'soldier'

35. **15 November 1940, Mooragh Camp, Ramsey, Isle of Man.** *In German.*

[Despite its date, this letter is postmarked a day later than its predecessor, and Grete Keller's numbering suggests she received it later.]

Dear Mutschili, Please let me know as soon as my application is turned down (or accepted). I have received the bow (wonderful), also the parcel with fruit, sugar etc. If the fruit is so expensive, don't send me any: we do occasionally get apple purée here, so fresh fruit is not absolutely necessary (though of course I enjoy eating it very much). I'm now leading a string quartet: second violin poor, viola middling, cello middling. We're practising the Rider Quartet and Mozart's first D major quartet, the only sheet music we have. I am stricter than Oscar, and plague the gentlemen for hours over a few bars. They are sweet and patient, only once was slight opposition detectable, when I took the upbeat to the Trio of the Rider Quartet with a glissando. (Adler will know what I mean.) Now they're all playing the upbeat with glissando. Something amusing: our 'camp supervisor' Rabbi Dr van der Zyl was released, and now we're having elections. Heated election campaign, storm in a teacup, election speeches etc. Now here in our house there is a dealer from Manchester by name of Naphtali (in Yiddish that would be pronounced: Naftuli) Zins, whom Uncle Hans always calls Naphtalin-Rent.[32] He deals here in old trousers and equally old cheese. Yesterday, Uncle Hans, in the middle of a deadly serious election meeting, made a fiery appeal on behalf of Naphtuli, demanding that he should be elected. He would, with his efficiency, make sure the camp had plenty to eat (although he himself wouldn't lose out financially in this matter). He speaks excellent English. I have never seen Uncle Hans laugh so much as he did at this his first-class election speech. Kisses, Hans

36. **19 November 1940, Mooragh Camp, Ramsey, Isle of Man. To Inge Kompfner.** *In German.*

Dear Inge, Please tell Mutti from me that I received her letter of the 12th, and that I really can't put into words how touched I am by all that is being done for me. Please tell her that she should continue with the artist application, as it is quite possible that I'll *be rejected* by the AMPC, or that I'll withdraw voluntarily, because very recently my goitre, which had already been diagnosed by two doctors here, has started to give me trouble when I lift heavy things. I have the parcel with more wonderful gloves, a sublime cake (about which it is impossible to speak, it's so good) and two eggs, which tasted better than almost anything I can think of. I will also try to get to see the English doctor about release because of my goitre. It's a shame, I was really looking forward especially to the Pioneer Corps, to the opportunity of being able to help at long last. Also tell Mutti that I'm eating plenty and I'm not starving (no scales here), so she really needn't worry. I should like to thank you, too, very much for all you've tried for me. Even if all efforts fail, and I stay interned for a long time, it will not dampen my spirits (or my health), if only Mutti wouldn't keep finding reasons to worry. One shouldn't be self-indulgent:[33] I am absolutely fine. Hans

37.   21 November 1940, Mooragh Camp, Ramsey, Isle of Man. *In German.*

Dear Mutschili, Well: you do know that I'd made my application to the A.M.P.C. *Today* was the medical inspection, and I was REJECTED ON MEDICAL GROUNDS: struma (goitre). 'There is no possibility of your joining the army,' I was informed by the (incidentally charming) English army doctor. Funny, I hadn't really bothered much about my swollen neck, until the day I helped to carry a bed, when I suddenly became breathless and had a very tight throat. On the same day, our GP Dr Kohn, watching me swallow, said: 'You have a swollen neck'. Ever since then I had worried, of course, that I might not be able to cope with the heavy work in the AMPC. – So, Mutschi, perhaps it will be easier for me to get released, since I have proved my pro-British attitude so much beyond doubt. You did write, didn't you, that Bloomsbury House wants to submit yet another application? Is Dr Meyer some hope as well? And over and above that, the goitre should be grounds for release. The day after tomorrow I shall be giving a concert (Kegelstatt Trio, Mozart Sonata). It's a pity, as I had already hoped that in the A.M.P.C. I could help the people of London: this is now out of the question for ever. Please, if you get the chance, send another set of strings. The 'Jewish Chronicle' still comes via Huyton. Many, many kisses, Hans

Despite Keller's protestations that he had been looking forward to the Pioneer Corps, the medical rejection probably came as a bit of a relief. He had evidently worried about the goitre, and probably more generally about how he would cope with heavy physical work. His thyroid trouble was apparently genetic: has father also had a goitre.[34] So did Arnold Schoenberg – in the light of Keller's later keen interest in his music, it is interesting to discover the coincidence that Schoenberg in 1915 was also rejected from military service because of a goitre.

The speed at which Keller's application to the Pioneer Corps was processed – only 5 days from start to finish – shows how keen the authorities were to get internees into the Corps. Even though Keller's application came to such a swift end, it was not without benefit. Within a few days, his hope that 'perhaps it will be easier for me to get released, since I have proved my pro-British attitude so much beyond doubt' was to prove well founded. Morrison's speech in the Commons on 26 November, as well as outlining the importance of the Pioneer Corps for internees seeking their release, did not forget those it excluded:

> As regards those who are not eligible for enlistment or are rejected on medical grounds, the Government, following a recommendation of the Asquith Committee, have decided that there shall be added to the White Paper a new category providing for the release of men who, being by reason of age or physical unfitness ineligible for the Pioneer Corps, can satisfy a tribunal that they are opposed to the Nazi or Fascist systems, that they are positively friendly towards the Allied cause, and that they will remain steadfast towards that cause in all circumstances. It is estimated that the number of men who under such a scheme might come before a tribunal or trubunals would be in the neighbourhood of 2,000, and the examination of 2,000 applicants would be a manageable proposition. I will make a statement at an early date about the steps to be taken to bring this scheme into operation.[35]

This became known as 'paragraph 23', because the October White Paper had contained 22 categories for release. It was to be another month before Morrison had got the scheme set up, and Keller made his application under this category on 23 December.

38.   24 November 1940, Mooragh Camp, Ramsey, Isle of Man.
In German.

Dear Mutschili, I've received your letter of the 17th; there is also a registered letter for me in the office, but I can't fetch it today (Sunday).

The eggs were wonderful, as I've already written. Regular newspaper subscription (apart from the Jewish Chronicle) is really not necessary, here we read the Daily Telegraph. Leather gloves are wonderful. I only lug coke for a few minutes twice a week. I am very grateful to Berend. As I already wrote, I was rejected by the AMPC on medical grounds (toxic goitre). For that reason, tomorrow I'll be sending off an application in which I also refer to your artist application which is coming soon. Maybe in a few weeks I'll be seen by the English doctor, as because of the goitre I'm unfit for internment. It wouldn't be bad if you were to put in your application also the request that I should be examined because of the goitre, because then the Home Office will request a report from here and I shall get to see an English doctor more quickly. Perhaps you could simply enclose this application with the artist application: what do you think? Obviously the AMPC rejection must be mentioned. My concert was sold out (120 people) – I earned 4/6. I shall repeat it on Thursday. I expect that Uncle Hans will be released soon. For the time being I won't apply to join Rudi, as the doctors here are already familiar with my condition. Mutschi, how do you really feel? I wish I were already in Bowness. Kisses, Hans

39.   28 November 1940, Mooragh Camp, Ramsey, Isle of Man. *In German.*

Dear, dear Mutschili, Received your parcel with the hot water bottle and wonderful eggs, suitcase and letter of the 20th. To answer it: as I've already written to you several times, I have been *rejected* on *medical* grounds (toxic goitre) from the AMPC. Date of medical exam: 21. Nov., my Nominal Roll: II/209. Thank you very much for the Eskimo hat! I should indeed love some honey. Received £2. I sleep on the camp-bed, have enough blankets, am not cold. We cannot heat the room itself, but the living rooms of all the houses are heated. Actually, the climate is quite warm (Gulf stream), and only the continual storms and rain exacerbate it somewhat. Morrison's statement is not quite clear to me, as you cannot see from it whether any difference will be made between those who were rejected by the AMPC on medical grounds, and others who are to be considered unfit only on the basis of a doctor's certificate or other proofs. In any case, the White Paper should clarify this. Apart from that, the following applies to me: in the best case I shall be released on medical grounds or as an artist before the tribunal hearing; otherwise, if the rejected ones don't form a category, I will come before the tribunal, where my joining cannot fail to count as an unambiguous proof of pro-Britishness. (I have in my possession a statement from the recruiting officer about my joining and medical rejection.) In spite of that, it would not be a bad idea if you sent me a letter from Roy, which will include the fact that he will support me after release, one from Berend about Red Cross Opera. To be cont'd. Hans

40.   1 December 1940, Mooragh Camp, Ramsey, Isle of Man. *In German.*

Dear, dear, dear Mutschili: from now on you'll have to pay postage again, as the 'free of charge' only applies to letters *from* internment. I have received your letter of the 23rd and Inge's letter of the 21st, also there is a parcel for me at the Censor's. Mrs Peach seems to have been the person who sent me the love letter to Huyton some time ago, but I still don't know who she is, a female board member[36] of some ethical or Steiner society? I ended my last letter with the request for 1) a letter of recommendation from Roy (mentioning the concentration camp and my pro-British attitude), and if we can trouble Berend yet again (perhaps you would draft the letter for him), a confirmation of that and in what manner I worked for the Red Cross, and will in future. Roy should also write that he will support me after my release, that because of my unfortunate rejection by the AMPC, I will offer my services as a musician in every respect. Perhaps a letter from Greig would not be bad either. I need all that for the tribunal. So that you don't believe I'm starving: in spite of all efforts, I can't fit into the jacket you sent me. When I read your letter to Uncle Hans, I said: better a goitre in the hand than ten lung infections in high-altitude fresh air, and he laughed a lot at that. Thank Inge for her letter. Have concerts every week. Kisses, Hans

~

Herbert Morrison's presentation of the Pioneer Corps as an opportunity for the internees to prove their opposition to Hitler raises interesting questions about 'loyalty'. One group of internees who had particular difficulty in persuading the British to accept them as allies – despite their passionate opposition to Nazism – were the communist refugees. The difficulty of their position in Britain is well illustrated by the story of what happened to Yvonne Kapp, the Assistant to the Director of the Czech Refugee Fund, who (it will be remembered from chapter 4) had done so much create employment opportunities for refugees, including the agricultural scheme which Keller had been about to join at the time of his arrest.

In the autumn of 1940 Kapp, like Keller's family, was living in the Lake District. She was no longer in the employ of the Trust, having been dismissed on the orders of the Home Secretary on account of her membership of the Communist Party. At the time of her dismissal, the staff of the Trust had been evacuated to Berkshire (where some of them were living in a 'decrepit Victorian vicarage'). Kapp had been continuing her successful deployment of refugees to farms and factories when she was abruptly summoned to the Home Office. The historian Charmian Brinson has described what happened then:

> It was while she was working on her employment scheme that she was summoned to London to a meeting, called by a representative of the Home Office, ostensibly to be questioned on the *bona fides* of certain refugees employed by the Trust. It soon became clear, however, that it was primarily she who was under investigation. Sir Henry Bunbury [the retired senior civil servant who was the Trust's Director] was also interviewed about her at some length and was obliged to ask her 'whether I was or had ever been a member of the Communist Party'.[37]

At the next meeting of the trustees, events apparently came to a head, as Kapp described in her memoir *Time Will Tell*:

> I was asked to wait outside the room where we usually foregathered and spent an uncomfortable half-hour before being invited to enter when I was formally addressed by the Chairman, Sir Malcolm Delevingne. In a doleful voice he announced that with deep regret he had to inform me of the Secretary of State's decree that I should no longer work for the Trust in any capacity. They, the Trustees, who had the fullest confidence in my loyalty and integrity, would be profoundly sorry to lose my services, and he advised me to write to the Home Secretary appealing against the decision.[38]

She and Sir Henry Bunbury returned to Berkshire, and the dilapidated vicarage, to break the news to her colleagues. She was not the only Trust member to be dismissed by Sir John Anderson at that time, and there was considerable consternation among the other staff.

> Sir Henry posted a notice announcing our dismissal and declaring his personal regret. For a week or more, debarred from our offices, we held court in the vicarage, to which many members of the staff came with little offerings and friendly words. Then with six months' salary in lieu of notice and a glowing testimonial both from Sir Henry and also the Trustees, together with Margaret, I left for the Lake District.[39]

Kapp's considerable abilities were a serious loss to the Czech Refugee Fund Trust, which, like most of the organisations set up to assist refugees, could not afford many experienced salaried staff. Too heavy a reliance on volunteer workers, as the historian Louise London has pointed out, 'resulted in amateurism and a lack of both systematic administration and effective financial controls'.[40] This was the reason why Sir Henry Bunbury, on his appointment as Director when the Trust was originally set up, had laid such stress on the importance of providing it with professional staff.

> Advising how the new organisation should be run, he insisted that experience had shown the need in such work for 'the type of trained ability which can usually only be obtained on a salaried basis, and for an office-trained and disciplined clerical staff'. Qualified staff were particularly necessary in key management posts, Bunbury declared: 'Mediocrity, however well meaning, is always costly in the long run, and especially so when it is organising and directing the work of others.'[41]

But despite the support of Kapp's colleagues, including Sir Malcolm Delevingne, the Trust's Chairman, who helped her draft the appeal, the Home Secretary would not relent. One must remember that this was the time of the Nazi-Soviet non-aggression pact, when communists were viewed with particularly deep suspicion. Indeed, the pact did present British communists with a dreadful dilemma: while the Soviet Union was labelling the war as 'imperialist' their loyalties were pulled between official Party doctrine and the incompatibility of their socialist beliefs with fascism. Yvonne Kapp herself wrote of the 'appalling confusion' she felt when the pact was signed and her dismay that communist Russia was not going to fight against Nazism, with whose victims she was so passionately involved. Hitler's invasion of Russia in June 1941, and the subsequent realignment of the Soviet Union with the western allies must have been an enormous relief.

Of course there were a great many communists among the refugees – especially among those who fled from Hitler on political rather than racial grounds. Despite their often impressive anti-Nazi credentials, they found themselves the object of considerable suspicion in Britain. Some of the original refugee tribunals, for example, had refused to grant category

C status to any refugee of communist sympathies, and some communists even ended up in category A. As Yvonne Kapp later wrote, 'it sometimes happened that the refugee was asked if he would be prepared to take up arms against the Soviet Union … and if he said he was not, he was automatically included in Category 'A' as hostile'; indeed, Kapp suspected that there were many cases in which refugees were interned 'because, although they were recognised as having escaped from Nazi oppression and were not suspected of Nazi sympathies and connections, their left-wing politics evoked an ineradicable prejudice in some reactionary tribunal presidents.'[42] One such example was publicised in March 1940, when the *New Statesman and Nation* took up the case of the prominent economists R. R. Kuczynski and his son Jürgen Kuczynski – the latter of whom had been active in the communist underground in Nazi Germany, and was interned in Britain under category A as a result. As the anonymous author of the paper's 'London Diary' wrote,

> I cannot understand why R. R. Kuczynski could ever have come under suspicion at all, as he is a researcher with a world-wide reputation, and has never had any connections with a political party. But the judge seemed to find grounds for suspicion even in his trips to America and asked him, to the old man's surprise, whether he had any connection with an espionage system in Bloomsbury House! Finally, in summing up his case, the judge remarked 'I am not going to intern you *to-day*,' and in granting his wife a 'B' certificate stated that the ground was that she was living under the subversive influence of her husband. When her husband protested and reminded the judge that he was teaching at the London School of Economics, the judge replied ominously, 'I know all about the London School of Economics.' J. Kuczynski was subjected to an even severer cross-examination. It seemed to be held against him that he had written *Hunger and Work* and *Freedom Calling*, although the Ministry of Information has given the latter pamphlet its blessing. … The result of this remarkable examination was a 'B' licence for the elder and internment for the younger Kuczynski. The judge seemed suspicious of any trace of anti-Nazi activity.[43]

The reference to Bloomsbury House is telling. This was simply the headquarters of all the main refugee welfare organisations. As Lafitte has described it,

> Early in 1938 the need for co-ordination of refugee work became so acute that a Central Co-ordinating Committee – now the Joint Consultative Committee on Refugees – was set up in London, with Lord Hailey as

Chairman. In 1939 it was decided to centralise in one building the offices of the main organisations under the Committee, and the Executive of the Baldwin Fund leased a hotel in Bloomsbury, which was renamed Bloomsbury House and became the headquarters of all the major organisations working for refugees.[44]

Yvonne Kapp felt strongly that the sort of prejudices as were shown by the judge at the Kuczynskis' tribunal were very common, and had done much to exacerbate the situation of those who sought asylum in Britain:

> If the word 'Communist' evokes a violent reaction in some people, the words 'foreign Communist' more than double the effect; one has no need to magnify the menace conjured up by those two words in order to excite the deepest prejudice. When, moreover, these people are associated with that other prejudice-provoking word, 'Jew', there is no limit to the fear and hatred which artful propaganda may arouse, as has been amply testified in Germany itself. Since these reactions in their most naked form can only occur in persons addicted to emotion rather than reason, to feeling rather than fact, the actual numbers and the personal conduct of these Communist refugees could in no way modify those views or their expression.[45]

Lafitte felt too that this sort of bigotry ran deep in the Establishment of the time, and even forty years later he still wrote angrily against 'that combination of ignorance and prejudice against foreigners so prevalent among the civil and military Upstairs-Downstairs set who had run Britain during the past decade, with their tendency to assume that foreigners who disliked Hitler (who had dealt with the "Bolshevik menace") and Mussolini (who had at least "made the trains run on time") were very likely to be Communists wanting to overthrow the established order.'[46]

Kapp realised that her chances of re-employment with the Trust or any other refugee organisation were slim. She therefore used her six months' money to do another service for the refugees. When she went to the Lake District, she took with her her former colleague Margaret Mynett, also dismissed from the Trust's employ for communist sympathies – and together they wrote a book.

British Policy and the Refugees, 1933-1941 is a remarkable work, drawing on the extensive experience of both women to chart in detail how the British had responded to the influx of refugees from 1933 onwards – laying bare all the harm, both intentional and unintentional, which had been done. Yvonne Kapp did most of the writing, but it was Margaret Mynatt who was responsible for the majority of the research. A refugee herself, from Vienna via Prague, where she was briefly imprisoned, Mynatt had first-hand knowledge and extensive contacts among Czech refugees, all of which had been of enormous help to the British Committee for Refugees from Czechoslovakia's attempts to rescue those still stranded there – indeed she has been described by one of her colleagues as 'the heart and soul of our entire enterprise'.[47] In the same way that François Lafitte used his Austrian connections to gather detailed information about what was happening to the refugees, Mynatt used her many connections with Czech refugees to produce a clear exposition of their situation and critical analysis of the British response.

Kapp and Mynatt were unfortunately too late. Their book was not finished until early in 1941, and although it had already been accepted for publication the previous autumn, the enormous success of Lafitte's *The Internment of Aliens* caused their publishers to fear that Kapp and Mynatt's work was too similar. They dropped publication, but the book survived in manuscript, and was taken up by other publishers in the 1960s and the 1980s. On both those occasions it still failed to make it into print, but such was the continuing scholarly interest in the manuscript that it was finally published by Frank Cass in 1997.

~

Back on the Isle of Man, Hans Grotte's 'hypotrophic prostate' finally justified his delight with it, and his release on medical grounds was officially authorised on 30 November.[48] He left the camp on 6 December, and his departure marked a big change in Keller's life. Uncle Hans had been his companion and advisor throughout all the trauma of the last two years. Keller's mother being trapped in London after the Anschluss, it was Uncle Hans who saw Keller through the death of his father and his flight to London. He had been there through all the months of internment, and despite the more abrasive aspects of his character, Keller held him in great affection and was profoundly aware of the debt he owed him. As he wrote in his letter of 13 October, 'From the beginning he has been unbelievably nice and kind to me'.

41.   5 December 1940, Mooragh Camp, Ramsey, Isle of Man.
In German.

Dear, dear Mutschili, So, Uncle Hans is leaving early in the morning: thank God a happy event[49] at last. Just received your letter of the 29th and yesterday your second small parcel; the tins are all fantastic and I don't know which to give preference to. The cake is wonderful, but if it's black inside instead of white it's even better. The gloves are first class and the margarine is a rare pleasure. Uncle Hans is very excited, although he pretends he's calm. I hope he has a good crossing; in any case I'm giving him several pills to take with him. 6 Dec.:- Uncle Hans has gone. I hope he'll stay a day in Douglas because the weather is terrible. Next Monday all of us from No.3 will move into No.15 (the main kosher house and nicest hotel here). I will move to No.14, a transfer which Uncle Hans had already been considering himself. As I have large expenses for shoe-repairs etc, I'm asking for another 2 pounds, please. A long time ago I asked for another little bottle of iodine, as I'm treating my corns with iodine with great success. That letter doesn't seem to have arrived. If you send granulated sugar again, then please wrap it really well: it always arrives all leaked out. Uncle Hans will have told you that my dictionary has gone astray. Could you send me any English-German German-English one? Tomorrow Dr Ferdinand Rauter, the pianist with whom I've been playing here, will be released (artist application). In any case, I'll give you his address: 28 Clarendon Rd., W11; Phone: Park 6224. Are you getting news from Georg? I have written to Muni a while ago, but except for the one letter, which she still sent to me in London, I have had no post from her, though you once said there was a letter coming. I haven't heard anything from Kollmann either. How is the playing of the lady violinist? Are you getting back to your old form? Tonight is the farewell concert for Rauter. I'll be playing the Brahms C minor Piano Quartet with him. The Jewish Chronicle *is* coming. Many kisses, Hans

42.   9 December 1940, Mooragh Camp, Ramsey, Isle of Man.
In German.

Dearest Mutschili, I'm writing today from the really beautiful living room of No.14, where I'll be living from today. The reason why I didn't go into the kosher house No.15, at least on a trial basis, is that Dr Kohn, meaning well, wanted to put me together with the visually impaired Pander (because we are roughly the same age). As Uncle Hans will confirm, there's something fishy about Pander's eye-trouble, so I decided to move into this house straightaway. I live on my own in a small attic at the top, and I'm very content with that. I did not accept the room that Uncle Hans had recently selected for himself, because on close inspection it turned out to be really damp. The move was harder work than I had expected: it is incredible how much stuff one accumulates after a while. If anything, the house rules here are more to my liking than those we had in No.15: kitchen duty once a week (morning, midday and evening washing-up), housework once a week, carrying rations once a week. Although only 4 people go for this latter task, I immediately volunteered to do it and didn't notice the goitre at all. Since Uncle Hans left, Dr Kohn applies to me every available father-complex with a vengeance and is charming. Dachinger, too, with whom I have now become closer friends, sees to it that I eat enough. I've also become friendly with Pastor Hansen. He says that Judaism must not disappear, because its mission is to carry the moral law around in the world. There can't be many priests who don't say that Jews should convert, don't you think? I need money: I'm really stuffing myself, shoe-repairs etc. Kisses, Hans

43.   11 December 1940, Mooragh Camp, Ramsey, Isle of Man.
In German.

Dear Mutschili, Well, I'm in dire financial straits: the ski boot repairs will be very expensive, I've got to go to the dentist's, I often have my evening meal at No.5 (1/6), because, as you know, the evening meal here is practically non-existent. In addition I buy something from the baker's nearly every day, must pay the people who do the heaviest work for me (the work the young people have to do; then I realized that, though in this house I immediately volunteered for all jobs, the heavy containers from the kitchen, when filled with water, can only be carried with difficulty by more robust and goitre-less people, and much else), washing, darning socks, bathing – in a word, my expenses will soon rise to pounds. I have only 5½ pounds left in the bank, and in my pocket around 15 shillings. If the dentist has to do several fillings, God forbid, then my money will shrink. What sort of expenses does Rudi have? I'm really not throwing money away, but if, for example, I really indulge myself foodwise, then in spite of the parcel I'll spend 2/3 a day for food alone. Of course I don't do that now. I'll also cancel the newspaper. So please send several pounds: I will be very careful. By the way, the Commandant has announced that rationed foodstuffs may no longer be sent to internees. – Just received the lovely parcel of the 5th (cake, eggs), which of course alleviated my worries *considerably*. Now I can eat at home for a long time. Just now the doctor has prescribed milk for me (free every day). Please *cancel* the Jewish Chronicle: I can borrow it here. I'm feeling very well, have many friends. Just received a letter from Kollmann. What's the situation with the artist appl.? *How was Hans's sea crossing?* Kisses, kisses, Hans

44.   13 December 1940, Mooragh Camp, Ramsey, Isle of Man. *In German.*

My dear, dear, dear Mutschili, Just received your letter of the 8th; I'm always very happy when a letter comes and so unendingly thankful for all that is being done for me. Please always keep me up to date about things, even if an application should be refused; I should like always to be clear about my position. I've received Mowgli's letter of the 6th and will write to her separately as soon as I get a chance. My neighbour at table, a certain Jeitteles, just saw the envelope of your letter and said, 'That is a wonderful hand, a typical classic handwriting'. I've always said you are the female Goethe. Peter Altenberg[50] agrees with me, and you have the same star-sign, too. Greig's medical application is a wonderful step, which I wouldn't have expected of him, for if there's an enquiry from the Home Office, I will get to see an English doctor much more quickly than through the local treatment: Dr Roll says he must observe me for some considerable time before he can put me forward; if he presented me right away, all that would happen is a telling-off by the English doctor and I wouldn't get any advantage from it because he would have to continue keeping an eye on me. But if the Home Office requests it, I should be put forward without any delay so that a report can be sent. I am very, very worried about Georg's fate. How is his frame of mind? What does he do all day? Where is he living? Where did Mowgli see him? Could you send him something for Christmas? What does he live off? Who is looking after him? Have you already received Dachinger's picture of me? Yesterday, at a Jewish arts-evening (in which I didn't take part because I found the date was too short notice to practise) 'Jacob's Dream' by Beer-Hofman was read aloud. It contains these words, 'The Jew wears his yoke like a crown'. Lovely, isn't it? Servus, *dear* Mutschi? Kisses, Hans

45.   **17 December 1940, MS. Mooragh Camp, Ramsey, Isle of Man.**
In English and German.

Dearest Mutschili, The day before yesterday the following notice was officially issued: Notice for the information of Male Enemy Aliens in Internment. – The following category of eligibility for release from internment has been added to the categories in the Home Office White Paper:- 'Any person who is ineligible by reason of age for the A.M.P.C., or who, having applied for enlistment in that Corps, has been rejected on medical grounds, and in regard to whom the Tribunal appointed by the Secret. of State for the purpose reports that he is opposed to the Nazi or Fascist System and is actively friendly towards the Allied cause and that the Tribunal is satisfied that he will remain steadfast towards that cause in all circumstances.' Applications for release under this category should be addressed to the Under-Secretary of St., Aliens Department, P.O. Box No. 2, Bournemouth. This application should state the applicant's age and whether he has applied to enlist in the A.M.P.C. and has been rejected on medical grounds, and should give sufficient particulars of his history to indicate that he is a person who comes within the category. The applications will be referred by the Home Off. to the appropriate Tribunal, who, after considering all the information available, will advise the Secretary of State whether the applicant is eligible for release. -I have already finished the rough draft of the application and am only waiting for the arrival of all the statements of recommendation (I've already got Greig's) to make the fair copy and send it off with the reference letters. I should like to do that as soon as possible, as the applications will be processed in the order of their arrival. I have received Rudi's letter of the 9th in which he tells me he will be released the next day. I am glad to be the last one, as I was always afraid of the unpleasant feeling of being released while knowing that one of our people is still interned. Please let Rudi know that I've always considered Purcell to be the greatest English composer. Yesterday I saw the doctor again, I'm to come again on Thursday, he will put me forward soon. Servus, dear Mutschili, greetings to all! Hans

Keller was now the last of his family to be left in internment. Rudi Kompfner's release was authorised on 5th December, and he left the Isle of Man on the 12th. He was released under category 6 – 'Persons who occupied key positions in industries engaged in work of national importance', because his work as a physicist had been noticed by the Admiralty: 'Before his internment he had sent a paper on magnetrons to the *Wireless Engineer*, whose editor, Hugh Pocock, showed it to the Admiralty. This brought Kompfner's abilities to the attention of Frederick Brundrett, who sent him to the physics department at Birmingham University when he was released in December 1940.'[51]

TO:
Mrs. GRETE KELLER
32, HERNE HILL
LONDON, S.E. 24.

SENDER:
HANS HEINRICH KELLER
A.I.C. 9,2 No. 75107, TENT 220
HUYTON NR. LIVERPOOL
CAMP 2.

Dearest mother;-Roy and Mowgly, as British subjects, are
permitted to visit me and uncle Hans provided that
they obtain the permission from the Home Office. They, or
one of them, should do so at once. They should bring, or
you should send me immediately the following things in
face of the fact that I don't know how long I stay in this
camp: warm underwear, a warm cap (ski-cap), warm gloves
a violin with reserve strings, fruits, cheese, chocolate and
other eatables (I probably have not to carry my luggage
for long distances), some soap, perhaps ski-shoes with warm
stockings, about 10 £ and my training suit. I have made an
application for release to the War Office, but, as this will
take months till it is there, I ask you urgently to make an
application, too. I am told that my face-neuralgia, my hay-
fever, my nervous and physically infirm constitution as well
as my testifiable pro-British attitude, and the fact that I
am a Jew, that I have volunteered for casualty service etc.
will be considered as valid reasons. Oscar is with us,
though in a house; he and we are quite all right. Give my
things in a case. Mention in the application my having been
in a Nazi Concentration Camp. Write soon. Try to speak to
Uncle Rudis friend Mr. Vansittard about the application.
For the rest don't worry about me. Yours affectionately Hans
5th July, 1940.

Director of Prisoners of War
War Office, (A.G.3/P.W.)
Hobart House
Grosvenor Place, S.W.1

*Facsimile of one of Keller's early letters from Huyton Camp (letter 2, p. 53). In line
with the regulations governing internees' post at the time, this letter is written on
official note-paper and limited to the permitted 24 lines in length. For the benefit of
the censor, Keller has printed the letter in a style quite unlike his normal handwriting.*

Illustrations

Keller's maternal grandparents, Josef and Sofie Grotte, with their children.
Back row (l-r): Gustav, Hans, Fritz, Grete, Paula; seated: Sofie, Irma, Josef.

The young Hans with his half-sister Mowgli (left) and with his mother (right).

Roy Franey, Keller's brother-in-law, in a photograph taken in the year of his marriage to Mowgli. 'Without him, the gas chamber would have been an absolute certainty.'

Keller's half-sister Gertrude, known to the family as 'Mowgli'. This photograph was taken in the year of her marriage to Roy Franey (1933)

Keller's parents, Fritz and Grete Keller, with his sister Mowgli, on holiday at Kritzendorf.

Keller's sister Mowgli outside 13 Nusswaldgasse, the family home in Döbling, Vienna, in 1931. The house was burned down in 1945, but when Keller revisited Vienna in the 1970s he found that 'the fir tree, which was planted when my sister was born (she is ten years older than I), looked the same in 1976 as it did in 1938'.

Keller's class at school in 1931, when he was aged 12 (Keller is in the back row, on the left in the corner).

The Franey family packs up to leave Vienna after their last visit before the Anschluss. Roy later returned alone, as part of his efforts to secure visas. In this picture, Grete Keller stands in front, holding Ena and Nora, with (l-r) Inge, Paula? (Inge's mother) and Roy behind, and the Kellers' cook at the extreme left.

'Enemy aliens' arriving at Huyton Alien Internment Camp , May 1940.
© Getty Images

Huyton Alien Internment Camp near Liverpool.
Keller was interned there from June to October 1940. © Getty Images

Internees stuffing straw into sacks to use as mattresses in Huyton Camp
(Belton Road from the corner of Altmorr Road, 21 May 1940). © Getty Images.

Hugo Dachinger, *Officer standing behind barbed wire fence*, painted in Huyton Alien Internment Camp, 1940. © Walker Gallery, National Museums, Liverpool.

Hugo Dachinger, *Dead End*, painted in Huyton Alien Internment Camp, 1940. © Walker Gallery, National Museums, Liverpool.

The boarding houses of Mooragh Alien Internment Camp, Ramsey, Isle of Man.
© Getty Images.

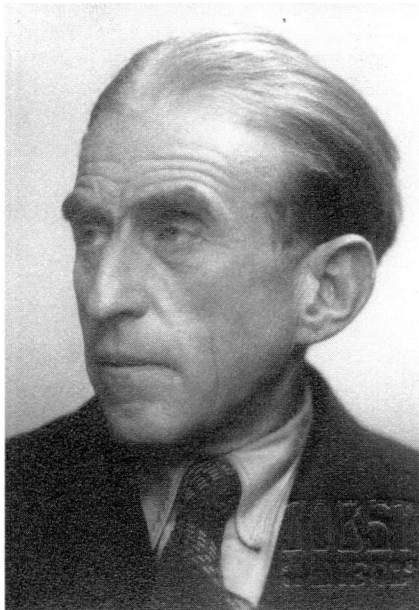

Keller's uncle, Hans Grotte, who facilitated Keller's escape from
Vienna and later kept him company in the internment camps.

Glebe House in Bowness, where the family moved in 1940 to avoid the London Blitz, and where Keller went after his release from internment.

Mowgli, Roy, Ena and Nora Franey at Glebe House after Roy's call-up.

Keller at Glebe House after his release from internment,
with his nieces Ena and Nora Franey and a friend.

8   *Release, 1941*

In all its discussion of the fate of the foreign internees, this book has so far paid little attention to the British internees, those detained under section 18B of the Defence (General) Regulations 1939. It will be remembered that Roy Franey was taken to Brixton police station to be interviewed under this regulation, on account of all the Austrians in his house. It may be that other British citizens who were simply trying to help their foreign friends were caught up in internment, for it certainly seems that suspicion was sometimes attached to refugee work. One wonders whether Yvonne Kapp's communism would have caused her quite so much trouble had she not been so prominently involved in helping enemy aliens.

But for the most part, those who were interned under 18B were members of the British Union of Fascists, most prominently Oswald Mosley and his wife. Reading it now, the text of the amendment to this regulation passed by Parliament on 22 May 1940, which led directly to Mosley's arrest two days later, appears to have granted the government remarkably sweeping powers. Under it, the police could detain any member of any organisation if 'the persons in control of the organisation have or have had associations with persons concerned in the government of, or sympathies with the system of government of, any Power with which His Majesty is at war.'[1] Thus, had the Nazi-Soviet pact hardened into an actual alliance, for example, and Britain been at war with Russia, all British communists could have been subject to arrest. This possibility may even have been in the minds of the legislators, hence perhaps the reference to 'sympathies with the system of government' of an enemy country.

Given his initial driving support for alien internment, Churchill's attitude to the arrest of the Mosleys is interesting. Socially, he was in a difficult position, because Diana Mosley (née Mitford) was a cousin of his wife's and very much a friend of the family in her youth. His private secretary, Sir John Colville, remembers the Prime Minister's embarrassment at the arrest of some of his relatives:

> While he was at Chequers on June 29, Churchill received from the
> Home Secretary a list of 150 prominent people who had been arrested

under Regulation 18B and interned. Of the first three on the list, two were cousins by marriage of Clementine Churchill, 'a fact,' Colville noted, 'which piqued Winston and caused much merriment among his children.'[2]

The two cousins on the list were Oswald Mosley and George Pitt-Rivers. The latter apparently believed in 'a conspiracy of Jews, Free-Masons and Communists as the deliberate cause of the war'[3] and was the author of such books as *The Clash of Culture and the Contact of Races* (1927), *Weeds in the Garden of Marriage* (1931) and *The Czech Conspiracy* (1938).

Not surprisingly, Churchill was subject to sustained pressure from friends of the Mosleys, first to allow them to be interned together, and then to secure their release. Such friends included many in the aristocracy, as fascist opinions had reached the highest level of British society, extending even to the circle around Edward VIII. The wife of one of the ex-King's closest friends, Lady Alexandra ('Baba') Metcalfe – whose nickname at the time of 'Baba Blackshirt' says something about her political sympathies – was one of the principal campaigners on the Mosleys' behalf. Churchill was persuaded to enquire into their situation in December 1940, and he duly wrote to his Home Secretary Herbert Morrison about the conditions in which they were being held:

> Does a bath every week mean a hot bath, and would it be very wrong to allow a bath every day? What facilities are there for regular outdoor exercise and games and recreation under Rule 8? If the correspondence is censored, as it must be, I do not see any reason why it should be limited to two letters a week. What literature is allowed? What are the regulations about paper and ink for writing books or studying particular questions? Are they allowed to have a wireless set? What arrangements are permitted to husbands and wives to see each other, and what arrangements have been made for Mosley's wife to see her baby, from whom she was taken before it was weaned?[4]

Shortly afterwards, Oswald Mosley was transferred from Brixton Prison to Holloway, to be with his wife. They remained there until 1943, when a deterioration in Sir Oswald's health caused the government to consider his release. Churchill was then with Stalin and Roosevelt in Tehran, so Herbert Morrison was left to deal with the issue – much to Churchill's frustration. He sent Morrison several telegrams on the subject, which make interesting reading. Writing on 21 November, he advised his Home Secretary not to stick simply to the issue of Mosley's health, but to address the wider question of whether it was justifiable to lock up a British citizen on account of his political views:

I expect you will be questioned about the release of the Mosleys. No doubt the pith of your case is health and humanity. You might, however, consider whether you should not unfold as a background the great principle of Habeas Corpus and trial by jury which are the supreme protection invented by the British people for ordinary individuals against the State. The power of the Executive to cast a man into prison without formulating any charge known to the law, and particularly to deny him judgment by his peers for an indefinite period, is [in] the highest degree odious and is the foundation of all Totalitarian Governments whether Nazi or Communist. It is only when extreme danger of the state can be pleaded that this power may be temporarily assumed by the Executive, and even so its working must be interpreted with the utmost vigilance by a Free Parliament. When the danger passes, persons so imprisoned, against whom there is no charge which Court and Juries would accept, should be released, as you have been steadily doing, until hardly any are left. Extraordinary powers assumed by the Executive with the consent of Parliament in emergencies should be yielded up when and as the emergency declines. Nothing can be more abhorrent to a democracy than to imprison a person or keep him in prison because he is unpopular. This is really the test of civilisation.[5]

Morrison appeared to be inclined to stay with the humanitarian argument, so Churchill wrote again four days later urging him 'Do not quit the heights', and even to countenance the termination of the government's powers under 18B, 'which we fully admit are contrary to the whole spirit of British public life and British history'.[6] In a second telegram sent the same day, Churchill made his position clearer:

I am convinced 18B should be completely abolished as the national emergency no longer justifies abrogation of individual rights of habeas corpus and trial by jury on definite charges. I doubt very much whether any serious resistance would be made to this. There are of course a number of totalitarian-minded people who like to keep their political opponents in prison on lettres de cachet, but I do not think they constitute a majority. I have already on more than one occasion expressed in Parliament my distaste for these exceptional powers and my hope that success and security would enable us to dispense with them. However, as these views conflict with the line you have adopted I shall not press them at this stage.[7]

Although he told Morrison he was not going to press this line on him, Churchill's impatience is still evident in a sarcastic remark later in the same message: 'I am sure we shall not need to go to Stalin for help in defending the principles of British liberty and humanity.'

In his letters to his wife Churchill's frustration at Morrison burst out with a vengeance:

> I am burning to take part in the debate on 18B, and if I were at home now I would blow the whole blasted thing out of existence. So long as Morrison presents the case as exceptional treatment for Mosley naturally he is on difficult ground and people can cry 'Favour'! He really would lose very little to sweep the whole thing away, which he could do by the overwelming arguments I have mentioned to him in the various telegrams which you will have seen by now.[8]

She agreed:

> I wish indeed you were here to handle all this 18B stuff. Morrison has shewn political courage, but he trails his coat & gets everyone's goat. I feel it ought not to have been entered upon in your absence. You have the conviction about the injustice of 18B which would command respect, & you could lift the whole thing.[9]

The whole issue was particularly difficult for Morrison because his Labour colleagues in the House of Commons were overwhelmingly against the release of any of the interned fascists. It was one of the most difficult moments of his career, as it threatened to split the wartime coalition. Many in the Labour Party were already unhappy with the coalition, which they felt weakened the Party's identity at a time when the public was clearly moving to the left. The enormous public outrage at the news of the Mosleys' release added to their desire to distance themselves from the decision, and to their determination that 18B would stay. A mass demonstration outside the House of Commons on 23 November, while the embattled Herbert Morrison was defending himself inside made matters worse. This was only one of several mass protests held to demand Mosley's return to gaol – on one occasion '20,000 factory workers had handed in a petition to No.10 Downing Street and had stood in Whitehall in protest.'[10]

Clementine Churchill described to her husband what was happening:

> Yesterday Mr. Morrison lunched with me. He seemed battered by what he is going thro' in the Mosley affair. I feel very sorry for him as I think he is shewing political courage of quite a high order. The manifestations have been surprising & various. The crowds at various points in London quite large but good tempered; I ran into hundreds streaking thro'

parliament Square – good looking girls & middle-aged men rather like a foot-ball crowd.[11]

Clement Attlee, the Labour leader and Deputy Prime Minister, warned Churchill of the growing revolt in his party over the issue, but Churchill had got the bit between his teeth. He wrote again – with clear impatience – to Morrison to stiffen his resolve:

> Considering you are supported by the entire Cabinet with one exception and by me as Prime Minister you have no choice whatever but to fight the matter through and you will no doubt be supported in any direct issue by a very large majority.
>
> There is no hurry about the general question of 18B. I certainly recommend however that you express your distaste for such powers and your regret that dangers of the country have forced you to assume them and of your earnest desire to return to normal. This is a becoming attitude in a democratic Minister and costs you nothing.[12]

Churchill's statement that there was 'no hurry about the general question of 18B' was a relief to Morrison, who had feared that the Prime Minister was now going to go all the way and push for the release of all the remaining 18B internees – a move which he felt neither the Labour Party nor the public would stand. The Mosleys were released from Holloway, but kept under house arrest for the rest of the war, and 18B remained in force.

~

All this drama happened in 1943, by which time the vast majority of the foreign internees had already been released. Fears of a German invasion were long gone – indeed it was now a question of when the Allies would mount a new attack on the Western Front, something for which Stalin was pressing Churchill hard during the Tehran Conference.

Back in December 1940, when 'Baba Blackshirt' was starting her campaign on behalf of the Mosleys, the refugee releases were gathering pace, and Keller could see – from the releases of his friends and family, from the new routes to release application opened up by Morrison's announcement and Vaughan Williams's committee, and from the continual reduction in the size of Mooragh camp – that the end of his imprisonment was now in sight. As he said to his mother on 31 December, 'the camp is shrinking more than when Huyton was being reduced.'

The release of his cousin, Rudi Kompfner, and more especially of Uncle Hans, marked a new phase of Keller's internment. It is possible that his statement 'I am glad to be the last one' was true in more ways than one, as these last few months in the camp represented the first time Keller had been quite alone, separated from everyone in his family. Daily life was settled and evidently enjoyable in some ways, and the anxiety of the earliest part of his internment was only a memory. By now it was clear that release was only a matter of time – indeed it was a race between his various applications as to which succeeded first: the 'artist' application to Vaughan Williams's committee, the medical application on account of the goitre, the long-shot attempt under the 'student' category, or the new application he was about to make under Herbert Morrison's 'paragraph 23'.

A medical release was thought to be probably the speediest route, if the goitre were considered sufficiently serious, and Keller and his refugee doctor were now waiting for the request for a medical report to arrive from the Home Office (which they thought would greatly improve his chances with the English doctor). Keller wrote about this to his mother on 23 December, 'I've spoken to Dr Roll [the refugee doctor], and he will put me forward whenever I want, but thinks that it would be far better if I wait for the enquiry which is to be expected as the result of Greig's request. The request takes an average of 3 weeks to arrive from the time application was made, so it should come any day now.'

Although a medical release looked like the quickest route, Keller felt that his best chance of success lay with his 'paragraph 23' application, so he began busily preparing for the tribunal at which he was to prove his loyalty to Britain. Witness statements by friends and family were prepared, with particular importance being attached to that of Roy Franey, as Keller's original sponsor.

46.   19 December 1940, Mooragh Camp, Ramsey, Isle of Man.
In German.

Dearest Mutschili, Received your letter of the 11th with enclosures and pound, a parcel (still at the post office), Uncle Hans's letter. As you know from my last letter, I don't go before the tribunal in person, but make an application to it, which will be dealt with without my being present. I want to send the application as soon as possible, to prevent almighty delay. For this purpose, I'm asking Roy, with much appreciation, to send his letter of recommendation (about which I've already written quite some time ago) *not to me* but direct to the Undersecretary of State, Aliens Department, P.O. Box No. 2,

Bournemouth, with the request that it be *forwarded* to the tribunal which is dealing with my case. The letter should be described as an *enclosure* to my application sent from here at the *end of December*, and should contain: my H.O. ref. no. K11049, the paragraph of my application to which this enclosure refers, namely: the most recently added paragraph – rejected from AMPC – my personal details; a statement about my pro-Allied, anti-Nazi attitude, about my detention at the concentration-camp in Vienna, my expulsion, the payment of the Reich emigration tax, my stammering because of the detention, my physical abuse by the SS and Gestapo, my very close ties to England, and the undoubtedly unwavering nature of my feelings. In my application I myself mention Roy's letter, which I ask him to send by registered post, please. Don't forget; my application is being made on the basis of the latest paragraph newly added to the White Paper, his letter is an enclosure. Please [could all this be done] as soon as possible: forgive the trouble. Tins and cooker I'll send as soon as I've finished with the application. New category is my greatest chance. Kisses, Hans

At this point, the postal system for internees began to worsen again, much to Keller's frustration, as it forced him to repeat the above instructions to his family again and again. 'It seems that a lot of letters are getting lost at the moment (you still don't seem to know that shortly after Hans left I moved into House 14),' he wrote to his mother on 26 December. Because of all these repetitions, some of his next letters are omitted here (and hence the gaps in numbering).[13]

49(a). 31 December 1940, Mooragh Camp, Ramsey, Isle of Man. To Hans Grotte.[14] *In German.*

Dearest Uncle Hans! I thank you very much for your detailed, fascinating and instructive letter, as well as for your parcel, the contents of which were exactly what I need. I am puzzled that you still don't seem to know that a few days after you left I went to live at House 14: houses 1-9 were cleared, the camp is being reduced. House 3 was split between Houses 15 & 16, and I took the opportunity to take myself off elsewhere. I'm living in a top-floor attic facing north (alone), as on more detailed inspection the room that you had chosen turned out to be damp. It's not very warm here, but otherwise OK: after all, I have enough blankets and I don't spend a lot of time in the room during the day. – I still go to No. 15 every so often to visit Kohn, Fischer, Wolf etc. – not to mention Naphtuli. You will be interested to hear that Wandstein is released (medical). Roll thinks that I should wait until Greig's enquiry arrives, as there would be more chance then. I have made an application to the tribunal (category: ineligible for AMPC). It will be judged without my being present. I've received Roy's letter of recommendation & tried to send it after the appl., nevertheless I ask Roy to send a detailed letter (anti-Nazi, pro-Allied attitude, Nazi prison (concentration camp) date of my appl. 23.12., H.O.Ref. No. K.11049, personal details, his securing of my subsistence, cat. of my appl.: ineligible for, rejected from AMPC, the unchangeability of my mind) *as an enclosure* to my application; which mentions his letter, to the Undersecr. of State, Aliens Dep., P.O. Box 2, Bournemouth, registered with the request that it be forwarded to the tribunal that is dealing with my appl.. This new cat., in case you don't know it yet, allows all those to be released who – rejected from PC or too old – can prove to the tribunal, by means of their appl. on the basis of their past history, their impeccable anti-Nazi opposition and pro-allied attitude, in all eternity and under all circumstances. This I have done. Nebenzahl, with whom I now live in the same house, described the appl. as excellent. Dachinger is released, but still in the camp because he doesn't want to go without his pictures: permission to take them with him has not yet been granted. The camp is shrinking more than when Huyton was being reduced. Played in concerts with Gellhorn twice, am very friendly with him. I don't understand why Greig's enquiry still hasn't arrived! It usually takes an average of 3 weeks from sending it. Please send this letter on to Mutti. Sincerely Hans

50.   2 January 1941, Mooragh Camp, Ramsey, Isle of Man. *In German.*

Dearest Mutschi, received: Roy's telegram, registered letter with Roy's enclosures, fantastic parcel with cake, strings, your letter of 25th – thank you very, very much for everything. *So I hope* that Roy sent basically the same letter as the one you sent me together with a copy, to the H.O.. I'm innocent in what seem to be a number of misunderstandings: I gave perfectly clear instructions and never wrote that I was keeping the appl. back *in order to enclose Roy's letter*, and I only demanded a copy in case I should still have the appl. when the letter arrived. Furthermore I repeat that I shall not appear in person before any tribunal, but that my appl. will be dealt with by the tribunal in my absence. Roy's letter is very lovely and I thank him very much for all his trouble, please confirm in any case that he sent a letter to the Home Off. which is similar to this one (of the 29th). I personally don't think much of the student appl., apparently not many students are being considered, on the other hand I have the advantage of the AMPC; I assume that the Home Office will send the student file to the tribunal dealing with the medical rejection from the Pioneer Corps. As far as my propitious horoscope is concerned, please ask Oscar for me which year he is actually talking about. Surely not January this year? In that case, the best that it can mean is that I shall get lots of cakes in January. By the way: I had already tried sending the tins off, but at first I couldn't for lack of paper; now I have your paper, but I'll wait until I've finished the new cake. The beard is fairly similar in colour to the hair on my head, but it seems darker. I intend to keep it, though in a more civilised form: no violin eczema, no pimples, no shaving etc. Perhaps I shall have it shaped and trimmed before my release so that you're not too shocked. Otherwise, in the camp it got me the nickname 'Jesus'. Received the dictionary: thank you very much. Lilli Geller wrote; she's marrying an Engl. Jew. Thank you *very much* for the directions for the journey and tel. no.: I shall manage to go the wrong way anyway. *Of course* I shall take a taxi from Windermere, as truly as I am the goitred son of my father ('What you've inherited from your fathers ...').[15] Sandwich spread is delicious. Dentist is giving me fillings. I thank Roy yet again for everything, from now on there should be no more hassle: either I'm going to be released or I won't be released. – Never again will I have the opportunity to gather so much insight into human nature as I have here, and in this respect internment was useful. These people! When they're without women they become childish. I happen to live here in a very wealthy house (as opposed to scrounger-house No.3). People chuck their money about, & I always take good care not to join in. Recently three of them managed to get on the outside of a goose that had cost 15 sh. I'm getting to know all strata of Jewish society here. How is Uncle Hans? How's Rudi? Is Georg's illness completely incurable? Will he never be able at least to limp along? Lovely that perhaps we will be able to play quartets. I'd love to play the Rider Quartet. Or Mozart's first one in D major, with the difficult cello passage in the finale. Kisses, Mutschi, Hans

The letter that Roy Franey wrote in support of Keller's 'paragraph 23' application is still extant. He wrote as follows:

> My brother-in-law, Mr. H. H. Keller, is making application for his release from Mooragh Internment Camp under the category of persons volunteering for the Pioneer Corps, but rejected on grounds of ill-health. He has been known to me since he was eleven years old. He was born in Vienna, on 11th March 1919, the son of Jewish parents. In November 1938 he was arrested and maltreated by the Gestapo in the notorious 'Purge', and he has never quite recovered from the shock of the treatment he received. Although ordered to leave the country, he was only allowed to go after all the family's money and property had been surrendered to the Nazis. He has lived with me since his arrival in this country in Dec. 1938 and in consequence I am able to state that his attitude is completely pro-British and most definitely anti-Nazi. I guaranteed for this young man when permission was granted for him to enter this country and if he is released he will live again with my family and his mother and continue his musical studies.[16]

~

Grete Keller was becoming more anxious again, now that her son was alone in the camp without any family member to support him. She suggested that she herself should write to plead with the Camp Commander, but Keller discouraged this and tried to reassure her that he was not unhappy: 'I'm never lonely when I'm on my own: you know that; and besides, I have numerous very dear friends.'[17] They included 'a solicitor and judge called Dr Nebenzahl (56 years old), who is very much like Uncle Hans, but more interested in intellectual matters. He will only make an application (§23) when he has somewhere to go.' Keller asked his mother if she would be able to find 'a boarding house or bed and breakfast in the Bowness area' for him.[18]

The most important of Keller's friends at that time, 'by far my closest friend,' was the pianist, conductor and composer Peter Gellhorn. He was more than six years older than Keller, but they formed a firm friendship in the camp which continued into later life. Gellhorn had come to England soon after the Nazis came to power in 1933, and before his internment was teaching at Toynbee Hall, the influential centre of social reform in Commercial Street, Whitechapel. After the war he conducted the Carl Rosa Opera Company, before becoming head of the music staff at the Royal Opera House, Covent Garden. After that he became conductor and chorus master at Glyndebourne and then of the BBC Chorus. He was with the BBC Chorus during the 1960s, when Keller was in charge of the orchestral and choral section of BBC Music Division.

Another musical friend Keller made at this time was the pianist Paul Hamburger, with whom he was also to work in later life. As a writer Hamburger was a frequent contributor to *Music Survey*, the journal that Keller edited with Donald Mitchell from 1949 until 1952, and he also wrote two chapters for their 1952 symposium on Britten. His career as pianist and répétiteur took him to Britten's English Opera Group, and then to Glyndebourne, where he worked at the same time as Peter Gellhorn. Hamburger later joined both Keller and Gellhorn at the BBC, where he was first staff accompanist and later Chief Producer, Artists. He apparently enjoyed his time in internment – 'it was such fun being among so many artists from my homeland'[19] – and was a cheerful presence in the camps.

Max Jekel, the violinist with whom Keller had played quartets in Huyton Camp after Adler's departure, had unfortunately been sent to a different Isle of Man camp from Keller. It was, however, the same camp where Rudi Kompfner had been held – the Central Promenade camp in Douglas – so Jekel had met Kompfner, and Keller was able to have news of him. Jekel had the good fortune to meet several other good string players in his camp, to the envy of the quartet-starved Keller. 'Did Jekel play in the Central Promenade Quartet? With whom?' he asked his mother on 23 December. One of those with whom Jekel played was the young Siegmund Nissel, to whom he apparently gave some lessons while they were interned together.[20] Nissel later remembered that 'There was lots of music in camp; I played string quartets with Max Jekel and remember playing the Bach E major concerto with Reizenstein at the piano.'[21] Nissel was apparently transferred between different Isle of Man camps, and in Onchan Camp he met the Austrian violinist Peter Schidlof, with whom he had in common the traumatic experience of coming to England on the Kindertransport. These 'children's transports' had brought thousands of refugee children to Britain in 1938 – but without their parents, to whom visas were not granted. Sometimes the parents managed to get to Britain another way, but many were trapped and their children never saw them again. Siegmund Nissel never forgot the awful moment of saying goodbye to his father at the station, 'conscious that this could be the last time'. He was fortunate: his father later managed to get a temporary visa, leaving Vienna 'on what proved to be the last possible train, at the end of August 1939'. But Schidlof's parents died in concentration camps.[22]

Peter Schidlof had earlier been interned at Prees Heath in Lancashire, where he had met the violinist Norbert Brainin, a pupil in Vienna of the great Carl Flesch himself. Before that, he had met Ferdinand Rauter in Ladbroke Grove police station, where both men were taken during the initial round-up. It was Rauter who got Schidlof, Brainin and Nissel out of internment (through his work on Vaughan Williams' committee) and introduced them to their teacher and mentor Max Rostal. He then, through his Anglo-Austrian Music Society, brought them together with other young musicians, both Austrian and English. One of the English musicians whom they met in this way was the 'cellist Martin Lovett. Brainin, Schidlof, Nissel and Lovett went on to form the most famous artistic product of the internment camps: the Amadeus Quartet.[23]

51.   8 January 1941, Mooragh Camp, Ramsey, Isle of Man.
In German.

Dearest Mutschili, I forgot to thank Inge very, very much for her enclosure in the last parcel. I had a Christmas card from the Adlers: thank them very much. Miss Tooth wrote to me a charming, amazingly unconventional letter. Dr Roll informed me yesterday that the Home Office enquiry pertaining to my state of health (through Greig's appl.) has arrived here. Because of that I shall be summoned before the English doctor in the next few days. Gellhorn and I are very great friends. Consummate musician (pianist, conductor), profound human being. Director of a music school in the East End. If you want to read a book in which all possible tragedy is to be found, read D. H. Lawrence's 'The Trespasser'. A wise book. Berend has re-opened his orchestra – writes Tooth. One can see that the summer is approaching again: evening roll-call now at 6 o'clock (before it was at 5). Sir John Emerson (chairman of the Asquith Comm.) was in the camp.[24] According to him, it will take a long time yet until Category 23 (my category) will be released. He says that everyone in this category will come before a tribunal, but the way it's phrased in the White Paper, as I've already written, says the opposite: presumably Sir John got it wrong. But to be on the safe side, I must ask Greig to send me yet another letter of recommendation, as I enclosed his letter with my appl. It really shows now what a good thing it was that you sent me Roy's letter, if – according to Sir John's version – I have to appear in person before the tribunal after all. However, I don't think it's likely. In any case it is of immense importance that he also sent this letter after the appl., & I thank him yet again especially for that. What does Oscar do all day? What about Paula? Has she already seen Rudi? Could you send me some old tie in case of a tribunal hearing, or for when I'm released. 9 January: I have lent Dachinger, who is going to be released, £1 travel money. Please send it back to me: he will send it to you as soon as he arrives. – Mutschili my dear! – Just received your parcel of the 4th. *Many* thanks for handkerchiefs, eggs, fruit. 10th January: I'll send my next letter, if nothing worth telling happens in the meantime, to the 'Manchester Youth Relief and Refugee Council', who are sending a letter to the Guardian with the request that young people should come forward for 'entertainment in shelters and rest centres'. (The request is directed explicitly at refugees.) For the time being I shall enquire in more detail what it is all about. Therefore some time will probably pass between this and my next letter. Mutschili, what do you do all day long? Where are you doing your 'governing'? Please, if the student appl. should be refused, tell me immediately. The eggs in the last parcel were packed much better (in this firm tin) than in the penultimate one: then one was broken, but still useable in so far that I could put it in the soup. How large is the house there? Don't you suffer from air-raids there at all? Why don't you play quartets with that new violinist? Apropos, is the lady violinist young and pretty? As she doesn't have any technique, we can at least assume that. Is Inge practising regularly? And what is your average sort of mood? Does Uncle Hans play tennis again? No na. That's all for today. Servus Mutschi, *many* kisses, Hans

52. 14 January 1941, Mooragh Camp, Ramsey, Isle of Man. *In German.*

Dearest Mutschili, It is very likely that next Monday I shall be seen by the top English doctor (Colonel) after I saw another *English doctor* yesterday who gave a *positive* medical report. The Colonel can now either confirm this report, which means I should be released in about 3 to 8 weeks, or he can change the report from positive to negative, on the strength of which I would be considered fit for internment. Making any prognosis is impossible: experience shows that he refuses as well as confirms. The Home Office has informed me that my appl. under §23 will be put before the tribunal in due course. Received your letter of the 7th with great joy. A rucksack would be *very good*. Mozart sonata at Christmas went pretty well, it's just that the violin is bad. I've given up my battle with the corns and am not treating them at all at the moment, when I am free I shall simply have them removed. I have enough cocoa. I shall send the tins as soon as I've finished the last cake. I am absolutely delighted to hear about your playing in public, so to speak, & the success. – Of course I have mentioned Uncle Rudi in my §23 application. Is Georg really well (I mean: better) or has the doctor just persuaded him that he is? Our camp will be transferred to Peel in due course.[25] It was cold here, too, but I think not as unpleasant as with you. Is there such a thing as a boarding house or bed & breakfast in Bowness or its surroundings? Dr Nebenzahl intends to go and live there. 16.1.: Just received your letter of the 9th & as always really delighted. I like Mr Geschwind very much too. Thank Roy for his efforts. I have resigned the leadership of the quartet because of the incompetence of the other members. They really tried hard, but I can't face studying 5 bars for 2 hours. The strings are comparatively good. I have breakfast with the others. The chocolate etc I drink later in the evening among my circle of friends. I'm going to have two fillings, not painful. The Liptauer was absolutely marvellous. Gellhorn's musical maturity and at the same time technical perfection, plus his human qualities, bear only one comparison: Oscar, as he must have been when he was young. I am of course happy when, during his studies, at which I am usually present, I can give him some advice which he will accept with enthusiasm. The thought of Mrs Geschwind makes me feel awful even now. I cannot even imagine the change in Mrs Adler. *Many* kisses, Hans

53.   20 January 1941, Mooragh Camp, Ramsay, Isle of Man. To Paula Kompfner. *In German.*

Dearest Pauline, I really must tell you that, for me, by far the nicest things that happen in the camp are the cakes. You know how much I enjoyed them when I was in Oakbank, here I enjoy them even more: 1) I am not so spoiled foodwise as I used to be, 2) I immediately gobble up so much of the cake in one go that I can hardly move, 3) it has even been known to happen that I indulge myself with a piece *before* dinner. That thick filling! I can't stop grunting with delight like a pig. – Gellhorn will be released in the next few days. 21 January: Gellhorn has now been released. Has Dachinger already sent Mutti the pound I lent him? The Home Office doctor didn't come this week because of the drifting snow (he lives in Douglas), so I expect that I shall have my examination next week. Lilli Geller (who is getting married some time about now) sends her special regards to Mutti. The honey that Mutti sent a while ago was bliss. I occasionally buy honey here, but a small jar of nowhere near the quality of the aforementioned type costs 1/- sh. Immediately after my release I must look round for wartime music work. Could Mutti send me some Weights cigarettes *direct from the shop*: you can only buy the expensive varieties here. 22 January:

Just now I received a letter from Rudi, and I was *very* pleased with
it. Please be sure to tell him so. He told me about some books he
is going to send, to which I'm looking forward enormously. I thank
him very much!! Today I received Mutti's parcel, no, Mowgli's parcel
(rucksack & fruit); thanks very much. I wish I needed the rucksack
now. *24.1:* Received socks with great joy, Mutti's letter of the 20th with
all the enclosures. There is a real jinx on those tins: now I have happily
finished the cake, but I have to go to the (refugee) dentist every day
at the time when parcels are accepted. I'm having a long course of
treatment (nerve treatment, I'm wondering what the bill will be) and
yesterday, after weeks of trying to save it, he pulled the nerve out. He
is fantastically skilled, saving teeth which have been declared lost by
50 dentists, and in the camp he is therefore a notorious saint. He was
Kitchener camp dentist.[26] Because of that alone, but also because I
must have my jacket made larger & my shoes seen to, the £2/- are of
immeasurable value to me. Has there really not been any answer to
the student appl.? Dachinger is fully Jewish; Gellhorn half.[27] Referring
to Mowgli's letter, it wasn't a matter of not writing something to
Mutti, but of when I should write it to her. Which Bach solo sonata
is Mutti playing? Thank you so much for the detailed description of
your lives. Uncle Hans's appl. very good, and will, if there is a positive
outcome, serve to speed matters up. So servus, Pauline! Hans

Peter Gellhorn's release had taken Vaughan Williams some time: there could
be a considerable delay between the recommendation of an internee for
release and the date when he was actually allowed to leave the camp. Vaughan
Williams wrote gloomily to E.J. Dent on 13 December, 'We recommended
Gellhorn for release about 3 weeks ago. I have written to tell him so – But I do
not in the least know whether any attention is paid to our recommendations.'
It was to be another 5 weeks before Gellhorn finally got to leave.

As more and more 'artist' applications were successful, the remaining
music-making in the camp grew less satisfying, though Keller was lucky
enough still to have Paul Hamburger to accompany him. But he often thought
longingly of the quartets at home with Oscar Adler; as he wrote to his mother
on 17 February, 'Playing quartets is what I'm looking forward to particularly –
I've quite forgotten how to do it.'

Keller's mother was primarily a pianist, taught in her younger days by the
composer Franz Schreker, who fell in love with her (and even threatened to
commit suicide over her). She did not take up the 'cello in earnest until she
was about 40 years old – inspired to do so by her admiration for Oscar Adler's
playing. Keller was then about four years old, and her many hours of practice

were a strong childhood memory. As he recalled, 'In her twenties, she had taken cello lessons for a few months, until the arrival of her first child. As soon as her second child could be left to his own devices, which was fairly soon, she took up the cello again, practised five hours a day (from 5 a.m. till 10 a.m.), and played with me in a concert-giving string quartet after we had emigrated.'[28]

As has been seen, Keller felt later that the double dose of mothering he had received by having a sister so much older than himself had been a marvellous way to grow up – 'I can strongly recommend this set-up: it makes for a smashing childhood,' he wrote later. 'Whenever anything goes wrong between you and your parents, you have a mediator at hand, an acting mother as it were.'[29] As the next letter shows, however, Mowgli did not always agree with her brother. Such was the force of Grete's personality (say other members of the family) that people tended to take her part – Keller himself included.

'I can see that there's going to big battle about my beard, which I won't want to get rid of (for all sorts of practical reasons)' wrote Keller to Grete on 20 December, 'but I suppose it should be possible to give it a more civilized shape'. In the event, he did decide to sacrifice it, rather than argue with Mutti – much to the disappointment of his cousin Inge, who remembers that 'everybody was looking forward to seeing him with his beard'.[30] But he kept the moustache – then and for the rest of his life.

54.   1 February 1941, Mooragh Camp, Ramsey, Isle of Man.
In German.

Dearest Mowgale, many thanks for your sisterly letter of the 25th which I received today. Now, though I'm particularly sorry to have given the impression of having been careless in respect of the points you raise, I do have to respond by stating that I am innocent on nearly all counts, because: 1) the sorry saga of the tins: when Mutti wrote for the first time that I should send the tins back, I had to go, for several days running, to the various offices because of the §23 appl. (at the time allocated for handing in parcels). When I'd finished with that, I couldn't find any paper in which to wrap the tins. When at last after several days I had scraped together enough paper, I took the tins to the Censor & then to the post office, where they were rejected because they weren't packed well enough. When finally after a fortnight I received the paper from Mutti, my root treatment at the dentist's began – again, every day at the time the post office accepted parcels. The dental treatment took weeks. If occasionally I had a day off, then they happened not to be accepting any parcels. A few days ago I finished at the dentist's & immediately despatched the tins (before I received your letter). Over and above all this I kept Mutti informed all the time about why the tins still weren't on their way. – 2) As soon as Mutti had written that I should have my beard trimmed, I looked around for a barber, but at the moment none seem to be officiating any more. Either in Liverpool (if there is time, as I hear that one doesn't have to go to the police any more) or in Windermere, I'll have my hair cut & my beard trimmed. 3) The bow is not at all badly haired; I only asked for the other one to be sent, because having only one is impossible for performances & anyway I wanted to have, or to have sent to me, a reserve bow, as long as it's possible. I hadn't written about it in my reply to Mutti's letter about this, because I had more important things to put into the 24 lines. The fact that I forgot to explain this in my next letter represents my only fault. 4) I don't know Bestemm[31] any more, I chose the Yiddish word 'Tsore' because it describes a more melancholy concept than 'Sorge' or 'sorrow'. Otherwise I don't quite understand where the lapse is supposed to be. – I don't always collect the milk, but when I do I drink it boiled. Therefore, I hope that you see that, apart from my forgetting to write about the bow, I'm not guilty in any way. – I still remember when Nora's father was criticised by you and Mutti for putting his shoes, soles down, on the upholstery. Alfred Adler would have loved to see how the next generation overcompensates. Of course I'll take over Ena. But isn't she still a bit young? I hope you're not cross any more. Kisses, Hans.

When Keller said here 'I'll take over Ena', it meant as a violin pupil. In the event, however, Ena did not take to the violin, and remembers only one lesson from Keller. Some fifteen years later, Keller began to teach violin to another member of his family, Nina Trott, the daughter of his cousin Inge. It was Grete Keller who first noticed her musicality, and Keller gave her a few lessons before finding her a permanent teacher in Maxi Bakony, whom he had met at Dartington. Nina's violin-playing flourished, and she eventually became a professional jazz violinist. She has many memories of being in Herne Hill in the 1950s listening to Keller play quartets with his mother and Oscar Adler, and one particularly special memory of an afternoon spent with Keller shortly before his death:

The afternoon with Hans in 1984 stands out in my memory as being quite significant in my musical life. I'd previously had no idea that Hans would 'approve' of jazz, and was touched by his interest and enthusiasm. During that conversation we talked about Stephane Grappelli and his facility for improvisation, and I vividly remember Hans expressing great interest in the fact that I'd taught myself to improvise. He seemed amused and gratified by the idea that I'd become a bit of a 'maverick' and gave me the impression that he was going to follow my progress in jazz with great interest.[32]

Keller gave her his violin, on which she still plays.

When Keller burst on the London musical scene only a few years after his release from internment, he wrote and spoke with a remarkable confidence and commanding authority, sparks of which are visible in his detailed instructions to his cousin Inge in his next letter from the camp. Musicians from all walks of life began to seek his advice, which meant that he was in increasing demand as a teacher. Despite his many other roles, his teaching remained a central part of his life, and it was evidently inspiring – but never dogmatic (although he could certainly appear dogmatic in print). As a teacher 'he was full of questions,' wrote one of his friends. 'He was a marvellous listener, and I really believe he found listening as much a *learning* process for himself – like teaching.'[33]

One of the most important elements of Keller's teaching was his coaching of string quartets. This ranged from children's quartets at the Yehudi Menuhin School (where he continued teaching right up until his death) to established professionals like the Chilingirian Quartet. Many lessons and coaching sessions were followed by voluminous correspondence: Levon Chilingirian, for example, still has in his possession a remarkable series of letters Keller wrote to him in 1974, when their busy diaries had interrupted their coaching sessions:

> Dear Levon,
>   I was depressed last night … because we only got through less than 1½ Haydns. I thought to myself that while a few words (if they stimulate what you want to do, anyway) can change your approach out of all recognition and make it strikingly meaningful, we won't meet again until September – and then it will be Schoenberg, not Haydn. … I decided, at 0007 precisely, to act realistically, if unconventionally: that's what life usually is about, and art always. I shall devote about ½-hour per day (not, perhaps, every day) to one of the forty-five, sending you notes about what to avoid, and what might be overlooked on superficial acquaintance. …
>   *Op. 9 No. 4* first movement: The 'Boccherini tempo' (my term) should not induce one, on the one hand, to split the music into half-bars – nor, on the other hand, to play it too fast by way of over-compensation. The beginning is mysterious, contained, slowly developing, especially in view of the double start (bar 7). The gravest danger in the movement is an unintended accent on the semiquaver upbeat in bar 2 and all

corresponding places: The motif plays a dominating role, not only here, but also in the development. The danger is heightened when three instruments answer one (bar 3). If this phrase and its reply is thought of as a contrasting variation (but still very much a variation) of the end of the first phrase (middle of bar 2) and its echo in the second violin, the interpretation is bound to be logical. The more de-accentuation on the upbeat, the better. There is a danger of an unconscious quickening of pace when the second violin has the triplets – and, on the other hand, of an insufficiently light flow where the first has the demisemiquavers (second subject). In the recapitulation, there is an almost historic wrong accent – in bar 29 after the double bar, on the syncopation (first and second violins). It remains to be said that the opening cello quavers have to contribute to the mystery, and that accompaniments tend to be too loud unless one does something about them. ...[34]

Some of Keller's remarkable insight into quartet-playing is preserved in his last book, written shortly before he died and published in 1986 by Dent: *The Great Haydn Quartets: Their Interpretation*.

56.   2 February 1941, Mooragh Camp, Ramsey, Isle of Man.
In German.

Dearest Mutschili, Yesterday I received Inge's letter of 22nd-23rd and was especially pleased with it. Although I continually get letters from all sorts of different people, I don't know anyone who writes letters so well, so true to life & so vividly. What sort of studies is she playing? I'm pleased that she has taken on my quartet-chutzpah to a certain extent; everything else will come by itself. Referring to the solo in No.46 (if I remember rightly) she has to be careful to maintain the rests between the semiquavers without breaking the line of the melody: in a word, to play the rests. The demisemiquaver runs as calmly as possible, there she has unlimited time, as she is leading, so the more controlled and apparently slowly she plays them, the faster they will sound. No rit. at the end, but in such a way that it sounds as if there were one. Restrained increase of intensity in the sequences before the end, with an inner urgency, upbeats with strong resonance but nevertheless leading to the 1st beats of the sequences. Live with the rests between the sequences, that is, with the playing of the others (even when you're practising), that's the only way to achieve a continuously developing intensification. Right, and now she must practise all that, & when I come it has to be first class. She should say to herself 'don't rush' three times before she starts. – What is happening about the orchestra? Aren't you playing with them? If so, is the intonation bearable? Do they need a cracking good leader? (I mean me.) 3rd Febr.: Today I went to see Roll to ask him if he would please ask the H.O. doctor who was supposed to be coming tomorrow, how my case is doing. Unfortunately, the Home Office doctor had unexpectedly come today instead of tomorrow, and of course Roll had forgotten to ask him. He promised to ask him next week, I am to remind him again on Saturday. Today a parcel came from Uncle Hans: many thanks. Unfortunately he had put in a packet of margarine, which was of course confiscated. Could you tell him that sending rationed food is not permitted. Because of my nagging conscience, I am now collecting my milk every day, and force it down. Schiff from Bloomsbury House was here: the tribunal for §23 will decide in London, *without the applicants' presence*, on the basis of the application that was submitted & of any other writt. information. It is therefore as I understood it to be, & also as it emerges unambiguously from the amendment to the White Paper. Sir Emerson must have got it wrong, or those here trying to understand him got it wrong. Those different types of chocolate which you always send are heavenly. 5. II.: Today I received a touching letter fr. Roy: I am always amazed that such a person exists. From Lilli Geller I've suddenly started receiving regular enormously long stormy letters, due to the fact that she is now getting married, & accordingly she is setting up some back-up for the purpose of preventing sexual monotony. People go on a lot about polygamy, but rather less about one woman with lots of men. Next week I shall be performing Mozart's little G major trio. The books that Rudi sent are giving me great pleasure, please let him know when you have the opportunity. Mr Peake, the Under-Secr. of State, says that the loyalty of those who are released later will not be held to be in question in *any* way. *Kisses*, Hans.

57.   **8 February 1941, Mooragh Camp, Ramsey, Isle of Man.** *In German.*

Dearest Mutschili, Thank you very much for the parcel of the 5th with all the lovely things. However, sending rationed food to internees is not permitted. The censoring office turned a blind eye this once, because he was touched by the labelling and the small amounts, but he has charged me with writing to you that you shouldn't do that any more, next time it will be confiscated. From Gellhorn I received a very lovely letter, in which he also sent me the 2/6 which I lent him half a minute before his departure, as he had no change nor any vouchers (Camp money) to pay for a telegram; I thought that he hadn't even noticed that I had paid for the telegram for him. Next week I shall hear whether Colonel Barker, the Home Office doctor, has confirmed my medical report. If he has done so, it takes 7 weeks to 2 months from the signing to the release. In my case the wait might be on the longer side, because at the time when the report might be expected to arrive at the Home Office, my file will probably be at the §23 tribunal, resulting in further delays, as I know from medical releasees[35] who had also made an appl. under one of the tribunal paragraphs (§19).[36] Has Mowgli received my reply to her honoured sisterly missive? Have you received the tins? Have you got a radio over there, now that it's allowed again?[37] 10th Feb.: Dr Roll has just told me that Col. Baker *confirmed* my positive medical report and sent it to the Home Office. (About a fortnight ago.) Today I received a letter from Uncle Rudi in which he sent me a copy of a letter which he has sent to the tribunal c/o the Home Office. I thank him greatly for his efforts. So, with God's help, the medical report will meet up at some stage with my Home Office file, & I shall be released. For weeks already we've hardly had any cigarettes (3 or 4 cigarettes once a week). Could you ask Inge, or someone who has nothing to do, to send me directly through a tobacconist (otherwise it won't be handed out here) cheap cigarettes (perhaps Player's Weights)? The weather here is warm now, it seems we've survived the worst of the winter. By the way, are both violins in Bowness? Which one is Inge using to practise? I hope that Adler uses mine when you play string duos. (I mean when he plays with Inge). The eggs are excellent and a great pleasure, as are the fruit and the chocolate bars. I suppose that for the time being one is quite cut off from Muni and Kollmann? How is Mariedl Jaray? Could you be so good as to take the trouble of writing to Greig's office, asking them to let me know immediately when the Home Office letter announcing that my release has been granted eventually arrives, by sending a wire straight here (Keller, Mooragh Camp, Ramsey, Isle of Man). It would be nice for me to know a few days in advance, not only because of the packing, but also because of the various farewell celebrations and concerts. Servus, kisses, Hans

This letter that Rudolf Keller wrote to the Home Office on Keller's behalf is still preserved:

I beg to draw your attention to the case of my nephew H. H. Keller, House 14, Mooragh Internment Camp, Ramsay, I.O.M. My nephew is a very gifted young violinist, who stood before the L.R.A.M. exam of the Royal Academy. He had been interned in Vienna, beaten and tormented. I am afraid he was persecuted by the well informed Gestapo, because he is my only relative of this name. He has done absolutely nothing politically, was strongly pro-British, but lived only for his musical studies. My late brother was paralysed when he heard of the maltreatment of his only child and died a few weeks later, my sister-in-law was blackmailed by the Gestapo to send from this country all her money and that of her child to get the permission for him to leave Germany. He had very great nervous troubles and looks – although not yet 22 years old – like a 35 year old man. You may believe me after these facts that my nephew is absolutely anti-Hitler and, as the nephew of the under-signed publisher of 'Prager Tagblatt' and 'Neue Leipziger Zeitung', the most radical anti-Hitler papers of Central Europe, is hated by the Nazis. I think it is absolutely safe to release him from internment.

I am, Sir, your obedient servant

Dr. Rudolf Keller

Subjekt of a Nazi police 'Steckbrief' (warrant) with photo.[38]

~

The family tried their utmost, but still the time went by without news. On 17 February, as Keller told his mother, 'Today official attention was drawn to the possible delays in cases of medical release as the civil servant in the Home Office who is handling all the reports & applications has been away on an inspection trip & has now got a backlog of work to catch up on.'[39] This was disappointing: 'As things stand, the medical cases take, on average, so long that it's unlikely I will be home for my birthday.' Keller's birthday was on 11 March, and he did indeed spend it in internment.

Although he told his mother 'you must not think that I don't do anything day & night but ponder the date of my release,' it must have been difficult to keep his mind off the subject – and such speculation would have featured constantly in camp conversations. Writing after his release to his psychological colleague Margaret Phillips, Keller described himself and his fellow internees as suffering from a 'release obsession':

> During the whole period in which I had opportunity to witness the camp life a 'release obsession', i.e. a desire after release which was much more intense than it would have been if emanating only from personal rational considerations, made itself felt among almost all members of the camp. … Having been myself a victim of it, yet fully aware – even during the period of its actual operativeness – of its irrational character, I attempted to study it in myself and others.[40]

Rumours constantly circulated in the camps:

> Today I heard of four people who were informed today that the Home Office had refused their positive medical appl. As far as I hear, they do not want lots of sick people on the mainland, as the hospitals are needed for other things; therefore – such is the rumour – a new modern hospital is being set up in Peel here on this island. But since my case doesn't need any hospital treatment (i.e. wouldn't improve because of it), & over and above that, I am financially independent in that I wouldn't be a burden on any committee outside, it is to be hoped that my case will not be refused.[41]

Keller had also heard that the 'paragraph 23' tribunal had started its work, which raised his hopes as he would rather be released that way:

> Although §23 release would take longer, I should be *much happier* to be released *explicitly* for reasons of *loyalty*. On the other hand, medical release would have the advantage that it would probably happen soon, whereas one can't tell how long the tribunal will take to work through the 400 cases it has so far.[42]

~

60.   21 February 1940, Mooragh Camp, Ramsey, Isle of Man.
In German.

> Dearest Mutschili, The honey from the last parcel is excellent, I much prefer it to sandwich spread. The hospital intends to send

the Home Office an urgent list with all those medical cases whose release is overdue, i.e. those whose reports were sent a very long time ago. I don't know whether I can count amongst those yet. There is one case whose report was sent as early as December. I can't compete with that. Just received your letter of the 15th. Never realized how talented a letter-writer you are. The whole letter a real delight. Really, that typewriter will be a ray of sunshine for the next 100 years. Oscar's verdict on tuning made me laugh more than I have for ages. Could you send me a little money again before too long? Obviously one's playing deteriorates greatly in orchestras, intonation even more than solo-playing, but if one is very careful (particularly afterwards), no damage will be done. Middle movements of the 2nd Beethoven are easy. Titus Overture difficult. What are you playing by Handel-Beecham? Water Music? I think that Eine Kleine Nachtmusik has already been so played to death by amateur orchestras that you will not succeed in bringing it back to life. Watch it: the Romance you will play like a funeral march, at the beginning of the Finale there will be 25 different first violin entries, and in the fourth movement, the second violins and violas will play the quavers as if they were suffering from consumption, & not together. And the Finale will sound like a slow Bourrée. I believe, however, that one also does learn a lot in an orchestra, and I know *what* fun it is, even when the playing is exceedingly provincial. I for one am ever so pleased that you're playing in an orchestra, and I try to imagine you. Berend was not exactly a model of strict conscientiousness, but Read was. Weber (music composed specifically for the piano) must be difficult to arrange for violin. *What* has he arranged? Surely not bits of the A-flat major sonata? Pianino wonderful. Nebenzahl has the same attitude to music as Uncle Hans, to whom in certain respects he bears an astonishing resemblance. He thanks you very much for the information on places to live. So my prognosis has come true: the appl. was submitted under §23. Hamburger plays the piano, an amateur and ignoramus the cello. Yes, I should love to have sardines: the last ones were wonderful and, as I was told by a professional on the topic, a factory owner who lives in our house, they are the best ones there are. In my circle of friends there is always a tin-opener (in this case the factory owner). Biscuits would also be very good. Well, well, that typewriter! I keep thinking of it. Just like the Christmas tree when I was a child. Today a lady gave a lecture here about 'Mental Hygiene & Prevention of Nervous Troubles'. Hans.

'That typewriter' seems to have been a present bought for Keller in ancipation of his release. The typewriters in his father's office had been among Keller's favourite toys in childhood: 'my father … would take me to his office when he had to work at the weekend and his staff wasn't there, seat me in one of the outer rooms and put a typewriter in front of me. It was bliss. All afternoon I'd sit there, typing, and when I finally heard him call from next door, "Let's go home now," my heart invariably broke.' [43] After his release, Keller did type all his writings until after he joined the BBC. He switched then to longhand and dictating, partly because of the availability of BBC secretaries (whom he often employed to type his writings after hours), and partly because of the onset of the first symptoms of motor neurone disease (which also put an end to his violin-playing at that time). During the 1940s and 1950s, while he was doing his own typing, he usually kept carbon copies, which is why that period of his life is particularly well documented in the Cambridge Keller Archive.

62.   3 March 1941, Mooragh Camp, Ramsey, Isle of Man.
In German.

Dearest Mutschili, There have been another one or two medical releases. All the overdue cases, i.e. all those who had been judged as positive by the Home Office doctor Colonel Barker before 20. 1. (& for whom he sent an urgent letter to the Home Office a few days ago), so including me as well, were re-re-examined in the course of the last few days by the camp medical officer Dr Templeton. He selected a few cases whose release he considers particularly desirable, and I'm one of those. Tomorrow he will send me to the Home Office doctor's deputy, & the latter will decide whether my case and the other cases chosen by Dr Templeton should be put as urgent. My personal guess is that because of my positive medical report, there's a possibility that the Home Office will ask the §23 tribunal for a decision, & that while this is being awaited, I'll then be released under §23. – Otherwise you must not think that I don't do anything day & night but ponder the date of my release, just because that is always the main theme of my letters; after all, in any correspondence between 2 people the crux of their relationship will get preferential treatment in their letters, & the crux of our relationship is the moment when we are reunited. I've received Inge's letter of 22.II and I particularly enjoyed it. Regarding the passage in the Haydn G minor quartet: as far as I can remember, we are dealing with the accompaniment to the second subject of the first movement (in B flat major) (I mean: the second subject is in B flat major). Rapidly bowed triplets in this key are always *very* difficult. It is best to practise slowly in 2nd position, just bearing in mind that once the B flat will come on a down-bow & then on an up-bow. Initially emphasize the B flat. Don't use much bow. Don't hurry, the first violin at this point rarely maintains the opening tempo, rather it becomes a little more sedate. If (as is easily possible & doesn't really matter) she still isn't on top of this passage when it comes to playing the quartet, then the day before she should practise the second and third notes of each triplet, slurring them. It is sufficient that the metric sound character is maintained, and if she does it skilfully, Oscar won't even notice. When later on she comes up against that same theme, she must not allow herself to be rushed by the (partly slurred) accompanying (ornamental) triplets in the first violin. That's all for to-day. Kisses, Hans

63.   4 March 1941, Mooragh Camp, Ramsey, Isle of Man.
In German.

Dearest Mutschili! These long letters, like yours of the 25th which I received yesterday, are really wonderful. The £2 is downright generous, and I am ever so grateful to you. I always felt, whenever I played it (and that was unfortunately very often) that Tchaikovsky's Elegy is an unbearably horrible piece, but perhaps I am wrong. In any case, the Waltz (in G major) from the same serenade is really lovely, aren't you going to play that as well? That composer whose name you don't know, & by whom you're playing something in the string orchestra, is likely, according to my calculations, to be Holst? – I don't know whether I know all the Beethoven string trios: if you only knew 2, then it will be the same for me. Which Mozart Andante are you playing? Nebenzahl thanks you very much again, he hasn't decided yet where to go. Shortly before the arrival of your letter, I, too, learnt that cigarettes are only allowed to be sent direct from the manufacturer. As we hardly ever get any any more, it would be wonderful – if it isn't too much trouble – if even a small number reached me every week, which could be achieved by a one-off order with the manufacturer, as I know from the many house-mates who get their cigarettes this way. But *please* really only if it isn't any trouble. Whenever the children say something that sticks in your memory, please write it to me: they keep my spirits up. Recently I gave a concert: Brahms G major sonata and the above-mentioned Mozart trio in the same key. There were 95 people there, surprisingly many in view of the number of people left in the camp now (400). During the Brahms I even got applause between the movements. My net earnings: 2 sh. I had great pleasure from a letter from Liane (69 West 68th Street, New York City, U.S.A.) and even greater joy from one from Muni (Women's College of the University of North Carolina, Greensboro, N.C., U.S.A.), both of them have written to you, too, they implore you to write to them from time to time to let them know how I am doing (in the case of Liane, a postcard will do). Muni has a scholarship at the above institute, Liane is working as a typist. The examination of the nine selected cases (including mine) by the deputy Home Office doctor, Col Flowerdew, did not bring about any change in the situation. 5.III. Today I received Mowgli's parcel with apples, 'Black Magic' & dates & thank her very much for them. In 14 days I shall play the Mozart trio again for the camp youth (admission free). Have you had any news from Georg? 7.III. Just now I received your parcel with the cake, eggs, sardines, honey etc – bless you.[44] Today I heard of a young lad whose positive medical report was re-routed to §23. Probably that's what will happen to me. Thanks for the parcel! Kisses, Hans

64.   11 March 1941, Mooragh Camp, Ramsey, Isle of Man. *In German.*

Dearest Mutschili, I'm lying in bed with a mild case of 'flu. Treatment & care first class: I've never had the doctor so near to me (a certain Dr Frankl, formerly Hernals, on first-name terms with Uncle Hans). The wonky writing & the ink-blots aren't caused by the fact that I'm already at death's door, but because I'm lying down, writing against my knees without anything to rest the paper on. Top temperature (yesterday) 38.5, since then it's been going down, and since midday today I've not had a fever at all. Because of Nebenzahl's insistence, I've moved to the ground floor into a lovely heatable room from which someone was recently released. I received Mowgli's and Roy's birthday present (£1 each) with great joy: it came at just the right time, as I shall have some extra expenses through being ill. I was also very happy to receive the 50 Player's Weights: I shall only appreciate them properly when I'm well again. Received your letter of 3.III. and was ever so pleased with it. I don't know this composition by Handel-Beecham. By the way (Lalo): you might have a go at studying the Cello Concerto by Lalo? Oscar is likely to have played the Brahms sonata (G major) which I have played here? I am most impressed by your pedagogical discoveries and I consider them to be 100% correct, but I can't try them out for myself because I haven't got a mirror. Shall I send the tins right now or wait until there are six of them? How did Inge play the Rider Quartet? Could you thank Roy and Mowgli very much for me? People are looking after me very well, and I get so much nursing that I'm already feeling quite sick. So servus Mutschi, kisses, kisses, kisses, Hans

65.   13 March 1941, Mooragh Camp, Ramsey, Isle of Man.
In German.

Dearest Mutschili, Well, I'm well again now, & because of that I'm writing again even today, though there is nothing new to report. This coming Sunday, the Home Office has arranged for the folk singer Engel Lund to come and sing here. Rauter, Lund's permanent accompanist, had applied to the Home Office for permission for Lund to sing here. He's not coming himself, I don't know who will accompany her. Rauter, by the way, is another member of the committee of musicians about whom you have written to me (which Mayer & Knepler are on as well). Lund will probably also sing some Yiddish folk songs. Rauter sang them to us when he was still here. I've just received a very lovely letter from Mowgli (of 3.III.). Well, now that I know that the cigarettes are from Mr Holiday, they taste twice as good! Recently we were taken to see the Chaplin film. Mowgli, too, has seen it, as she reports in her letter. I found the overall atmosphere of the film really excellent, though it does go on at times. The power of irony, which never leaves Jews, even when they're sitting up to their ears in the muck, becomes clear. And irony is one of the strongest weapons, particularly against the two dictators. The various characteristics are spotted so well and ridiculed so well. (I mean the character traits of the dictators.) Please can you give Mowgli birthday greetings from me; as you know I'm not allowed to write another letter this week. And I'm sorry I can't send her a present either; the most I could do would be to send her the £ which she sent me for my birthday. But I need that £ to give presents to those who helped me while I was ill. Can Inge already do childcare? Are Rudi & Peggy living in Oakbank again? I really want to thank Mowgli very much for her letter. I still have to forego practising the violin for a few more days because I am not yet allowed to sit for hours in a cold room. Well, at least the worst of the horrors of winter have been overcome. So Roy wants to become a doctor in September? And Uncle Hans plays tennis. Mowgli writes that as if it were something new. So you

practise for 4-5 hours a day? Good for you. That is something you
haven't done for a very long time. Incidentally, where did the Adlers
rehearse before their performances? Have they got their piano with
them? Evening: now, in order to complete my recovery, I was given
a glass of sherry by a bank director & I cracked an egg in it (on his
advice). Kisses Hans.

The 'Chaplin film' to which Keller and his fellow internees were taken was
The Great Dictator, Chaplin's first 'talkie', which was released in October 1940.
It was perhaps an appropriate choice, for the film satirised Nazism, with
Chaplin playing 'Adenoid Hynkel'. Keller had long been interested in film, as
his surviving letters from Vienna show, and after the war he became intensely
interested in film music, on which he wrote frequently and fascinatingly for
many years. He was a particular champion of the achievements of British
composers, many of whom became his personal friends. As a critic, his
interest in film music foreshadowed his later concern for broadcast music –
'film music is capable of becoming a weapon of musical mass destruction,' he
wrote, and he urged the critical establishment to pay it more attention, writing
for the British Film Institute a 24-page pamphlet on *The Need for Competent
Film Music Criticism* in 1947.[45]

As Keller mentions here, Roy Franey was at this time embarking on a
change of career. Trained as a chartered surveyor, he originally worked with
his father in the family building business, 'Almond Franey and Son Ltd, Estate
Managers and Builders, London'. When he met his wife, she was a medical
student, and this may have influenced his decision to train as a doctor himself,
as a mature student. He started his medical training shortly after the birth of
his two daughters, and finally qualified in May 1942. He was called up and
served as a Medical Officer in the army until the end of the war. After 1945 he
worked as a hospital doctor for a year or two, before returning to his original
profession of surveyor – having managed to keep his building business going
throughout the war.[46]

The many references to cigarettes in these letters show that Keller was
already a smoker – and he remained one all his life. He never attempted to
give up entirely, though he and his friends did operate a 'Reduced Smoking
League'. His BBC colleague Julian Hogg, who was secretary of the League,
remembers that one had to smoke fewer than 12 cigarettes a day (or 84 over
a week) to get into the First Division. Over 84 took one into the Second
Division, 96 into the Third, and 126 (18 a day) into the Fourth. Many of
Keller's extant letters to Hogg begin with things like 'Week ending May 10:
Cosman 98, Keller 75' – Keller here managing to get into the First Division,
while his wife languished in the Third!

However, the cigarette mailings to Mooragh Camp, which Mutti had just set up with Mr Holiday, the tobacconist across the road from the Franeys' Herne Hill House, could now be cancelled. Halfway through his next letter, Keller received momentous news ...

66.   19 March 1941, Mooragh Camp, Ramsey, Isle of Man.
In German.

Dearest Mutschili, Really, all the things I received last week from you are quite wonderful. After the things I already acknowledged in my last letter, on Saturday I got Ena's card, which gave me immeasurable joy. The picture is so marvellous, the facial expressions are so amazing, that I can look at it for hours. Then next came your parcel of the 12th with the wonderful tin of pears, first-class sardines, eggs, chocolate etc. Then came the Adlers' card, for which I'd like specially to thank them, if I were allowed to write more often, I would obviously send them a reply. And finally came your letter of the 11th, heralding [Carl Flesch's book] 'The Art of Violin Playing',[47] about which I'm quite speechless with joy, and the pound, which will end all money worries (of course, there never were any real money worries). I am not disappointed that the whole thing is dragging on so much, because apart from the fact that I have always seen that most others are waiting, or had to wait, even longer than me, I came into this world as an old Jew and as an onlooker on my own life, and therefore I am well suited for situations in life in which one must have patience. I've already told you I've received the cigarettes. I have no other wishes: just one request: – could Mr Holiday be asked to send the cigarettes regularly every week? I have presented Dr Frankl with two boxes of cigars (you can get cigars here) as he took no money for treating me. For a change, I can feel a tooth and will take myself off to the dentist again. My next letter will go to Uncle Hans, because I want to ask him to write another letter trying to speed things up in the medical matter, to the Home Office (through Greig's office). 20 March: yesterday Greig's telegram arrived, *that my release is authorised.* I am *so* happy that I can't really write about it. Obviously now I won't need to write to Hans about another reminder. Nor, probably, will the cigarette mailing be necessary any longer. 'The Art of Violin Playing' will be forwarded to me in Bowness if it arrives here after I've been released. The bed and mattress I'll be taking with me. I hope that the order of release will arrive here soon. Tomorrow I shall gradually start packing. Today was given over to the strenuous occupation of eating up all my stock of food. I shall of course telegraph

you as soon as I know when I am sailing. Until then, many kisses &
many greetings to everyone, Hans

~

Keller left Mooragh Camp on 23 March 1941, and joined his family in Bowness.
It is not certain whether he actually knew which of his various applications
had finally secured his release, and doubtless it hardly mattered to him in the
joy of being free again. The index of internees in the National Archives records
that he was released under 'Category 3' – that is, on medical grounds.[48] Keller,
however, seems to have been unaware of this, thinking instead that he owed
his release to Ralph Vaughan Williams. In an interview towards the end of his
life, in which he was asked about his time in internment, he gave this account:

> I was interned – if I remember aright – in 1940, and I spent nine months
> in internment. Actually Vaughan Williams got me out: he had heard me
> in a concert, and he wrote a letter of protest to the Home Secretary.[49]

This interview took place nearly 45 years after the event, but Keller's family
and friends are all under the same impression. As we have seen, Keller had
indeed made a release application to Vaughan Williams's committee, and
since this was being considered at the same time as his medical application
(as well as his student and 'paragraph 23' applications), there may have been
some confusion in the family as to which was the one that had actually
worked. Or they may have received an indication from the Committee for
the Release of Interned Alien Musicians that it had approved his application.
Certainly Ferdinand Rauter, who worked closely with Vaughan Williams, had
heard Keller play – indeed, had played with him on many occasions in the
camp. But it might also be true that Keller wanted in later years to believe that
he was released by Vaughan Williams as a musician, because this would have
been an endorsement of him as a violinist – something that might have been
important to him when he could no longer play. The first symptoms of the
motor neurone disease that was eventually to kill him manifested themselves
very early – around 1960 according to his wife – and his violin was one of the
first casualties. Keller determinedly ignored his symptoms for more than 20
years, finally getting a diagnosis only a year before his death.

~

After Keller left the Isle of Man, the numbers of internees still held there continued to decline, as the Home Office tribunals steadily worked through the remaining cases, and most of those in category C gained their liberty within the next few months. The numbers still on the island a year after Keller's departure were down to around 5,000, a tenth of whom were British subjects held under 18B. By the time Mosley was released there were even fewer, and the camp at Peel was closed, dispersing the British fascists among the other camps, so that the friends and enemies of Nazism once again rubbed shoulders. The numbers held on the Island were briefly swelled by the arrest of Japanese nationals after Pearl Harbour, but these were repatriated within months. Also increasing the numbers temporarily were internees returning from Canada and Australia, as they waited on the island for the Home Office to review their cases. There was consternation when one such former deportee hanged himself at the news that the Home Office had finally turned him down, and the Island Commander had to try to keep the news out of the papers.[50]

By the end of the war, the numbers left were tiny, and the whole issue was buried under a combination of relief that the conflict was finally over, and horror at the death and destruction elsewhere. As Lafitte later acknowledged, 'if one uses man-made megadeaths as the measure of war-engendered misery, this whole lamentable operation comes close to the bottom of the scale.'[51] Only about a thousand internees had actually died as as result of their arrest, the majority by drowning as they were deported, but some through suicide or ill health brought on by their confinement. Britain had lost fifty times as many lives in the Blitz.

But are numbers all? What so incensed François Lafitte, Yvonne Kapp, Eleanor Rathbone, 'Judex', 'Scipio' and all the other passionate British campaigners against mass internment in 1940 was that to lock up indiscriminately the same people who had just been locked up by the Nazis seemed to contradict everything they thought Britain was supposed to be fighting for. 'When the war broke out,' said the MP Graham White in the first Commons debate on internment, 'we were not, according to the then Prime Minister, fighting the German people. We were fighting Hitlerism ...

> That vision has now been shattered and, as we know, the utmost use is being made in Germany of this fact, with appropriate headlines from the English Press, with the object of showing that the enemies of Hitler in Germany are now the enemies of England. They ask, 'Where are the much-vaunted cultural values of Democracy?' ... That may seem to some people a matter of small consequence, but it is, in reality, of the utmost consequence, because the regeneration of Europe depends upon people who have still, in Germany and in other countries, democratic

and reasonable sentiments. These beliefs are being shattered by the treatment of refugees in the last few weeks.[52]

Essentially he and his colleagues were seeking to uphold, on behalf of the foreign refugees, the same principles that Churchill invoked in 1943 on behalf of the Mosleys, and described as 'the supreme protection invented by the British people for ordinary individuals against the State' – that 'the power of the Executive to cast a man into prison without formulating any charge known to the law, and particularly to deny him judgment by his peers for an indefinite period, is [in] the highest degree odious.'[53] Churchill himself, despite being the initial driving force behind mass internment, seems to have moderated his position fairly rapidly, and he acknowledged in his later writings that the policy of 1940 had entailed 'grave affronts to the rights and liberties of the individual'.[54] Those rights and liberties, however, seem to have been considered more seriously in the case of British citizens: it is significant that when mass internment began it was applied to foreigners before British fascists.

As Yvonne Kapp and Margaret Mynett so eloquently put it, an interned and deported refugee 'must have wondered, long before he found himself lying on straw in a rat-infested wharf behind barbed wire, or being shipped to Canada under military guard without the consent or the knowledge of his family, what the British thought they were fighting for if the first anti-Nazis in Europe presented such a menace.'[55]

For some, however, the self-interest and defence of Britain as a nation state should override all such arguments. In times of war, ideals like this could be thought to be a luxury which it was unfair to impose on a government dealing with a national emergency. Sir Edward Grigg MP, for example, also speaking in that first internment debate on 10 July, had no doubt as to what the proper priorities should be:

> There has been going on this afternoon, I suppose one of the greatest air battles of the war. At this moment – I do not know whether it is so – bombers may be over a number of our towns … In the approach of many Members of this House to this problem there was an atmosphere of unreality which to me was positively terrifying.
>
> I wonder how many Members have ever tried to put themselves in the place of the men who are actually responsible for the security of this country and are not concerned with merely making speeches.[56]

This sort of ethical question, about the extent to which the sacrifice of individual liberty for the sake of a 'higher' cause can be justified, was something on which Hans Keller later wrote with passion and originality, perceiving clearly the dangerous ease with which appalling decisions can be made if obligations to the individual are removed: 'Where humanity has been abolished, there are no more human problems.'

When he reflected in later life on his own experiences under the Nazis, Keller always saw the link between such extreme situations and the way in which the same moral questions operate in everyday life. During his life at the BBC, for example, he constantly pointed out the diminishing and stifling effect that corporate life had on individuals – to the frustration of some of his management colleagues. But, to Keller, if 'what the Nazi story teaches me is that I am behaving wrongly to my subordinates or not wrongly enough to my superiors,' the consequent duty to implement such insights could not be avoided.

Ultimately, what Keller wanted to impress on those who heard or read things like his account of his imprisonment in Vienna was that 'if there is any lesson to be drawn from any crime against humanity, it is that its sources, inevitably, are actively around us all the time, and within us too, otherwise it could not possibly have happened.' He was deeply suspicious of all 'crusades', seeing even in the best of them the seeds of human disaster if they threatened to put the cause above the individual human being, or to suborn the individual conscience, the independence of which he described as 'the ultimate value'.

As he wrote about his 'Vienna, 1938' broadcast:

> You miss [the] point if it makes you feel sadly good about our (your) own goodness, and 'thoughtful' about those terrible Nazis, or terrible anybodies for that matter: what I am on about is what happens to conscience, yours, mine, anybody's, once it is projected on to a group idea. The end of humanity happens long before any ensuing massacre. It happens when somebody starts to save the world, or his country, or his corporation, or anything that needs other people's consciences … it isn't me that's controlling you, it's Germany, Marxist ideology, BBC 'policy', something that's bigger than both of us. As a matter of fact, there's nothing bigger than either of us so long as we retain our moral integrity.[57]

That there was a positive side to the internment of refugees might be viewed as almost an indecent thing to say. But for Keller, there was most definitely a positive side to his time in the camps, and it is only now becoming clear just what that was. He was, it must be said, one of the more fortunate internees. His arrest came in the last of the mass round-ups, so his experience of the chaotic early months of internment was briefer than some. He avoided being deported, and he had at least one family member with him in the camps most of the time. He also had many friends and family supporting him on the outside, with the resources to alleviate some of the practical discomforts of camp life. Because of his youth, his natural disposition and his earlier experience in Vienna, he quickly made the best of things, and his insatiable intellectual hunger eagerly absorbed all the opportunities that his many talented and distinguished fellow internees were able to give him.

Because of the restrictions on the length and frequency of letters, their censorship, and the large amount of practical information to be conveyed in those 24 lines, there are few details in Keller's letters from internment of the rich intellectual life of the camps. Brief references to G. K. Chesterton, J. S. Mill and D. H. Lawrence show that Keller was continuing to some extent his former exploration of English writing. But in general – and musically in particular – internment seems to have meant a plunge back into the lost world of Vienna, as the internees created for themselves a community in which they could try to feel at home. For a young man like Keller such an experience was an important stimulus, heightening his awareness of his Viennese heritage. The months of enforced inactivity also provided the mental space in which to re-examine it, re-think it – and, for Keller, re-discover much of which he had previously been unconscious.

The importance of the internment episode to Keller's intellectual development really becomes apparent when one begins to read what he wrote after his release. Typing furiously on his new typewriter, the words poured out in their thousands and, fortunately for biographers, he kept many of them. His months in the camps included a crucial discovery, which set in train an enormously fruitful burgeoning of ideas with which, over the next few years, he found his own inimitable voice as a writer and worked out what it was that he wanted to say.

Hans Keller (Milein Cosman)

9   Afterwards, 1942-48

Reading Keller's letters from internment is fascinating from an historical point of view, but rather more frustrating for a biographer. Among all the repetitive detail about food and release applications, these short, censored letters contain little indication of the enormous intellectual development that was undoubtedly taking place inside Keller while he was confined alongside many distinguished minds, uprooted from his former life, with little to occupy him but music, reading, conversation and thought.

Since he brought no papers with him out of the camps, evidence as to what was going on in his mind at that time has to be gleaned mainly from the voluminous writings that survive from immediately after his release. His cousin Inge's evidence is that Keller returned from the camps full of psychoanalytic theory,[1] and indeed his letters, notes and writings dating from 1941-45 show clearly that this subject had become a consuming obsession. But whom he met or what he read while interned that sparked this interest is still a mystery.

Keller published very little during the rest of the war, but he was writing all the time. Looking back in later years on his younger self, he stressed the importance to a developing writer of not rushing too quickly into print – 'I was well aware that I had to wait'.[2] He also described what he was waiting for: 'The first requirements [of a writer] are (a) discovery of as yet unrecognized essentials, and (b) a firm knowledge of one's understanding and one's incomprehension.' Many of his papers from this time of discovery and self-analysis still survive, and were published posthumously by Christopher Wintle in *Music and Psychology: Vienna to London 1939-52*.[3] What follows here serves as something of a companion to that volume, which is recommended to readers interested in reading more of the genesis of Keller's unique blend of music and psychology, and his immediate response to his enforced change of language and culture.

When Keller finally left the Isle of Man on 23 March 1941, just after his 22nd birthday, he travelled straight to Bowness to join his mother, sister, nieces, aunt and cousin at Glebe House. Glebe House was not small, but with only three bedrooms it was not really big enough for so many people. 'There was no room for Hans,' remembers Inge; 'I can't remember where he slept.'[4] Keller's niece Ena remembers there being a boarding house behind Glebe House, and she thinks Hans moved into it not long after his release.[5] Grete Keller remained in Glebe House until the end of the war (at which point she acquired the house next door to the Franeys in Herne Hill), but the rest of the family was more mobile. Roy Franey was called up into the army as a medical officer, so Mowgli would sometimes go to London to meet him on leave. Uncle Hans and his partner stayed in London, and Inge and Paula Kompfner returned to live in Herne Hill in February 1942, to be nearer medical facilities after Paula had had a heart attack. Keller seems to have remained mostly in Bowness until the end of 1943. There he played quartets with Oscar Adler (who was living in Ambleside) and prepared for his LRAM examination, which he passed in April of that year. By the beginning of 1944, however, he was back in London, thoroughly immersed in psychoanalytical research.[6]

Although Freud is not mentioned at all in Keller's letters from internment, there is a clear difference between the more general philosophical and sociological concerns of his pre-internment writings, and his intense study of psychoanalytic theory afterwards. After his release he made contact with several eminent British psychoanalysts, including J. C. Flugel of University College, London, founder of the British Psychoanalytical Society, and John Rickman, co-founder with Ernest Jones of the Institute of Psychoanalysis in London, and editor of the British Journal of Medical Psychology (which was to publish Keller's first major article). Keller also knew Willi Hoffer of the Vienna Psychoanalytical Society, one of several of Freud's circle who fled to London in 1938. Though Hoffer was not himself interned in Britain, he probably knew colleagues who were, and it is more than likely that Keller's keen interest in psychoanalysis was stimulated by encounters with émigré analysts in the camps. Hoffer was considerably impressed by Keller, whose knowledge of psychoanalytic literature he later described as 'unequalled'.[7] He arranged for Keller to be admitted to the library of the Institute of Psychoanalysis, and even sent to him a musical schizophrenic patient of his, on whom Keller attempted a 'musico-psychological treatment'.[8]

But the most significant of Keller's many mentors in the field of psychology at this time was Margaret Phillips. Ironically, she was not a psychoanalyst, but an educationalist with strong interests in social psychology; when Keller first encountered her she was a lecturer in education at Stockwell College in Torquay, and shortly afterwards she became Principal of Borthwick Training College in south London, one of several Emergency Teacher Training Colleges set up in the wake of the 1944 Education Act to meet the anticipated post-war shortage of teachers.[9] She had published her first book, *The Education of the*

Emotions, in 1937, and during the war she embarked on a long study of the psychology of social groups. As she later explained, the impetus for this study came from the widespread disruption in society that followed the outbreak of the war.

> The mass evacuation of women and children and the direction of much of the population to the defence services and to the war industries meant that many of the groupings in which people's lives were normally lived – family and neighbourhood, school and church, working and leisure-time groups – were violently disrupted. There followed first a period of social chaos and deprivation painful to experience or to witness and then a movement both spontaneous and sponsored – in the villages and country towns, the new factories, the camps, aerodromes and wardens' posts – towards new groupings which might to some extent replace the old.
>
> Here was an opportunity for a social inquirer of much the same kind as the physical and mental damage of wartime offered to medicine. This burgeoning of new groups might not recur: now was the moment to observe their formation and development as and where circumstances allowed.[10]

Her method in both this study and her previous one on emotional development was to assemble a large amount of primary material by means of questionnaires, diaries and interviews (she cites some 275 contributors to her first book), which she interpreted in the light of different psychological theories. Phillips generally found her contributors from among her own acquaintance: 'Since much more was involved than the answering of a formal questionnaire, it was only possible to approach those on whose time I had either a personal or a professional claim, i.e. friends and pupils, the latter mainly teachers in training. Friends produced a third group, their own friends, valuable as giving me a greater variety of type of contributor than I should otherwise have secured.'[11] And this was how Keller first became aware of her work, when a mutual friend passed to him Phillips's questionnaire on social groups towards the end of 1942.

Although, as Keller told Phillips, 'I have not had very much experience with groups, nor have I ever directed my attention in more than a superficial way to the problems which this subject offers',[12] he seized on her study with alacrity. He replied to her questionnaire immediately and in enormous detail, sending her 26 closely typed pages. He took as his subjects two very different groups, '(a) the population of an internment camp in which I resided for several months [this is clearly Mooragh Camp], and (b) a string quartet of which I have been a member for several years.'[13]

Keller's response is interesting for more than one reason. At first sight, it seems paradoxical that such a passionate individualist as he was later to prove himself to be should have found the study of social groups so compelling. He later described 'collective life' in the most unflattering terms ('the seamy side of human existence'), and he fought hard throughout his own life to avoid becoming a comfortable insider anywhere:

> The evil, that is to say, is collectivity as we know it and accept it, with effective power on the one hand and the happy abrogation of individual judgement on the other ... The ultimate value is the independence of individual conscience, while the ultimate vice is its cession, capitulation, loving surrender, arrested development, collective envelopment. There is no collective wisdom: there is only unacknowledged, collective stupidity. Man has lived for quite some time now and still hasn't discovered, once and for all, that a group doesn't think.[14]

Keller's eager response to Phillips is also interesting because what he produced was so completely at variance with Phillips's intentions. Her original (very open-ended) questionnaire made it clear that what she was looking for were empirical observations of the day-to-day workings of a group:

METHOD PROPOSED

> The study of particular groups over a period of time either by members of the group or by observers in close contact with it. Where possible it is suggested that a diary should be kept, and notes written up whenever developments occur. It is likely that a study of the same group by two or more members (observers) independently would yield good results.[15]

Keller provided very little in the way of actual observational details – for example, to one question about the common pattern of life within the internment camp and whether it contributed to group unity, he simply replied, 'This can be imagined without illustrations or deductions.' Instead, he chose to concentrate more on applying Freudian theory to his experiences. This, for example, is his response to a question about leadership in the camp:

> For those members of the community (a considerable percentage) for whom the camp leader, and often the Officer in charge of the camp, appeared to be a father surrogate, there was thus given a very powerful connective element, of course with its negative accompaniments of jealousy and rivalry ... This whole state of affairs was splendidly illustrated by the fact that in the internment camp in which I stayed at first, the (refugee) supervisor of the camp had the generally chosen

name 'camp-father', whilst the house-leaders (who were often members of the camp's parliament) were distinguished by the name 'house-fathers'.

These numerous fathers owed their position, I mean their father-position, to a number of psychological conditions: (i) the general tendency of individuals to regard their group as a family, and to find a loving and advising father for it; (ii) the fact that the majority of internees were jews, and therefore had often a very strong ... family sense, which suddenly, through the internment, had been robbed of the possibility of direct satisfaction; (iii) the fact that, [being in] a situation of distress, ... regression to earlier stages of development, when ... a father had been much more of a necessity, took place as a matter of course; (iv) the aptness of many individuals, when greatly in need of a father and at the same time unable to get one after the pattern of their own father imago, to identify themselves with the father and thus to compensate for the absence of the father with the fact of being one ... many of the 'sons' wanted to become fathers themselves.

The fact that no females were within the community facilitated the father-constructions ... in consequence of psychic energy flowing along a single channel, which otherwise partly could have been distributed along several heterosexual lines.

There was to be noticed, however, also an intense opposition against the father-terminology; this opposition eventually, in the second camp in which I resided (composed to a considerable part of members of the first camp, and as far as I know, of other camps which also used the father-nomenclature), gained the upper hand by abolishing the father-designations; the former camp-father was termed Supervisor, and the house-fathers changed into house-leaders. ... Supervisors and house-leaders, when once dispossessed of their intimate names, would encounter perhaps less opposition than formerly. ...

And this was his response to a question about common internal grievances in the camp:

During the whole period in which I had opportunity to witness the camp life a 'release obsession', i.e. a desire after release which was much more intense than it would have been if emanating only from personal rational considerations, made itself felt among almost all the members of the camp, including myself.

As you know, psychologists have tried very hard to explain the problem, the different aspects of which are (often alternatively) called 'collective emotion', 'herd instinct' (Trotter), 'mutual suggestion of individuals' (le Bon), 'emotional contagion', 'mass-hypnosis', 'mass-suggestion' etc., etc., etc., and there has been a great row going on: you will perhaps remember, for instance, that McDougall's principle of direct induction of emotion by way of the primitive sympathetic response, by which he tries to explain the intensified emotional reactions of crowds, has been brushed aside by Freud and has been emphatically re-stated by McDougall. I cannot allow myself to be so arrogant as to give my opinion in reference to this hot dispute, which has been raging even within the sphere of hormic psychology (of which Freud could be considered a ¾ member), because my scarce and incomplete observation of the phenomena give me no right to do so. I have always felt this problem to be a very burning one, and have followed with keen curiosity the development its explanations took from the New Nancy School up to the post-Freudian analysts including Brill and Jones, with the radical 'transference' solutions which one of the latter, I forget who, has offered. ...

Now this [release] obsession took possession of the group-members in a varying degree, but it was nowise discernible what exactly was the reason for this very marked variability, and, as far as a few members were concerned, even for the total absence of the obsession. Having been myself a victim of it, yet fully aware – even during the period of its actual operativeness – of its irrational character, I attempted to study it in myself and in others ... [but] I very much doubt whether any light can be thrown on the mechanisms of processes of this sort, except with the help of psycho-analytic technique, which I had not at my disposal.

The importance, however, of this collective depressive state with reference to your points I & II [the unity or otherwise of the group] is undeniable, for it helped to bring about strong internal emotional unity. That a group the members of which suffer from the same complaint will often for that reason exhibit the achievement of a greater degree of unity than the same group would display without the collective pain is not psychological news, and therefore I need not long detain you at this aspect of the obsession. I want only to remind you in addition that the process of rationalization was facilitated through the obsession being collective, because the individual felt that ... the behaviour of the others sanctioned his own attitude ... Noting all this we yet must not overlook the fact that a collective suffering, though doing so much for emotional unity, does also work – to be sure, in an indirect way – in the opposite direction, though not with the same intensity, indeed, often only to a very small degree. In the present case, however, this second aspect (which brings us to the negative side of your points I & II) showed quite remarkable significance. One of the effects of the obsession being a general tendency towards psychic inertia, indolence and indifference towards everyday life and everyday duties, this general emotional state could not fail to affect in an unfavourable way the conduct of some individuals in respect to others, and to the rest of the group. I say 'of some individuals' because many of the campmembers countermined successfully the danger which, as they realized in time, threatened from the endo-psychic side, and though they could not suppress fully their depression, they at least succeeded in frustrating much of the evil effects which the tendency towards indifference, if it would not have been perpetually checked, would have brought about. In this way even part of the negative aspect showed itself as causative factor for the positive aspect, because the intra-individual countermeasures at least in some cases, did not stop at equalization (or less than that), but progressed towards over-compensation: towards special interest in group life and group duties.

A question about the effect on group unity of 'differences of age, sex, class, temperament, race or nationality among members' stimulated a particularly long response from Keller, in which he described the frustration caused by the absence of women (which 'showed itself in an over-accentuation of the individual's past sexual experiences – especially the older members of the group were prone to narrate to the younger ones sexual events from their past'); the 'Eonistic tendencies (transvestism)' of those who took the female roles in camp shows ('The fact that some of the audience enjoyed the male female much more than they would have enjoyed a she-player would be the object of an interesting investigation'); the instances of tension between different classes ('I must say that this factor has played a greater role than I would have expected under such exceptional circumstances'); the lack of significant differences of nationality (diverting such tensions to distinctions like that between 'an individual who for the most part of his life had lived in England and one who only recently had fled from Germany'); and the difficulty of abstracting differences of age 'from other interrelated conditions', as in this example:

> A middle-aged man, by profession a professor of mathematics, gathered around himself a number of younger individuals, mostly artists, and between them and him there developed intense intellectual intercourse. Upon observation of this little group-life, I can state with a high degree of certainty that he could be considered as being homosexual, or rather bi-sexual, in the wider meaning of the term. Father-impulses played a great role in his conduct also, of course, but there was a great difference between the attachment he formed for the younger ones and that

which other 'fathers' exhibited. He obviously seemed to be spiritually in love with his protégés. I personally, as far as I knew him, did not like him very much, but this must not prevent me from saying that his contribution, and the contribution of others who were like him, to unity between campmembers, those who were his 'sons' as well as those who indirectly benefited through coming into contact with the high intellectual and moral standard which he often succeeded to arouse in his protégés, was certainly considerable. The negative side of the picture consisted mainly in the fact that he was extremely jealous of any other middle-aged man who tried to form friendships with younger individuals of his group.

This anecdote apart, there are relatively few factual observations in Keller's long letter. Instead, theory predominates throughout – and the last nine pages are entirely taken up with an extended theoretical critique of Phillips's project. As Christopher Wintle has observed, the comparison of Phillips's questionnaire with Keller's response brings together the two cultural approaches Keller describes in his 1939 essay 'An Emigrant Searches for England': 'by drawing up categories for observation, Margaret Phillips works in the English way, from the "outside in"; by probing the internal dynamics of the group, Keller works in the Continental way, from the "inside out".'[16]

And yet, despite their radically different approaches – and their radically different personalities, age and background – Keller and Phillips came to form a strong working partnership over the next three years. Since Phillips was living in Cornwall and Keller in the Lake District, they did not actually meet until August 1943, and only sporadically thereafter, so their acquaintance was conducted primarily by letter for some time. At first they simply exchanged ideas and discussed psychological matters of mutual interest (including the problems of the friend who had introduced them). In terms which were both intense and bantering in turn, they also enjoyed energetic debates about the validity of their respective methods – Keller having followed up his response to Phillips's questionnaire by sending her one of his own:

> I believe that Miss Marle has told you that I am working on a study of the psychology of modesty and shame; if I understood her correctly, you would be prepared to give me some information about this subject in return for the present letter.

The aims of Keller's study, as he stated them, were exhaustively broad. As well as studying shame and modesty in sexual and social contexts 'along the lines proposed by Flugel in his *Psychology of Clothes*', he proposed also to examine 'the appearance of shame-modesty processes in mythology, religion, poetry, art and perhaps even in music (Brahms' later works)'.[17] His questionnaire to Phillips, however, concentrated on the more personal aspects of the phenomenon, with questions like 'Have you ever had, as a child, the wish to be a boy?', 'Give details of your sexual enlightenment', 'Do you remember at what age you began to feel shame in relation to the excretory functions?', 'Have you ever, during your adolescence, been conscious of slight homosexual tendencies?', 'Do you blush easily?', and so on.

He asked for the 'utmost sincerity and shamelessness' in her response, and she replied with a frankness impressive in a single woman born in the nineteenth century (she was then about 50), writing to a man half her age whom she had never met. This led to a long debate on the value of such enquiries. 'What [do you] want to know this for?' Phillips wondered:

> Is there really anything to find out which Havelock Ellis did not find out? And look what a humourless person Havelock Ellis turned out to be – after all that was said about his wisdom … and what a mess [he and his wife] made of their marriage … Why do I feel all this to be so trivial and unreal? Because you can't isolate sex like that from a total state of mind. Stephen Spender said – just when his wife had left him and he was thinking the whole thing out – keep sex inside love and love inside the world. And that's sense. But this is nonsense.[18]

Keller's notes of the time show that he had indeed read Havelock Ellis thoroughly, and fragmentary drafts survive of essays with titles like 'An Attempt to Contribute to the Psychology of Pudency' and 'Some Comments on the Causes and Effects of Shame and Shyness'. By 1944, however, he had abandoned this project and formally joined Phillips in her work on social groups. Together they worked on a joint book, which was provisionally entitled *The Psychology of Social Unity*. The Keller Archive contains a considerable amount of material from this project, showing that it occupied a major proportion of Keller's time during 1944 and 1945. Several of their individual case studies survive, examining groups as diverse as an 'ATS billet', a 'Factory Group (Surgical Instruments)' and 'Miss Everness' Bridge Party'. Margaret Phillips's search for source material from among her own acquaintance led to a certain predominance of groups connected with education, such as a 'Group of 5 Students at a Training College', the 'WEA Committee, Mill Hill and Edgware Branch', an RAF training school, and the staff of Anna Freud's nursery (though this last may well have been a contact of Keller's through Willi Hoffer).[19]

It seems from the many draft outlines for the book that Keller's role was to provide a psychoanalytical commentary on Margaret Phillips's interpretation of this material. Each of her chapters was to be followed by one of Keller's reviewing the same material from a Freudian perspective. Working in this way, Keller thought, would mean that 'the resulting treatment of evidence will perhaps be marked by a greater degree of realism than would be possible without that kind of collaboration. The occasions on which conclusions compatible with each other were arrived at by the [different] investigators were numerous.'[20] Several of Keller's commentaries survive in draft, under titles like 'From Community to Association', 'Evolution of the Family Pattern', 'Uniting and Disrupting Factors in the Group', and 'From Intra-familial to Extra-familial Group Life'. In addition, Keller wrote some chapters of theoretical exposition, such as 'Freudian Theory of the Group', 'Psychoanalytic (Freudian) Group Theory and Its Critics', and 'Object-cathexes in Group-relations'.[21]

Margaret Phillips evidently valued Keller's work highly, despite the way in which she often countered his earnest Freudianism with a rather more sceptical approach, accusing him at times of 'Freudian fundamentalism':

> Even assuming Freud as the greatest genius ever, surely he need not have discovered the whole truth for all time? Especially in view of the number of corrections he made in his own system while he was alive? Have you ever thought where your own passion for Freud has come from? ... If not I begin to think you had better...[22]

She urged him not only towards a broader approach, but also towards a more original one:

> The fruitful thinking & writing now is being done not by Freudian fundamentalists but by people who are moving on from Freud into new territory, modifying Freud as the theory comes into contact with new phenomena. Whereas – and here we come again to the question of our respective methods – when you are dealing with this group material your urge is not to find anything new in it but just to show that however much it dresses itself up it is really all the same old stuff and to leave the bits for the birds. I go into these enquiries expecting to learn something from them. What you will have learnt, I gather, is just how right you are already (or rather how right Freud is!). Should you be accused of having said something original or of having found something out, you would indignantly repudiate it ... for fear that anyone but Freud should get any credit.[23]

This was evidently an old argument between them, and a letter from Keller written two months previously shows that he was well aware of the criticism and able to anticipate it with amusing irony:

I decline to accept any praise for interpretations which may be my own as far as their actual formulation is concerned because I am fully convinced that all available praise for such analyses should centre round psycho-analysis and its founder. ... If your comment on this [is] that I am displacing narcissism on to psycho-analysis and that I have introjected the latter partially, I can only say that if I have done so I have done so in accordance with the reality-principle – a reply which in itself could be taken to justify your comment.[24]

Although his interests were later to broaden ('chewing the Freudian cud began to bore the pants off me'),[25] the importance he placed on Freud's insights did not diminish. Writing thirty years later, he evidently still felt the same:

I came to the definite conclusion that what, outside analysis, are known as the psychoanalytic dogmata, are in fact a single man's discoveries of world-shaking truths (shaking the mental world, that is): the dynamic unconscious, repression (*Verdrängung*) in the strictly analytic sense, infantile sexuality and its consequences, the Oedipus complex (at least in Western civilisations), and the validity of free-association technique.[26]

~

The years between his release from internment and the end of the war were a period of intense internal exploration and self-examination for Keller. Prevented by intermittent health problems and his status as an 'alien' from embarking on a career,[27] and without too many financial worries,[28] his wartime life was primarily one of reading and writing, punctuated by violin-practice and occasional chamber music concerts with Oscar Adler and, later, Otto Hüttenbach. This was also the time when he undertook a course of self-analysis, which he often said in later life had been crucial to helping him understand himself and channel his considerable mental energy – though it might be said that his association at the same time with Margaret Phillips was just as important.

I consulted a close collaborator of Freud's [Willi Hoffer], who told me how much a training analysis would cost me. Well, that was out of the question. I subsequently decided to analyse myself. Which I did, and I showed that close collaborator of Freud's the results – after a time, of course – and he told me that in some respects I got less deep than hetero-analysis, but in other respects I got deeper. So he was intensely interested. And I did this for five years, self-analysis, every day one hour. I can strongly recommend it. ... You have to have the personality for it. The form it took was that I sat down every day for an hour, with a pencil, and wrote free-associations: whatever came into my mind. My knowledge of psychoanalysis proved a grave obstacle, because I always started interpreting instead of letting it out. So that obstacle amounted to a defence against my unconscious. Once I had firmly decided, however, not to interpret but just to let it flow, it went much better. Five years of it – changed my life. At the end of it I knew far better who I was, and I could distribute my psychic energies far more economically. So I strongly recommend this approach to a suitable personality. Freud himself did nothing but self-analysis – that's how he made his major discoveries.[29]

Keller's cousin Inge has expressed some surprise at the idea that it was lack of money that prevented Keller from formally training as an analyst – 'Is that what he said? Money?'.[30] His friend Donald Mitchell is also sceptical:

If for Hans there were to be any analysis at all, it would have had to be self-analysis. Can anyone imagine him submitting himself to – for – analysis? I can't. He was the most independent person I've ever met, and I cannot see how anyone so resistant to submission could ever have managed a relationship with an analyst.[31]

It is also not clear why Keller never attended a university, as he had originally intended (and as Margaret Phillips at least was urging him to do – 'If you want to live by psychology you have to have either a medical or a psychological degree'),[32] but again there are hints that the real reason was not financial. Writing to Keller about 'the problem of you & a degree', Phillips told him 'I do sympathise about the boringness for you of life with students (though it is a brand of boredom which you will inevitably I am afraid come in for, one way or another, all through life).'[33] Keller's own letters on this subject have not survived, but something of his feelings on the matter might be gleaned from a letter he wrote over a decade later to the musical analyst Rudolf Reti. Reti had written enthusiastically to Keller when he first became aware of Keller's 'functional analysis' of music, hailing him as a 'kindred mind' and suggesting that they and other like-minded musicians should 'unite as a "group"'.[34] The idea was far from appealing to Keller:

If I don't take up your idea of a group it is simply for reasons of personal character: emotionally I am quite gregarious, but intellectually I am basically a recluse who does not profit by discussion – except more or less accidentally, e.g. when teaching. This does not mean that I deem myself cleverer than everybody else, but when somebody has something important to say and is able to say it clearly, he will write it (as you have done) and I will read it and profit by it or not, as the case may be. Whenever I am drawn into a discussion, I find that from my own point of view it is a waste of time.

Nor, frankly, do I think that one could 'nourish compositional movements' in any essential way: if they aren't nourished by individual creative needs, the food won't be much good anyway. But this is a minor point.

Please do not think that I regard your idea as worthless; only, I am not the man for it, and what you call my 'dynamic approach' only functions when it serves individual expression. In a group, moreover, one has, inevitably, to make intellectual or artistic concessions – of which, again, I am characterologically incapable. I do hope you understand.[35]

The return of peace in 1945, and the whole family's decision to stay in Britain and apply for naturalisation, meant that the question of Keller's future became more pressing. His 1945 diary shows that he was playing quite a lot of music by then, principally with Adler, Hüttenbach, Berend and Paul Hamburger (all fellow émigrés – it appears that Keller never really broke into the English musical scene as a violinist), but it is not clear how productive this was financially. Although he was very involved with Phillips' social groups work, publication of their book still seemed a long way off, and Keller began to explore the possibility of earning some money by publishing some of his other writings. He approached various magazines and journals to see if they would be interested in articles, stories and aphorisms on psychological themes – this, for example, was what he wrote to the editor of *Onward* in September 1945:

Dear Sir,

Kindly let me know whether any of the following articles would interest you.

Metaphysics and Psycho-analysis.
Musical Composition and Dream Formation.
Psycho-analysis and Religion.
Artistic Resistances Against Psycho-analysis.
Philosophical Resistances Against Psycho-analysis.
An Ethical Implication of Psycho-analysis.

Should you feel inclined to consider any of these, please let me know about the desired length of articles you require.[36]

Many such articles written around this time survive in manuscript,[37] under titles like 'Religion: the Psycho-analytic Standpoint', 'War, Peace and Psychology', 'Peace and Pessimism', 'Sexual Hesitancies', 'The Need for Pets', and 'Self-knowledge'. They are generally short pieces written in a relatively popular style (sometimes under the pseudonym 'A Psychological Observer'), and they were intended for journals like *The Spectator, The Psychologist, Horizon, New Statesman and Nation, The Fortnightly*, and *Leader*. Short stories like 'Appointment with Boredom', 'Mens Sana in what?', 'Freedom from Freedom' and 'A short story without point', were sent to publications like *New Writing* and *The Writer*. Some of these were entered for various writing competitions, such as 'Ladies and gentle males...', an unsuccessful entry in a BBC competition for variety scripts.

In July 1945, Keller succeeded in having a set of aphorisms ('On Maturity...') accepted by *The Psychologist*; his letter on the subject 'What Shall We Do With Hitler?' was printed in the *Evening Standard* in April ('Subject him and as many of his collaborators and followers as possible to extensive and intensive psychological research ...'); and one of his short stories appeared in the magazine *Kite* in December.[38] His first substantial article to be published was 'Male Psychology', which was written in 1944 and published in *The British Journal of Medical Psychology* two years later.[39] He and Phillips also made a few joint forays outside their specific work on their book: in September 1945, for example, they gave a presentation of some of their ideas to the British Psychological Society, and in early 1946 they produced a long report on the 'Psychology and Ethics of School Staff Groups'.[40]

~

With hindsight, what is most striking about Keller's writing up to the end of 1945 is that almost none of it is about music. It is as though he lived two separate lives, thinking with two separate minds. On the one hand he was a violinist and violist, taking his LRAM, studying music theory, playing in Fritz Berend's orchestra and in Adler's and Hüttenbach's quartets. On the other, he was obsessed with psychoanalysis, reading in the Institute's library, corresponding with its members, and working busily with Margaret Phillips. All his many writings, despite the variety of different forms with which he experimented (including aphorisms, short stories, a play and even the odd poem) sprang solely from the psychologist side of him. This sometimes gives a rather claustrophobic feel to the writing, especially in the fiction, where it can seem as though Keller is reducing the variety of human behaviour to a study of textbook types.

Whether Keller ever felt at that time that he was writing with only half of himself is not known. But Margaret Phillips certainly felt that something was missing. She was evidently a fairly frequent critic of Keller's style of writing, and what she described as 'my third attack on your literary style' (made when they had still not yet met) makes interesting reading:

> What I want to ask you is: have you in the course of your self-analysis shed any light on the question of when you use each of your styles, and why? It is certainly not a matter of difficulty with English, because your other style is potentially a beautiful one, as I have said before. That style seems to me like the quality of your thinking when your whole personality is involved and not merely your intellect; then it is like the quality of Dr Adler's playing; properly speaking one would not speak of a style at all; it merely says what it has to say; the communication reaches one directly without the apparent intervention of an instrument or a person or a technique. So another way of putting the question is; when is the whole of your personality behind what you want to say and when only your intellect? And yet that does not represent it either. Better say; what are the occasions on which you retreat to a pillbox and snipe at the enemy with words; which are those on which you exude clouds of sepia-coloured words into the water? And what part does formal logic play in these tactics?[41]

Writing many years later, Keller described the psychological and musical sides of himself as not merely separate, but operating at different levels of his being:

> My psychological interests have, in fact, always been overriding. Music is not an 'interest'; I'm a musician, and to suggest to a musician that he is interested in music makes as much sense as suggesting to you that you are interested in liquid, food, or sleep.[42]

Writing about music, rather than simply playing it, therefore felt to him like an activity bordering on the unnatural:

> There is no art that produces as much comfort for the mind feeling and thinking it, and as much discomfort for the mind thinking about it, as the so-called art of music. I say 'so-called', because it is questionable

whether music is an art at all; we call it one because we find it difficult to call it anything else. I should prefer to call it a mode of thought, and hence of life.[43]

Keller's almost total silence about music for the first 26 years of his life suggests that his later insistence on the distinct and separate nature of musical thought – and the way in which it operates according to laws which he described as 'the definable opposite' of those of conceptual thought[44] – was very much a product of his own early experience. It was to lead, in 1956, to his famous method of 'wordless functional analysis', in which he undertook to analyse music solely in its own terms: writing music about music.[45]

When Keller first tried to write about music in words – in a tiny handful of fragments written around 1942 – he did so only in psychological terms. Rather than approach the subject through the wealth of the repertoire he knew so intimately from his Viennese childhood, he treated 'music' as another psychoanalytic case study, in terms which were general rather than specific. Finding 'Holy Freud'[46] disappointingly unmusical, and stimulated by a remark of Hoffer's that no one else had written on this subject, Keller searched through the psychoanalytical literature for any possible references to music he could find.[47] 'It is unfortunate that Freud was almost totally unmusical,' he wrote in a draft of the opening of the first of a planned series of *Studies in the Psycho-analysis of Music*. 'Otherwise he would have been in a position not only to make the most essential contribution to the psychology of music, but also once more to prove many of his discoveries by the analysis of musical mental processes which, to the non-psychoanalytical observer, represent a bewildering picture of psychic phenomena largely isolated from the rest of mental life.' Keller's own attempts at the psychology of music (which are among his earliest surviving post-internment manuscripts) were intended to address this gap, but they were still written for psychologists rather than musicians to read. Writing in both German and English, under titles like 'Manifestations of the Primary Process in Musical Composition' and 'Dream-Work and Development in Sonata Form', he attempted to explain his sense of the singularity of musical processes by showing them as products of the unconscious mind.

These essays were all left incomplete, and his frustration at the failure of this attempt to define in words the nature of music convinced Keller that musical thought and conceptual thought were 'two mutually exclusive logics'. Defining the former in terms of the latter was bound to fail, he later thought, because of 'conceptual thought's fear of losing its grip, of giving in to the chaos of the unconscious, once the laws of conceptual thought are not only abandoned but positively replaced by their opposites. The fear is realistic, for music is the one art which … has actually rationalised the primary process [of the unconscious] with its displacements, condensations, representations through the opposite.'[48]

~

The moment when Keller stopped treating music as a 'branch of applied psychology'[49] and discovered other ways of writing about it, was no less than epiphanic. It gave him the opportunity to unite his 'two minds' as, with astonishing speed, he switched from psychology to music as the subject of his writing, and from playing to writing as the expression of his musicality.[50] By the end of 1946, the transformation was complete, and Keller was writing almost exclusively about music. His work for Margaret Phillips quickly dwindled and their book was shelved, as Keller concentrated on breaking into the burgeoning post-war musical scene.[51] The change had been triggered by a single evening in the summer of 1945: the night when Keller first heard Benjamin Britten's new opera *Peter Grimes*.

Keller said in later years that his presence at Sadler's Wells that night was a complete accident. Alan Blyth, after interviewing Keller for his book *Remembering Britten*, reports what happened as follows:

> Hans Keller first heard Britten's music by mistake. After the war he used to attend almost every performance of *Così fan tutte* given by Sadler's Wells Opera. One evening, instead of the overture to Mozart's opera, he found himself listening to something quite strange – it was *Peter Grimes*. He immediately regarded it as a masterpiece. From then on he determined that he would acquaint himself with as much of Britten's music as he could.[52]

If this recollection is accurate, Keller must have heard *Peter Grimes* during its first run in June-July 1945, when it was performed alongside *Così fan tutte* (as well as *La Bohème, Madame Butterfly, Rigoletto* and *The Bartered Bride*).[53] His 1945 diary marks all the various performances of each opera, with *Così fan tutte* emphasised on several occasions by a box around the title, presumably to indicate Keller's intention to attend. It is not clear on which night Keller actually heard *Peter Grimes*, but it might have been 21 July, the last night of the run, which is the only one of its performances not noted in his diary. On this date Keller had marked instead a concert (Mozart's Clarinet Concerto) at Central Hall. This apparently took place at 4.30 in the afternoon, so he could conceivably have gone on to Sadler's Wells afterwards. The idea of his having heard the opera only once during its first run might be supported by the fact that it was its second staging (the following February)[54] rather than its first which released Keller's flood of writing on Britten. By that time, Keller had clearly been giving Britten some thought, had already begun to try his hand as a music critic, and was in a position to review the opera for two different publications.[55]

What attracted Keller so much to *Peter Grimes* was the way in which it opened up to him new ways of applying his psychoanalytical knowledge to music. First, it presented him with a drama of considerable psychological interest, set by a composer of remarkable insight in this direction. Up to this point, Keller had been seeking a way into the psychology of music through sonata form – drawing parallels, for example, between the way in which the development section of a sonata transforms the material of the exposition, and the way in which a dream transforms the material it draws from everyday life. Such abstract general speculation (he rarely mentioned specific works) had borne little fruit. Close analysis of the libretto of *Peter Grimes*, however, gave Keller a way into thinking about Britten's setting, as he explained a couple of years later with the concept of 'applied music' (i.e. music which is attached to a drama, such as opera and film music):

> The psychology of music is the most difficult branch of applied psychology, but the psychology of what we might call applied (as distinct from absolute or pure) music offers a comparatively easy approach to the musico-psychologist. The reason, therefore, is clear. Whereas in pure music we encounter processes which, at any rate on the surface, bear little relation to such mental phenomena as have already been elucidated by psychological analysis, the processes that make up applied music, though in themselves as mysterious psychologically as those of pure music, are at least definitely related to extra-musical mental processes that have already been successfully subjected to scientific research.[56]

The result was *Three Psycho-analytic Notes on 'Peter Grimes'*.[57] Outside his work with Margaret Phillips, this was one of Keller's most substantial essays so far, consisting of some 50 pages of typescript (of which the first seven are unfortunately lost). He never published it (and there is no evidence of his trying to do so), but he thought highly enough of it to consider sending it to the composer.[58] The *Three Notes* examine in turn 'Grimes's Character' (which Keller diagnoses as 'anal'), 'Grimes and His Mother' (in relation to Ellen, the 'inter-uterine phantasy', and the sea), and 'Grimes and His Father' (in relation to Balstrode, and also the two apprentices in the 'reversal of generations phantasy').

In actual content, the *Three Notes* could be seen to represent the last of Keller's purely psychoanalytical work, rather than the beginning of a new musico-psychological fusion; for it is to Montagu Slater's libretto that Keller here addresses himself – to the extent to which the music is almost entirely excluded.[59] Indeed, in the only place where he makes a specific musical point (when he notes the 'indication of Peter's unalterable fate' by the dominant seventh on D in Act II, Scene 2, and its possible link with the 'mother'), Keller suddenly becomes noticeably more tentative, and remarks that 'my whole emotional approach to music is not such as to make extra-musical associations particularly easy for me'.

Nevertheless, whether he was yet able to express it or not, it was Britten's music, and not just the story, that had made such a profound impression on Keller, as his subsequent writings confirm. He really did 'acquaint himself with as much of Britten's music as he could' and, as Christopher Wintle has remarked, 'devoted himself with extraordinary energy and single-mindedness to propagating the composer and his music'.[60] The idea of writing about the psychology of music through 'applied music' (which *Peter Grimes* had inspired) Keller also pursued with remarkable vigour, and it is this that led to his huge output of film-music criticism during the next few years – a genre of writing which he did much to create, beginning with his pamphlet *The Need for Competent Film Music Criticism* in 1947.[61] It seems that Keller needed to begin his life as a musical writer away from his natural repertoire, so his early articles are almost all concerned with Benjamin Britten or film music. The *Peter Grimes* experience did provide one crucial link with the past, however, in the way in which Britten seems to have cast new light for Keller on the music of Mozart – as will be seen.

The second new way of writing about music which his encounter with Britten opened up to Keller also had a large extra-musical dimension, and drew particularly on the sociological aspect of his groups work with Margaret Phillips. Keller was intrigued by the response of critics and audiences to Britten's music. In particular, his attention was caught by the paradox of a composer who was both unusually popular – he thought that 'Britten's popularity needs a special explanation'[62] – and also the object of what he thought was unjustly harsh criticism. He was further struck by the fact that Britten's critics continually singled out 'the most immediately striking of his musical endowments and attainments'[63] for special denigration, and that English critics were more negative than continental ones.

Criticism of critics, analysis of their motivation, the reception of music, and audiences' projections were important themes in Keller's writing for the rest of his life. Related to these were issues of musical nationality – or perceived nationality – which naturally featured in Keller's writing about Britten in the 1940s. One such idea about Britten and 'Englishness' which drew particularly on his wartime work with Phillips was 'group self-contempt'. This phenomenon he had first encountered 'in the diary of an Auxiliary Fire Brigade's group life during the war', and subsequently in many other groups – always those 'whose members are, or regard themselves as being, in some way persecuted by members of other groups which occupy an authoritative position'.[64]

> Since the dominated group inevitably feels the dominating group to be *in loco parentis*, the former's members project part of what might loosely be called their common superego on to the dominating group, with the result that they turn part of the aggression which they would but can't release towards the dominating group back against their own group.[65]

Among the many examples Keller cited were Jewish antisemitism, female misogynism (including prostitutes' contempt of their own profession, a subject on which he conducted some research in 1945), and – noting that 'Britten's work meets with far more understanding and far less resistance abroad than in his own country' – 'British anti-Brittenism', which was, he submitted,

> a prominent aspect of British musical group self-contempt, though in this case the dominating group which, together with the contempt it displays ('Das Land ohne Musik'), serves as a model for the group-self-contemptuous attitude, has its centre – the bulk of the Austro-German tradition's exponents and followers – in the past and only its periphery – the Adornos – in the present.[66]

One particular event which interested Keller was the première of Britten's *Spring Symphony* in 1949, the reactions to which showed clearly the psychological importance to English musicians of the question of symphonic form. It was, he thought, the continental symphonic tradition which was the primary cause of British musical inferiority feelings. Quoting Wilfred Mellers's description of Elgar's symphonies as 'the culmination of a symphonic tradition that had never happened', Keller went on to guess that 'group self-contempt had played an active part in Elgar's musico-mental make-up':

> Elgar's deep-seated wish for, and unconscious fantasies of, a symphonic tradition whose factual absence we have recognised as one of the chief causes of group self-contempt, must in that case have been so powerful that he embarked upon the task of crowning, and thus proving the existence of, this non-existent British symphonic tradition: his was, if I may say so, a supremely successful flight into reality. His

genius enabled him to realise what early psychoanalysis called the infantile 'omnipotence of thought' to an extreme degree that even the most imaginative critic would have been unable to foresee. The British symphonic tradition became, a posteriori, so much of a reality that we can say for certain that Wilfrid Mellers would have taken its existence for granted if he hadn't known it wasn't there.[67]

This question was a very topical one in the years immediately after the Second World War, when British enthusiasm for symphonic form was very evident. Even the new CEMA-educated popular audience wanted to hear symphonies,[68] while the newborn festivals and other arts organisations of the post-war revival commissioned symphony after symphony from British composers. It was a form in which British composers were only too happy to write: for example, the new Cheltenham Festival of British Contemporary Music commissioned 25 symphonies from British composers in the first two decades after the war, but those same composers during the same period wrote nearly five times that number.[69]

The third way in which *Peter Grimes* helped Keller apply his psychological knowledge to music – and the one which has its roots most deeply in Keller's own feelings and musical perceptions – lies in his acute observation of individual creative character. We know from the reference to 'shame-modesty processes' in Brahms which appears in one of Keller's earliest letters to Margaret Phillips that this was an element of his thought which pre-dated *Peter Grimes*. Indeed it also pre-dated Margaret Phillips' role as midwife to so much of Keller's psychological thinking. But it remained unexplored until Keller's encounter with the particular creative character of Benjamin Britten.

At the end of the *Three Psycho-analytical Notes on 'Peter Grimes'* there is a very brief reference to Britten's 'admirably productive empathy regarding such phenomena as need for punishment, nemesism, rebirth- and death-phantasies', which, Keller says, impressed itself upon him again when he heard the 'deeply conceived, and, accordingly, deeply moving, settings of *The Holy Sonnets of John Donne*' (given their premiere by Britten and Pears at the Wigmore Hall in November 1945). It seems that it was Britten's 'empathy' which was the part of the composer's character which so overwhelmed Keller when he heard *Peter Grimes* for the first time. As he subsequently sought out more of Britten's music, this same quality impressed itself upon him again and again:

> Empathy is a very predominant part of Britten. It seems to me that he has developed it, even measured against an artistic standard, to an unusual extent, and it is fascinating to observe its emergence in different fields, e.g. in that of Lieder accompaniment. A still more subtle expression of

it – so it seems to me – comes out when he accompanies Pears in his (Britten's) own compositions. For there he does not only play what he has composed, but also at the same time Pears' version of it.[70]

In this context, the fact that Keller first heard *Peter Grimes* when expecting to hear *Così fan tutte* is most significant. The parallel between Britten's 'empathy' and what he called Mozart's 'unsurpassed artistico-psychological insight'[71] was the first of many more parallels Keller identified between the two composers. It unlocked Keller's musico-psychological way of writing not only about Britten, a composer who was new to him, but also about Mozart, in whose music he was already soaked to the very bones.

The impact of hearing *Grimes* in the context of *Così fan tutte* was magnified for Keller by Peter Pears' performance in the title role, which seems to have impressed him almost as much as the work itself ('his Grimes is unsurpassable').[72] Pears was also singing the role of Ferrando in the Wells production of *Così fan tutte* that season, and it was in this that Keller first heard him.[73] This first encounter with Pears' voice had astounded Keller all the more because Pears was singing music about which Keller then thought England had nothing to teach him. Eleven bars were apparently enough to convince him he was wrong, and he returned to listen again and again. The impression stayed with him, and he recalled it for *Opera* magazine a few years later:

Somewhere in the Wells gallery, years ago. The Overture to *Così* has started. I am not yet a music critic; just a musician. I am lying on my back across three seats, with my mac as a pillow. I'm rather young and one production is as bad as another, so why should I see it? In any case the music will tell me more about the stage than the stage. As for singers, one is worse than another, particularly in England, particularly when you don't know it. So I haven't bought a programme. I wouldn't know the names, anyway. The opening trio is unfolding. The vocal triplets are pretty poor, but then they always are. Yet, do what I will, that tenor is not down to my decided expectations. Oh well, he'll soon make a mess of it all. Just wait for No. 3, the third trio with that marvellous start in, or from, the dominant, and the tenor's liberating opening in the tonic 'To my lady her fond lover such a banquet then will offer.' He won't sense the harmonic meaning of his entry. He won't get what is, comedy or no comedy, the heroic touch of the melody. He'll never recreate that jubilating tension in C major for which another composer would have needed one-and-a-half keys at the inside. He'll never ... but here, the third trio starts. It makes me, literally, sit up. The old Viennese axiom that apart from cellists the most unmusical people in the world are tenors vaporizes somewhere at the back of my mind. For once a singer who isn't a poor substitute for an instrumentalist! A voice of character which carries farther and deeper than any voice thrice as strong! A musician who knows, lives, what Mozart and he are doing, and who therefore knows how to define it. Within eleven bars, I have turned from a stern examiner into an admiring pupil. From now onwards the performance becomes – for me of all people – an impatient waiting for the tenor.[74]

Having gone to listen to Pears singing Ferrando (for probably the seventh time), Keller's experience of hearing him unexpectedly in this remarkable new opera must have been overwhelming. Pears also provided direct inspiration for Keller's *Three Notes* in a short *Radio Times* article he wrote to accompany the broadcast of *Peter Grimes* on the BBC Third Programme on 13 March 1946. Writing to the singer a few weeks later, Keller told him that the *Three Notes* 'can be regarded as a complement, on the psychological level, to what you expounded on the more sociological one',[75] and indeed on the front cover of Keller's manuscript there is a pencilled note of a possible fourth *Note* which was to discuss one of the points Pears made in his article.[76] Keller also specifically included Pears among the addressees of a 'Letter to the Authors of *Peter Grimes*' written to accompany his *Three Notes*, in which he described him as 'a reproductive genius of exceptional calibre, with a distinct accent on "productive"'.

With Pears' help, the parallel between Britten's creative character and that of Mozart became abundantly clear to Keller. It formed the subject of the very first of his essays on creative character, 'Britten and Mozart', in which Keller undertook to cross the barriers of nationality and history to show that 'for the first time Mozart, the universal musician who masters everything with a somnambulistic surefootedness and grace, has found a companion'. Written at about the same time as the *Three Psycho-analytical Notes on 'Peter Grimes'*, this essay represents a fundamental turning-point for Keller as a musical writer. If the *Three Notes* represent the last of his purely psychological work, 'Britten and Mozart' can be taken as the beginning of his new blend of music and psychology. It was also in this essay that Mozart became the first of Keller's 'own' repertoire to appear in his writing.

The description of Mozart's 'somnambulistic surefootedness and grace' reveals another significant encounter Keller had at precisely this time; it followed hard on the heels of his *Peter Grimes* epiphany and helped consolidate his new direction as a writer. In 1946 Alfred Einstein's book *Mozart: His Character, His Work* was published for the first time in Britain, providing Keller with a literary example of the sort of ideas on musical character that he was wanting to write about himself. The influence this book had on Keller is unmistakeable, and he was generous with his acknowledgements to Einstein. 'Britten and Mozart', when it appeared, was introduced as one of 'a number of diverse articles supplementary to Alfred Einstein's *Mozart – His Character, His Work*', and peppered with quotations from the book; Keller's next few articles on Mozart are also marked as belonging to 'a series of supplementary notes and articles' to Einstein's work.

Notwithstanding its eminent forebear, 'Britten and Mozart' still took two years to get into print.[77] But despite the series of rejections, the article caused something of a stir among the editors who read it, and they received Keller's future work with interest. Some, while turning it down, still took the trouble to send rather fuller reactions to Keller than their usual rejection slips. Cyril Connolly of *Horizon* read it 'with great interest' before 'regretfully' turning it down.[78] William McNaught of *The Musical Times* seemed to suspect he might be missing something significant, but found Keller's writing style too much of an obstacle:

> I don't like joining the wrong queue; but I must follow my opinion. I have respect for the observation, thought and critical faculty that produced the matter at the core of the article (is that wide and narrow enough?); but I find no merit in the way it is expressed. The use of language is awkward and often obscure in its junctions, implications and allusions.[79]

Geoffrey Sharp of the *Music Review*, on the other hand, took heated issue with the central theme of the article in a letter which is no longer extant, but which was apparently long and – according to Keller's reply – 'frank' and 'somewhat emotional'.[80] To judge by one of Sharp's later letters to Keller ('who is Benjamin Britten to merit such detailed investigation of his work??'),[81] it was the matter more than the manner of Keller's article which he disliked.

But despite their differing views on Britten, Geoffrey Sharp was intrigued by Keller, and it was he who gave Keller his first real break as a music critic. A few months after turning down 'Britten and Mozart', he accepted for publication Keller's first major musical article not on Britten or film music – 'Mozart and Boccherini'[82] – after which Keller joined his team of regular reviewers, writing for the journal every month from then on. The *Music Review* was very important to Keller: even after he had edited his own journal he still described it as 'home',[83] and he continued to send it some of his most important articles (such as his 'Unity of Contrasting Themes' articles in 1956),[84] remembering with gratitude the 'total freedom'[85] Sharp had given him in those early days (Britten excepted!) – which even extended to setting up a regular column for Keller to review film music. It was also through the pages of the *Music Review* that Keller met the person with whom he laid the last foundation stone of his writing, and with whom he was to make his name: Donald Mitchell.

~

In 1948, Keller turned twenty-nine. He was now writing regularly for the *Music Review*, and also for film publications like *Sight and Sound, Contemporary Cinema* and *Film Monthly Review*. The little magazine *Music Parade* began to print his writings regularly from the beginning of that year, and Keller was managing to place single articles in a variety of other publications with increasing ease. His efforts during the previous two years to establish himself as a music critic were paying off, and he could now say that 'I am depending entirely on my writing for my living'.[86]

One of those to whom he had sent 'Britten and Mozart' and who read it with interest was Erwin Stein. A former pupil of Schoenberg and close friend of Berg and Webern, Stein had been artistic advisor to their publisher, Universal Edition, until forced by the Anschluss to flee to London. He and his fellow émigré Ernst Roth then joined the staff of Boosey & Hawkes, who at that time were Britten's publishers. Stein became interested in Britten, and keen to help publicise his work. He sent Keller's article to Ernest Chapman, editor of Boosey & Hawkes's house journal, *Tempo*:

> I am enclosing a Number of 'Con Brio' and a letter of a Danish paper, also the article on Britten and Mozart which I mentioned. As to the last, I think it very interesting but in reading it again I have some doubts about the English. Do you think the man can be employed?[87]

Chapman did not immediately publish 'Britten and Mozart' – 'I got it into my head that it would require a lot of alteration' (a view which he subsequently changed)[88] – but he did think Keller worth employing, and straight away commissioned him to write an article on Britten's Second String Quartet, which Boosey & Hawkes had published a few months earlier.[89] This was an article which Keller seems to have found particularly difficult to write, to judge by the number of draft versions of it that still survive.[90] Part of the problem may have been that neither Stein nor Chapman was happy with the way he wanted to write it. Stein's concerns were primarily stylistic, as he wrote to Chapman:

> Keller is doing some alterations which I suggested but is sending it tonight, so you will receive it, I hope, in the morning. I am by no means

sure of this article. The man is a bit of a disappointment. He has some imagination but is not clear and likes to stress minor points. See what you can do with the English. I think some expressions are not very clear, but you will find the meaning. Anyhow, I am quite prepared to help.[91]

Chapman obliged with the sort of rigorous editing that Keller would later apply to contributors to his own journal. One of the sections which ended up being deleted, however, was the original opening, which, in taking its starting point from the work's reception and the question of English musicians and sonata form, was particularly characteristic:

> Britten's second String Quartet had a lukewarm press. One distinguished critic calls it 'a clever manipulation of not very fertile ideas', another, while recognizing 'moments of great beauty' and 'an undeniable largeness of approach', does not 'find the music emotionally or spiritually meaningful'. Unfortunately, the emotional or spiritual meaning of music is nowise a matter for argument. But it may at least be worth noting that some of us do find such significance in the quartet. For 'to find' means, according to my dictionary, 'to come upon', and one does not usually come upon things that aren't there, while one often doesn't come upon things that are. However, rather than emotional content, the architecture of music is a fit subject for rational discussion. From this standpoint, the Quartet's first movement, being in sonata form, is of special interest. If it is true that English composers have so far 'never taken naturally to sonata form',* one is eager to learn how Britten, whose formal mastership is widely acknowledged, manages the sonata movement. One's interest is enhanced by the fact that the first movement occupies a solitary position within the quartet, succeeded as it is by two movements more of the 'English' – i.e. of essentially monothematic – type.[92]

* 'English Chamber Music', by the Music Critic of *The Times*, January 17th, 1947.

Chapman may have been unhappy at Keller's implied criticism of other critics. As he later explained to Keller, 'It's more or less a tradition here that critics shall not criticize critics'.[93] This was a piece of advice which Keller was later to ignore in the most spectacular fashion, as will be seen later at the close of his essay 'On Musical Understanding'.

At the time, however, Keller was receptive to all their comments, and was keen to contribute more to *Tempo*. Since it was a journal concerned particularly with contemporary music (with a natural stress on those composers published by Boosey & Hawkes), he needed to find another modern subject:

As regards my next contribution to *Tempo*, I have been trying to think of something novel which would interest the average reader: What about a research into the difficulties encountered by the listener to modern music? Questionnaire method. Replies to represent cross section of our musical society. If the answers to the questionnaire should prove sufficiently interesting, one might perhaps devote an entire article to quoting and reporting on them, while another article, in the succeeding issue, would suggest how to counter the difficulties elicited. The enquiry should have a strong practical as well as a strong theoretical interest; moreover, it ought to pump some life into the sleepy part of contemporary aesthetics.[94]

This was actually a question of considerable personal interest. Until his encounter with *Peter Grimes*, Keller had not taken any interest in modern music. 'I was never interested in music I couldn't understand,' he later wrote, and 'since conservative Vienna did not press the understanding of contemporary music upon me, I grew up without it.'[95] London, on the other hand, did press contemporary music on him – not least because he now wanted to make his living there writing about music, and in the new post-war world a refusal to engage with what was happening around him would have made that difficult. Writing about Britten and the music of current films went some way to making Keller's articles topical. But for a Viennese émigré in particular, there was one figure it was going to be impossible to avoid: Arnold Schoenberg.

Indeed, one of his next commissions for *Tempo* was a review of Dika Newlin's book *Bruckner – Mahler – Schoenberg*.[96] Though it was a book whose primary aim was to defend Schoenberg's most radical works by showing them to be part of a continuing Viennese tradition – 'the culmination of several centuries of historical development, rather than the products of a wilful iconoclasm', as Newlin put it – Keller's review hardly mentions the title figures, concentrating instead on Newlin's 'disturbing' omission of the more conservative Franz Schmidt, 'an important post-romantic composer (four symphonies) who remains to be discovered in this country'.[97] Schoenberg's name appears only once, and then only to be quoted saying that Schmidt had 'too much talent'.

This piece of hearsay Keller probably heard from his great musical mentor, Oscar Adler – 'my teacher and most intimate musical friend'[98] – who knew both composers. When Keller was young, Schmidt was part of Adler's 'chamber-musical world' in which Keller grew up. He heard Schmidt as 'cellist in Adler's quartet, and as pianist accompanying Adler, and he remembered for the rest of his life the 'revelational quality' of these performances. Keller even had the chance as a teenager to play quartets himself with Schmidt, and he also heard him conduct his own music, 'which, to date, I have never again heard with anything like the vitality and simultaneous textural transparency of those performances.'[99]

For Oscar Adler, his friendships with Schmidt and Schoenberg, though years apart, had much in common:

> In my whole life there was only one man with whom I had as profound a friendship as with Franz Schmidt. That was in my youth, and the man was Schoenberg: at the time, we made our first steps into the field of chamber music ... Despite his defective technique, a similar spiritual power radiated from his playing as, later, from Schmidt's.[100]

For Keller, however, the two relationships were very different. Schmidt was a living presence in his own life, as composer as well as performer. Schoenberg, on the other hand, he never met, for that friendship with Adler dated primarily from their youth in the early 1890s.[101] Nor does Adler's chamber-musical world seem to have included much of Schoenberg's own music. Despite Adler's intense respect for Schoenberg's gifts – 'I regard you as the only one with the vocation of continuing Beethoven's work' – there are hints in their correspondence that Adler may have found his friend's later works as difficult to comprehend as did Keller. Certainly, Keller does not seem to have had any recollection of Adler ever playing any of Schoenberg's quartets. When Schoenberg in 1949 asked his old friend for a direct opinion of his later works, this was Adler's – slightly evasive – reply:

> Reading Heine's writings recently one sentence particularly caught my attention. He says – with regard to paintings: 'Modern art needs or requires new eyes'. Applied to music one could say: 'New music requires new ears'. And I think that you were already born with these 'new ears', with this 'Weithörigkeit', within which the diatonic way of expression of the older tradition is only a historical special case of the possible, from which the direction of development logically has to lead to other possibilities.[102]

– an answer which appears to imply that Adler may have felt himself to lack the 'new ears' required by his friend's new music.

When Keller reflected on his own early exposure to Schoenberg's music, he could remember only two specific occasions when he heard it:

> As a child, I found Schoenberg incomprehensible, though I smelt a master and suspected a genius. I chiefly know this from my letters to a girl friend; what I remember most clearly myself is his

incomprehensibility ... Of the two Schoenberg performances I recall, one was by the Kolisch Quartet, whom I chiefly remember for their intellectualized Mozart. The work was Schoenberg's Fourth Quartet, of which this may have been the first Austrian performance. At any rate, they played the work twice, and I dutifully sat through it all. The 'duty' was self-imposed, of course: that inkling that here might be greatness did not altogether leave me in peace. But understand I did nothing. All I noticed was the recurrence of the recitative-like theme of the slow movement; and if that hadn't been in unison, I probably wouldn't have noticed it either.

The other Schoenberg performance, of *Pierrot lunaire*, I heard on the radio. I was quite a devoted musician by then, and my reaction was proportionately hostile: the simultaneous absence of key and (in the 'speaking voice') of pitch was more than I could bear; both my sense of harmony and of true intonation were deeply offended. I remember wanting to smash the wireless set; I certainly switched it off. Paradoxically, by that stage, my suspicion of genius and indeed any feeling for the mastery of it all was as intense as my aversion. I came to the conclusion that this, very probably, was a great composer, and that he was probably not for me.[103]

It must have been only shortly before the Anschluss that Keller heard that performance of the Fourth Quartet (of which the Kolisch Quartet gave the world première in America in January 1937), by which time he would have been eighteen years old. The radio experience of *Pierrot lunaire*, which Keller implies took place rather later, may well therefore have been in England.[104]

Apart from Oscar Adler, the other major musical influences on Keller when he was young were of course his parents, both of whom were highly musical. Keller described his father's repertoire as catholic but quite conservative: 'anything ... up to and including Bruckner'.[105] Keller himself could not even go that far:

Throughout my childhood, whenever he thought he was only playing to himself, [my father] reconstructed the Bruckner symphonies on the piano, and bored the pants off me if I happened to sit next door. And in my early adolescence, between the ages of twelve and thirteen, he bought me tickets for a subscription series comprising all those intolerable Bruckner symphonies. ... The last comprehensible word my father spoke before he died was 'Bruckner'. I was nineteen by then: it was a day or two before my escape from Austria. I took my deafness to the composer's music with me, and it was only in this country that the truth about this towering genius gradually dawned on me – though it was a difficult dawn, since at the time performances were few, bad, and far between, Bruckner being considered an unexportable Austrian provincial, like Mahler.[106]

It was therefore only in exile that Keller came to understand the more recent music of his compatriots. As far as Schoenberg was concerned, the 'suspicion of genius' which Keller recalls resisting so fiercely must have been frequently reactivated by Adler's affection for and confidence in him. Adler's conviction that Schoenberg was Beethoven's true heir was something that remained with Keller and appeared in many of his later writings, though he had not been able to perceive it in Vienna. The 'weithörigkeit' of Beethoven himself, however, was clear to him from an early age:

> The most advanced things I knew and loved as a boy were the late Beethoven quartets, which of course were more advanced than Brahms or Reger, and are more advanced than many things which appear nowadays. But then, with Beethoven, 'contemporary' music – the problem – started, however intermittently. When one played the late Beethoven quartets, one felt one was alone – alone even inside oneself, for one part of one's mind fathomed the bottom of what the rest felt to be bottomless. This was my first and most important lesson in contemporary music, and music was never the same again after it. Previously one had felt on top of it; now one yearned to get at the bottom of it.[107]

Schoenberg may have been brought particularly to Keller's mind at the time of his escape from Vienna because Adler was then in frequent correspondence with the composer, as Schoenberg (already living in California) tried to help him find sanctuary in America. Later, in Huyton Camp, Keller and Adler were interned alongside David Josef Bach, another of Schoenberg's youthful friends, and Keller may well have received further reminders of Schoenberg in the shape of their reminiscences about their remarkable old friend.

But if Keller was moved by this to re-examine Schoenberg's music, the impulse was shelved during his discoveries first of Freud and then of Britten. Each of these 'epiphanies' was characterised by Keller's complete immersion in his new discovery, leaving little room at the time for other new insights. At the end of 1948, however, the time was ripe, and Keller's Schoenberg-epiphany came on 15 November that year. Once again – as with Phillips in the case of Keller's discovery of Freud, and (in a different way) Pears in the case of his discovery of Britten – Keller needed a 'midwife' with whom to work out the implications of his new insight. This was Donald Mitchell, whom Keller met for the first time only two days later.

'It amuses me now to find that in one respect I was actually ahead of Hans!' recalls Mitchell:

> I enjoyed listening to Schoenberg, while Hans at the time, when he overheard a broadcast of *Pierrot*, in his own words, was 'looking round for something to throw at the radio to stop this awful noise'. Here again I was indebted to my mother. As I have remarked elsewhere, she used to sing 'Es sungen drei Engel' from the *Gurrelieder* and it cast a spell on me – what a melody, what harmony! – that has never diminished. ...
>
> That mention by Hans of an offending radio reminds me of what I was just occasionally aware of in my earliest encounters with Hans: an unexpected vein of conservatism. I recall babbling on about Mahler and the books I wanted to write about him and was somewhat taken aback when Hans halted the flow by declaring that the book that *really* needed to be written was one about Franz Schmidt – a composer of much merit, no doubt, but one to my ears bound by convention and tradition as Mahler was not.[108]

Donald Mitchell was then just 23, but he had already founded a musical journal of his own – *Music Survey* – of which he had so far published four issues, revealing a breadth of musical taste unusual for a young Englishman of that time. His mother was a singer who had trained in Leipzig, and this meant that his childhood was full of 'all kinds of music that I think would not have been much of a domestic presence in England at the time, for example songs by Pfitzner, Reger and Schoenberg.'[109]

In 1948, Mitchell began to contribute to the *Music Review*, where he was immediately struck by the writing of one of his fellow-contributors:

> I was reading a copy of that very journal one day and it had in it this most extraordinary review by Hans Keller – a name entirely new to me – of an opera at Covent Garden, I think by Mozart. I had never read a review like it. ... and when I was idly turning over the pages of the correspondence at the back (I think) of the same issue, there was a letter from the same Hans Keller ... and to my utter astonishment I found that he was living at ... Herne Hill which was just down the other end of the street in south London, very, very near to me.[110]

Mitchell describes himself as being 'knocked out' by the 'precision' and 'confidence' of Keller's writing, which was in such stark contrast to the wordy generalisations which he felt characterised British musical criticism of the time:

Gone were all those boring generalities and tedious descriptions, stuffed with modifiers and qualifiers – our Sunday-paper review sections are still littered with them – and in their place, detailed observations on rhythm, pitch, tonality, modulation, dynamics, nuances of expression, which left one in no doubt that here was a critic who knew what he was talking about. And even more amazing, knew the work he was talking about, from the inside outwards, as Hans himself might have said. Moreover, I seem to remember that, lest anyone might think that this critic had not done his homework, there were footnotes in which he laid out his sources. It was an astonishing performance – and there were many others of a like kind – which punched a big hole in the facade of English music criticism as it was practised in the 1940s and 1950s. It has never been – or looked – quite the same since.[111]

Mitchell wrote to Keller, and they met on 17 November 1948 at a concert in the Central Hall, where Keller was reviewing for *Music Review* the LSO's performance of Gordon Jacob's Second Symphony. Keller's diary for that evening notes: 'Mitchell top of staircase (buffet) *MR* in his hand, red shirt & tie, interval or before'. Two days earlier, on 15 November, underneath a note that 'Mitchell may ring', there is another significant note: '3rd Scherchen 1st perf 2nd Kammersy Schönb'.

This refers to the broadcast that night on the BBC Third Programme of a performance of Schoenberg's Second Chamber Symphony by the Philharmonia Orchestra, conducted by Hermann Scherchen. It was for Keller the moment when Schoenberg's genius finally became clear to him. After his violent reaction to *Pierrot lunaire*, he had pushed Schoenberg to one side while his *Peter Grimes* experience led him to begin a gradual exploration of other – more conservative – contemporary music. As he later explained, it was atonality, exacerbated in *Pierrot* by the imprecise vocal pitch – that had kept Schoenberg's music beyond the pale: 'Tonal new music I had meanwhile begun to understand … but with the atonal Schoenberg I entered upon an armistice: he left me in peace and I left him …

Then came the revelation, by way of another radio event. One night I twiddled about on my set and got into the middle of a fascinating piece, transmitted from somewhere abroad. My excitement mounted as the music developed. The more complex it got, the clearer it seemed – an experience which doesn't happen to you every day. Whoever the composer was, he was a neglected genius; as the work ended, I had come to feel quite protective and pioneering about him.

It turned out to be Schoenberg's Second Chamber Symphony, a latish work reverting to an earlier, tonal style. Schoenberg had, in fact started it before he grew atonal; he returned to it with the experience of twelve-tone technique behind him – which therefore trickled into this music. I could not have encountered a better introduction to the understanding of his most mature atonal style, which here, as it were, expressed itself tonally. In a flash – well, in about quarter of an hour, anyway – I got the hang of his thought, and once the thought, with the feeling inside it, had impressed itself on me, the style didn't matter so much any more. Much later, Schoenberg wrote an essay entitled 'Style and Idea'; even the title immediately clicked with me.

The door was now open not only to the understanding of Schoenberg's atonal and twelve-tone music, but to contemporary music in general. Schoenberg was so much more complex than the rest, that the rest seemed easy in comparison, even where it was, in time, more 'advanced'; and that went for Webern too. . . .

I familiarized myself with a great deal of Schoenberg's music before I started bothering about twelve-tone technique as such. With me, the emotional click must always come first, and the intellectualization, which my mind does ultimately require, has to be spurred on by emotional understanding, or rather, by understanding emotion.[112]

This account was written some years later, but Keller did briefly review this broadcast at the time, both for *Music Parade* and *The Music Review*:

The Schoenberg left a powerful impression after one hearing even on me, an uninitiate, for whom indeed there is not the faintest doubt that this is a work of genius. Its outer movements are strongly in E flat, while the middle movement, a scherzo, is atonal, i.e. apparently written in twelve-tone technique. The compelling way in which these different idioms are combined in one and the same work – in point of fact the last movement develops without a break out of the scherzo – has to be heard to be believed.[113]

Begun on 1st August, 1906, it was finished, I think, some eight years ago. It thus contains elements of the composer's earlier style. Is the quick, first part of the second movement new, and are the first movement and the slow final section of the work of earlier origin? The first movement never loses sight of its strong tonal centre, E flat, though there is a leaning towards the subdominant, and the end-section returns in no uncertain manner to the initial tonality. But far from resulting in inconsistency, the 'atonal' part of the second movement emerges as a locial, tensing contrast, to be relieved at the end. It is interesting to note here that the *Ode to Napoleon*, 'which employs all the techniques of "atonality"' (Newlin,

Bruckner, Mahler, Schoenberg, p. 261), also ends tonally, in fact in the same key as the present work. For the rest, this Chamber Symphony corroborates what I have previously suspected, *i.e.* that whenever Schoenberg is foreign to me, this is not his fault, but mine. I recognize the master.[114]

Meeting Donald Mitchell immediately after that experience was a remarkable stroke of luck. The importance of the relationship to both of them is shown by the speed at which they absorbed each other's ideas. Within three months Mitchell had asked Keller to join him as co-editor of *Music Survey*,[115] and by the time their first joint issue was published in summer 1949, it would have been impossible for readers to guess that, contrary to what they might have expected, it had been the Viennese Keller who had brought Mitchell to appreciate Britten, and the English Mitchell who had done the same for Keller and Schoenberg.

Mitchell's first article on Britten ('Let's Make an Opera') appeared in their second issue in the autumn of 1949, alongside an article by Schoenberg (defending himself against Thomas Mann's fictional appropriation of the twelve-note technique in Doctor Faustus), whose presentation by Keller (citing his correspondence with the composer, his 'authorized' translation, and his personal knowledge) showed clearly that Keller no longer felt himself to be 'an uninitiate' where Schoenberg was concerned. It is not certain exactly when Keller began to correspond with Schoenberg, but it was probably in April 1949, when Stuckenschmidt's biography of the composer describes Keller contacting Schoenberg initially on Adler's behalf: 'In April the young London writer on music Hans Keller had written that Oscar Adler, with whom he studied viola, was longing for a sign of life.'[116] Schoenberg wrote to Adler on 2 July – 'For such a long time I didn't have your address and now the chance has come to write to you' – and communication was re-established. That summer was the year in which Schoenberg wrote his essay 'My Evolution', in which he recalled his youthful friendship with Adler and what it had meant to him.[117] When he read it, Adler was profoundly touched:

> Your mentioning our close connection of long ago has moved me deeply: it never ceased in spite of our external separation. Your memory has strengthened my confidence, because in those articles I encountered many thoughts which I myself reached. It is encouraging to a high degree when such thoughts are pronounced by somebody who is himself standing in the chain of creative geniuses as one member of this heirarchical row which supports the other members of this chain in the same way as it is supported by them.[118]

Adler told Schoenberg about Keller in several of his letters:

At last I have put together an efficient string quartet which gives private chamber music evening concerts as shown on the enclosed programme. Keller plays viola; he has developed as an excellent chamber musician. He has also become a respected writer about music and he may be able to get a publisher for you here; he will write to you about it. ...

You have a fervent admirer in Hans Keller, who is valiantly and with relish fighting various music critics. At present much is written about you and 12-tone music.[119]

Keller was indeed taking up the cudgels with relish, and Schoenberg was delighted to encourage him: 'Now sharpen your pen,' he told Keller, when sending him 'a very unpleasant review' which he wanted Keller to counter.[120] This 'combative manner' of Keller's criticism was another characteristic that particularly attracted Donald Mitchell, and indeed it was the passion and aggression of *Music Survey*'s attacks on the critical received opinion of the day that made it so disproportionately influential. As the *Musical Times* of 1951 colourfully described it,

The tower inhabited by *Music Survey* is also armed with machine guns; and it is a dull number that does not hit twenty targets. ... Undoubtedly one wants to read *Music Survey* for its *bravura*, its ungoverned cleverness, and (let us, too, be just) the large amount of scholarly and musicianly comment that fills the spaces in between.'[121]

Though Mitchell later credited the polemical character of *Music Survey* to the 'new editorial set-up' after Keller joined him as co-editor – and even went so far as to say 'I should be nonplussed if anybody asked me why in fact I started the paper' – the early issues of *Music Survey* show clearly that Mitchell did have a mission of his own.

What really worried me as a young man was the awful parochialism of English musical life, the complacent provinciality of the opinion-makers. ... Whereas I may not have developed an identifiable platform or programme, nonetheless those early issues of *Music Survey* bear witness to my attempt to bring to the notice of readers those composers who I felt were neglected or cold-shouldered in England, or to whom the English were indifferent.[122]

As well as Schoenberg – on whom Mitchell published two substantial articles by Dika Newlin – these under-rated composers included Mahler, Pfitzner and Reger, as well as re-evaluations of older figures like Haydn and Mendelssohn. Mitchell had found that many of the established journals and newspapers 'showed attitudes to [these] composers, with which I was totally out of sympathy. Therefore I didn't expect to find much of a market for my particular interests.' Such frustration with the established press was less of a motive for Keller – 'on the whole I should say that I did not feel frustrated, and that no such negative feeling was responsible for my enthusiasm for *Music Survey*'. By his own account, his motive was more of a positive mission to share his own discoveries:

> Behind all such polemics was something which had nothing to do with aggression, which was sheer enthusiasm, musical enthusiasm for great composers who were not yet recognized as being great.[123]

One of these composers was of course Britten, to whose music Keller and Mitchell devoted a whole issue of *Music Survey*, followed by a (not uncontroversial) book of essays.[124] Another was Schoenberg, on whose behalf Keller and Mitchell made the following announcement in the Spring of 1950:

> As long as any great music needs partisanship we shall be found to be partisans. From now on, every issue of this journal will reserve space for the special subject of Schoenberg until, with our help or without, he has ceased to be a special subject. If we are the first who, while not members of the Schoenberg school, decide upon such constant support, this is Schoenberg's merit as well as a reminder of history at which we are ourselves, as it were, surprised.[125]

Keller's conversion to Schoenberg's music had been astonishingly rapid – perhaps because of the number of years he had spent trying to ignore it. As with his previous discoveries of Freud and Britten, Keller's devotion to Schoenberg was complete and lasting (as he said himself, 'to discover means to over-estimate'),[126] but in some respects it went even deeper this time, amounting almost to an identification. While he often said that he was not particularly interested in Britten as a person (and was frustrated at times by Britten's reticence and conventionality), he became deeply interested in Schoenberg's personality, as his 1965 radio *Portrait of Schoenberg* clearly shows.[127] Schoenberg the exiled Jew, the inspired teacher, the individualistic uncompromising autodidact – the composition of Keller's portrait (right down to the descriptions of Schoenberg playing table-tennis with fellow musicians) does indicate a certain consciousness of parallels with his own life. As one of his later colleagues at the BBC put it:

> I always felt the Schoenberg worship was psychologically a strange phenomenon. We all worshipped various composers ... [and] we

were all enthusiastic about those causes to which we subscribed. But in Hans's case, Schoenberg could do no wrong, and he really did seem to be totally dedicated.[128]

One of the most important things that Keller shared with Schoenberg was his sense of a continuing, developing musical tradition. Partly a result of his musical upbringing, this also harmonised with his new Freudian aesthetic, in which the new is interpreted in the light of the old, the adult in the light of the child, and the cultural present is dependent for its meaning on its inevitable echoes of the past. Such an interpretation received powerful support from Schoenberg's 'conservative revolution', and it is not surprising that Keller was assiduous in his attempts to demonstrate the strength of Schoenberg's links with tradition and his position as guarantor of that tradition's continuing vitality. Nor is it surprising that the Second Chamber Symphony (in which he could clearly perceive atonality's tonal background) should have been the work which showed Keller the way into Schoenberg's music. When, at least two decades later, he revisited his painful early experience of *Pierrot lunaire* in a 1965 essay 'Whose Fault is the Speaking Voice?', he had this to say about the nature of revolution:

> The conscientious revolutionary 'revolves' history and indeed his own psyche, turns it upside down, so that what was at the forgotten bottom comes out on top, and is new only inasmuch as it had been forgotten – that is psychologically speaking, repressed. It is resented, not because it's never been there before, but because it has. In this sense, the true revolutionary, the innovator who remains psychologically truthful, is the most radical conservative imaginable: he conserves things which had already been forgotten.[129]

The 'unexpected vein of conservatism' that Donald Mitchell detected in Keller, and which he felt was so paradoxical a feature in a character who was 'so plainly sceptical, radical and innovative',[130] was an absolutely fundamental part of Keller's musical understanding and essential to his passionate search for meaning. The underlying unity of apparent contrasts became his lifelong concern, manifest not only in his analytical searching for the internal unity of individual musical works, but also in his insistence that the newest and most modern works are still dependent for their musical meaning on their relationship with the past.

∿

From the time of that first joint edition of *Music Survey* in 1949, Keller's development as a musical writer was essentially complete, and he altered very little from then on. Since this was also the point at which he began to become well known, his creative character has always appeared to his readers to be remarkably consistent. Indeed so finished and confident did he already seem by 1949, that readers would have been surprised to know how much he had changed in the preceding decade.

Keller's aphoristic prose style, incisive insight and fondness for controversy were all part of what made him stand out as a writer, but the two things that really made his name were his unusual combination of music and psychology, and his fervent advocacy of Schoenberg. Naturally, in the England of 1949 these did make him appear particularly Austrian, and many assumed that his focus on Freud and Schoenberg had been brought intact from Vienna, his devoted faith in them bred into him from an early age. The truth was much more complicated, as this book has shown, and it was bound up with the shock of exile. The Viennese culture which was so prominent a part of Keller in 1949 was very different from that with which he had arrived ten years earlier. The story of his first decade in England was not the simple importing of a foreign culture (so feared by Vaughan Williams), but rather one in which that culture was reinvented as a result of its new setting.

Keller's 'sunny early years', as he himself described them, were both secure and culturally rich. Intellectually, the home in which he was brought up was highly stimulating, dominated by his remarkable mother, who collected around her a dazzling array of writers and musicians, including Oscar Adler, whose 'chamber-musical world' was such a profound influence on her son. The musical repertoire in which Keller was so deeply educated, however, was that of the First Viennese School rather than the Second: 'since conservative Vienna did not press the understanding of contemporary music upon me, I grew up without it.'

All this was abruptly broken up in 1938. For Jews in Austria, the Anschluss meant that Hitler's antisemitic legislation came upon them much more suddenly than it had in Germany. From that moment, as Keller later described it, 'one was, intermittently, running for one's life,' and his previous concerns then assumed, 'to put it mildly, a dream-like quality'. Cut off from his mother, his father dying, the world around him collapsing into irrational hatred, everything he had valued suddenly meaningless, Keller escaped eventually to a new and alien country, where, although the remnants of his family did their best to re-create their former life, nothing was ever the same again.

This first traumatic uprooting was then followed by a second. Internment meant that Keller's new life in England was also broken up, almost immediately and at first seemingly indefinitely. The indeterminate state in which he was then suspended, however, seems to have been of considerable importance to his intellectual maturation. The cultural life of the internment camps was extraordinary, and for Keller this period of confinement alongside many distinguished representatives of German and Austrian arts and letters seems to have provided an opportunity to begin to re-examine his own heritage from a new angle.

Among the many aphorisms he wrote which date from his early years in England there is this:

> With a single stroke, the contented émigré was robbed of his protective routine of daily habits that defined the nature, value and purpose of life. Bereft of this apparently protecting rampart, he is forced either to go under for lack of any real aim in life or, rather, to live a meaningful life.

It is not quite certain exactly when Keller wrote this, but it is possible that it is a description of how it felt to be interned. Keller here describes the disruption of the life of a 'contented émigré' – someone already beginning to settle down in his new country when he is abruptly reminded that he does not belong. All the external supports with which he was reconstructing his life were removed, leaving only the life of the mind. For Keller, the search for 'a meaningful life' did indeed become a fundamental driving force for the rest of his days, and it found its initial focus in the three profound discoveries that he made during his first decade in England: his three 'epiphanies'. All three of these discoveries were, in fact, *re*-discoveries of things that had already been part of his life in Vienna, though their importance for him had not been apparent at the time. As Keller put it when talking about Schoenberg and revolution, he 'revolved his own psyche'.

The first discovery was made in internment, when Keller encountered Freud. He must have known of Freud's theories in Vienna, but this time he seized on them with an almost desperate fervour. 'Have you ever thought where your own passion for Freud has come from?' Margaret Phillips later asked him; part of the answer may have been that psychoanalysis gave him a way to try to make sense of what had happened to him, to understand the complex motives behind irrational behaviour, and indeed his own thoughts. Keller's writings before he was interned were a rather diverse miscellany, and his correspondence surviving from that time shows that he had no clear idea what he wanted to do in his life; afterwards he pursued psychoanalysis single-mindedly, combining it at the same time with a most intense self-examination.

As Keller made his rediscoveries of Freud and later of Schoenberg, he needed a partner with whom to work through the implications of what he had found. In both cases he chose an English partner – and this *was* a choice, for there were Viennese émigrés at hand who could have filled this role. But it was not Willi Hoffer who helped Keller understand psychoanalysis, but

Margaret Phillips, and it was not Erwin Stein (or even Oscar Adler) who helped Keller come to terms with Schoenberg, but Donald Mitchell. It is also noteworthy that Keller did not choose recognised authorities, the disciples of the great men, but relative outsiders. Margaret Phillips was an educationalist, not a psychoanalyst, and she was an (unmarried) woman to boot. Donald Mitchell was very young, self-educated, and out of step with the majority of current English critical opinion.

Like his discoveries of Freud and Schoenberg, Keller's *Peter Grimes* epiphany was also in a sense a rediscovery, a reworking in exile of his own past. This was the moment in which he discovered himself as a musical writer. He had been both a musician and a writer all his life, but had never put them together until now. Again, this discovery was only achieved with the help of an English partner – or rather two partners: Benjamin Britten and Peter Pears. Again, they were to some extent outsiders, because of their youth and their homosexuality (though they fast became the new musical establishment). Significantly, Keller's writing laid particular emphasis on Britten's 'outsider' status, by constantly drawing attention to critical opposition to his work.[131]

Despite the crucial importance to him of Britten's music, Keller's real breakthrough as a musical writer came when he finally started to write about his own repertoire, beginning with Mozart. This was such a major step for him that it seems to have needed the stimulus of a completely new musical repertoire to achieve it. After the initial dislocation of his obsessive writing about Britten and film music, however, Keller's instincts were all towards the integration of this new repertoire with the music of his past – hence, perhaps, his interest in finding sonata form in Britten's quartets, for example, or serial technique in Mozart.

Mozart – the understanding of whom 'gives me a standard by which I judge what I understand and what I don't' – had a special importance for Keller. During his childhood, Mozart's music had been 'a central point of agreement' between him and his father, and Mozart was the first composer whom Keller felt the urge to defend. At the time, this was a purely private and and entirely musical defence, but it might have sown the seed for Keller's later public vindication of many other composers.

> We were both much concerned about what was then still the established underestimation of Mozart – a great genius, of course, it was said, but lacking the depth of a Beethoven. Week in, week out, therefore, we were engaged upon the rehabilitation and revaluation of Mozart within our four walls.'[132]

In writing about his own repertoire, the music he had known so well from childhood, Keller was not only reconnecting himself with the past: he was also connecting his intellectual and emotional understanding. Margaret Phillips had made a very significant point when she told Keller in 1943 that the problem with his writing was that, too often, he was writing with 'only your intellect'. It may have been the case that Keller's emotional understanding was so bound up with music, and his musical and verbal thought were then so separate, that it was almost inexpressible in words. Yet, as he came to realize later, the understanding of emotion was essential:

> With me, the emotional click must always come first, and the intellectualization, which my mind does ultimately require, has to be spurred on by emotional understanding, or rather, by understanding emotion.[133]

The first editorial that Keller wrote for *Music Survey* contains a lyrical description of such an 'emotional click' when Keller recalled the moment when his ears were newly opened to the full glories of an old favourite.

> I had been passionately in love with *Figaro* since my childhood. I had always been delighted with, indeed intensely moved by the sextet. I had every wrong reason to believe that I understood this piece completely, for I knew it inside out. Until one day I discovered that what I had known inside out was not much more than its outside. It had been an exhausting day; I arrived at the opera later in the evening, and on the verge of going to sleep. When I entered, the sextet was just starting, and now, for the first time, I heard everything it revealed and concealed. Its cogency, its universality, the heavenly resignation underlying this understatement of all that moves, divides and unites the world, the easy victory over deep tragedy that is its humour – it all overwhelmed me and, to be frank, I cried. From then onwards, I was convinced that the sextet was *Figaro*'s best number, and when some time later I read that Mozart himself thought so, my belief that I understood Mozart received a confirmation it did not need.[134]

The ability to express in words such moments of musical insight and to analyse their meaning was hard won. Whether the bridging of the gulf in Keller's mind between music and words would have been achieved without his exile – without his need for psychoanalytical explanation, his surprise at the English Pears' revelatory singing of Mozart, and his admiration of Britten's psychological empathy – is a matter for speculation. But it may be that his sudden arrival in another culture and the consequent mental dislocation were what finally jolted Keller's instinctive musical understanding into verbal consciousness.

The strange limbo of the internment camps was where the process began, when Keller made the first of the three re-discoveries on which he was to build his future life. The camps were a psychological no-man's land – neither Austria nor England – a place where, as Keller put it, one was 'robbed of the protective routine of daily habits that defined the nature, value and purpose of life'. Those habits were not only practical, but intellectual and cultural, and the loss of their 'protecting rampart' proved strangely liberating. What Keller called 'those inevitable, almost instinctive prejudices with which one's civilisation, especially if it happens to be an old one, has burdened one almost from birth'[135] were there pulled into the light, to be revalued and refashioned in a new land. After he left internment, Keller went on to bring Vienna to London; but it was now a very personal Vienna – and very much more his own in 1948 then when he had left it ten years before.

To illustrate Keller's style as it first crystallised, there now follow four of his early articles:

(i) **'Britten and Mozart'** was the essay that heralded Keller's new blend of music and psychology, the first of his many studies of musical character. Written in 1946, it was first published in the January 1948 edition of *Music and Letters*, which was then edited by Eric Blom. Blom was clearly struck by Keller, but once Keller began to write about Schoenberg, and more particularly to seek to demonstrate Schoenberg's links with Viennese tradition, they clearly ceased to see eye to eye. After the publication of Keller's essay 'Strict Serial Technique in Classical Music', which undertook to show that Schoenberg's new technique was foreshadowed in Mozart and Beethoven, Blom was particularly negative, writing in *The Observer* that 'if anybody ever succeeds in making me hate Mozart's music, it will have been Hans Keller's boast to have done so.'[136]

(ii) **'Così fan tutte'**, on the Sadler's Wells performance of 28 January 1948, was probably the review that first attracted the attention of Donald Mitchell to Keller's writing, and so led to their famous *Music Survey* partnership. It was published in *The Music Review* in May 1948.

(iii) **'On Musical Understanding'** was the first editorial the Keller wrote for *Music Survey* after joining Mitchell as co-editor. It appears in Vol. II, No.1, the first issue that Keller and Mitchell edited together, at the beginning of 1949, and is perhaps something of a critical credo.

(iv) 'Schoenberg and the Men of the Press' is a more specific lesson from Keller to British music critics. It was published in *Music Survey* in March 1951 (Vol. III, No. 3), about half-way through Keller's tenure as co-editor.

(i)   'Britten and Mozart'

A Challenge in the Form of Variations
on an Unfamiliar Theme

Ars adeo latet sua (OVID)

Remarkable similarities between Benjamin Britten and Mozart obtrude themselves on the suitably prejudiced observer, prejudiced, among other things, in favour of the view that presence of similarities does not imply absence of differences. People are wont to harp on the relation of Britten to Purcell (and to other composers, such as Mahler, whom they know Britten to admire). With Purcell, however, Britten has obviously established what in psychoanalysis one would call a superego identification – Purcell, that is to say, is Britten's father, and there is a limit to one's interest in the continuous pointing out of evident family resemblances.

Yet there is a way in which both comparisons between Purcell and Britten, and between Mozart and Britten, are equally beneficial: they counteract the current over-emphasis on the historical aspect of music, to which, in the case of the comparison with Mozart, is to be added action against the over-emphasis on the ethnological and geographical aspects.

To be sure, the exaggerated importance attached to historical factors has itself to be considered historically, as a sign of our times: the significance of the temporal environment for human activities, mental or otherwise, has once again been discovered, and to discover means to overestimate.

In music, moreover, historical explanations are particularly welcome, for the factors that go to make the individual musical character are a rather mysterious affair, and it is one of the tragedies of the mind that it prefers mysterious explanations to waiting for the facts to become a little less mysterious.

Proceeding to Britten's work itself, one of those who overdo its historical aspect is Britten. 'It is largely a matter of when one was born. If I had been born in 1813 instead of 1913 I should have been a romantic, primarily concerned to express my personality in music ...'* I don't think he would. True, he would have been more of a romantic, but in the sense in which he uses the word not primarily one: of all romantics he would have been least romantic. Taking into account everything that depth psychology teaches us about character formation in early childhood, it is fairly safe to assume that, other things being as nearly equal as they can be, a Benjamin Britten born in 1813 would not tend (again in his own words) towards the 'point at which the composer would be the only man capable of understanding his own music'. This is not to say that nature is necessarily more important

---

*   [Anon., 'Profile – Benjamin Britten,' *Observer*, 27 October 1946.]

for a man's artistic character than nurture, character-building elements whose dependence on historical circumstances – given a large cultural frame like 'western civilization' – is negligible. In early childhood (between minus nine months and six years) contemporary aesthetic trends are not usually of great importance even to a precocious individual such as Britten. To quote two instances cited by him, Picasso and Stravinsky did not just come because history told them to, but because they liked being told. History is of course always clever afterwards: had Picasso and Stravinsky not worked against individualistic art, she would not have betrayed that she had told them to, but would have told us that they behaved according to her previous precepts.

One does not, then, understand Britten as soon as one knows that he belongs to the twentieth century and why, and that he is an Englishman and why.* Trying to neutralize the over-stress on historical and also on geographical interpretations (important as these admittedly are) this article will, but for a small exception, disregard them altogether. Yet I think that Britten will on the whole agree with my suggestion 'Britten often parallels Mozart'. What is less, I believe that this suggestion is so glaringly obvious that any musical person must agree with it as soon as he starts thinking or merely dreaming about it. A few days ago I met a colleague whose musical judgment I have learnt to value. 'I say, I want to write an article on Britten and Mozart', I told him. He thought for a while, then said: 'Yes, that's true'. Whereby the subject was closed. (It wasn't, of course: we talked for an hour about it. But it could have been, had we not felt compelled, assured of mutual admiration, to show off our insight.) Since, however, there are some musical people who are not sufficiently acquainted with Britten, and a great number of musical people who are not sufficiently acquainted with Mozart, for me to rest satisfied with just the title over the present article, I must put something under it. At the same time the musical reader will not require me to go into details, e.g. to produce some of those crippled musical quotations that often give to an article an added significance that is ornamental rather than illustrative.

I thought a good deal about the order in which to present the points of similarity between the two composers until I arrived at the conclusion that the best order will be not much of an order. For the relations, both psychological and aesthetic, between the various points are so manifold that any stringent order would be misleading, i.e., would automatically distract from the fact that a lot of other orders have also to be kept in view.

Often when another writer's view of either composer approximates to my own, I shall give his instead of or in addition to mine, in order to exclude as far as possible

***

* It may at the same time be worth mentioning that 'from his childhood days on, [Mozart] was especially fond of England and the English'. Alfred Einstein, *Mozart – His Character, His Work*, London, Cassell, 1946, pp. 88ff.

the objection that I am begging the question. And, wherever convenient, I shall of course, also let the composers speak for themselves.

Here, then, we go: –

The most obvious common characteristic of Britten and Mozart, their youthful maturity, need not detain us long; it has indeed already reached the pages of a popular magazine. Thus it just remains to point out that in both Britten's and Mozart's case youthful maturity has a double sense: maturity early attained and maturity retaining a youthful aspect. Busoni on Mozart: 'He is young like a youth and wise like an aged man – never out of date and never modern …'

Both composers manifest their maturity in artistic behaviour that is largely classical. To me they seem to be masters in the solution of a paradox inherent in all classical art: the paradox of restrained, yet explicit emotion.

Both have an impeccable sense of form. With Britten this particular asset is even acknowledged by his sternest critics, while Mozart's sense of form can only be called, with Busoni, 'extra-human'.

Both are liable to be severely misunderstood (yes, *are*, for even in Mozart's case this is not yet a thing of the past), not only by their critics, but also by a great number of their followers. For their music is approachable on various levels, each seemingly giving a complete picture in itself, so that the superficial listener, moving on the most superficial level, may yet be strongly impressed and may think he knows all about what he hears. In this connection Mozart's attitude towards the 'popular' should be noted. Writing about the first three Vienna piano concertos he says (letter of December 28th 1782):

> These concertos are a happy medium between what is too easy and too difficult; they are very brilliant, pleasing to the ear, and natural, without being vapid. There are passages here and there from which connoisseurs alone can derive satisfaction; but these passages are written in such a way that the less learned cannot fail to be pleased, though without knowing why …

Are we not here reminded of Britten's popularity, as well as of the fact that he is at times reproached with 'making concessions'? In any case, Mozart and Britten are the only two composers I know who strongly and widely attract people who do not understand them.

Both composers are clever, supreme craftsmen, hence both are accused of trying to be clever and of lacking in the deeper emotions.

> It is a pity that in his truly artistic and beautiful compositions [he] should carry his effort after originality too far, to the detriment of the sentiment and heart

of his works. His new [compositions] ... are much too highly spiced to be palatable for any length of time.

One of Britten's more favourable critics? No, one of the most favourable among the then contemporary critics of Mozart's six quartets dedicated to Haydn. 'It is perhaps the one work ... in which he achieved real sublimity.' But this, surely, is one of Britten's 'favourable' critics, talking, I don't know, of *Grimes* (referring to 'Now the Great Bear and the Pleiades'), or of the Donne Sonnets (referring to the sixth), or of *Lucretia* (referring to the English horn and strings passage at Lucrèce's last entry)... No, it is a critic of Mozart again, this time one of our own age, a very favourable one: nor is he just a scribe. It is in fact one who is elsewhere above criticism – Professor Dent on *The Magic Flute* (1940). 'The "splendid isolation" of Mozartian music from the standpoint of biographical interpretation caused this music to be explained, in a period of romantic afflation, as *"academic in form, cold, empty frivolous, superficial"*.'* Precisely the same descriptions are not seldom given of Britten's music to-day, though we are not living in a period of romantic afflation. And if it be objected that Britten, as distinct from Mozart, actually *is* cold and empty and superficial, we who find warmth and a rich and deep content in his music have at least this to be said in our favour: while one does not usually find things that are not there, one often does not find things that are. I would suggest that both composers sublimate not only their depths, but also their heights, *i.e.* they even sublimate their sublimity. (Richard Strauss, incidentally, calls Mozart 'the sublimest of all composers'.)

In the music of neither Mozart nor Britten is there a sign of inhibitions (as distinct from restraint). In this respect their exact contrary is Brahms. It is this freedom from inhibitions that makes a certain class of neurotic listeners belittle their works: we cannot easily bear it if others do not suffer from what we deny suffering from ourselves. Hand in hand with the absence of intra-musical inhibitions goes a delight in accepting, and working within, given limitations. With Mozart this point is self-evident. And when we come to Britten, I must ask the reader not to believe the composer too much when he gives a variety of practical reasons for the scoring of Lucretia and Albert Herring; for it is clear that these reasons offer him a welcome excuse for trying what he can do within the limitations of the chamber opera.

Ease, facility, effortless skill – these points are obvious in the case of either composer. Among their admirers both Mozart and Britten are known to be able to 'manage anything'. I hope there will never be any opportunity of proving that Britten can even manage things that bore him stiff; in Mozart's case such proof is furnished by the F minor Fantasy for what is called a barrel-organ (*Orgelwalze*) or clock (*Uhr*), 'a kind of composition which I detest', as he writes to his wife. But the general fact that both composers can write on commission as if they did not write on commission is of course established. The essence of such music for a special

---

*   Einstein, 1946, p. 109. Italics mine.

occasion does not with them betray external compulsion. Here the history of the Mozart Requiem is symbolic: an outer impulse is changed into an inner one.

The continued success of such impulse-changing does not depend merely on versatility, but also on deep-reaching agility. Britten is perhaps the most agile composer of our time. Busoni on Mozart: 'He is universal through his agility'. Universality itself has many aspects with Mozart and Britten. Two of these are particularly significant, both aesthetically and psychologically:

1   A German writer on music, Carl Gollmick (1796-1866), divides composers into two classes (he would!), *i.e.* 'melodists' and 'contrapuntists', and proceeds to show that Mozart satisfies the requirements of both these classes. If one wants to use this objectionable division – as a stenographic makeshift – for showing that it cannot be used in Mozart's case, and why not, one can also apply it, in almost the same way, to Britten.

2   Both composers have a sense at once of humour and of tragedy which they manifest quite clearly and which tends to go unrecognised by many of us because we do not easily permit ourselves to indulge, in our turn, in this double sense, and because we often find it difficult to bear contrary standpoints in the same man or work, or expressed at the same time. Yet, as the psycho-analyst [Otto] Rank has clearly recognized apropos of *Don Giovanni*, music is uniquely suited 'to express, at the same time, different tendencies'.

This [second] point merits a little further attention, for which purpose I must, alas, once more differ from Professor Dent, high esteem for whom it is needless to stress. Replying to the time-honoured question whether *Don Giovanni* is a serious or a comic opera, he says: 'The simplest plan is to take the opera as its author and composer intended – as an amusing comedy, with a touch of social satire and a great deal of fantastic impossibility'. One is all for taking the opera as all this, but Dent wants it to be taken as this alone. The libretto may stand such a one-sided interpretation, but the music does not. The question whether *Don Giovanni* is a serious or a comic opera does not indeed exist: it is both.* Similarly, *Così fan tutte* is not just 'an elaborate artificial comedy' (Dent). The great E major aria, for instance, suggests otherwise.

With Britten the whole story has started all over again. A prominent and otherwise perspicacious critic has made me very unhappy with his remark, apropos of *Lucretia* (which, upon thorough study, I deem a great work), that the composer's

---

*   The two schools of interpretation, the 'tragic' and the 'comic', both equally one-sided, *can* be roughly located along historical and geographical co-ordinates. As far as the latter magnitude goes, the tragic school is predominantly German, the comic predominantly English.

bent was not for 'tragic or even human feeling', but solely 'for artificial comedy'. Meanwhile, Britten's first comic opera, *Albert Herring*, has itself shown that he is able, in the words of Charles Stuart, to take 'excursions into a rarer world, with the earthiness of comic opera left behind and below'. We must recognize that there are two sides to Britten.* In fact I personally think that whenever there is only one side to an artist it is a wrong one.

Both composers create in the same way. Britten: 'Usually I have the music complete in my head before putting pen to paper.' In this respect their exact contrary is Beethoven. They also create, if I may say so, in the same way:

> When not flying or sailing to foreign opera houses and concert halls ... Britten is perpetually rushing off to catch trains for voice-and-piano recitals with Peter Pears in remote provincial towns. The business of musical creation goes on serenely among the bustle and the baggage. Looking unseeingly through train windows ... Britten composes as fluently as if he were sitting in a soundproof cell, with quires of manuscript paper before him and a grand piano at his elbow.†

> And travel does not interrupt Mozart's creative activity; it rather stimulates it. When long journeys are out of the question, as for example, during the last ten years in Vienna, he is constantly changing his residence ... from the town out into the suburbs, and from the suburbs back again into town.‡

Britten's parallel manoeuvres proceed of course from London to Snape and from Snape to London.

Scoring: strictly speaking, this problem does not appear to be one with Mozart and Britten (except where they are concerned with other composers' works: *Messiah*, *Matinées musicales*). 'With Mozart', Arthur Hutchings aptly observes,§ 'such problems [of balance, tone-colour, variety, etc.] do not seem to exist. He may have been lucky; the band may have been at just the right stage of development to make

---

* On the basis of psychological reflections such as I have sketched above, *sub* (2), I ventured the prediction some time ago ('Glyndebourne Preface', in the June issue of *Sound*), that 'the *serious* musical aspect of [*Albert Herring*] will tend to be underestimated, or even neglected'. Many reviewers have, unfortunately, proved me right. Among the exceptions there is, of course, Desmond Shawe-Taylor who, apropos of the threnody in the last act, points out that 'it is such moments as these which make it a superficial judgment to write the work off as a farce or a charade.' (*New Statesman and Nation*, 28 June 1947).

† 'Profile – Benjamin Britten', *Observer*, 27 October 1946.

‡ Einstein, *op. cit.*, pp. 4ff.

§ 'A Note on the "Additional Accompaniments"', *Music Review*, Vol. VII, No. 3, p. 161.

instrumental thinking but one element in musical thinking as a whole …'* (Dear old History again, though it is true that Hutchings later rejects her claims.) Compare this with what one of the most discerning critics of Britten, Desmond Shawe-Taylor, says about this composer's 'musical thinking as a whole':

> One difference between Britten and most of his contemporaries is that, in the process of composition, his imaginative 'inner ear' is listening, all the time and at full stretch, to what he is doing; fascinating as his music looks on paper – for he is a master of figuration and every kind of musical device [as Mozart is. – H.K.] – I feel tolerably sure that his ideas never occur to him as anything but sheer sensuous sound, and that it is to this fact that they owe the force and freshness with which they strike the listener's ear.

Thus, for instance, Mozart's and Britten's compositions for orchestra are not orchestrated, but orchestral.

Both composers seem to 'derive much from melodic inspiration. More materially, they are liable to be inspired by the human voice (as also by language, including foreign language), and indeed influenced by individual voices (as well as by instruments and instrumentalists). As regards Mozart, 'opera was always composed for a special occasion and for particular singers; the choice of singers influenced the vocal style and other characteristics as well'.† The same is true of the three operas Britten has written so far; even Grimes was 'considerably influenced' by the Sadler's Wells Opera Company.‡ It would seem to me that when Britten writes for tenor or soprano he is in advance of himself in a similar way as Mozart when writing a piano concerto (in which he can let himself be inspired not only by his piano playing but also, in various ways though indirectly, by vocal ideas). At the same time Britten the pianist has for me some striking similarities with what I picture to be Mozart the pianist; but as I have not heard Mozart I shall not enlarge on this point. In any case Mozart's piano concertos and Britten's tenor compositions are instances of their common love for virtuosity which, together with their common love of the dramatic, is also part of their intense common love for opera. Both, moreover, carry their symphonic thinking into opera, and their operatic thinking into extra-operatic music.

---

*   Hutchings's sentence ends thus: '… as it is to a composer writing a chamber work'. The relevance of this phrase, however, escapes me: surely it needs qualifying. Brahms, for instance, certainly conceived music in an abstract manner even where he was concerned with chamber music, much of which clearly exhibits his surmounting instrumental problems.

†   Einstein, op. cit., p. 465.

‡   Benjamin Britten, 'Peter Grimes: Introduction', in Peter Grimes, ed. Eric Crozier, London, Boosey and Hawkes, 1945.

As for the more extra-musical aspects of their operas, the psychological and sociological theme of rebellion plays an important part. Even *The Magic Flute*, it must be remembered, 'was a work of rebellion';* *Grimes* and *Lucretia*, as well as *Herring*, centre on the motive of opposition to (society's) tyranny.

Operatic technique (Mozart to his father, October 13th 1781):

> Why, an opera is sure of success when the plot is well worked out, the words written solely for the music and not shoved in here and there to suit some miserable rhyme ... I mean, words or even entire verses which ruin the composer's whole idea. Verses are indeed the most indispensable element for music – but rhymes – solely for the sake of rhyming – the most detrimental. These high and mighty people who set to work in this pedantic fashion will always come to grief, both they and their music. The best thing of all is when a good composer, who understands the stage and is talented enough to make sound suggestions, meets an able poet, that true phoenix; in that case no fears need be entertained as to the applause, even of the ignorant.

Britten:[†]

> This working together of the poet and composer seems to be one of the secrets of writing a good opera. In the general discussion on the shape of the work – the plot, the division into recitatives, arias, ensembles and so on – the musician will have many ideas that may stimulate and influence the poet. Similarly when the libretto is written and the composer is working on the music, possible alterations may be suggested by the flow of the music, and the libretto altered accordingly ... The composer and poet should at all stages be working in the closest contact, from the most preliminary stages right up to the first night.

Joseph Gregor[‡] has pointed out that, in spite of what there was before him, Mozart may in some respects be regarded as a founder (a 'second founder') of opera. The same can already be said to-day, as far as the modern British – perhaps not only British – field goes, of Britten. We cannot leave the subject of opera without quoting a criticism of *Don Giovanni*, or rather of a review of *Don Giovanni*, whose resemblance with various criticisms of allegedly too favourable reactions to Britten's operas is, it will be admitted, almost uncannily striking. Einstein[§] rightly reminds us that

---

*   Einstein, *op. cit.*, p. 465.

†   Benjamin Britten, Preface to *The Rape of Lucretia*, London, Boosey and Hawkes, 1946.

‡   *Kulturgeschichte der Oper*, Zürich, 1941.

§   *Op. cit.*, p. 134.

> No biography should fail to reproduce ... – as evidence of contemporary presumption, especially characteristic of Berlin – the dictum of an anonymous writer who was moved by an enthusiastic description of *Don Giovanni* by Bernhard Anselm Weber in the *Musicalisches Wochenblatt* of 1792 to the following reprimand: 'His report of Mozart's *Don Juan* is highly exaggerated and one-sided. No one will misjudge Mozart, the man of great talents and the expert, prolific and pleasing composer. Yet I do not know any well-grounded connoisseur of art who considers him a correct, not to say finished, artist; still less will the critic of sound judgment consider him, in respect to poetry, a proper and fine composer'.

When they are not accused of striving after originality, Mozart and Britten are accused of lacking originality, of eclecticism. In Mozart's case such an accusation will necessarily be indirect, because unfortunately it isn't done. (If it were, the lack of understanding in many a half-hearted 'admirer' would more easily be seen.) One way of thus indirectly attacking Mozart is to discover too much of him in Christian Bach, and to end up by playing Christian Bach instead of Mozart.*

With regard to Britten's 'eclecticism', the accusations are of course direct and numerous. Instead of allowing ourselves to be detained by them, let us look at the whole question from the other, understanding side. To begin with, Mozart again. Here is an eminent musicologist on his 'eclecticism'; we shall easily see how this applies to Britten:

> ... [Mozart] united the musical treasures of all nations of his time. This could easily have led to a mixture without character, but ... Mozart did not imitate anyone or anything; the external appearance of music was but a means of expression to him, never technique ... It is not enough ... to say that content and form balance each other in Mozart's music, for this unity is style, and while the style is constant the variety of its manifestations is as great as the number of his works. Mozart never created really new forms, but by regarding, the existing styles not as unities but as phenomena which contribute towards a general style, he created a universal all-inclusive style ...†

> We must not forget that Mozart was the child of an era customarily called the 'golden age' of musical art. Such a golden age ... offers to the genius the richest treasures of the various artistic forms. ... He simply takes the gifts of his epoch, intact, and, as self-evident matter, utilizes them at his will. ... Mozart

---

*   *Pace* Christian Bach's mastery and all that Mozart owes to it.
†   P. H. Lang, *Music in Western Civilization*, New York, 1941, p. 636.

> shuffled [the creations of the eighteenth century] like a pack of cards and the result was a strikingly original and individual world.*

This is all true, I suggest, except for the over-stress on history: Britten is doing a similar shuffling without being the child of a golden age.

Let us now hear Britten's own words on his 'eclecticism'. After implying that he passes from manner to manner 'as a bee passes from flower to flower', he declares: 'I do not see why I should lock myself inside a purely personal idiom. I write in the manner best suited to the words, theme or dramatic situation which I happen to be handling.' We here remember that Einstein speaks of Mozart's 'astonishing capacity for imitation, assimilation and elaboration of whatever suited him',† of his being 'the greatest master of style, or rather of all musical styles'.‡ Indeed Mozart himself wrote to his father (February 7th 1778): 'As you know, I can more or less adopt or imitate any kind and any style of composition.' Einstein suggests§ that this capacity accounts for Mozart's super-nationality, and I would add that it also accounts for Britten's, whose success among foreign musicians in this country and abroad is remarkable. It may be interesting to note in this connection that Britten's solution of the modern sonata problem in his C major Quartet has perhaps been most strongly appreciated by two Austrian musicians: Erwin Stein¶ and the present writer.** According to the music critic of *The Times*, the sonata form 'is for all its universal validity an essentially Austrian way of thinking in music'.††

Britten's afore-mentioned remarks on his 'eclecticism' also include a reminder that has already been partly quoted at the beginning of this article: 'The romantics became so intensely personal that it looked as though we were going to reach a point at which the composer would be the only man capable of understanding his own music.' And Mozart writes to his father (December 28th 1782): 'The golden mean of truth in all things is no longer either known or appreciated. In order to win applause one must write stuff which is so inane that a cabby could sing it, or so unintelligible that it pleases precisely because no sensible man can understand it ...' Again, could not the following, too, have been written, *mutatis mutandis*, by Britten?:

---

*   *Ibid.*, p. 137.

†   Einstein, *op. cit.*, p.110.

‡   *Ibid.*, p. 129.

§   *Ibid.*, p. 103.

¶   Erwin Stein, Analysis of 'Benjamin Britten – String Quartet No. 2, in C, Op. 36', Hawkes Pocket Scores, Boosey and Hawker, London, 1946.

**   Hans Keller, 'Benjamin Britten's Second Quartet', *Tempo* 3 (Old Series 18), March 1947, pp. 6-8.

††   'English Chamber Music', *The Times*, 17 January 1947.

This is what I think [of a Concerto for two flutes by Friedrich Hartmann Graf, 1727-1795]. It is not at all pleasing to the ear, not a bit natural. He often plunges into a new key far too brusquely and it is all quite devoid of charm. When it was over, I praised him very highly, for he really deserves it. The poor fellow must have taken a great deal of trouble over it and he must have studied hard enough. At last a clavichord, one of Stein's, was brought out of the inner room, an excellent instrument, but covered with dust and dirt. Herr Graf, who is director here, stood there transfixed, like someone who has always imagined that his wanderings from key to key are quite unusual and now finds that one can be even more unusual and yet not offend the ear.[*]

Reflecting upon Mozart's temperament, Einstein says:

He yielded to an influence quite ingenuously, quite in the feminine fashion. He strove least of all for originality; because he was entirely certain of the Mozartian, personal stamp of his product. *Facile inventis addere* cannot apply to him; this adage applies indeed only to science or technique. What he derived from others was for him a fertilization, which eased the course of the spiritual and musical pregnancy and birth.[†]

And Desmond Shawe-Taylor, after mentioning, inter alia, Verdi's and Handel's influence upon *Albert Herring*, remarks that 'in spite of such links, the whole score remains immensely characteristic of its composer'.[‡] The whole problem of Mozart's and Britten's originality and eclecticism can, I think, be summed up in Einstein's words: 'Mozart belongs, like Bach, to the rare species of the conservative revolutionaries, or the revolutionary conservatives.'[§]

In a paragraph on the youthful aspects of Mozart, Láng[¶] thinks that in the composer lives all the eighteenth century's

youthful delicacy and feminine grace, ... its brightness and naturalness, ... its flexibility, its loving care for the little and the fine, its fondness for variation and for the characteristic ... But this lovable youthfulness ripens into maturity, and playful freedom and moodiness are harnessed by schooling and discipline, ingenuous feelings are formed by classic measure, ideas are deepened to symbols of universal significance.

---

[*]   Mozart to his father, 14 October 1777.
[†]   *Op. cit.*, p. 122.
[‡]   'Britten's Comic Opera', *The Listener*, 12 June 1947.
[§]   *Op. cit.*, p. 162.
[¶]   *Op. cit.*, p. 624.

Note how very exactly the spiritual tendencies here enumerated apply to Britten, although – neo-classicism apart – one does not find the affinities between our own time and the eighteenth century very striking.

One may at the same time concede that the form in which Britten's fondness for variation quite often manifests itself, i.e. the ostinato, is in part historically determined.

In and beyond the art of variation, the fundamental musical principle of repetition is treated in a similar way by the two composers. Both mechanical reiteration and narcissistic re-citation are absent; thematic relationships, though frequent and really simple, often go unrecognized by the superficial listener because in the process of transformation or transplantation of themes or fragments far-reaching changes of emotional significance are secured, though of course at the same time an underlying emotional identity is preserved. The strong drive of either composer towards economy (as distinct from poverty) of thematic material is just as obvious as the fact that economy, in either case, also radiates in other directions, e.g. the instrumental. In an article entitled 'Back to Mozart?' Felix von Weingartner once remarked:

> ... thus I want to give the following answer to the question put in the title: To create, with our modern means of expression, *in Mozart's spirit* – this would perhaps be the right thing. ... But ... can there be any question of 'back'? I think it must much more truly be said: '*Forward* to Mozart!'[*]

Can it be chance that Weingartner was, as far as I know, the first to call Britten (after hearing the oboe Quartet in 1934) a genius?

Before I try to round off my thesis I should like to quote some more of Busoni's aphorisms on Mozart. Their relevance will, I trust, be appreciated at this stage without further comment. 'He doesn't risk anything foolhardy.' 'He is capable of saying very much, but never says too much.' 'He carries all characters within himself, but only as an exhibitor and portraitist.' 'Together with the puzzle he gives you the solution.' 'He can always draw water from any glass because he has emptied none.' 'His smile is not that of a diplomat or actor, but that of a pure nature – yet that of a man of the world.' 'He is spirited without any nervousness – idealist without becoming immaterial, realist without ugliness.' 'It is the architectural that is most closely related to his art'.

'In respect to universality,' writes Einstein, 'Mozart may be compared only with other great masters; and in our comparisons we shall limit ourselves to the eighteenth and nineteenth centuries.'[†] He would not, I believe, thus limit himself if he knew Britten's music.

---

[*]   His italics.
[†]   *Op. cit.,* p. 103.

> Nearest [to Mozart], perhaps, is Handel, the master of the cantata, the opera, the oratorio, the concerto grosso, the sonata – but we are stopped short already. Did not all this flow from one unified, mighty source, Italian vocalism, the *bel canto* of the monumental aria?[*]

On the basis of the present article, I submit, we cannot be stopped short in this or any other way when we compare Britten with Mozart. Britten, that is to say, is not only immeasurably nearer to Mozart than Handel because his (Britten's) universality does not spring from one unified source, but also because, beneath, above and beyond the sphere of universality, Britten and Mozart have far more in common than Handel and Mozart. 'And was Bach universal? To be sure, he left no corner uncultivated in the fields of instrumental and vocal music. ... Actually, however, all this, too, grows from one root –instrumental music ...'[†] And so it goes on. Gluck, Einstein's next object of comparison, need not, it will be admitted, detain us. 'Both Haydn and Beethoven are cramped by the word, they speak most freely in the instrumental fields.'[‡] And even putting the question of universality apart again, can it be suggested that Haydn-Mozart comparisons or Beethoven-Mozart comparisons are comparable with a comparison between Britten and Mozart?

> And this would bring us to Schubert, the composer of the 'Unfinished' and the D minor Quartet, and of hundreds of perfect songs, the only one who could be compared to Mozart, if it were not that, although he wrote operas too, the dramatic, the scenic, the feeling for the stage, were denied to him.[§]

I submit that Britten stands far nearer to Mozart than does Schubert, once more not only in respect of universality (cf. particularly 'the dramatic, the scenic, the feeling for the stage'), but also – as I hope the present paper tends to show – in almost every other respect. In fact, to me personally it seems that the only deep-rooted musico-characterological difference between Britten and Mozart is that the one is often strongly inspired by nature while the other is an indoor composer. Passing, for obvious reasons, over the rest of Einstein's list of composers to be compared, or rather not to be compared, with Mozart, we arrive at this admirable summing-up of Mozart's universality:

> When one considers the somnambulistic surefootedness and grace with which Mozart masters the vocal and the instrumental, mass and opera, quartet and

---

[*]   *Ibid.*

[†]   *Ibid.*

[‡]   *Op. cit.*, p. 104.

[§]   *Ibid.*

concerto, one's admiration grows immeasurably at the phenomenon of his uniqueness as a universal musician.[*]

This is not the time, and I am not the man, to decide about the relative greatness of Mozart and Britten; to assess how far with Britten, too, 'the world-spirit wishes to show that here is pure sound, conforming to a weightless cosmos, triumphant over all chaotic earthliness, spirit of the world-spirit';[†] but as one who is soaked in the music of both Mozart and Britten I may be allowed to claim that for the first time Mozart, the universal musician who masters everything with a somnambulistic surefootedness and grace, has found a companion. It follows that I regard Britten as the greatest of all contemporary composers whose music I understand.

---

[*]   *Op. cit.*, p. 105.
[†]   The concluding sentence of Einstein's book, p. 471.

(ii) 'Così fan tutte'

Ex. 1a

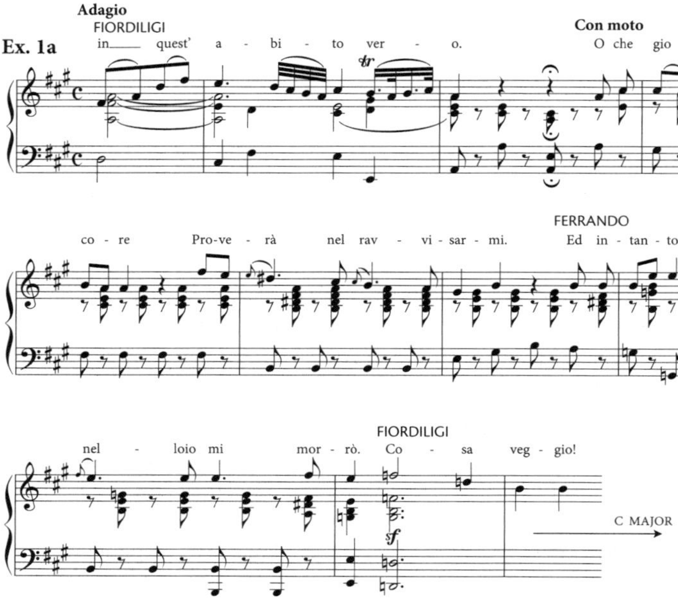

Ex. 1b

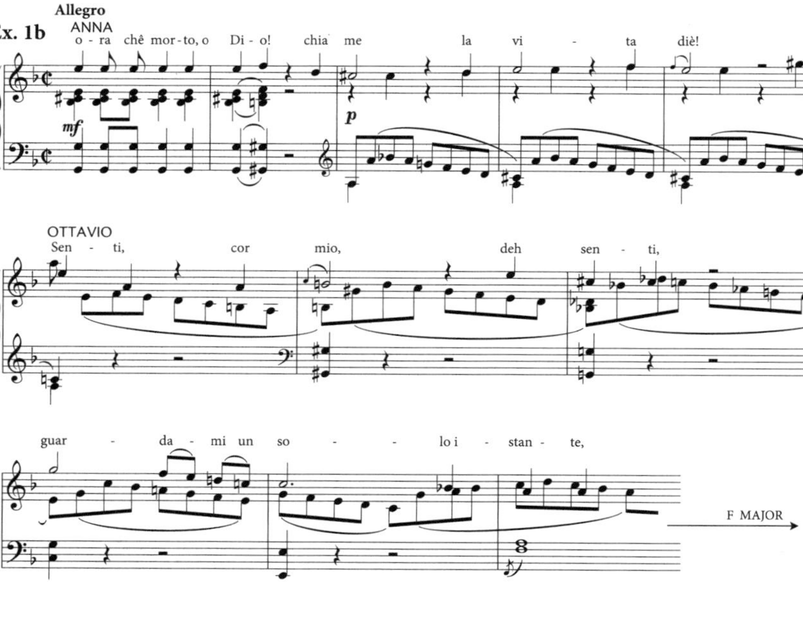

Ex. 2a

Allegro
DORABELLA

A mor - re mi fac - cia vi - ven - do pe - nar,

Ex. 2b

Adagio
ELVIRA

il mio__ tra - di - to, tra - di - to a - mor,

Ex. 3a

Allegretto

Ex. 3b

Andante maestoso

Why do the cuts in opera productions escape criticism, whereas interpretational mishaps, which vary from performance to performance, don't? Why, for instance have Fiordiligi's B flat aria(-)* in, and her supremely important E major aria(+)[†] out? Because the latter is too difficult? But then Miss Lowe – *pace* her musical and vocal qualities – can't manage the former's triplets, either. Why again have Despina's comparatively unimportant G major aria (-) in (though shortened), but deprive Ferrando and Dorabella of their arias in Act II (-)? To give Miss Bower a bit more to do? But then – *pace* her good performance – a singer is not as important as all that. One is grateful, on the other hand, for the inclusion of No. 20 (*Prenderò quel brunettino*)(-), and for the full version of No. 23 (*Il core vi dono*), shortened in the previous Wells production; nor does the omission of No. 7 (*Al fato dàn legge*)(-) matter. Brannigan makes an excellent Alfonso, and Miss Pollak splendidly builds up her aria (not her *arias*, as we read in *The Times*).

This number (No. 11, *Smanie implacabili*), which 'would do credit to any fury robbed of her serpents',[†] was mutilated by a hair-raising cut in the recent Vienna State Opera production. In the A major duet No. 29 (cf. Ex. 1a) one misses Pears, all the more because Lewis (a good singer) imitates him. The unexpected, indeed overwhelming, dominant minor entry (see Ex. 1a), in particular, does not receive sufficient intensity. I remember only two other vocal ensembles of Mozart's wherein the entry introduces the dominant minor, namely, the first duet in *Don Giovanni* (Ex. 1b) and the *Requiem's Tuba mirum*. In all three instances, the entry in question is the tenor's. In Exx. 1a-b one further observes the parallel modulations

---

*   (-): Omitted in the previous Wells production.

†   (+): Included in the previous Wells production.

‡   Einstein, A., *Mozart: His Character, His Work*, London 1946.

to C and F respectively; there are other (e.g. motivic) relations between these two numbers which are not apparent from the quoted excerpts. The similarities in the psychological content of the two dramatic situations are striking; one here remembers Dent's sensitive observation that if Anna 'had been Italian, and not Spanish, she might have been Fiordiligi'.[*] Dent does not, however, note the present, as distinct from other, less important parallels between *Così* and *Don Giovanni*. Neither does Einstein, who is averse to the search for Wagnerian *Leitmotive* in Mozart,[†] but who will, I feel sure, admit the great significance of such inter-operatic *Leimodulationen*. The beginning of Ex. 1b is, incidentally, an intra- and inter-operatic *Leitmotiv*. See the beginning of scene xix in *Don Giovanni* (D minor!), and the beginning of the Queen of the Night's D minor (!) aria. Exx. 1a (*Così*, first duet)– 2b (*Don Giovanni*, first finale, end of scene xix), and 3a (Despina's first aria)– 3b (*Don Giovanni*, first finale, end of penultimate episode) are among those motifs which you would expect Mozart to use frequently, but which he actually seems to use only on these occasions. Both Ex. 3a and Ex. 3b are immediately repeated, the latter twice. The utilization of this cadential motif at the *beginning* of Despina's aria (Ex. 3a), while playful, is at the same time perhaps more beautiful than it is serious, but more ordinary than its application at the *end* of the Andante maestoso in the *Don Giovanni* finale (Ex. 3b).

We know how well Dent describes the sham aspect of *Così*, but it seems to me that he does not define what is perhaps the most intriguing aspect of *Così*'s simulations. Occasionally, I mean, Mozart only pretends to be pretending.

---

[*]   Dent, E. J., *Mozart's Operas* (1913), second ed. 1947, London, OUP, 1947.

[†]   Einstein, A., Preface to the Eulenburg minature full score of *Don Giovanni* (1930?).

(iii)   'On Musical Understanding'

Nihil est ab omni parte beatum (HORACE)

To describe musical understanding to the musical is unnecessary; to explain it to the unmusical is impossible. But it is desirable to reflect on the when and why of its absence – questions which each of us must decide in his own mind before he can claim the right to criticise. Two of the three chief enemies of musical understanding are (a) lack of technical knowledge, (b) technical knowledge. The third obstacle in the way of our understanding something is our understanding of something else.

To stress the need for technical knowledge at this time of the day is luxurious. Nowadays only music critics do without it. They represent the public; hence their duty is to represent ignorance. Good music, however, unlike a pudding, is the result of a revelation which necessarily creates much of its own technique. What is more, while there is no technique left once the pudding is on the table, music develops a good deal of its technique each time it is played or imagined; technique and result overlap. The technique of a good pudding and of bad music is of course of little interest to the consumer – the former because it is satisfactory, the latter because it isn't. But it will not do to neglect an inspired technique. Since, however, the good composer does not arrive at what he has to say via his technique, we don't either. Technical studies must be inspired by an understanding of the revelation which inspired his technique. Without technical knowledge we cease to understand when the composer's inspiration leaves us. With technical knowledge, we then begin to understand, and to write highly competent, unfavourable reviews. Misunderstanding can be an enjoyable activity, but from it there is a longer way to understanding than from lack of understanding.

How, then, should one try to understand the composer's revelation? One shouldn't. 'Wenn ihr's nicht fühlt, ihr werdet's nicht erjagen' (Goethe, *Faust* I). The grasping of inspiration, like inspiration itself, has nothing to do with effort or expertness. Wherefrom some will deduce their own pet view that good music is there to be understood by Everybody rather than by the Expert, a view fashionable nowadays among those who base their scientific investigations into the position of art in society on their complete ignorance of the science of the mind. The truth is that given money, time, inclination, and a sufficient dose of unconscious guilt for making him enjoy hard, futile work, more or less everybody can become what among other everybodies is known as an expert. But only few get anywhere near understanding the full, terrific meaning of, for instance, what I have shown to be Mozart's inter-operatic Leitmodulations,* and some of them may neither know nor

---

*   *The Music Review*, May 1948, pp. 110 ff., and November 1948, pp. 298 ff. [see essay (ii) on *Così fan tutte*].

care what I wish to convey by this term. In a word, only a small minority of us is musical through and through, and the understanding of great art is at the time of writing limited to a spiritual aristocracy. How far this regrettable state of affairs may be improved through changes in early upbringing remains to be seen; that it cannot be improved by adult education is obvious from the established fact that character formation is determined in childhood.

And how are we to know if and when we belong to the few who really understand? If and when we belong, we know. But we do not always know if and when we don't belong. And example from my own experience: I had been passionately in love with *Figaro* since my childhood. I had always been delighted with, indeed intensely moved by the sextet. I had every wrong reason to believe that I understood this piece completely, for I knew it inside out. Until one day I discovered that what I had known inside out was not much more than its outside. It had been an exhausting day; I arrived at the opera later in the evening, and on the verge of going to sleep. When I entered, the sextet was just starting, and now, for the first time, I heard everything it revealed and concealed. Its cogency, its universality, the heavenly resignation underlying this understatement of all that moves, divides and unites the world, the easy victory over deep tragedy that is its humour – it all overwhelmed me and, to be frank, I cried. From then onwards, I was convinced that the sextet was *Figaro*'s best number, and when some time later I read that Mozart himself thought so, my belief that I understood Mozart received a confirmation it did not need.

Now it is my understanding of, for instance, Mozart which gives me a standard by which I judge what I understand and what I don't. I think that nobody should talk or write about music unless he has developed such a standard. That there is no further standard by which one can objectively ascertain the existence of one's criterion of understanding is unfortunate, but does not get us round the need for it. Doubtless the composer(s) on whose understanding our standard is based must be part of our lives. One trouble here is that one meets and reads people who have made a composer part of their lives while showing a none too exhaustive understanding of his music.

The other trouble is that once you have lived yourself into the music of one composer, your understanding of other composers may suffer, especially of those whose artistic tendencies are in some way opposed to the individual traits of your favourite. This risk does not simply stand in inverse relation to your musicality, but depends to a great extent on your character. The strongly original and revolutionary genius shows less broad an understanding for other composers than the more conservative and eclectic genius; otherwise, indeed, the former could not be revolutionary, nor the latter eclectic. Similarly with the listener, according to whether or how far he tends to be single- or many-minded.

The greatest danger to music is mindless, seeming many-mindedness, a danger that has become acute since there are more composers, musicians, critics, and music-lovers than musical people. I do not deny the beneficial aspects of the Music-for-the-Masses (and -by-the-Masses) policy, but I marvel at the naiveté with which its adherents overlook the fact that while not every bad thing has a good side, every good thing has a bad one, which in this case happens to be pretty awful. It is they who deplore the present-day cleft between the composer and the public, but instead of blaming the public they blame the composer, and ask him to climb down to the greatest and uncommonly common measure of idiocy which is the inevitable consequence of bringing music to the unmusical.

The public always, and the composer and executant artist rarely, get the critics they merit, for it is the public who pay for the critics, and it is the artists and the few able critics who, being after all human, are far too cowardly to pronounce openly what a racket the greater part of musical criticism is — as each of them will gladly tell you in private. Since at the present time the majority of audiences lack even the faintest criterion by which to measure their understanding, they welcome everything from a critic as long as it makes nonsense, giving particular preference to factually wrong criticism. One or the other reader may remember the controversy I recently had with one of our leading critics in one of our weeklies. He had written an extremely unfavourable review of Britten's *Beggar's Opera*, basing his irrelevant criticisms of the composer's harmonies on verifiably wrong observations, e.g. the imputation of keylessness. While I had not at that time seen the score (a fact which I pointed out), I enumerated the keys of, *inter alia*, the numbers which showed strong chromatic intensification. In his reply to my stressedly factual protest this critic had not the courage to admit that he had been, simply and provably, wrong. Instead, beside discharging an undue amount of hostility, he suggested that the proof of the pudding lay in the eating, a retort which in this case was more than usually absurd since I, too, knew the work only from hearing.

The point I wish to make is that a leading critic can, without an uproar on the part of the musical public, criticise *harmonies* without (among other blunders) noticing the presence of *keys*; and that, when one points this out, he is still allowed to believe that he sufficiently understands the stuff to criticise it. The gravity of such a symptomatic incident can hardly be overestimated, once we are agreed that wherever the proof of the music is to be found, it does not lie in the ear of the deaf.

(iv)   'Schoenberg and the Men of the Press'

The decisive happens despite (NIETZSCHE)
The critic stumbles along behind the artist (J. ISAACS)

We gather that Schoenberg's new book *Style and Idea* will very shortly be published in this country (Williams & Norgate). This seems the moment, then, for dispelling some of the prejudices which may have been aroused against the work by certain reviews of its American edition (1950), immoral at their worst and ignorant at their best. With Richard Capell's *Daily Telegraph* review, entitled 'Schoenberg's Ideas', I have dealt in an article (under my present title) in the February issue of *Colophon*, where I have also examined John Amis's (*Tribune*) and Frank Howes's (*The Times*) latest verdicts on Schoenberg's music. Richard Capell himself bequeathed this subtly ironical title to Winton Dean, inviting him to produce what turned out to be an extended tirade on the book in *Music & Letters*, and it is against this article-review as well as against Richard S. Hill's review in *Notes* (Washington) and Professor Gerald Abraham's emissions *ex cathedra* Monthly Musical *opinionis* that I here propose to defend the composer. Nothing is easier, and nothing more convincing to the ignorant, than to sweep over the deep. Nothing is more relieving than to talk about what one doesn't know, for it's the easiest thing to be done about it; besides, it promotes solidarity among the light-minded, promotes that jolly good highbrow fellowship which keeps the music critic's conscience ever supple and easy. Artistic stupidity hides behind anti-artistic intelligence which takes everything into humorous account except genius. Genius tends to be a disturbing phenomenon for the critic, for its recognition depends upon the creation of new standards of evaluation. Music criticism justifies itself where an inspired vision of the future supersedes all acquired illusions of the past. Otherwise, it merely judges itself: perhaps it is because the critic criticizes himself that he doesn't want to be criticized by anybody else. Or perhaps it is because he feels more certain than secure. In any case, one has to grant him that his certainty is based upon his professional knowledge; but, alas, most professionals who construct this body of knowledge are amateurs without the imagination of amateurs. They know enough to judge the past by its future, but when it comes to the present they judge it by its past. As for the future – that, they say, can look after itself. 'Can' and 'must', however, have no future tense, and what can and must be known and said, can and must be said now.

It may seem unfair to reproach Gerald Abraham with insufficient knowledge, not only because he stands far above the common music(ologic)al pressman both as a scholar and as a musician, but more particularly because he has written on Schoenberg for *Grove's* Supplementary Volume (4th Edition). A *Grove* article, however, depends on exoteric knowledge, whereas the appraisal of genius, and of the man in whom genius burns, depends on esoteric knowledge. In simpler words, in matters out of the emotional or spiritual ordinary, it all depends on whether you know things outside in or inside out.

In the case of Winton Dean, however – a valued contributor to this journal upon other subjects – there does not even seem to be any exoteric knowledge capable of utilization. In fact, all that emerges from his piece is his staggering ignorance of every aspect of Schoenberg's work, mind, and background. A real knowledge of the twelve-tone technique, to be sure, can only be derived from the actual compositions; just as a real understanding of Schoenberg's work, including his writings, can only be arrived at by way of one's insight into the development of his genius, or rather *into strongly developing genius in general* (Beethoven, for instance, or Freud, or Picasso). Mr. Dean, however, far from realizing as much as his factual ignorance, and quite unconscious of the dangers of spiritual ignorance, writes about Schoenberg's essays as a teacher would write about the efforts of a none too gifted, if far too self-satisfied pupil. He is careful to grant Schoenberg no more than a 'reputation' and a 'position', whereas he uses the words 'genius' and 'master' for the purpose of ironisation. I am indeed in a difficult position, for humility in the face of genius is not half as readable as humour in the face of the unfaceable. Before we plunge into the morass, moreover, we have the ungrateful task of teaching the editor of a leading musicological journal *mores*: that he should have entrusted an article on Schoenberg's book to someone whose knowledge of Schoenberg equals mine of Sibelius is inexcusable.

There is good humour, there is bad humour, and there is the worst kind of humour, which is good humour misapplied: 'Schoenberg's latest work is written in the twenty-six letter system.' Thus Mr. Dean sets the mood of his article, and the *Musical Times* was quick to quote the sentence with relish. Upon the following excerpt from Schoenberg's essay 'On Revient Toujours' –

> ... a longing to return to the older style was always vigorous in me; and from time to time I had to yield to that urge. This is ... why I sometimes write tonal music. To me stylistic differences of this nature are not of special importance. I do not know which of my compositions are better; I like them all, because I liked them when I wrote them.

– Dean comments: – 'The [penultimate sentence], which belies a great deal elsewhere in the book, will perhaps disconcert both friends and adversaries; the [last sentence] reveals a parental tenderness and fidelity almost unique in creative artists.' Mr. Dean here proves himself unable to distinguish between the evolutional, historical point of view, wherefrom the stylistic differences are of special importance, and the extra-historical evaluational standpoint, from which they aren't. And sure enough, Mr. Dean's complete mis-interpretation of the excerpt's last sentence, which he has not understood at all, brings us to the crux of most criticisms of the book: the critics' inability to view Schoenberg *in terms of his development*. What

Schoenberg means is what, in the simplest possible words, he says: he likes all his compositions because *each is true to the stage of creative development at which it was written*. Now, Schoenberg's more recent tonal compositions correspond to the stage where, having fully mastered his most advanced style, he is able to progress by regressing: to let the older methods gain by the new. The mastery he has achieved in his new technique makes it possible for him to revert to the old techniques without slackening his ever further urging development, without impeding his extra-diatonic thinking: he can now symbiotically combine contradicting methods without contradicting himself. Of course, if you cannot grasp his development, he seems to contradict himself, in his music and in his writings. He contradicts himself as much and as little as Beethoven's late B$^\flat$ quartet contradicts his early one. If Schoenberg did not thus 'contradict himself' – that would be a ground for criticism! Genius's first debt to art is dynamic evolution, while the critic's original sin is static evaluation. Thus Mr. Hill: '... there are constant indications in the lecture on "Composing with Twelve Tones" of how his method has changed and evolved. Obviously, he could not have been "right" both before and afterwards, and Schoenberg would be the first to admit it.' Being the author of a study on 'Schoenberg's Tone-Rows and the Tonal System of the Future' (*Musical Quarterly*, New York, January 1936), Mr. Hill is most unfortunately regarded as an authority on Schoenberg, and his pseudo-favourable review of the present book is doubly dangerous: a trap for the virginal reader, all the more effective because the trapper doesn't know that he is trapping. Exactly what right has he to give categorical information on what 'Schoenberg would be the first to admit'? If he understood what lies behind Schoenberg's 'changing method', if he had a musical approach to the development of Schoenberg's music, if he knew it from the inside, he would not be able to pronounce such overbearing nonsense. Those who experience Schoenberg's musical contents know that he wouldn't admit anything of the sort. On the extreme contrary, he would say that he was right both before and afterwards, that in creative growth what was right yesterday won't be right tomorrow; and that what is wrong for the pupil is right for the master. A truism? Not many apply its truth to the case of a genius who, once his own pupil, became his inner master's master.

Discussing this essay on twelve-tone composition, Dean lets Schoenberg appear 'convinced that the old tonality had been outmoded'. Nowhere does Schoenberg – himself still (better: again) in creative touch with 'the old tonality' – express or imply such a conviction. If Mr. Dean knew something about Schoenberg apart from the present book, he would perhaps realize the naiveté of his ideas of 'Schoenberg's Ideas'; he would know, for instance, Schoenberg's often-expressed aphorism that 'there is still plenty of good music to be written in C major.' In today's labile state of musical history, one and the same *time* comprises a bewildering variety of historical, developmental stages: history does not altogether [resist] parallel chronology. What is already valid for one creator (and listener) is not yet valid for another, and manybody's today is somebody's yesterday; while different stages of development may, moreover, co-exist and collaborate in the same musical mentality. That the complete emancipation of the dissonance represents an extreme advance in the inevitable evolution of music does not mean that all preceding stages are past; on the contrary, it means that Schoenberg's new style is the future's emissary in the present. The consequent sense of a mission which goes through Schoenberg's writings, however, is stigmatized as arrogance. 'Intellectual arrogance abounds,' says Prof. Abraham. 'One is tempted to call him egocentric and almost unbelievably conceited,' says Mr. Hill. 'Is it not the height of arrogance,' asks Mr. Dean, 'to assert that "the time will come when the ability to draw thematic material from a basic set of twelve tones will be an unconditional requisite for obtaining admission into the composition class of a conservatory"?' I should say, that depends on whether the time will come. But Mr. Dean does not even comply with primitive logic: he does not admit the mere possibility that Schoenberg's is a realistic prognosis, in which case the term 'arrogance' does not apply, for to arrogate means to claim unduly. In other words, Mr. Dean, who never tires of reproaching Schoenberg with begging questions, begs (among others) the most fundamental question of all, though he professes to leave it unanswered at the end of his article. Likewise Mr. Hill: 'The world has not caught much warmth from his fire yet, and no one can possibly say whether eventually it will turn towards or away from that fire.' I beg Mr. Hill not to prescribe to us what we can or cannot possibly say. Predictability is a function of knowledge. If, on the one hand, one recognizes the scientific validity of the twelve- note method, while on the other hand partaking of Schoenberg's (as of all good music's) secret science,* i.e. if one isn't what Schoenberg calls 'one of these non-musicians who look in my music only for the twelve notes – not realizing in the least its musical content, expression, and merit'; if, in short, one is a musical scientist (accent on either word) who understands Schoenberg's music, one is in no doubt about its future. If, on the other hand, one thinks, with Prof. Abraham, that 'the lecture on "Composing with Twelve Tones" tells us, what most of us already know, how to "understand" twelve-tone music – that is, how to read the cipher – but contributes nothing toward its aesthetic justification,' one should not perhaps write about twelve-tone technique. For this sentence contains three radical fallacies. Firstly, inverted commas or no, the essay definitely doesn't tell us how to understand twelve-tone music (no musician's essay ever tells us how to understand music), nor does it encourage us to go twelve-tone hunting for the pleasure of the hunt. It describes the development and application of a method and is addressed to the musician who likes to know about what, emotionally and spiritually, he already understands, as well as to the potential

---

*   Schoenberg says in his essay on *The Blessing of the Dressing*: 'Secret science is not what an alchemist would have refused to teach you; it is a science which cannot be taught at all. It is inborn or it is not there.' [This essay of 1948 also appears in: *Style and Idea. Selected Writings of Arnold Schoenberg*, ed. Leonard Stein, with translations by Leo Black, London, Faber, 1975, pp. 382-86.]

pupil. Secondly, there is no 'cipher' in twelve-tone music; in fact, with the greatest precision, Prof. Abraham uses the wrongest possible term: a cipher conceals, whereas the tone row clarifies. Thirdly, the evolutional theory, the genesis of the twelve-tone technique is the aesthetic justification of its application, and Prof. Abraham appears to ask for an aesthetic justification of an aesthetic justification. The theory of twelve-tone music cannot, of course, be more complete than its history: what absurdity to expect the first twelve-tone musician to complete it!

But in spite of his howlers, in spite even of his unwarranted and unpleasant slight at Schoenberg's 'mental character' – 'terribly like the portrait drawn by his enemies' – [Prof. Abraham] does not quite descend to the schoolboy level of Mr. Dean, who does not shrink from giving Schoenberg a lesson in the Rudiments of Tonality; one need not be an admirer of Schoenberg in order to marvel at Richard Capell's temerity in printing this among many instances of equal insight: '[In tonal music] the basic motive is not [as Schoenberg says] a derivative of the tonality, it is expressed in terms of the tonality, just as a Latin poem is expressed in terms of the Latin language – a very different thing …'. I do not propose to prove to Mr. Dean that 2 x 2 is not 5 before someone supports him; but meanwhile he might try to translate a tonal motive of his own choosing into other terms, 'just as' one translates a Latin poem. He is indeed enamoured by comparisons; they work like miracles to prove the rightest wrong: 'Why should a reference to tonal harmony [in twelve-note composition] be "disturbing" in a pejorative sense? The modes did not cease to fertilize music the moment composers began to use the classical tonic and dominant system,' the absurd implication being that diatonicism is to modality as dodecaphonism should or could be to diatonicism. But the classical major and minor *are* modes, representing the survival of the fittest by artistic selection, whereas all atonal technique grows out of the disintegration of tonal unity and the emancipation (increasing intelligibility) of the dissonance. Thus, Mr. Dean's didactic comparison does not apply if we do not outright condemn an atonal approach; and if we do, we are asked to improve the unimprovable. '"False expectations of [tonal] consequences and continuations" which, by the very fact of their existence, could have been of the greatest artistic service are condemned outright. Not the least subtle device at a composer's command is his ability to open up one vista and lead his listeners down another.' Mr. Dean has not the faintest inkling of the radical change in compositional technique that manifests itself in twelve-tone music, whose evolutional aspect he is therefore once again unable to grasp. So-called deceptive devices in music – say an interrupted cadence (Trugschluss), or a 'deceptive' (discontinued) imitation – are not intended to deceive anyone (good music never is), but, on the contrary, to show the listener that and how he has been deceived by his platitudinous prejudices, by his automatic expectations. For this purpose, the disillusionment must be stronger than the illusion. Now Mr. Dean proposes that a radically new method of unification should, while it is still in the making, 'open up one vista' of an age-old and deeply ingrained method of unification, 'and lead his listeners down' the new way. But how can they thus be led, if the illusion is stronger than the disillusionment? Optimistically supposing that the composer did not himself fall a victim to the *fata morgana* he had conjured up, that, dead certain of the journey's end, he unhesitatingly continued on the new way – he would find, upon turning round, that his listeners had gone and perished the other way which promised to lead home but led to nowhere. This would be a real deception. Of course, the seasoned master of the twelve-tone technique can, as Schoenberg has shown in his music, lead the master-listener to new destinations by routes at once new and familiar, by routes whose unfamiliarity reveals itself all the more to the traveller when he becomes familiar with them; but then Mr. Dean does not perhaps realize that the twelve-tone lecture is not addressed to masters. If, on the other hand, he does, he might re-consider one of its reminders: '"Everything" has always been allowed to two kinds of artists: to masters on the one hand, and to ignoramuses on the other.' But what can one do with ignoramuses who proceed to teach the masters how to teach?

When Mr. Winton Dean, who by the evidence of his article has not gone through a single twelve-tone composition, declares the teachable part of Schoenberg's method to be a '"preconceived formula"* with a vengeance, hedged about with all manner of rules and prohibitions'; when he criticises this method as if he had ever tried to apply it, one realizes that the time has come when the ability to draw thematic material from a basic set of twelve tones ought to be an unconditional prerequisite for obtaining permission to criticize the twelve-tone method qua technique (as distinct from any particular result of its application). Any criticism of the technique's alleged rigidity is quite irrelevant if the limitations imposed upon horizontal construction are not considered against the freedom gained in vertical combinations. But so far is Mr. Dean's mind removed from the actual compositional processes involved in the application of the technique that such an elementary independent thought would never occur to him; he closely sticks to his misreading of Schoenberg's essay, for that is all he knows. In my opinion, once the twelve-tone technique has securely established itself, has become second nature, the genuinely musical world will realize that no change at all has taken place in the degrees of freedom and of discipline: the limitations of tonal harmony will be seen to have given way to a harmonic freedom which corresponds to the relative melodic freedom in tonal structures, and to have changed their residence from the harmonic to the melodic and contrapuntal field. Meanwhile, it is absurd to suggest, as Mr. Dean does, that Schoenberg 'has sought to elevate his own procedure to a universal rule.' The essay on twelve-tone technique stresses very thoroughly how the development of his technique has been bound up with the development of his

---

*   Apropos of Schoenberg's definition of a 'method' as 'a *modus* of applying regularly a preconceived formula.'

own creativity, and in the essay on 'The Blessing of the Dressing' he points out that all his pupils

> differ from one another extremely and though perhaps the majority compose twelve-tone music, one could not speak of a school. They all had to find their way alone, for themselves. And that is exactly what they did; everyone has his own manner of obeying rules derived from the treatment of twelve tones.

It is only the twelve-tonal, i.e. essentially extra-tonal principle on which his technique is based that claims universal validity (as distinct from universal applicability), and a creator whose technique is not based on a principle so universal that it is in harmony with the psychic universe may as well pack up and steal away before someone discovers the swindle which unwittingly pronounces its own death-sentence by calling itself 'contemporary'. Art is never contemporary, journalism always is; which is why the musical journalists mistake journalistic music for art. Nobody minds the critics' going about their 'quiet little jobs as cemetery watchmen' (Sartre), but when they start to employ themselves and one another as new life's grave-diggers … But stop, says Mr. Dean. He is not, he would tell us, passing final judgment on Schoenberg as a composer. Sartre: 'Our critics never bet on uncertain issues.' 'But,' says Mr. Dean, 'Schoenberg has ventured into the field of criticism.' He hasn't. He speaks as a teacher whom you mistake for a critic when he talks about the work of others, and for a 'doctrinaire' when he talks about his own. From what you and your colleagues-in-arms have written, readers who do not know much about Schoenberg must conclude that his prime concern is to push his compositional method down other people's throats, and that for the rest you can't learn anything from him, except 'things that were commonplace to Prout' (Abraham). A mere musician, however, and not a twelve-toner either – Otto Klemperer – recounts:-

> Originally a pupil of Hans Pfitzner, I had the opportunity of studying with Arnold Schoenberg in Los Angeles during the years 1935-37. I showed him a number of my compositions, which he criticised; he also analysed for my benefit many works of the masters, such as, for instance, the motets of Bach. I consider him the greatest living teacher of composition, although, strangely enough, during our long conversations he never mentioned the twelve-tone system.

Whereas Prof. Abraham's musicological conclusion is – 'For the sake of their own reputations, let composers keep to lined paper!' In fact, the critics of the book have not even derived any benefit from its masterly analyses of the masters; but then, the best teacher is the bad pupil's worst. As for more than one reviewer's criticisms of Schoenberg's sense of humour, it is a particular pity that the humour of the following paragraph from the essay on 'The Blessing of the Dressing' should have gone unobserved:-

> I once had a pupil who had started harmony with me. About two months later he stopped taking lessons. He had been offered a position as second music critic on a great newspaper and was afraid too much knowledge might have an unfavourable influence upon the spontaneity of his judgment. He made a career as a critic and even as a pedagogue.

MUSIC SURVEY

(KATHLEEN LIVINGSTON   WILLIAM W. LIVINGSTON   DONALD MITCHELL)

VOL. III, No. 3   **CONTENTS**   MARCH, 1951

EDITORIAL CORRESPONDENCE should be addressed to the EDITORS, MUSIC SURVEY, OAKFIELD SCHOOL, WEST DULWICH, LONDON, S.E.21. Annual Subscription, including postage, 11s. U.S.A. $2.50.

All enquiries relating to advertising space in this journal should be made to MUSIC SURVEY at the above address.

Epilogue:
'Hans Keller in the Early Days'

An Interview with Donald Mitchell

This is an edited transcript of an interview with Donald Mitchell that took place on 23 April 2001 as part of a Hans Keller Conference held at the Arnold Schoenberg Institute in Vienna. The interviewer was Christopher Wintle.

CW Good afternoon and welcome to you all! Our 'paper' this afternoon takes the unusual form of a discussion between two people who, in different ways, knew Hans Keller well. It is a great honour to introduce the first of them, Donald Mitchell, who is our main speaker and one of the very closest of Keller's friends and colleagues. The second is myself: I am Christopher Wintle, I come from King's College London and I've been editing Hans's papers for some years now. I therefore know him mainly through his work, though I too dealt with him personally. I should add that I've also had the pleasure of knowing Donald for many years.

Donald has had (at least) four lives. First, he has become a world authority on Gustav Mahler, about whom, as we all know, he has written voluminously. Second, as former Chair of the Britten Estate and a senior trustee of the Britten-Pears Foundation, he has done a tremendous amount of work for Benjamin Britten – during the composer's lifetime and after – and has again written about him in all sorts of valuable ways. Third, he has been a prodigiously prolific critic in his own right, and one who set a benchmark in the 1960s with his challenging book *The Language of Modern Music*. And fourth, he has done distinguished editorial service in various fields, most notably as co-editor with Hans Keller of the journal *Music Survey*. It is this fourth life, obviously, that we are going to talk about today – though all the activities somehow belong together. Now Donald has already written about his collaboration with Hans in his collection of essays, *Cradles of the New*, which was published by Faber in London five or six years ago …

DM It seems a hundred years ago!

CW Well, it wasn't quite *that* long! 1995, if I remember correctly. Anyway, it brings together three bits of writing that are important from our point of view. One is the funeral address for Hans, a poignant piece that Donald himself delivered at Hans's cremation in Golders Green. This was first published in *Tempo* in 1986. Another is a tribute originally published in the *London Review of Books* in 1987, 'Remembering Hans Keller', a much more extensive piece, and a heartfelt one too – the then editor of the *London Review of Books*, Karl Miller, was a great admirer of Hans, not least because of their shared enthusiasm for football. And the third, which came out before either of the others, is taken from the reissue in hardback (by Faber in 1981) of the journal *Music Survey*, the '*New Series*' covering the years 1949 to '52. Here Donald took part in a three-way discussion with Hans and Patrick Carnegy on the gestation and purpose of this unique publication. It only had a distribution of about 500 copies, but its impact at the time was big. Indeed, as Hans might have said, it has continued to have an impact even though it has been out of circulation for 50 years! Now, obviously, I want to ask Donald about this period of Hans's life, and I will begin by putting a question he has more or less answered in his writings, and that is, how did he come to meet Hans in the first place? At the same time, I want to add in a new question, what sort of reputation did Hans have at the time?

DM Well, the answer to that is that you must remember I was a very young man, younger than Hans, of course. I was 21 or 22 years old. I had been a conscientious objector, a pacifist, in the war, and had finished with that, and was teaching in a preparatory school in south London to try to earn something to live on and have somewhere to live and to make my way as a writer on music at that time, above all, perhaps, to think about music. And one of the journals which I read was the *Music Review*, edited by a rather eccentric figure, Geoffrey N. Sharp, and published in Cambridge. An interesting guy, nonetheless, even though he started off by rejecting for publication one of Hans's most important articles. I think it never appeared in *Music Review*, and appeared in fact in *Music and Letters*.

CW 'Britten and Mozart', which appeared in 1948.

DM That's right. So he wasn't quite eccentric enough to accept it. I was reading a copy of that very journal one day and it had in it this most extraordinary review by Hans Keller – a name entirely new to me – of an opera at Covent Garden, I think by Mozart. I had never read a review like it. It had all kinds of detailed bar references, footnote references and God knows what else. And also probably complete instructions as to how the conductor could do it better next time! This I found entirely enthralling and when I was idly turning over the pages of the correspondence at the back (I think) of the same issue, there was a letter from the same Hans Keller actually taking to task somebody in a previous issue who had got something wrong; and to my utter astonishment I found that he was living at – where was it? – 24 Herne Hill which was just down the other end of the street in south London very, very near to me …

CW   … At 30 or 32 Herne Hill, both addresses he used.[1]

DM   And I thought, good heavens, I simply must get in touch with this chap, and wrote him a letter. We then spoke on the phone and arranged to meet at a concert. I remember, amazingly, since it's so long ago, which concert it was. You must remember I am talking about 1947 or '48 so it really was a long time ago. We arranged to meet in fact at a performance of the Monteverdi *Vespers* somewhere in central London – at the Central Hall, was it? – conducted by Walter Goehr, who had quite a bit to do with Britten.[2] It was he who conducted the very first performance of the Serenade for tenor, horn and strings in wartime London in 1943 at the Wigmore Hall.

CW   Indeed, a watershed performance for many musicians of the time!

DM   That's right. Hans had given me a description of himself, and I had done likewise, and we met at the door of the hall. Odd that it was music by Monteverdi that Hans and I listened to, sitting side by side for the first time! Afterwards we had coffee together, as became our habit. From that time onwards, we really became very, very firm friends and later, of course, colleagues. But it was the discovery of a wholly unexpected proximity that started off an enthralling friendship which lasted until the very end of Hans's life.

CW   In those early days, were you involved with his relatives at all?

DM   Certainly I was. I had the luck to be part of the family, and I have often told people how one Christmas a new recording of *Die Fledermaus* with Julius Patzak on top form was brought into the drawing room and the entire family was there – Mowgli (Hans's sister), her daughters, Hans and Hans's mother. We listened to the whole work, and you should have witnessed Hans's response – I mean, he was visibly captivated by this incredible music. And that's what mattered to him. Whether it was Schoenberg, Britten or whichever Strauss, he responded with unreserved feeling, passion and warmth to the music. That's why I loved him! And why I loved listening to music with him.

CW Before that first meeting you yourself had already started *Music Survey*. Can you tell us just a little bit about yourself, your early background and the kind of things that *Music Survey* was doing when you invited Hans – soon after that meeting, I believe – to join you on the editorial team, or rather to form a duo with you?

DM Absolutely: five issues of the journal in question, *Music Survey*, had already appeared before Hans joined me, although the very first issue was called something else.[3] I can't remember now what it was, but I immediately got an angry letter from a solicitor saying I was infringing some other journal's copyright and would I please change the title immediately, which I did. And so it became *Music Survey* from the second issue onwards. I think the interesting thing about the early issues was that they reflected something of my specifically European cultural heritage. I am not, I am entirely happy to say, wholly British in origin. My mother, in fact, was half Swiss. My Swiss grandfather, her father, came from Basel, and so as a boy I visited him with my brother, and after the end of the Second World War, which was to see the death of my mother, I was in Switzerland for a time almost every year. My grandfather, Carl Brenner, had sent his favourite daughter, my mother, to the Leipzig Conservatoire before the First World War because she was a highly talented singer and musician. A remarkable woman, perhaps a shade eccentric too. I think she meant to get out of Leipzig and return to Switzerland when the war started in 1914 but somehow missed the train or possibly was simply happy staying put. In fact, she remained in Leipzig – unthreatened – throughout the war. She lived there with a Jewish family – the Rosenthals – and I am very, very proud of my parents because, when the Nazi persecution of the Jews began in Germany, it was my Mum and Dad who helped get the family which had looked after her out of Leipzig – and they came to London and finally found refuge partly in Britain and partly elsewhere in the world, in India, I believe. So there is a bit of European history too mixed up in that part of my family life.

CW And the culture?

DM As a result of this, and my mother's musical education – Nikisch for her was still a living memory! – I was in contact as a boy with all kinds of music that I think would not have been much of a domestic presence in England at the time, for example songs by Pfitzner, Reger and Schoenberg – it was my mother's voice that first introduced me to the *Gurrelieder*! All the more reason for my fascination with what Ulrike Anton told us in her paper, and especially those negative comments of Vaughan Williams's that she quoted. Perhaps I might claim to be an early manifestation of the 'Euro' in human guise! More seriously, the culture that I was fortunate enough to enjoy as a child was already evident in the philosophy, agenda and aesthetic of those early issues of *Music Survey*.

CW In what ways particularly?

DM For example, two of the earliest of Dika Newlin's articles on Schoenberg appeared in those early issues, two very, very important articles indeed. There was something about Pfitzner, which I think Harold Truscott may have contributed. Reger was another who enjoyed a bit of prominence because my mother had seen him about in Leipzig when she was a student. There are lots of wonderful songs by Reger, and I still think about those from time to time.[4]

CW And Hans obviously shared these enthusiasms?

DM I certainly think that my modest European dimension, if it may be so described, was one of the reasons why Hans and I did, as it were, hit it off. Although, as I say, I was naive and ignorant in some ways, nonetheless I was educated in others that must have made a strong appeal to Hans when bringing his 'portable culture' (as we have been hearing from an earlier speaker). I was somebody, Hans may have thought, who was at least a little bit more open minded and receptive than Vaughan Williams.

CW Isn't it ironic, though, that it was Vaughan Williams who helped Hans (and others) out of his internment camp on the Isle of Man in 1941?

DM Vaughan Williams was a very splendid human being. There's no doubt about that. But I think you should bear in mind that his was a cultural view which I – all of us, in fact – inherited. That made it all the more unusual that 22-year-old Mitchell was branching out in cultural areas, initiating cultural explorations, talking about music, thinking about music, far removed from or even in opposition to the current culture of his day.

CW So Vaughan Williams apart, who exactly *were* you opposing?

DM Well, here is an excerpt from a lecture given in 1921 by Arthur Bliss in the United Kingdom. Now, he was undeniably a gifted musician – at one time, indeed, he was thought to be a kind of English *enfant terrible*. And in fact it was my mother who gave some first performances, or certainly very early performances, of Bliss's vocal music on the radio in the very earliest days of broadcasting (Savoy Hill!). So there was an intriguing, perhaps ironic, family connection here with a composer regarded at the time as 'advanced' and internationalist. His taste, if his choice of works can be taken seriously, was certainly catholic, and I am glad as I am sitting in the Schoenberg Institute in Vienna that Schoenberg's *Five Pieces* met with his approval! But as his text makes clear, his dislikes were sharply focused, providing him indeed with his point of departure, 'overpowering grand opera with its frothy Wotans and stupid King Marks.' He continued: 'Give me such works as *Le Sacre du printemps*, *L'Histoire du soldat*, the *Sea Symphony* (Vaughan Williams) and *Savitri* (Holst), *The Eternal Rhythm* (Eugene Goossens) and *The Garden of Fand* (Bax), the Ravel Trio and de Falla's *Vida breve*, *L'Heure espagnole* (Ravel) and *Five Pieces* of Schoenberg, and you can have all your Strauss *Domestic* and *Alpine* symphonies, your Scriabin poems of Earth, Fire and Water, your Schreker, your Bruckner and your Mahler'. He concluded: 'There is abroad amongst [composers] now a hatred of padding, a contempt of laborious super-texture; they are, in other words, anti-Mahlerites. I fear I cannot say a good word for German music; it is to me anathema, not because it is Teutonic but because to my mind it is at the same time ponderous and trivial, or, in the jargon of present-day science, boundless, yet finite.' And if anyone asks me today "Why, young man that you were, were you trying to start a journal?", one reason was exactly the prevalence of those sorts of view, which even in the pre-Hans days I was trying to contest; and I think Hans recognized that. But of course the dynamics of the whole process intensified dramatically after he had joined me as co-editor.

CW Can you re-live for us something of the excitement of talking to Hans for the first time and planning the future of *Music Survey*? I mean, what sort of ideas did he want to bring to it and what sort of personnel did you and he assemble – were they English or mainly émigrés?

DM You make it sound as if our editorial activities were more systematic perhaps than they were. I think a lot of it involved friends – and we have a very distinguished and very old friend in Paul Hamburger with us today, who was very much in the thick of *Music Survey*. He wrote a lot of reviews and some articles whose importance does not diminish with time. I think a lot of people were drawn in as the editors' joint spheres of musical friendships developed and evolved. Likewise, and for that same reason, the contents of the journal evolved. I don't think, to be honest, that we sat down and held planning sessions.

CW And you had enough 'copy'?

DM We always had many more things we would have wished to publish than we actually succeeded in publishing. There were often postponements and delays. But I think some very remarkable work appeared: not only Hans's work, of course, though some very important things by him did appear in *Music Survey* during those years, but two profoundly interesting articles by Luigi Dallapiccola, quite exceptional articles. Nobody then was rushing to publish that sort of thing. 'Notes on the Statue Scene in *Don Giovanni*' was one, and 'On the Twelve-note Road' the other. Extraordinary stuff.

CW Another contributor was Robert Simpson, who was to become a close friend of Hans's when, much later, they were colleagues at the BBC – Glock's BBC, perhaps one ought to add! Did you bring Keller and Simpson together?

DM Probably, because I saw a lot of Bob both during and after the war, along with Harold Truscott and Harry Newstone (the founder and conductor of the Haydn Orchestra). We met at Bob's place – was it in Catford or Crofton Park? I can't remember precisely – and during the times of blackout and air raids, we would listen to those great unknowns, Bruckner (Bob's favourite) and Mahler (mine), surrounded by towering stacks of shellac 78 rpm discs, with thorn needles and needle sharpener to hand. Bob too was an implacable pacifist and undoubtedly influenced me. I certainly respected the strength of his views, musical and political, and perhaps envied the total certainty with which he held them.

CW Erwin Stein wrote for *Music Survey* too and was to become a close friend of Hans ...

DM Yes, we published Erwin's obituary of Schoenberg in 1951. I myself had two great experiences of Erwin during the war years. The first was with him and Noel Mewton-Wood on the top floor of the Steins' flat in London. It was the first time I ever heard in live performance any part of Mahler's Fifth Symphony – it was not heard in a public orchestral concert in England, believe it or not, until October 1945! Erwin, who was a passionate but wildly eccentric pianist, and Noel, a superb professional, played the work in a duet version. It was altogether unforgettable. The other occasion was when Erwin gave a famous performance of *Pierrot lunaire*, in Hampstead I think. I remember him standing there, conducting of course with great authority and with Peter Stadlen at the piano. Because Erwin was so tiny a man, the tails of his dress coat were almost on the floor, a riveting image seen from behind. There was some misapprehension that Erwin had in some way abandoned Schoenberg and taken up Britten. But that was certainly not the case. What an astounding thing in wartime to put on this performance of *Pierrot* in somebody's drawing room in Hampstead!

CW And how was your working relationship with Hans?

DM We were great, great friends. I can't remember a quarrel. We travelled a lot together at one stage, particularly to Holland. In those days and on those occasions life was full of laughter and animation, not to mention provocation.

CW There is something that has always puzzled me about Hans in the late '40s and early '50s. I said you were leading four lives; well, he was leading six or seven, because he was steeped in psychology, sociology, fiddle-playing, film-music criticism, concert criticism – and so forth. So how did he organize his life, or rather – what I'm really after – did he do any composition as well?

DM That I don't remember. It is very important to keep in mind the dates of our collaboration on *Music Survey*, from 1949 to 1952; and then that was crowned by the big book on Britten in 1952, the famous *Commentary* on all his works that up to then he had composed. It was a continuous development: the book was a kind of vastly inflated issue of *Music Survey*, dedicated to Britten. Although, don't forget, during the lifetime of *Music Survey* we had already produced, in 1950, a Britten number, the first time maybe any journal in England had devoted itself to a living twentieth-century composer. In fact, we produced two numbers of this kind, the Britten number and then, in 1952, a Schoenberg number. These two represent the extraordinary confrontation of cultural extremes, I believe, that was the consequence of Hans and I finding ourselves neighbours in South London. But I don't recall from this period any evidence of Hans himself composing.

CW Was it Hans who kindled your enthusiasm for Schoenberg?

DM It amuses me now to find that in one respect I was actually ahead of Hans! I enjoyed listening to Schoenberg, while Hans at the time, when he overheard a broadcast of *Pierrot*, in his own words, was "looking round for something to throw at the radio to stop this awful noise". Here again I was indebted to my mother. As I have remarked elsewhere, she used to sing 'Es sungen drei Engel' from the *Gurrelieder* and it cast a spell on me – what a melody, what harmony! – that has never diminished. All the more riveting when, years later, I learned from one of our contributors to *Music Survey*, Hans Nachod, the famous tenor, that it was that very number that

Schoenberg asked him to sing before inviting him to participate in the preliminary premiere of the *Gurrelieder* when the 'orchestra' (if I remember aright) consisted of Berg and Webern at two pianos. A case of history catching up on a musical experience that had been stored away in my youthful memory, a moment of revelation. In a flash I totally understood why it had to be that number that Schoenberg himself wanted to hear. Incidentally, that mention by Hans of an offending radio reminds me of what I was just occasionally aware of in my earliest encounters with Hans: an unexpected vein of conservatism. I recall babbling on about Mahler and the books I wanted to write about him and was somewhat taken aback when Hans halted the flow by declaring that the book that *really* needed to be written was one about Franz Schmidt – a composer of much merit, no doubt, but one to my ears bound by convention and tradition as Mahler was not.

CW So far, we've heard about the reactions to Austro-German music from Arthur Bliss and Ralph Vaughan Williams. But can you tell us what people thought of *Music Survey* and, more particularly, what they thought about the book you've mentioned, the oddly titled *Benjamin Britten: a Commentary on His Works from a Group of Specialists* put out by Rockliff in 1952?

DM The reception given to *Music Survey* in its early days was unequivocally hostile, especially by the established, 'professional' critics of the establishment. They had no time for our specific enthusiasms and our supposed bad manners. In the first series, when I was flying solo, so to speak, I pursued a polite English tradition of not attacking colleagues and maintaining the possibility of discourse. The later issues, however, were deliberately polemical. Hans had taught me how to be usefully and legitimately impolite. And that development had arisen naturally out of discussions with Hans about the treatment meted out to composers whom we especially valued.

CW Was that really a matter of personal loyalty?

DM I think what everybody should understand about Hans – and this is one of the things I remember him for, and always shall – was his profound, unfettered musicality. In that dialogue we had with Patrick Carnegy when *Music Survey* was republished in volume form, Hans says somewhere that our ambition was to establish a musical criticism and a musical musicology – that at least was our ambition although we didn't always live up to it. It was precisely that kind of commitment, rooted in genuinely musical experience, that was rarely encountered in the UK at the time – and we were polemically trying to generate change!

CW So who were your targets this time?

DM Let me try to give you a couple of examples of the dismaying attitudes and practices common at the time. Do you recall Eric Blom, who was a noted critic in those days? I got to know him a bit, after a rather shaky start. I remember him coming up to me (we had had several controversial exchanges but in the end we did at least speak to one another) – he came up to me with a look on his face that was a combination of disappointment (how could anyone be so silly?) and reproof (you should really know better) – you have to remember, he was an established, major figure among critics, and I was nobody special – and uttered words that I am afraid I have never forgotten: "You know, Donald," he said, "we just *don't want Mahler here*." Those last four words were given unmistakable emphasis, as if he were declaring Mahler to be a prohibited immigrant. It reads pretty oddly today, in the light of Mahler's ascendancy, but in Hans's and my day it was the prevailing establishment view.

CW And your other example?

DM As for the *Commentary*, the review that I remember most vividly – to be sure there were many and the majority of them highly critical – was a long review – an article in fact – entitled 'The Cult of Benjamin Britten', which approached our entire enterprise as if it were the product of a religious faith. This appeared in *Scrutiny*,[5] a very famous, prestigious literary journal edited by F. R. Leavis, an eminent critic and leading figure at Downing College, Cambridge. *Scrutiny*, for a number of years, had been running what, in effect, was a campaign against the literature of the Thirties, and the poetry of W. H. Auden in particular. Because Britten had set a lot of Auden texts, and there had been much creative exchange between them, this was a black mark for Britten so far as *Scrutiny* was concerned. It shows you how far sometimes wholly extraneous motives can influence the way people write, think and make judgements. In the course of the article, the author, Robin Mayhead, made a really extraordinary claim. 'There is, in fact', he wrote, 'a depressing sameness and monotony about too much of Britten's vocal music. Whole passages from *St. Nicolas* could, one feels, be interchanged with fragments from *The Rape of Lucretia* or *Billy Budd* without anyone being the wiser.' Perhaps not Mr Mayhead, but I guess the rest of us would have noticed something was amiss. Bits of *St. Nicolas* interpolated into *Billy Budd*? Wow!

Hans and I wrote a letter to Leavis demanding a detailed bar-by-bar illustration of what our reviewer had in mind, but silence was the only response. It surprises me still today that this sort of thing could pass for criticism in the Fifties, above all in a learned literary journal, but it was by no means rare in England in the years we're talking about.

CW And you went out to meet it head on …

DM Yes, we did, by naming the critics and exposing the laughable basis on which their adverse opinions were all too often based. I don't think there was much justification for our opponents' surprise at our policy. Can I remind you what Hans wrote about himself in the blurb for the *Commentary*? 'Although Keller's almost suicidal attacks on the work of many of his fellow critics soon prompted them to brand him as the bad boy of music criticism, Donald Mitchell invited him in 1949 to become Joint Editor of *Music Survey* (1947-53). A frictionless collaboration was started between two markedly different personalities which were united in their passion for COMPETENCE and CONSCIENCE, and the challenging contents of *Music Survey* came to be admired by leading musicians all over the world, while at the same time becoming notorious among sundry musical journalists.' *Scrutiny*, one might claim, had been duly forewarned!

CW And of course, Donald, in your own reviews you examined the reviews of other critics, whom you too were quite happy to name and shame! I remember, by the way, a particularly effective shaft of Hans's against a critic who left the concert hall before the piece he went on to review had even been played!

DM By no means an unknown practice in earlier times! I certainly did one big article entitled 'More Off than On *Billy Budd*', in which after the work's premiere I reviewed almost all the reviews of it, including of course Eric Blom's …

CW … and Ernest Newman's?

DM That's right. You'll be amused to know that people kept on saying that we were great personal friends of Britten's, and what we had done was the equivalent of laying bouquets of roses on an altar. Well, neither of us in fact had even met Britten! When the book came out Hans and I had a polite letter, a nice letter, from him, expressing his gratitude and adding: 'I don't see why we should continue to please our detractors by remaining strangers – can't we *really* meet and have a good talk, some day when this opera [*Gloriana*] is finished and we can all be in London?' He was invited to the launch party but didn't come. I was very touched, much later on, when I knew him really well, and he told me how much the 'More Off than On *Billy Budd*' article had meant to him. It had done something, it seems, to mitigate the hostility, triviality and ignorance of the general run of the opera's critics. It was the only occasion he ever said anything of that kind to me. I'm glad to this day I wrote it.

CW And the book itself?

DM We heard that Britten would ask friends and family if they had seen the *Commentary* and indeed read any of it. The chapter he always mentioned was Paul Hamburger's on the chamber music, and in particular his analyses of the first and second string quartets. "Read that chapter," he would say, "and you'll find out how really clever I am!" He also told me that he had read my *Language of Modern Music* twice, which rather unnerved me because I don't think he ever read many books about music at all. We only talked briefly, but I do remember his stressing that for him the concept of tonality was absolutely fundamental to his composing. He could not have conceived composing in its absence. What he had really enjoyed, I remember, were some late additions to my original text in which I castigated the more extreme manifestations of Darmstadt. That he applauded!

CW Were there any other attacks of note on the *Commentary*?

DM There were two memorable adverse views, though very differently expressed. One was the attitude of Britten's publishers at the time, who feared that our combative championing of their composer would do his reputation irreparable harm. There were many of course who thought the same, which enabled them, alas, to overlook its many serious merits. For example it was in the *Commentary* that the first step was taken to compile not only a bibliography but also a list of works – as comprehensive as was possible in the early 'fifties – which included the unpublished works and the incidental music, hitherto uncharted territories. I think the new waves of Britten scholarship since his death all owe a debt to that process of documentation and discovery that was initiated in 1952 and passed at the time virtually without comment.

CW And the second view?

DM This took the shape of a review broadcast on the BBC Third Programme on 29 January 1952 and given by William Glock. Hans and I were chastised for 'adolescent standards' at the start of the review, but Glock's main complaint was what I think he described as our 'shabby treatment' of Stravinsky. This prompted a characteristic response from the editors of the *Commentary*, though I'm not certain it got published in the BBC journal to which it was addressed (the *Listener*).

Sir,

As editors of the Britten symposium William Glock 'reviewed' on the Third Programme (29 January) we are in a weak position in taking exception to his talk, but at least we know the contents of our own book of which Mr. Glock's tendentious mis-citations did not give the very vaguest glimpse. Since whenever he functioned as reviewer of the book, Mr. Glock proved factually and demonstrably incompetent, it is fortunate that he spent the greater part of his time on a talk – liberally illustrated – about Stravinsky. It is obvious that we trod on Mr. Glock's Stravinskian toe; he should have consulted a professional chiropodist and refrained from a public exhibition of self-treatment.

Yours etc.
(Donald Mitchell)
(Hans Keller)

In retrospect I'm not at all sure that Glock did not have a point; and when the *Commentary* came to be re-issued in 1971, I tried to persuade Hans to revise or at least acknowledge what I felt to be an inadequacy – to put it mildly – but without success. However, it led to a truly vintage riposte from the Hans Keller of 1971, who believed he had no right, as he put it, "to criticize the Hans Keller of 18 years ago: the latter is not around to defend himself." The real irony of all this, of course, was what we could never have imagined in 1952 that Hans would eventually find himself working as a very close colleague of Glock's and significantly contributing to the revolutionary impact the latter achieved when he was appointed Controller of Music at the BBC in 1959; and William and I, no less, were to enjoy a cordial relationship when I was busy with Britten's publishing affairs.

CW I am keeping my eye on the time and we must start to draw things to a close. But I must ask you one last question about your friendship, and this concerns the years following your editorial collaborations, and the extent to which Hans was, or was not, a political animal. He said he wasn't, of course. But if you look through his papers or read his letters you see that on certain issues he was strongly committed. On capital punishment, for example …

DM What I chiefly remember him for outside the world of politics pure and simple was indeed his tireless campaigning for the abolition of capital punishment in Britain. Within our own circles of friends and acquaintances, at almost every meeting or social gathering at the time this matter was before Parliament, Hans would produce an appropriate petition and request – no, badger – anybody and everybody to sign up. And he was unrelentingly single-minded. He would not give up until he had succeeded in getting the signatures he was after. I very much respect the vital role he played. If capital punishment were restored, then this old Euro-fan would have to make an exit – I could not live in a country which sanctioned it.

CW That's fascinating because, in the *Jerusalem Diary*, which he kept in 1977 and 1979, he reports writing repeatedly to the *Jerusalem Post* expressing his fears that Israel too might bring back capital punishment. To conclude, though: looking back on those early days, how do you assess your joint achievement?

DM When I open the Britten *Commentary* these days, or an issue of *Music Survey*, there are many things that make me blush a bit. But I don't feel impelled to apologize. The intent and the ambition were, I believe, honourable, and the achievement remarkable. Whenever I think of Hans, which is often, I remember what a unique experience it was working with him, an honour and a privilege. We succeeded, I believe, in creating an essential awareness of shoddy critical standards that led to those standards discernibly improving. Post-1952, critics were more careful about what they said or wrote. As for the two composers, Britten and Schoenberg, who were so often at the centre of our editorial activities, both had to contend with incompetent judgements and attitudes handed out from on high by practitioners disseminating a predominantly negative culture of criticism. We did something to change that, something explosive, intendedly; and it was *Music Survey* and the Britten *Commentary*, for all their shortcomings, that lit the fuse.

Notes

Oscar Adler (Milein Cosman)

Notes

Note: Reference to the Hans Keller Archive held in the Cambridge University Library takes the form 'CUL HK Archive' throughout; the Oxford and Cambridge University Presses appear as OUP and CUP.

Preface

1   From the 'Open Letter to the Authors of *Peter Grimes*' Keller appended to his *Three Psychoanalytic Notes on Peter Grimes* (in: Hans Keller, *Music and Psychology. From Vienna to London 1939-52*, ed. Christopher Wintle, London, Plumbago, 2003, p. 139).

Acknowledgements

1   Richard Dove (ed.), *'Totally Un-English'? Britain's Internment of Enemy Aliens in Two World Wars*, Yearbook of the Research Centre for German and Austrian Exile Studies, Vol. 7, 2005, pp. 139-52.
2   Hugh Wood, in: 'Hans Keller: A Symposium', *Music Analysis*, Vol. 5, Nos. 2-3, July-October 1986, pp. 397-401.

Chapter 1: Looking Back

1   Unpublished review of Martin Cooper (ed.), *The New Oxford History of Music, Vol. X: The Modern Age: 1890-1960* (London, OUP, 1974), held in the CUL HK Archive.
2   Hans Keller, 'My Family, You, and I', *The New Review* Vol. 3, Nos. 34-5, January-February 1977, pp. 12-23.
3   *1975 (1984 minus 9)*, London, Dobson, 1977, p. 49.
4   *Ibid.*, pp. 49-50.
5   Peter and Leni Gillman, *'Collar the Lot!' How Britain Interned and Expelled its Wartime Refugees*, London, Quartet, 1980; Ronald Stent, *A Bespattered Page? The Internment of 'His Majesty's Most Loyal Enemy Aliens'*, London, André Deutsch, 1980.

6   The conference 'Internment Remembered' was held in May 1990. It was organised by the Wiener Library (London) and Parkes Library (University of Southampton) and hosted by the Association of Jewish Refugees. The resulting publication was Cesarani and Kushner (ed.), *The Internment of Aliens in Twentieth-century Britain*, London, Frank Cass, 1993.

7   *AJR Information* Vol. XV, No. 7, July 1960. The resulting pieces on internment were published the following September (*AJR Information* Vol. XV, No. 9, pp. 7-9). The only previous mentions of internment in *AJR Information* had been a brief review of Eugen Spier's *The Protecting Power* in 1951 (Vol. VI, No. 5, May 1951, p. 4) and a personal memoir 'Hutchinson Square Revisited' by F. I. Wiener in 1957 (Vol. XII, No. 9, September 1957, p. 11). The latter is fairly positive in tone: 'What has been the final judgement on that time? Few were really hurt and deeply offended, most accepted internment as a necessary evil, a governmental screening operation. From this point of view internment in the Isle of Man was just an inconvenience.' The reviewer of Spier's book also initially played down the negative aspects of internment: 'Most of us have already forgotten the days when we were guests of boarding houses at the Isle of Man or inhabitants of racecourse stables. Therefore at first sight it may seem a little odd that now, after 10 years, a book on the internment of aliens is being published.' The subject of internment has been revisited in recent issues of the journal (now known as the *AJR Journal*), with two front-page articles by Anthony Grenville in July and August 2007, and much subsequent correspondence. In his second article, Grenville makes the interesting point that the forgiving attitude of many 1930s central European refugees towards their internment may have its roots in the high degree of assimilation they had experienced in German-speaking countries. He also argues that to attribute their relative lack of criticism of British policy merely to a fear of antisemitism 'arguably falls into the error of imposing the historical model of Anglo-Jewry onto the refugees from Central Europe, a model dominated up to 1945 by Anglo-Jewry's overriding fear of arousing antisemitism. Hailing mostly from Tsarist Russia, Anglo-Jewry had had little experience of successful assimilation in its lands of origin, whereas the Jews in the German-speaking countries had known over a century of gradually advancing integration; some of them maintained even after 1933 that Hitler's rise to power was an unaccountable lapse into barbarism on the part of an otherwise highly civilised society. Consequently they did not believe that gentile societies were irremediably infected by vicious antisemitism – Britain less than most – and they were not prey to a consuming fear of it.' *AJR Journal*, August 2007, pp. 1-2.

8   From the preface to the revised edition of the book published by Libris in 1988, p. ix. He did, however, have one major correction: 'Rather astonishingly, I completely ignored the crucial role of Winston Churchill, Prime Minister from 10 May 1940, but a key Minister before then closely involved with the armed forces' chiefs as First Lord of the Admiralty. I had assumed him to be too busy rallying the nation and waging war to be bothered at all about what should be done to refugees.'

9   John Rickman, editor of the *British Journal of Medical Psychology*, on learning Keller's address asked him 'Herne Hill: have you taken over Havelock Ellis's house; he was No. 30, wasn't he?' (letter of 5 April 1947). 'No, I don't think Havelock Ellis was No. 30,' replied Keller (9 April 1947). Ellis's house was actually round the corner, at No. 24 Holmdene Avenue, though it is unlikely that Keller met him since he died in July 1939 and had in any case spent most of the previous two years living in Hintlesham in Suffolk. See: J. Weeks, 'Ellis, (Henry) Havelock (1859–1939)', *Oxford Dictionary of National Biography*, Oxford, OUP, September 2004; online edition, May 2006. [http://www.oxforddnb.com/view/article/33009, accessed 20 March 2008].

10 François Lafitte, *The Internment of Aliens*, London, Penguin, 1940, reissued by Libris, 1988, p. 15.

11 Statement in the House of Lords, 6 August 1940, Hansard 117, H. L. Deb., 5 s, cols. 124-25.

12 See Bernard Porter, *The Refugee Question in mid-Victorian Politics*, Cambridge, CUP, 1979.

13 Panikos Panayi, *The Enemy in Our Midst: Germans in Britain during the First World War*, New York/Oxford, Berg, 1991, p. 283.

14 Note of meeting on 8 June 1920, CID Sub-Committee on Treatment of Aliens in Time of War, Report, Proceedings and Memoranda, PRO CAB 15/10, pp. 64 and 66, quoted in: Louise London, *Whitehall and the Jews 1933-1948*, Cambridge, CUP, 2000, p. 21.

15 'Proposals of the Jewish Community as regards Jewish Refugees from Germany', undated memorandum signed by Neville Laski KC, President of the Board of Deputies of British Jews and others, PRO HO 213/1627, quoted in London, *op. cit.*, p. 28.

16 Hans Keller, 'Hitler and History', *London Review of Books*, Vol. 5, No. 18, Febuary 1981, p. 14.

17 Hans Keller, 'My Family, You, and I', *op. cit.*

18 Ena Blyth, oral communication, 26 June 2005.

19 'My Family, You, and I', *op. cit.*

20 Inge Trott, oral communication, 29 March 2004.

21 'My Family, You, and I', *op. cit.* Keller also referred to the story in 'Truth and Music', *Music and Musicians*, April 1970, pp. 21-3 and 74. The story has not yet been traced. Although Keller says in 'Truth and Music' that it was published in 'an Austrian childen's newspaper', it was probably the *Prager Kinderzeitung*, as this was a Saturday supplement for children of the *Prager Tagblatt* of which Keller's uncle was the publisher. The manuscript is no longer extant.

22 Inge Trott, 29 March 2004.

23 *Ibid.*

24 *Ibid.*

25 *Ibid.*

26 'My Family, You, and I', *op. cit.*

27 Inge Trott, 29 March 2004.

28 'My Family, You, and I', *op. cit.*

29 Inge Trott, 29 March 2004.

30   'My Family, You, and I', *op. cit.*

31   Ena Blyth, 26 June 2005.

32   According to the internment records in the National Archives, PRO/HO 396/182.

33   *Biographical Memoirs, Vol. 54*, 1983, National Academies Press, p. 160.

34   H. Myles Wright, *Small Houses, £500-£2,500*, London, The Architectural Press, 1937. The house was built in 1936, before which the Franeys lived in a flat in Rutland Court on Denmark Hill.

35   The visit is mentioned in a letter from Pritchard, Englefield and Co. (Roy Franey's solicitors) to the Under-Secretary of State, Aliens Department, Home Office, 10 May 1938 (CUL HK Archive).

36   Letter from N. Powell of the Home Office to Pritchard, Englefield & Co., 10 June 1938 (CUL HK Archive).

37   Letter from N. Powell of the Home Office to Roy Franey, 4 July 1938 (CUL HK Archive).

38   Louise London, *Whitehall and the Jews*, pp. 69-70.

39   *Ibid.*, p. 68.

40   *Ibid.*, p. 70.

41   Letter to Fritz Schonbach, 10 October 1938 (CUL HK Archive).

42   Inge Trott, oral communications, 29 March 2004 and 12 April 2006.

43   Hans Keller, 'My Family, You, and I', *op. cit.*

44   'My Family, You and I', *op. cit.*

45   Inge Trott, 29 March 2004.

46   'My Family, You, and I', *op. cit.*

47   'My Family, You, and I', *op. cit.* 'Hakoah' was the Jewish football team. The name means 'strength' in Hebrew.

48   Ena Blyth, 26 July 2005.

49   Ena Blyth, 30 October 2007.

50   Arnold Schoenberg, 'My Evolution', *Musical Quarterly*, October 1952, reprinted in *Style and Idea*, ed. Leonard Stein, London, Faber, 1975, pp. 79-92. The other two young friends whom Schoenberg credits with his education were David Bach and Alexander von Zemlinsky.

51   See 'The Chamber Music' in: H. C. Robbins Landon and Donald Mitchell (ed.), *The Mozart Companion*, London, Faber, 1956, p. 93.

52   Inge Trott, 29 March 2004.

53   Inge Trott, 12 April 2006.

54   R. M. Cooper (ed.), *Refugee Scholars: Conversations with Tess Simpson*, Leeds, Moorland Books, 1992, pp. 116-17.

55   Michael Graubart in: 'Hans Keller (1919-1985): A Memorial Symposium', *Music Analysis*, Vol. 5, Nos. 2-3, July-October 1986, pp. 382-84.

56   Nina Trott, oral communication, 12 April 2006.

57   Milein Cosman Keller, oral communication, 20 June 2007.

58   'My Family, You and I', *op. cit.*

59   Letters to Fritz Schonbach, 20 November, 26 November and 2 December 1938 (CUL HK Archive).

60   *1975 (1984 minus 9)*, London, Dobson, 1977 (later reissued in 1986 by Toccata Press (London) as *Music, Closed Societies and Football*).

Chapter 3: Testimony, 1939

1   This letter to Sister Mary Stephen of the Convent of the Assumption, Richmond, Yorkshire, 18 February 1974, was written in response to a letter from her thanking him for the 'haunting broadcast which I shall not easily forget' (CUL HK Archive).
2   Hans-Albert Walter, 'Leopold Schwarzschild and the *Neue Tage-Buch*', *Journal of Contemporary History* Vol. I, No. 2, 1966, pp. 103-16.
3   Luke 23:34.
4   Translators' note: literally, Keller writes 'become soul'.

Chapter 4: London, 1939

1   Inge Trott, oral communication, 29 March 2004.
2   Keller's cousin, Inge Trott's certificate of registration (which she still has), records her own arrival at 'The Galleon, Seaview Road, Angmering' on 29 August 1939 and her return to London on 4 November 1939 (private communication, 19 November 2007).
3   Hansard 351 H.C. DEB. 5 s, col. 366-67.
4   Letter from Frederick Peel, Superintendent of the West Sussex Constabulary, 18 September 1939: 'I have to acknowledge the receipt of your letter of the 16th instant respecting your intended change of address to London and have to inform you that you should obtain permission from the Police of the district where you intend to reside. On receipt of this permission I will then issue the necessary travel permit. On no account must you leave your address without a permit from me.' (CUL HK Archive.)
5   PRO HO 396.
6   Letter from the (unnamed) 'Careers Advisor' of the *Jewish Chronicle*, 19 December 1939 (CUL HK Archive).
7   Letters from John Dominic of the Norward Technical Institute, 29 January and 17 Febuary 1939; John Shaftesbury of the *Jewish Chronicle*, 19 April 1939; and Camille Palanque of the London School of Stenotyping, 10 February 1939 (CUL HK Archive).
8   Yvonne Kapp and Margaret Mynatt, *British Policy and the Refugees, 1933-1941*, London, Frank Cass, 1997, p. 83.
9   Louise London, *Whitehall and the Jews 1933-1948*, Cambridge, CUP, 2000, pp. 145-46.
10   *Writing Lives: Conversations between Women Writers*, London, Virago, 1988, p. 111.
11   Yvonne Kapp, *Time Will Tell*, unpublished manuscript quoted in Charmian Brinson's foreword to Kapp and Mynatt, *British Policy and the Refugees, 1933-1941*, pp. xiv-xv.

12   Letter to Fritz Schonbach, 10 October 1938 (CUL HK Archive).

13   These essays are all published posthumously in: Hans Keller, *Music and Psychology. From Vienna to London, 1939-52*, ed. Christopher Wintle, London, Plumbago, 2003: 'Lyons Corner House, Pissoir', p. 8; 'Amusements', pp. 6-7; 'Summary Report on the Revisionist Faction Within Your Youth Group, with a Proposal for a More Effective Scheme of Activities', pp. 27-31.

14   'National Socialism and "Being German"', *Music and Psychology*, pp. 23-4.

15   Letter to Keller from Margaret Phillips, 5 August 1943 (CUL HK Archive).

16   Letter to Fritz Schonbach, 7 February 1939 (CUL HK Archive).

17   Letter to Fritz Schonbach, 2 December 1938 (CUL HK Archive).

18   Internment letter 17.

19   'Motive and Guilt: A Novel by Hans Keller'. Only a few (handwritten) pages are extant (CUL HK Archive).

20   CUL HK Archive. Many more of Keller's aphorisms are included in *Music and Psychology*, 2003.

21   'Schonend, weil in Kürze', *Zeitspiegl*, 26 October 1941. Christopher Wintle and Irene Auerbach have translated the title as 'Shielding you with Brevity' (see: *Music and Psychology*, pp. 14-16).

22   'Film Music – The Question of Quotation', *Music Survey*, Vol. II, No. 1, 1949, pp. 25-7; reprinted in: Hans Keller, *Film Music and Beyond. Writings on Music and the Screen, 1946-59*, ed. Christopher Wintle, London, Plumbago, 2006, pp. 30-2.

23   See 'Music Now: An Autobiographical Sketch', Hans Keller interviewed by John Amis, broadcast on Radio 3 on 28 October 1972; copies held in the National Sound Archive and the BBC Sound Archive, BBC LP 34533. See also 'My Family, You and I', *The New Review*, Vol. 3, Nos. 34-5, January-February 1977, pp. 12-23, in which he describes his change of languages as 'retrospectively a blessing'.

24   'My Family, You and I', *op. cit.*

25   Letter to Fritz Schonbach, 2 December 1938 (CUL HK Archive).

26   This complete version of the essay was originally entitled 'England'. The more evocative title 'An Emigrant Searches for England' comes from the other (incomplete) version.

Chapter 5: Internment, June 1940

1   According to François Lafitte, 'The worst offenders by far were the papers of the Rothermere group, closely followed by some of the Kemsley papers.' (*The Internment of Aliens*, London, Penguin, 1940, reissued by Libris, 1988, p. 168.) The *Daily Mail* correspondent G. Ward Price and Beverley Nichols of the *Sunday Chronicle* were singled out for particular criticism, and Lafitte went on to link the anti-alien press campaign of the spring of 1940 with pre-war advocacy of appeasement in the same newspapers. David Cesarani and Tony Kushner have pointed out the continuity of the exaggerated fear about spies in 1940 with previous British anti-alienism: see Cesarani, 'An Alien Concept?

The Continuity of Anti-Alienism in British Society before 1940' and Kushner, 'Clubland, Cricket Tests and Alien Internment, 1939-40' in: Cesarani and Kushner (ed.), *The Internment of Aliens in Twentieth-Century Britain*, London, Frank Cass, 1993.

2   Home Office Defence (Security) Executive, chaired by Lord Swinton. Winston Churchill, defending this committee later in the House of Commons, described its creation as follows: 'About 10 weeks ago, after the dark, vile conspiracy which in a few days laid the trustful Dutch people at the mercy of Nazi aggression, a wave of alarm passed over this country, and especially in responsible circles, lest the same kind of undermining tactics and treacherous agents of the enemy were at work in our island. Several branches of State Departments are, of course, always charged with the duty of frustrating such designs. But they were not working smoothly. There were overlaps and underlaps, and I felt in that hour of anxiety that this side of the business of National Defence wanted pulling together. I therefore asked Lord Swinton to undertake this task.' 15 August 1940, Hansard 364 H. C. DEB. 5 s, col. 959.

3   *Daily Herald*, 31 May 1940, p. 8.

4   G. Ward Price, 'There is more to be done ...', *Daily Mail*, 24 May 1940, p. 4.

5   Beverley Nicols, 'I'd intern my German friends,' *Sunday Chronicle*, 26 May 1940, p. 2.

6   G. Ward Price, *Daily Mail*, 24 May 1940.

7   Sir Neville Bland, 'Fifth Columnists and Parachutists' Activities', broadcast on the Home Service (appended to the 6 pm News) on 30 May 1940 (BBC Written Archive Centre, Radio Talks Script film 43). Extracts from the talk were reprinted in *The Listener*, 6 June 1940, p. 1083, under the title 'Watch Your German Friends'. Other newspapers reported Bland's talk (e.g. the *Daily Herald* quoted above).

8   Memorandum dated 14 May 1940, PRO FO 371/25189/462 (W 7984/7941/49), quoted in Bernard Wasserstein, *Britain and the Jews of Europe 1939-1945*, Oxford, Clarendon Press, 1979, p. 88.

9   Ena Blyth, oral communication 16 September 2007. The exact date of Roy Franey's interrogation is unknown. Mosley and his colleagues were arrested on 24 May 1940 and imprisoned initially in Brixton Prison.

10   Quoted in Gillman & Gillman, *'Collar the Lot!'*, London, Quartet, 1980, p. 133.

11   Neville Chamberlain made the announcement to Cabinet on 11 June 1940. Quoted in Gillman & Gillman, *op. cit.*, p. 161. This was the moment when internment policy was removed from the control of the Home Secretary and given to the newly-created Home Defence (Security) Executive.

12   PRO HO 396/181 gives the date of arrest as 'circular 21. 6. 40'. It may have been a few days later.

13   Lafitte, *The Internment of Aliens*, pp. 102-03.

14   Judex, *Anderson's Prisoners*, London, Gollancz, 1940, p. 10.

15   Quoted in Judex, *Anderson's Prisoners*, p. 70-1.

16   Lafitte, *The Internment of Aliens*, pp. 111-13.

17   *Ibid.*, p. 95.

18   Account of one internee transferred from Paignton Camp to Prees Heath in July, quoted in Lafitte, *op. cit.*, p. 95.

19   Hansard 362 H. C. DEB. 5 s, col. 1212.

20   H. G. Wells, *'J'accuse'*, *Reynolds News*, 28 July 1940, p. 6.

21   Scipio, *100,000,000 Allies – If We Choose*, London, Gollancz, 1940, p. 105.

22   *Ibid.*, p. 108.

23   *Ibid.*, p. 97.

24   Hansard 364 H. C. DEB. 5. s, col. 1580-81.

25   Quoted in Gillman & Gillman, *'Collar the Lot!'*, p. 34.

26   See Keller's internment letter 3b.

27   Most of Keller's early papers were discovered after his death in a trunk in his loft in Hampstead. Since they were still in sealed bundles, wrapped in newspaper dating from 1953 and 1954 and labelled in his mother's hand, it was clear that he never looked at them in later life. Many of these early writings were published posthumously in: Hans Keller, *Music and Psychology: From Vienna to London, 1939-52*, ed. Christopher Wintle, London, Plumbago, 2003. The originals are now in the CUL HK Archive. The internment letters were found in a separate bundle of papers given by Grete Keller to Inge Trott, containing writings and correspondence of both Hans and Grete Keller.

28   Judex, *Anderson's Prisoners*, London, Gollancz, 1940, p. 69.

29   Quoted in Lafitte, *The Internment of Aliens*, p. 132.

30   Quoted in Gillman & Gillman, *'Collar the Lot!'*, p. 211.

31   An acknowledgement of 'your application to be granted a Permit to visit an Internee' was sent to Roy Franey from the Director of Prisoners of War on 8 August 1940. It states that 'this application has been forwarded to the Home Office', but there is no evidence as to whether the permit was granted.

32   This firm of solicitors, founded by William Fairchild Greig in 1919 (the year in which Hans Keller was born), is still active, now in Acton, West London. The current partners believe that it would have been William Fairchild Greig himself who acted for Keller in 1940, although his two sons Roger and Brian were also solicitors in practice with the firm at that time. (Chris Hutson, private communication to the author, 16 and 19 October 2009.)

33   Judex, *Anderson's Prisoners*, p. 79.

34   See *There Goes Kafka* by Johannes Urzidil, translated from the German by Harold A. Basilius, Detroit, Wayne State University Press, 1968, p. 157.

35   Letter from Dr. Rudolf Keller to the Under-Secretary of State, Aliens Department, 27 January 1941 (CUL HK Archive).

36   *Ibid.*

37   Inge Trott, oral communication, 29 March 2004.

38   Letter to Margaret Phillips, 29 October 1944.

39   Rathbone papers, XIV.3.34, quoted in Susan Pedersen, 'Rathbone, Eleanor Florence (1872–1946)', *Oxford Dictionary of National Biography*, OUP, September 2004; online edn., May 2008 [http://www.oxforddnb.com/view/article/35678, accessed 8 April 2009].

40   Pederson, *op. cit.*

41   Lafitte, *The Internment of Aliens*, p. 113.

42   'Dunera Boys' was the title of the television dramatisation of the fate of the transported refugees. Directed by Ben Lewin and starring Bob Hoskins, it was broadcast on Channel 4 on 15 and 17 October 1985, drawing shocked responses from viewers which featured on the channel's 'Right to Reply' programme afterwards. 'I don't believe the British *could* have behaved as they were portrayed here', as one protester put it. Fritz Schonbach (who now lives in America) is an artist, and one of his watercolours of the internment camp at Hay can still be seen on the following website http://www.holocaust.com.au/mm/i_australia.htm.

43   Gillman and Gillman, *'Collar the Lot!'*, London, Quartet, 1980, p. 278.

44   *Ibid.*

45   Louise London, *Whitehall and the Jews, 1933-48*, Cambridge, CUP, 2000.

46   Scipio, *100,000,000 Allies – If We Choose*, p. 98.

47   Wasserstein, *Britain and the Jews of Europe 1939-1945*, p. 8.

48   Lafitte, *The Internment of Aliens*, p. 118.

49   Schaefer, 'Aspects of Community Life: Some Recollections', *AJR Information*, September 1960, p. 7.

50   Arnold Schoenberg, 'My Evolution,' in: *Style and Idea*, ed. Leonard Stein, London, 1975, Faber & Faber, pp. 79-80.

51   Undated letter from Oscar Adler to Schoenberg, probably written around 1950. Their correspondence (in a translation by Inge Trott) appears in: Amy Shapiro, *Dr. Oskar Adler: A Complete Man, 1875-1955*, 2002.

52   Judex, *Anderson's Prisoners*, p. 76.

53   Esther Simpson – see page 13.

54   Walter Landauer – see page 100.

55   Daniel Snowman, *The Hitler Emigrés: The Cultural Impact in Britain of Refugees from Nazism*, London, Chatto & Windus, 2002, p. 107.

56   Leo Kahn, 'On Internment', *AJR Information*, September 1960, p. 7. It should be remembered in reading this account that contributors had been asked to steer clear of making political comments (see page 3).

57   Leo Black, Obituary of Paul Hamburger, *The Independent*, 21 April 2004.

Chapter 6: Protest, July 1940

1   Debate on internment, 22 August 1940, Hansard 364 H. C. DEB. 5 s, col. 1541.

2   Victor Cazalet in the adjournment debate on 10 July 1940, Hansard 362 H. C. DEB. 5 s, col. 1209.

3   Hansard 362 H. C. DEB. 5 s, cols 1210-11.

4   Cmd. 6217.

5   Hansard 363 H. C. DEB. 5 s, col. 587.

6   François Lafitte, *The Internment of Aliens*, London, Penguin, 1940, reissued in 1988 by Libris, pp. 195-96.

7   Writing to Lord Snell on 12 August 1940 to ask him to undertake this enquiry, Winston Churchill set out its terms of reference as follows: 'To inquire into the method of selection of aliens to be sent overseas in the ARANDORA STAR:

whether the actual selection of individuals was in accordance with the method determined; and generally the responsibility for the action taken; and to report to the War Cabinet.' Churchill Archive, CHAR 20/2 A, 40. The reason for the enquiry into this particular aspect of the tragedy was because the presence of Category B & C internees on the ship was politically awkward, in view of the Government's stated intention that only the 'most dangerous' internees would be deported (i.e. Category A and actual POWs).

8   Letters from William Temple to Winston Churchill, 22 and 23 July 1940, Churchill Archive, CHAR 20/8, 174-78.

9   Lafitte, *The Internment of Aliens*, p. 192.

10   Hansard 363 H. C. DEB. 5 s, col. 587.

11   Louise London, *Whitehall and the Jews 1933-48: British Imigration Policy and the Holocaust*, Cambridge, CUP, pp. 170-71.

12   PEP continued its work under its old name until 1976, when it merged with the Centre for Studies in Social Policy to become the Policy Studies Institute.

13   Lafitte, *The Internment of Aliens*, p. xviii.

14   Quoted in Alan Marsh, 'From PEP to PSI', in the Policy Studies Institute's 75th anniversary booklet, 2006.

15   *TUC Report, 1931*, p. 406, quoted in W. H. Greenleaf, *The British Political Tradition*, London, Taylor and Francis, 2003, p. 145.

16   Lafitte, *The Internment of Aliens*, pp. xviii-xix.

17   *Ibid.*, p. xxii. On her arrival in London in 1938, Eva Kolmer published a semi-autobiographical book, *Austria Still Lives* (London, Michael Joseph, 1938), under the pseudonym Mitzi Hartmann.

18   Lafitte, *The Internment of Aliens*, p. xxiv.

19   Minutes of the War Cabinet meeting held on 1 August 1940, Cabinet Papers, 65/14, quoted in: Martin Gilbert, *Winston S. Churchill, Vol. VI, Finest Hour, 1939-41*, London, Heinemann, 1983, p. 710.

20   Churchill speaking in the House of Commons on 15 August 1940, Hansard 364 H. C. DEB. 5 s, col. 959.

21   Midge Gillies, *Waiting for Hitler: Voices from Britain on the Brink of Invasion*, London, Hodder, 2006, p. 151.

22   See, for example, the booklet, *Helpful Information and Guidance for Every Refugee*, issued by the Board of Deputies to new Jewish refugees from the beginning of 1939 onwards.

23   Hansard 364 H. C. DEB. 5 s, col. 1545.

24   Cmd. 6223.

25   Letter from Rudolf Keller to the Under-Secretary of State, Aliens Department, 27 January 1941, pleading for his nephew's release from internment (CUL HK Archive).

26   Hansard 362 H. C. DEB. 5 s, col. 1211.

27   Lafitte, *The Internment of Aliens*, p. 194.

28   See note 19 above.

29   Letter from Churchill to the Earl of Lytton, 2 August 1941, Churchill Archive CHAR 20/6 A, 88.

30   Hinsley & Simkins, *British Intelligence in the Second World War, Vol. 4 (Security and Counter-Intelligence)*, London, HMSO, 1990, p. 59.

31   J. W. Brügel, *Czechoslovakia Before Munich: The German Minority Problem and British Appeasement Policy*, Cambridge, CUP, 1973 (first published as *Tschechen und Deutsche* in Munich, 1967.)

32   Johannes Urzidil, *There Goes Kafka*, trans. (from the German) Harold A. Basilius, Detroit, Wayne State University Press, 1968, p. 157.

33   *Ibid.*, p. 158.

34   London, *Whitehall and the Jews*, Cambridge, CUP, 2000, p. 155.

35   Margarete Buber-Neumann, *Mistress to Kafka: the Life and Death of Milena*, London, Secker & Warburg, 1966.

36   Buber-Neumann, *Mistress to Kafka: the Life and Death of Milena*, p. 156.

37   Quoted in Buber-Neumann, *Mistress to Kafka*, p. 157.

38   *Ibid.*, pp. 160-61.

39   Kapp and Mynatt, *British Policy and the Refugees, 1933-1941*, London, Frank Cass, 1997, p. 22.

40   Translators' note: the way this sentence is written in the original shows that Keller is trying to imitate a Yiddish accent.

41   Paula Zoepnek, Uncle Hans's partner and future wife.

42   Sir George Frankenstein, formerly Austrian Minister in London, who became involved with the Free Austria movement after the Anschluss.

43   Translators' note: 'Schames' is a Yiddish word meaning a verger, caretaker or odd-job man in a synagogue.

44   Gillies, *Waiting for Hitler*, p. 125.

45   H. Myles Wright (ed.), *Small Houses, £500-£2,500*, London, The Architectural Press, 1937.

46   Ena Blyth, oral communication, 30 October 2007.

47   Gwendolyn Tietze has managed to identify two of the popular Viennese songs parodied here:

'Mei Muaterl is a Weanerin, drum bin i interniert' is based on

Mei' Muatterl war a Wienerin,
Drum hab i Wien so gern,
Sie war's die mit'n Leben
Mir die Liebe hat geb'n
Zu mein anzigen, goldenen Wean.

'Es wird ein Huyton sein, und mir werd'n draussen sein, es wird noch Listen geben, u. mir wer'n nimmer leben' is based on

Hollodaro! Hollodaro!
Es wird a Wein sein, und mir wer'n nimmer sein,
D'rum g'niaß ma's Leb'n so lang's uns g'freut.
'S wird schöne Maderln geb'n, und wir werd'n nimmer leb'n,
D'rum greif ma zua, g'rad is's no Zeit.

48   'Mr Holiday' kept the newsagent's shop opposite the Franeys' Herne Hill house.

49   In the possession of Ena Blyth.

50   Inge Trott, oral communication, 19 November 2007.

51   Ena Blyth, oral communication, 16 September 2007.

52   Tony Kushner, 'An Alien Occupation – Jewish Refugees and Domestic Service in Britain, 1933-1948' in: Werner E. Mosse (ed.), *Second Chance: Two Centuries of German-speaking Jews in the United Kingdom*, Tübingen, Mohr, 1991, pp. 553-78.

53   Inge Trott, oral communication, 19 November 2007.

54   See F. N. H. Robinson, 'Kompfner, Rudolf (1909–1977)', rev., *Oxford Dictionary of National Biography*, OUP, 2004 [http://www.oxforddnb.com/view/article/31326, accessed 20 March 2008].

55   David Howell, 'Morrison, Herbert Stanley, Baron Morrison of Lambeth (1888-1965)', *Oxford Dictionary of National Biography*, OUP, Sept 2004; online edn., May 2008 [http://www.oxforddnb.com/view/article/35121, accessed 2 November 2009].

56   A. V. Hill, 'Now I Can Tell the Story' in: R. M. Cooper (ed.), *Refugee Scholars: Conversations with Tess Simpson*, Leeds, Moorland Books, 1992.

Chapter 7: The Isle of Man, October 1940

1   *The Island of Barbed Wire* is the title of a history of internment by Connery Chappell, London, Robert Hale, 2005.

2   Quoted in Gillman and Gillman, *'Collar the Lot!'*, London, Quartet, 1980, p. 135.

3   François Lafitte, *The Internment of Aliens*, London, Penguin, 1940, reissued in 1988 by Libris, pp. 11-15. The camp described here is actually one of the camps at Douglas, not Mooragh Camp, but, as Lafitte says, 'life in most of the men's camps on the island followed the same general lines', and this account seems to tally well with Keller's experience.

4   Andrew Marr, *The Making of Modern Britain*, Episode 6, 'Britain at Bay', BBC2, 4 December 2009.

5   Daniel Snowman, *The Hitler Emigrés: The Cultural Impact in Britain of Refugees from Nazism*, London, Chatto & Windus, 2002, p. 110.

6   See Jennifer Taylor, '*Weltschmerz* or "Something to make people laugh"? Acceptable Political Content of the Isle of Man Internment Camp Journals, July-October 1940', in: Richard Dove (ed.), *'Totally Un-English'? Britain's Internment of 'Enemy Aliens' in Two World Wars*, Amsterdam, Rodopi, Research Centre for German and Austrian Exile Studies, Vol. 7, 2005, pp. 139-52.

7   Cmd. 6223.

8   Lafitte, *The Internment of Aliens*, p. 107.

9   'My Family, You and I', *The New Review*, Vol. 3, Nos. 34-5, January-February 1977, pp. 13-23.

10   Translators' note: The original 'Pech im Umglück' is a joke on the phrase 'Glück im Unglück'.

11   Cmd. 6233.

12   Hugh Cobbe (ed.), *The Letters of Ralph Vaughan Williams*, Oxford, OUP, 2008, p. 303.

13   *Ibid.*, pp. 302-03.

14   Letter from Duff Cooper to Winston Churchill, 22 July 1940, Churchill Archive CHAR 20/6 A, 80.

15   Memo signed 'E. A. S.', 22 July 1940, Churchill Archive CHAR 20/6 A, 81.

16   In 1936 Malcolm Sargent had caused a storm when he spoke out against pensions for orchestral musicians, saying in an interview in the *Daily Telegraph* that 'As soon as a man thinks he is in his orchestral job for life, with a pension waiting for him at the end of it, he tends to lose something of his supreme fire.' The players of the London Philharmonic Orchestra reacted particularly badly, having suffered the sacking of several of their members by Sir Thomas Beecham only the year before. Sargent unwisely approved of these sackings in his *Telegraph* interview, and the orchestra never forgave him, despite the lifeline he gave them with the Blitz Tours during the war. When Sargent began conducting at the Promenade Concerts after the war, the LPO made a particular request to the BBC that their concerts should be conducted by somebody else. (BBC Written Archive Centre, memorandum from W. L. Streeton (Programme Contracts Director) to Kenneth Wright (Deputy Director of Music), 30 April 1947 (R30/2345/2).)

17   William Haley, BBC Director-General, speaking in 1945, quoted by Rex Keating in 'Third Programme problems in certain underdeveloped areas', UNESCO Reports and Papers on Mass Communications, No. 23, December 1956.

18   Letter from Vaughan Williams to Bantock, 28 August 1940, in: Cobbe (ed.), *The Letters of Ralph Vaughan Williams*, p. 303-04.

19   CUL HK Archive.

20   Letter to Ferdinand Rauter, Hugh Cobbe (ed.), *The Letters of Ralph Vaughan Williams*, p. 344-45.

21   Letter from Keller to Daniel Jones, 3 December 1959 (CUL HK Archive). Davies's original script is still preserved in the BBC Written Archive Centre. The other composers who provided the 'counter-blows' included Robert Simpson and Alexander Goehr ('Is There Only One Way?').

22   Translators' note: This is meant as a joke, referring to the common instruction to schoolchildren to 'schreibe, wie du sprichst' – 'write as you would speak' – as well as to Inge's hesitant manner of speaking at the time.

23   On 5 November 1940 Franklin D. Roosevelt was re-elected as U. S. President for an unprecedented third term. Although he had promised not to bring America into the actual fighting, he had been instrumental in combating his country's isolationist tendencies and supporting the Allied cause.

24   Exodus 23:19.

25   Undated letter from Keller to Margaret Phillips [late 1942/early 1943], CUL HK Archive.

26   Hansard 362 H. C. DEB. 5 s, col 1219.

27   Lafitte, *The Internment of Aliens*, p. 99.

28   Letter from André Deutsch to Keller, 17 March 1954 (CUL HK Archive).

29   Hansard 367 H. C. DEB. 5 s, col 79.

30   Hansard 364, H. C. DEB. 5 s, col 1554.

31   Inge Trott, oral communication, 29 March 2004.

32   Translators' note: 'Naphtalin-Rent' is a pun: one meaning of 'Zins' is 'rent'.

33   Translators' note: Keller here uses the phrase 'sich versündigen', which is a Roman Catholic phrase meaning to commit a sin by a mere thought or word. Presumably he means that it's wrong to complain when one is really not that badly off.

34   Milein Cosman, oral communication, 13 April 2006. She also remembered that Keller still had the goitre when she first met him in 1947.

35   Hansard 367 H.C. DEB 5s col. 79.

36   Translators' note: the word Keller uses here is *Vorständin*: an ironic invented word.

37   From Charmian Brinson's introduction to: Yvonne Kapp and Margaret Mynatt, *British British Policy and the Refugees, 1933-1941*, London, Frank Cass, 1997, p. xv.

38   From the unpublished manuscript of *Time Will Tell*, quoted in Brinson's introduction to: Kapp and Mynatt, *British Policy and the Refugees*, p. xv.

39   *Ibid.*, p. xvii.

40   Louise London, *Whitehall and the Jews, 1933-48*, Cambridge, CUP, 2000, p. 68.

41   *Ibid.*, p. 68-9. The quotation from Sir Henry comes from his memorandum of 15 May 1939, 'Liabilities in respect of refugees from Czechoslovakia', PRO HO 294/39.

42   Kapp and Mynatt, *British Policy and the Refugees*, pp. 97 (n. 13) and 90.

43   *New Statesman and Nation*, 9 March 1940, pp. 299-300, quoted in Brinson's introduction to: Kapp and Mynatt, *British Policy and the Refugees*, p. xi.

44   Lafitte, *The Internment of Aliens*, p. 48.

45   Kapp and Mynatt, *British Policy and the Refugees*, p. 61.

46   Lafitte, *The Internment of Aliens*, 1988, p. xv.

47   Emmy Koenen, 'Erinnerungen: Zum antifaschistischen Kampf der KPD in der CSR', *Beiträge zur Geschichte der Arbeiterbewegung*, 18, 1976, p. 1067, quoted in Brinson's introduction to: Kapp and Mynatt, *British Policy and the Refugees*, p. xvi.

48   PRO HO 396/175.

49   Translators' note: Keller here uses the term 'freudiges Ereignis', which was the standard petit-bourgeois term with which to announce a birth.

50   Grete Keller had known the Viennese poet Peter Altenberg earlier in her life. He died in 1919, the year Hans Keller was born.

51   PRO HO 396/182; F. N. H. Robinson, 'Kompfner, Rudolf (1909-1977)', rev. *Oxford Dictionary of National Biography*, OUP, 2004.

Chapter 8: Release, 1941

1   Martin Gilbert, *Winston S. Churchill, Vol. VI, Finest Hour, 1939-41*, London, Heinemann, 1983, p. 616 n. 2.

2   Gilbert, *op. cit.*, p. 616.

3   *Ibid.*

4   Memorandum from Churchill to Morrison, 22 December 1940, quoted in: Winston Churchill, *The Second World War, Vol 2: Their Finest Hour*, London, Cassell, 1949, p. 626-27.

5   Telegram from Churchill to Morrison, 21 November 1943, Churchill Archive CHAR 20/130, 9.
6   Telegram from Churchill to Morrison, 25 November 1943, Churchill Archive CHAR 20/130, 15.
7   Telegram from Churchill to Morrison, 25 November 1943, Churchill Archive CHAR 20/130, 14.
8   Letter from Winston Churchill to Clementine Churchill, Churchill Archive CSCT 2/32/45-6.
9   Letter from Clementine Churchill to Winston Churchill, 1 December 1943, Churchill Archive CSCT 1/27/34.
10 Mary Soames (ed.), *Speaking for Themselves: the Personal Letters of Winston and Clementine Churchill*, London, Doubleday, 1998, p. 488n.
11 Letter from Clementine Churchill to Winston Churchill, 26 November 1943, Churchill Archive CSCT 1/27/30.
12 Telegram from Churchill to Morrison, 29 November 1943, Churchill Archive CHAR 20/130, 1.
13 The omitted letters were sent on 20, 23 and 26 December 1940, 30 January and 12, 17 and 23 February 1941.
14 This letter is addressed to 32 Herne Hill, where Uncle Hans was living at the time with Roy Franey, who was working in London. The rest of the family was in Bowness, where Roy would visit them at weekends until he went into the army.
15 'What you've inherited from your fathers ...' is a jocular reference to Goethe's *Faust*. Keller seems to imply that he has inherited from his father not only his goitre, but also a fondness for travel by taxi (for which he was famous in later life).
16 Letter from Roy Franey to the Under-Secretary of State, Aliens Department, 29 December 1940 (CUL HK Archive).
17 Letter dated 26 December.
18 Letter dated 30 January.
19 Quoted in the obituary for Paul Hamburger in *The Daily Telegraph*, 29 April 2004.
20 Daniel Snowman, *The Amadeus Quartet*, London, Robson, 1981, p. 23.
21 Daniel Snowman, *The Hitler Emigrés: The Cultural Impact in Britain of Refugees from Nazism*, London, Chatto & Windus, 2002, p. 109.
22 Snowman, *The Hitler Emigrés*, pp. 94-5
23 See Snowman, *The Amadeus Quartet*, p. 19 and Connery Chappell, *Island of Barbed Wire*, London, Robert Hale, 2005, p. 145.
24 'Sir John Emerson' was actually Sir Herbert Emerson, who, as well as being on the Asquith Committee, was also the League of Nations' High Commissioner for Refugees from 1939.
25 The Peveril Camp at Peel on the south coast of the Isle of Man was almost empty by this date. After May 1941 it was used to house British fascists detained under article 18B of the Defence Regulations.
26 Kitchener Camp at Richborough in Kent was a civilian refugee camp, established in a disused army training camp by the Council for German Jewry

(later the Central Council for Jewish Refugees). By the outbreak of war it had 3,500 occupants, many of whom intended to emigrate to the United States or elsewhere. Although the government did consider trying to convert it to an internment camp, in the end it was dissolved and its remaining inmates (many had enlisted in the Pioneer Corps) dispersed to camps elsewhere.

27 Irene Auerbach says that this sort of 'horrible arithmatic' is the sort of thing that no one who fled from the Nazis will ever forget. The exact proportion of one's Jewishness could be deeply significant.

28 'My Family, You and I', *The New Review*, Vol. 3, Nos. 34-5, January-February 1977, pp. 13-23.

29 'My Family, You, and I', *op. cit.*

30 Inge Trott, oral communication, 29 March 2004.

31 This is a Yiddish word which means very serious trouble, worry or exasperation (it derives from the Venetian Italian *blastemare*, and refers to the consequences of being brought before a tribunal for blasphemy). However, the way in which the word was used in Keller's family was different: for them it meant contrariness, doing the opposite of what one is asked. I am grateful to Laurence Dreyfus for the first definition, and Ena Blyth for the second.

32 Nina Trott, letter to the author, 7 December 2007.

33 Susan Bradshaw in: 'Hans Keller (1919-1985): A Memorial Symposium', *Music Analysis*, Vol. 5, Nos. 2-3, July/October 1986, p. 377. Keller's last book, *The Great Haydn Quartets: Their Interpretation* (London, Dent, 1986) was a product of his decades of coaching quartets.

34 Letter from Hans Keller to Levon Chilingirian, 11 July 1974: this is an extract from the first of the series of letters which Keller wrote to him over the next few weeks on the Haydn quartets. Keller defines 'Boccherini tempo' in *The Great Haydn Quartets: Their Interpretation* (p. 21) as 'the kind of weighty tempo character … which induces the somnolent, quasi-orchestral lower-part player, even though he may not be slow-witted, to mistake half a bar for a whole one during rest- or also minim-time'.

35 Translators' note: Keller's word here is the invented compound 'releastern'.

36 Paragraph 19 of the October White Paper was for 'any person as to whom a Tribunal, appointed by the Secretary of State for the purpose, reports that enough is known of his history to show that by his writings or speeches or political or official activities he has consistently, over a period of years, taken a public and prominent part in opposition to the Nazi system and is actively friendly towards the Allied cause.' Cmd. 6233.

37 Enemy aliens were not allowed to have radios as a result of the Aliens Order of September 1939. Inge Trott, however, remembers the family having a hidden radio at one stage. (Oral communication, 19 November 2007.)

38 Letter to the Under-Secretary of State, Aliens Department, 27 January 1941 (CUL HK Archive).

39 Internment letter dated 17 February.

40 Undated letter from Hans Keller to Margaret Phillips, possibly from late 1942 or early 1943 (CUL HK Archive).

41 Internment letter dated 23 February.

42   *Ibid.*

43   'My Family, You and I', pp. 13-23.

44   Translators' note: Keller uses here an expression which is a mixture of German, Yiddish and Latin: 'gebenscht sollst du sein'.

45   Keller's writings on film music are collected in: Hans Keller, *Film Music and Beyond*, ed. Christopher Wintle, London, Plumbago, 2006.

46   Ena Blyth, letter to the author, 2 September 2007, and oral communication, 16 September 2007.

47   Keller later translated Carl Flesch's memoirs into English as: *The Memoirs of Carl Flesch*, ed. Hans Keller and C. F. Flesch, London, Salisbury Square, 1957.

48   PRO HO 396/181.

49   Hans Keller, interviewed in summer 1985 for the Channel 4 documentary *The Keller Instinct* broadcast after his death on 23 February 1986 and 28 June 1988. A transcript was published as 'Hans Keller in Interview with Anton Weinberg', *Tempo* 195, January 1996, ed. Mark Doran, pp. 6–12.

50   See Gillman and Gillman, *'Collar the Lot!'*, London, Quartet, 1980, p. 286.

51   François Lafitte, *The Internment of Aliens*, London, Penguin, 1940, reissued in 1988 by Libris, p. viii.

52   Hansard 362 H. C. DEB. 5 s, cols 1232-33.

53   Telegram from Churchill to Morrison, 21 November 1943, Churchill Archive CHAR 20/130, 9.

54   Churchill's later account of his position was as follows: 'I was concerned at the grave affronts to the rights and liberties of the individual which the safety of the State had required. Having been brought up on the Bill of Rights, *habeas corpus*, and trial by jury conceptions, I grieved to become responsible, even with the constant assent of Parliament, for their breach. In June, July, August, and September our plight had seemed so grievous that no limits could be put upon the action of the State. Now that we had for the time being got our heads again above water a further refinement in the treatment of internees seemed obligatory. We had already set up an elaborate sifting process, and many persons who had been arrested in the crisis were released by the Home Secretary, who presided over this field.' Winston Churchill, *The Second World War, Vol 2: Their Finest Hour*, p. 626.

55   Kapp and Mynett, *British Policy and the Refugees, 1933-1941,* London, Frank Cass, 1997, p. 76.

56   Hansard 362 H.C. DEB. 5 s, cols 1295-96.

57   'Thinkers of the World, Disunite!', preface to: *1975 (1984 minus 9)*, London, Dobson, 1977, pp. 9-27 (republished as *Music, Closed Societies and Football*, London, Toccata Press, 1986).

Chapter 9: Afterwards, 1942-49

1   Inge Trott, oral communication, 29 March 2004.

2   In a letter to Robert Turnball, 4 April 1981, Keller urged the 23-year-old not to try to publish before he was ready: 'When I was your age, I was well aware that I had to wait.' (CUL HK Archive)

3   Hans Keller, *Music and Psychology: Vienna to London 1939-52*, ed. Christopher Wintle, London, Plumbago, 2003.

4   Inge Trott, oral communication, 19 November 2007.

5   Ena Blyth, oral communication, 30 October 2007.

6   Keller's residence in London during most of 1944 is indicated by his surviving letters and postcards to his mother, to whom he wrote almost daily at this time. Some of these letters are marked as being written from the Institute of Psychoanalysis, in whose library Keller appears to have been spending much of his time.

7   See Hans Keller *1975 (1984 minus 9)*, London, Dobson, 1977, p. 87.

8   The treatment was brief and ultimately unsuccessful (the patient had a mental breakdown), but Keller's brief notes on the first session are still extant in the CUL HK Archive and have been published in *Music and Psychology*, pp. 233-34.

9   There were 55 such emergency colleges set up after the war, and they operated for about five years. Files from the Borthwick Training College for Women are preserved in the National Archives (ED 143/35-36) as one of two representative institutions. Borthwick closed down in 1951, after which Margaret Phillips was awarded the OBE for her work there. (I am indebted to Ken Blyth for this information.)

10   Margaret Phillips, *Small Social Groups in England*, London, Methuen, 1965, p. 3.

11   Margaret Phillips, *The Education of the Emotions*, London, Allen & Unwin, 1937, p. 26.

12   Letter from Keller to Phillips, undated, written in response to her original questionnaire (CUL HK Archive). Though the questionnaire is dated July 1942, it is likely that Keller received it several months later. To judge by their subsequent correspondence, this first letter may have been written either at the very end of 1942 or in January 1943.

13   The sections on the string quartet, together with Phillips's original questionnaire, are published in *Music and Psychology*, pp. 41-7.

14   See Hans Keller *1975 (1984 minus 9)*, pp. 13 and 22.

15   From Phillips's questionnaire, July 1942 (see *Music and Psychology*. pp. 41-2).

16   Hans Keller, *Music and Psychology*, p. 41.

17   In later life, Keller wrote many times about Brahms's inhibitions, such as 'his frequent inability to achieve climax – a single main climax in a movement' and 'his habit of interrupting his melodic invention, out of a fear of sentimentality.' ('Music and Psychopathology', *History of Medicine*, Vol. 3, No. 2, Summer 1971, pp. 3-7; reprinted in: Hans Keller, *Essays on Music*, ed. Christopher Wintle, Cambridge, CUP, 1994, pp. 29-34.)

18   Undated letter from Phillips to Keller, probably from very early 1943 (CUL HK Archive).

19   Anna Freud, having followed her father into psychoanalysis, came to London with the rest of the family in 1938. She was particularly interested in child psychology and set up the Hampstead War Nursery, having worked before the war at the Baumgarten children's home run by Willi Hoffer.

20   From the preface to a later (96-page) report on 'The Psychology and Ethics of School Staff Groups', 1946. Though written by Keller, it reported on his and

Phillips's joint work (CUL HK Archive).
21   Much of this material is published in: Hans Keller, *Music and Psychology*.
22   Letter from Phillips to Keller, probably of 25 January 1945 (CUL HK Archive).
23   *Ibid.*
24   Letter from Keller to Phillips, 9 November 1944 (CUL HK Archive).
25   *1975 (1984 minus 9)*, p. 88.
26   *1975 (1984 minus 9)*, p. 87.
27   The CUL HK Archive contains more than one reference to ill health, including a medical certificate dated 9 February 1944 and signed by Dr. Hans M. Cohn of Upper Wimpole Street, stating that 'Mr. Hans Keller, aged 25, suffers from glandular trouble and should avoid heavy physical work and overstrain. He is in need of sufficient periods of rest in order to maintain his working capacity.' There are also references in Margaret Phillips's letters to her attempts to find Keller work being frustrated by 'the old story – they would have nothing to do with an alien' (letter of 15 August 1943).
28   Keller's cousin Inge Trott says of his immediate post-internment years: 'He wasn't making any money … He didn't have to, because of his mother. There was always money there.' (Oral communication, 29 March 2004.)
29   Mark Doran, 'Hans Keller in Interview with Anton Weinberg', *Tempo* 195, January 1996, pp. 6-12. Keller claimed that his method of self-analysis had not been the same as Freud's: 'My model for self-analysis, or my inspiration anyway, was not Freud himself, but a chemist who, having found that he shut up on sundry hetero-analytical couches, decided to test analytic theory (which, to begin with, he loathed) all by himself. He published some of his impressive results, and Freud wrote him a charming preface, praising his contribution to psychoanalytic knowledge, and remarking that if he, Freud, had found himself in the same situation, he would probably have acted likewise – [having] proved [himself] unanalysable by any other person.' (*1975 (1984 minus 9)*, p. 87.) This description has led Mark Doran to identify Keller's model tentatively as E. Pickworth Farrow's *A Practical Method of Self-Analysis*, London, 1942. A few scribbled pages of Keller's free-association have survived, bearing dates from 1943 and 1944.
30   Inge Trott, oral communication, 29 March 2004.
31   Donald Mitchell, 'Remembering Hans Keller', *Cradles of the New*, London, Faber, 1995, p. 476-77.
32   Letter from Phillips to Keller, undated but probably from August 1943 (CUL HK Archive).
33   Letter from Phillips to Keller, 13 August 1943 (CUL HK Archive).
34   Letter from Rudolph Reti to Keller, 27 June 1956 (CUL HK Archive).
35   Letter from Keller to Rudolph Reti, 15 July 1956 (CUL HK Archive).
36   Letter from Keller to the Editor of *Onward*, 8 September 1945 (CUL HK Archive).
37   Several are published posthumously in: Hans Keller, *Music and Psychology*.
38   'On Maturity …', *The Psychologist*, July 1945. *The Psychologist* (a popular magazine rather than an academic journal) published four further sets of Keller's aphorisms on this subject in 1947, and a translation of the first set

appeared in *Die Weltwoche* on 27 December 1946. The set is reprinted in *Music and Psychology*, pp. 108-11. The letter to the *Evening Standard*, published on 3 April 1945, was written in response to the paper inviting its readers to write in on this subject. *Kite*, subtitled 'A Factory Journal', was a publication which aimed to present 'the best which the writer in industry has to offer'. According to the editorial in the edition in which Keller's story appeared, its contributors were 'all factory workers', and it is unclear from Keller's correspondence with the magazine why they decided to depart from this policy in his case. Certainly his contributor's biography looks unusual among those of the metal turners and electricians who appeared alongside him.

39   In 1944, 'Male Psychology' was first offered, at J. C. Flugel's suggestion, to the American journal *Character and Personality* published by Duke University Press. The editor never responded and Keller looked elsewhere. The article was finally published in the *British Journal of Medical Psychology*, No. 20, 1946, pp. 384-88, and was reprinted in *World Psychology*, Vol. 2, No. 7, July 1947, and again in Keller's *Music and Psychology*, pp. 112-17.

40   The paper to the British Psychological Society, given on 29 September 1945, was entitled 'The Psychological Significance of Some Sociological Conceptions of the Group'. Only Keller's sections of it survive (see *Music and Psychology*, pp. 69-73). The report on school staff groups seems to have been intended for publication as a separate article, rather than a part of *The Psychology of Social Groups*.

41   Letter from Phillips to Keller, 17 July [1943] (CUL HK Archive).

42   *1975 (1984 minus 9)*, p. 87.

43   'Towards a Theory of Music', *The Listener*, Vol. 83, No. 2150, 11 June 1970, pp. 795-96, reprinted in: Hans Keller, *Essays On Music*, ed. Christopher Wintle, Cambridge, CUP, 1994, pp. 121-25.

44   See 'Why This Piece is about *Billy Budd*', *The Listener*, Vol. 88, No. 2270, 28 September 1972, p. 419; reprinted in: Hans Keller, *Essays on Music*, pp. 198-200.

45   See A. M. Garnham, *Hans Keller and the BBC: the Musical Conscience of British Broadcasting*, Aldershot, Ashgate, 2003, pp. 29-61, for an account of the genesis of functional analysis and its early broadcasts. For a complete edition of Keller's analytical scores, see: *Hans Keller – Functional Analysis: The Unity of Contrasting Themes*, ed. Gerold W. Gruber, Vienna, Peter Lang, 2001.

46   As Keller jokingly called him in a letter to Phillips of 28 January 1945 (CUL HK Archive).

47   In a postcard written to his mother on 20 April 1944 from the Institute of Pychoanalysis, Keller told her delightedly that 'I just found not less than 4 articles or passages – in the International Journal of Psychoanalysis – dealing with the psychology of music; Hoffer had told me that there wasn't anything about music in psa. literature!' He later wrote that 'the psychoanalytical literature on the subject is far more scarce than that in any other sphere of applied psychoanalysis; on the other hand it is far more extensive than many psychologists and, indeed, psychoanalysts would think.' ('Studies in the Psychoanalysis of Music', unfinished draft, CUL HK Archive).

48 Keller, 'Why This Piece is about *Billy Budd*', *The Listener*, Vol. 88, No. 2270, 28 September 1972, p. 419.

49 Keller, 'The Psychology of Film Music', *World Psychology* Vol. 3, No. iii, March 1948, pp. 23-6; reprinted in: *Music and Psychology*, pp. 157-160.

50 Keller later referred to his having 'switched over, as far as my living was concerned, from playing to writing' (see the unpaginated preface to the reissue of *Music Survey*, London, Faber, 1981), but it is not clear whether he had made much of a living from his violin-playing anyway. He continued to play in Oscar Adler's quartet until the latter's death in 1955. Not long afterwards, all possibility of violin-playing was finally ended by the onset of the first symptoms of what was later to be diagnosed as motor neurone disease (Milein Cosman dates this at around 1960).

51 Phillips eventually published her research alone as *Small Social Groups in England*, London, Methuen, 1965. Her preface to the book paid tribute to Keller, recording the way in which 'my first draft was fully discussed with him', but none of his writing was included.

52 Alan Blyth, *Remembering Britten*, London, Hutchinson, 1981, p. 87.

53 In the 1946 season, *Peter Grimes* appeared alongside *The Marriage of Figaro*, *Hansel and Gretel*, *The Bartered Bride*, *The Barber of Seville*, *Madame Butterfly*, *La Bohème*, *Rigoletto* and Vaughan Williams's *Sir John in Love*.

54 Keller made a note of the dates of the new staging at the end of his 1945 diary as 'Peter Grimes Feb. 7, 12, 14'. Unfortunately his 1946 diary is not extant.

55 Keller reviewed the opera in *National Entertainment Monthly* and *Reconstruction* (New York). At the beginning of 1946, Keller had secured a regular column in the former publication reviewing and previewing musical events around the country (including BBC radio broadcasts). *National Entertainments Monthly* was a new publication, which Keller first approached (by sending them a 'musical quiz') in December 1945.

56 'The Psychology of Film Music', *op. cit.*

57 Keller's *Three Psychoanaytic Notes on Peter Grimes* were written during the spring of 1946 and published posthumously in his *Music and Psychology*, pp. 121-45.

58 'Do you think that Britten is at all interested in, or at any rate not opposed to, the application to art of the psychoanalytic body of knowledge? Naturally I would only like to show him my paper when it is finished, if I knew that I wouldn't just waste his time.' (Letter to Peter Pears of 4 May 1946, CUL HK Archive; reprinted in his *Music and Psychology*, p. 140.)

59 One wonders whether the title of Keller's later essay 'Peter Grimes. The Story; the Music Not Excluded' (in Keller & Mitchell ed., *Benjamin Britten: a Commentary on His Works from a Group of Specialists*, London, Rockliff, 1952) might contain a reference (unconscious?) to his exclusion of the music in his first study of the work. The title does of course also complement Arthur Oldham's 'Peter Grimes. The Music; the Story Not Excluded': it is not known which article was written first.

60 Keller, *Music and Psychology*, p. 156.

61   *The Need for Competent Film Music Criticism: a Pamphlet for Those Who Care for FILM AS ART, with a Final Section for Those Who Do Not*, London, British Film Institute, 1947. Keller's many writings on film music have now been collected in: Hans Keller, *Film Music and Beyond*, ed. Christopher Wintle, London, Plumbago, 2007.

62   From 'A Great English Composer', an unpublished essay written in 1947 (CUL HK Archive).

63   'Resistances to Britten's Music: Their Psychology', *Music Survey*, Vol. 2, No. 4, Spring 1950, pp. 227-36; reprinted in: Hans Keller, *Essays on Music*, pp. 10-17.

64   Letter to John Rickman, editor of the *British Journal of Medical Psychology*, 3 April 1947 (CUL HK Archive).

65   'Resistances to Britten's Music: Their Psychology', *op. cit.*

66   *Ibid.*

67   'Musical Self-contempt in Britain', paper given at J. C. Flugel's request to the Social Psychology Section of the British Psychological Society on 4 November 1950, and published posthumously in Keller's *Music and Psychology*, pp. 197-209.

68   Note, for example, the heavily symphonic programmes of the post-war Henry Wood Promenade Concerts.

69   I am grateful to Richard Witts for these figures.

70   Note written by Keller on the back of a letter to Margaret Phillips dated 13 April 1946 (CUL HK Archive).

71   'The Psychology of Film Music', pp. 23-6.

72   Unpublished letter [1946] to the editor of *Time and Tide*, quoted in *Music and Psychology*, pp. 139-40.

73   Peter Pears joined the Sadler's Wells Opera Company in 1943, and sang the role of Ferrando in both 1944 and 1945. The Britten-Pears Archive holds programmes for his performances on 31 August and 2, 4 and 9 September 1944 (Ref: PG/1944/0829 & PG/1944/0902) and 2 April 1945 (PG/1945/0402). There are no extant programmes for June-July 1945, but Pears's singing of the role at the time is confirmed by Joan Cross's cast books (which show Pears as Ferrando on 22, 23 and 27 June, and 12 and 19 July) and Benjamin Britten's diary, which has a note 'PP Così' for 19 July (presumably the night Britten himself went to the performance) (many thanks to Jude Brimmer of the Britten-Pears Archive for this information). Hans Keller's recollection that he first heard Pears from 'the Wells gallery' would imply a date in summer 1945 (i.e. after the Sadler's Wells Theatre had re-opened). The emphasis given to *Così* in his diary entries of June-July 1945, however, might suggest he had already heard Pears in the earlier season.

74   'People x: Peter Pears', *Opera*, Vol. 2, No. 6, May 1951, pp. 287-92.

75   Letter to Peter Pears, 4 May 1946 (CUL HK Archive). Pears's article is reprinted in Philip Brett (ed.), *Peter Grimes*, Cambridge, CUP, 1983, pp. 150-52.

76   The note reads: 'IV. The appeal of *Peter Grimes*: There are plenty of Grimeses'. This is a quotation from the last sentence of Pears's article: 'There are plenty of Grimeses around still, I think!'

77   It was eventually published by Eric Blom in *Music and Letters*, Vol. 29, No. 1, January 1948, pp. 17-30. A few years later, once Keller had started to write about Schoenberg, he and Blom had many public disagreements, in the course of which Blom once remarked, 'If anybody ever succeeds in making me hate Mozart's music, it will have been Hans Keller's boast to have done so.' (*The Observer*, 8 April 1956, p. 10.)

78   Letter from Connolly to Keller, 18 December 1946 (CUL HK Archive).

79   Letter from McNaught to Keller, 14 February 1947 (CUL HK Archive).

80   Keller's reply is dated 18 January 1947 (CUL HK Archive).

81   Letter from Sharp to Keller, 4 January 1953 (CUL HK Archive).

82   Published in *Music Review*, Vol. 8, No. 4, November 1947, pp. 214-17, and reprinted in Keller's *Music and Psychology*, pp. 176-85. This article is prominently subtitled 'A Supplementary Note to Alfred Einstein's *Mozart: His Character – His Work*'.

83   Letter from Keller to Sharp, 30 June 1956 (CUL HK Archive).

84   'The Unity of Contrasting Themes and Movements', *Music Review*, Vol. 17, No. 1, February 1956, pp. 48-58, and Vol. 17, No. 2, May 1956, pp. 120-29. These two articles constitute his first extended 'functional analysis', the wordless version of which was later broadcast by the BBC's Third Programme.

85   See the unpaginated preface to the 1981 reissue of *Music Survey*.

86   Letter to George Taylor, editor of *Radio Affairs*, 13 January 1948 (CUL HK Archive).

87   Letter from Stein to Chapman, 16 January 1947 (British Library, Add. 62948, f. 54).

88   'Your Britten-Mozart article has been on my conscience all along. I got it into my head that it would require a lot of alteration; but now I've carefully read it through again, I see that in fact it requires very little alteration at all.' Letter from Chapman to Keller, 21 June 1947 (British Library Add. 62948, f. 83). Chapman was not in a position to publish 'Britten and Mozart' at that stage, being no longer editor of *Tempo*. He evidently regretted not having done so, and offered Keller a number of suggestions for the work's improvement.

89   Chapman wrote to Keller commissioning the article on 23 January 1947, according to Keller's reply the following day (British Library, Add. 62948, f. 76). The Quartet was first performed by the Zorian Quartet on 21 November 1945. It is known that Keller heard their performance of it on 4 January 1946, as his annotated programme from that occasion is preserved in CUL HK Archive.

90   A large number of drafts are in the CUL HK Archive, with a further two in the British Library (Add. 62948, ff. 99-103). One of the former is marked '2nd draft according to Stein's suggestions', and one of the latter is heavily edited by Chapman.

91   Letter from Stein to Chapman, 10 February 1947 (British Library, Add. 62948, f. 55).

92   This version is that of the second draft, as Ernest Chapman would first have seen it.

93   Letter from Chapman to Keller, 21 June 1947 (British Library Add. 62948, f. 83).

94   Letter from Keller to Chapman, 25 March 1947 (British Library Add. 62948, f. 77). Keller's idea was lost in the internal reorganisation at Boosey & Hawkes which saw Chapman relieved as editor of *Tempo*.

95   'How I Got There', an undated and unpublished article for the *London Magazine*. The article reached proof stage, but was not published 'because I refused to change', as Keller noted on the proofs preserved in CUL HK Archive.

96   Newlin, *Bruckner – Mahler – Schoenberg*, New York, King's Crown Press, 1948. Keller's review was published in *Tempo* 9, Autumn 1948, pp. 28-9.

97   Interestingly, Robert Layton, reviewing Newlin's book for Donald Mitchell's new journal *Music Survey* (No. 2, Winter 1948), makes a similar point: 'Her thesis does not enable the reader to see clearly why she believes Schoenberg to be in the line of Mozart, Schubert, Bruckner and Mahler. Why should not Franz Schmidt be an equally eligible claimant to that position?'

98   See 'The Chamber Music', in: H. C. Robbins Landon and Donald Mitchell (ed.), *The Mozart Companion*, London, Faber, 1956, p. 93.

99   'Natural Master', *The Listener*, Vol. 112, No. 2881, 25 October 1984, pp. 34-5.

100   Quoted by Keller in 'Natural Master', *ibid*.

101   Adler and Schoenberg continued to correspond, but, judging by Adler's contribution to the collection of essays for Schoenberg's sixtieth birthday, it appears that a brief meeting in 1933 was all he saw of Schoenberg in later life: 'In 1933, after many years, I once again saw Schoenberg (whom I had known as a seventeen-year-old) at one of his lectures. Yes! It was the same young Schoenberg with his quality of living unboundedly in the present – a quality that reveals itself anew at every moment – and with the elemental power of this timeless vitality.' This tribute is printed in full as Appendix 5 of Willi Reich's *Schoenberg: a Critical Biography*, trans. Leo Black, Harlow, Longman, 1971. Schoenberg made considerable efforts to help Adler emigrate to America after the Anschluss, but he was unsuccessful and they never saw each other again. They continued to write to each other with undimmed affection until Schoenberg died in 1951.

102   Adler's letter is undated, but it was written in reply to one from Schoenberg dated 2 July 1949. (See Shapiro, *Dr. Oskar Adler: A Complete Man, 1975-1955*, 2002, pp. 131-32.) The untranslatable word 'weithorigkeit' was apparently Franz Schmidt's (coined after a performance of *Pierrot lunaire*, by which he was 'deeply moved') and means the ability to hear into the distance.

103   'How I Got There', *op. cit.*

104   The date of any possible British radio performance is somewhat difficult to establish, as the BBC's Programme Index was not kept up during the war years.

105   'My Family, You, and I', *The New Review*, Vol. 3, Nos. 34-5, January-February 1977, pp. 12-23.

106   'My Family. You and I', *op. cit.*

107   'How I Got There', *op. cit.*

108   See p. 271 of this volume.

109   See pp. 266-7 of this volume.

110   Keller's letter (responding to an article on Mozart by Redlich in the previous issue) appeared in the August 1948 edition of *Music Review* (Vol. 9, No. 3), the

same issue in which Donald Mitchell's first article for the journal was published. Sixty years later, Mitchell cannot now recall exactly which of Keller's reviews was the one that first attracted his attention – elsewhere (see Chapter 10) he has described it as 'most probably the performance of an opera (Mozart?) at Sadler's Wells or Covent Garden' – but it is very likely to have been the review of the 1948 Sadler's Wells production of *Cosi fan tutte* that had appeared in the previous issue of *Music Review*, and which is reproduced in this volume.

111   Donald Mitchell, 'Remembering Hans Keller', in: *Cradles of the New*, London, Faber, 1995, p. 467.

112   'How I Got There', *op. cit.* Keller also described the experience of hearing *Pierrot lunaire* for the first time in 'Whose Fault is the Speaking Voice?', *Tempo* 75, December 1965, pp. 12-17: 'I felt that if I had been confronted with the loss of key or, alternatively, the loss of singing pitch alone, I might have been able to stand up to the experience; it was the combined assault on my sense of musical security that almost finished me. It took me a very long time to be able to perceive the musical truths that *Pierrot* expresses.'

113   'New Music in the Old Year', *Music Parade*, Vol. 1, No. 10, January-March 1949, pp. 4-5 and 9. According to a letter of 5 October 1948 from the editor Arthur Unwin to Keller, this article would have been submitted 'towards the end of November' (CUL HK Archive).

114   'First Performances', *Music Review*, Vol. 10, No. 1, February 1949, pp. 40-42.

115   Keller told Geoffrey Sharp that 'Mitchell has asked me to co-edit MUSIC SURVEY with him' in a letter of 21 February 1949 (CUL HK Archive).

116   H. H. Stuckenschmidt, *Arnold Schönberg*, Zurich, 1951, trans. Edith Temple Roberts and Humphrey Searle, London, Calder, 1959, p. 502.

117   See above, p. 12. Schoenberg's manuscript of *My Evolution* is dated 2 August 1949. It first appeared in German translation in the September 1949 issue of the Berlin periodical *Stimmen* and the *Oesterreichische Musikzeitschrift* of Vienna, before being included (in its original English) in the first edition of *Style and Idea* in 1950.

118   Letter from Adler to Schoenberg, undated but probably written in 1950, after the first publication of *Style and Idea* that year (Shapiro, *Dr. Oskar Adler: A Complete Man, 1975-1955*, pp. 129-30 – Shapiro's sequencing of the letters may be erroneous at this point).

119   Letters from Adler to Schoenberg, undated – the first was written in response to Schoenberg's letter to Adler of 2 July 1949, and the second probably in 1950. (See Shapiro, *op. cit.*, pp. 129-33.)

120   See 'Unpublished Schoenberg Letters,' *Music Survey*, Vol. 4, No. 3, Summer 1952, pp. 449-71.

121   'Notes and News: The Quarterlies', *Musical Times*, Vol. 92, No. 1295, January 1951, pp. 38-40 (unsigned).

122   From the (unpaginated) preface to the collected edition of *Music Survey* published by Faber in 1981. This preface takes the form of a conversation between Donald Mitchell, Hans Keller and Patrick Carnegy.

123   *Ibid.*

124   The 'Britten' issue of *Music Survey* was Vol. II, No. 4, Spring 1950, after which
      Keller and Mitchell published *Benjamin Britten: a Commentary on His Works
      from a Group of Specialists*, London, Rockliff, 1952.
125   *Music Survey*, Vol. II, No. 4, Spring 1950, p. 251.
126   From 'Britten and Mozart' – see p. 234.
127   This 75-minute radio feature comprised interviews with twenty of Schoenberg's
      family and friends, including his widow, Gertrud, his cousin the tenor Hans
      Nachod, his brother-in-law the violinist Rudolf Kolisch, and friends such as
      Oskar Kokoschka, Egon Wellesz, Roberto Gerhard and T. W. Adorno. It was
      first broadcast on the Third Programme on 6 November 1965 and repeated
      on 1 December that year. Copies are held in the BBC Sound Archives and the
      National Sound Archive at the British Library (939W, 940W, 939R).
128   Robert Layton, oral communication, 11 November 1996.
129   'Whose Fault is the Speaking Voice?' pp. 12-17.
130   Mitchell, 'Remembering Hans Keller', p. 469.
131   Martin Cooper, for example, on reading Keller and Mitchell's 1952 *Commentary*
      thought that they had exaggerated the opposition Britten faced: 'Britten's
      extraordinary musical gifts were recognised from the start; he has met with a
      minimum of misunderstanding; and for many years each new work from his
      pen has been immediately hailed as a masterpiece of its kind. It is puzzling,
      therefore, to the ordinary reader to meet in several of the essays included
      here a note of defensiveness, even a hint of defence by aggression, as though
      Britten's music were deliberately underestimated or spitefully ignored by critics
      or public.' ('Crown for Britten', *Spectator* 6499, 16 January 1953, pp. 72-3.)
132   'My Family, You, and I', *op. cit.*
133   'How I Got There', *op. cit.*
134   See 'On Musical Understanding', p. 252.
135   '*Gloriana* as Music Drama: a Reaffirmation', *Tempo* 79, December 1966, pp. 2-5;
      reprinted in Keller's *Essays on Music*, pp. 89-92.
136   *Observer*, 8 April 1956, p. 10. 'Strict Serial Technique in Classical Music' was
      published in *Tempo* 37, Autumn 1955, pp. 12-24, and reprinted in Keller's *Essays
      on Music*, pp. 169-78.

Chapter 10: Epilogue – 'Hans Keller in the Early Days'

1   32 Herne Hill was the house of Mowgli and Roy Franey. No. 30 was the house
      next door that Keller's mother acquired after the war; Keller moved there with
      her. Keller's letter in the *Music Review* to which Mitchell refers was addressed
      from No. 30.
2   In fact, Keller's diary notes this concert as Gordon Jacob's Symphony No. 2 in
      C, conducted by Walter Goehr. The rest of the programme is not mentioned,
      however.
3   The first issue, published in the autumn of 1947, was originally called *Music-
      Journal*. The title was changed at the request of the Incorporated Society of
      Musicians, who felt that it was too similar to their publication *A Music Journal*.

4   Two articles on 'The Importance of Hans Pfizner' by Harold Truscott were published in issues Vol. I, Nos. 1 and 2. Dika Newlin's Schoenberg articles – 'Schönberg in America 1933-1948: Retrospect and Prospect' appeared in Vol. I, No. 5 (Donald Mitchell's last solo issue) and Vol. II, No. 1. Reger was represented by 'Four Unpublished Letters' in Vol. I, No. 4.

5   Vol. XIX, 1952.

Hans Keller (Milein Cosman)

Index

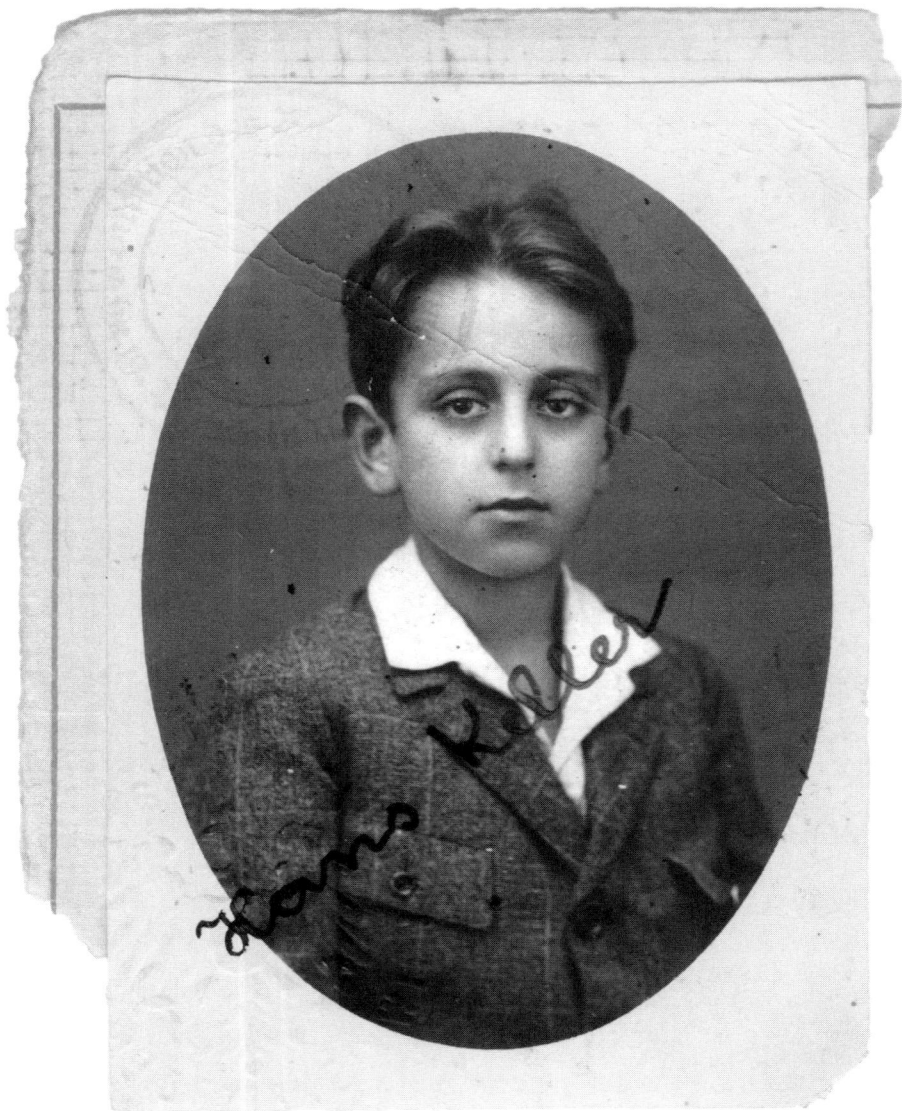

Index